Acknowledgements

This book is full of inspiring stories which document the first century of Apache Lutheran history. During 100 years more than 70 WELS missionaries and wives, beginning with my grandparents in 1893, shared God's love in Christ with generations of native Americans on Apache reservations in Arizona. Himself one of these missionaries, Hartzell's experience and research provide the inside scoop which makes this not only a monumental historical record, but also a tour which takes the reader on an informative and a memorable adventure.

—Rev. David J. Plocher, author of "Apache Lutheran Mission Beginnings —From the Letters of John Plocher."

The story line of the long succession of missionaries to the Apache from the Wisconsin Luther Synod is a long-neglected story. Until now, the portions of overall narrative have only been available in a few academic theses, early church newspaper articles and other reports, and a few journal articles. With this book, Pastor Hartzell, himself a modern-day product of the long line of Lutheran missionaries, has written a comprehensive history of this work. In telling the history of the numerous Inashood who faithfully undertook the mission's duties, Pastor Hartzell has not only expressed this longstanding commitment from the denomination's point of view, but, importantly, he also incorporates the roles of many Apache converts who aided the missionaries.

—Paul R. Nickens, Author of Old San Carlos

Pastor Hartzell has indeed written a love story, as he says in the introduction—a love story about a people and region and the Lutheran missionaries, wives, and families that came to bring the gospel of salvation to the Apaches. He is well qualified to pen this story, having lived on the reservation during his formative years and later serving as a missionary. One is immediately struck by his knowledge of the history and geography of the region and his understanding of the difficulties, challenges, and joys of work on this mission field. His love for precious souls for whom Jesus died is evident throughout. This book, however, is not a hagiography or panegyric that ignores human frailties. Pastor Hartzell understands human nature and God's grace too well not to reveal the faults and failings of both the missionaries and the people they came to serve. Yet he is sympathetic. The mission pioneers had no specific training for the work they were sent to do. Most had no pastoral experience before arriving on the field. They learned as they served. They had to work mainly through interpreters. Isolation, loneliness, and hardships of every kind took their toll. Some service was relatively brief. Others spent their whole lives in this ministry to the Apache people and are buried on the reservation. The Lord of the church blessed the efforts of all.

This volume will be enjoyed not only by those who have an interest in the story of the Wisconsin Synod mission to the Apache people, but also by all those who appreciate a compelling account of a culture, people land, and work beyond their experience. May it be widely circulated!

—Prof. John M. Brenner, Wisconsin Lutheran Seminary, Mequon, Wisconsin

Pastor Eric Hartzell has provided a fascinating history of the Lutheran church and the White Mountain Apache people of eastern Arizona. Utilizing historical documents and other sources, Inashood is a story of devotion, persistence, and God's redemptive work among an Indigenous community in the American Southwest. Readers will appreciate Pastor Hartzell's meticulous research, his personal anecdotes, and his remarkable ability in keeping the gospel at the center of the narrative.

—Matthew Sakiestewa Gilbert (Hopi), University of Arizona

INASHOOD

The Story of the Arizona Apache
Lutheran Missions and Their Pastors

Eric Hartzell

NORTHWESTERN PUBLISHING HOUSE
Milwaukee, Wisconsin

Cover Art: Painting by Eric Hartzell
Book Design: Pam Clemons

Northwestern Publishing House
N16W23379 Stone Ridge Dr., Waukesha, WI 53188
www.nph.net
© 2022 Northwestern Publishing House
Published 2022
Printed in the United States of America
ISBN 978-0-8100-3196-8

23 24 25 26 27 28 29 30 31   10 9 8 7 6 5 4

Contents

ARIZONA
Apache Reservations

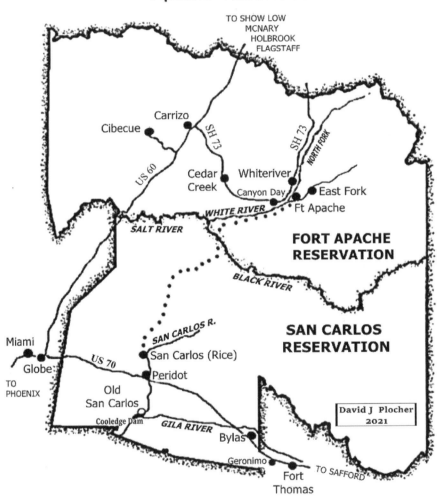

TO SHOW LOW
MCNARY
HOLBROOK
FLAGSTAFF

Cibecue

Carrizo

SH 73

SH 73

NORTH FORK

Cedar Creek

Whiteriver

Canyon Day

East Fork

US 60

WHITE RIVER

Ft Apache

SALT RIVER

FORT APACHE RESERVATION

BLACK RIVER

SAN CARLOS R.

SAN CARLOS RESERVATION

Miami

Globe

US 70

San Carlos (Rice)

Peridot

TO PHOENIX

Old San Carlos

David J Plocher
2021

Cooledge Dam

GILA RIVER

Bylas

Geronimo

TO SAFFORD

Fort Thomas

Introduction

Inashood

The poem is entitled to commendation for embalming pleasantly enough the monstrous traditions of an uninteresting, and, one may almost say, a justly exterminated race (THE NEW YORK TIMES' REVIEW OF LONGFELLOW'S THE SONG OF HIAWATHA).

If you are a linguist and know the Apache language and what makes it say what it says, when you hear the Apache word *Inashood*, you will hear something about the dragging of a long black shirt. This is the word that was used to describe the person who came to the people a long time ago and told them about Jesus and Christianity. The Lutheran *Inashood* sometimes still does wear a long black robe (or a white one these days) in his ministrations. As he made his rounds in the old days he often carried his robe in the window of his vehicle, and the blazing sun faded out the black to an unsightly brown. It dragged, and it picked up the dust of the place. (Those from Peridot on the San Carlos Reservation today still always have dust on their shoes as a matter of course. Everyone does, not just the *Inashood*.)

The *Inashood* called himself a missionary, and so did those who sent him to work among the Apache people. Not many of the missionaries ever became fluent in the difficult Apache language. Eugene Nida, the famous linguist and missiologist, said that Apache is one of the most difficult of all languages to master. This is perhaps supported by the linguistic cousins of the Apache, the Navajo, who became the Code Talkers to Japanese dismay during the Second World War. No one broke the "code" that was essentially the Navajos talking to each other in their own language. By the way, the word these Navajo soldiers used to stand for mission, as in some kind of military mission, was the word they brought from their homes in Arizona and New Mexico to describe the place where the *Inashood*-lived and worked. To this day the word is used to identify the place of work of *Inashood* and those with him. In Arizona by Keams Canyon and Window Rock the Presbyterians have their mission: Ganado Mission. On the East Fork River on the Fort Apache Reservation is East Fork Mission. Cibecue Mission is on the west end of the reservation. On the San Carlos Reservation, Peridot Mission and Bylas

Mission still do their work. All these missions had schools too. And *Inashood* is still there.[1]

The word *"Inashood"* is used today by those who speak Apache to describe a white pastor or a missionary. The word pastor is used when the conversation is in English. But *Inashood* is still *Inashood*. Not far from East Fork Mission early on a Sunday morning, a white pastor made his lonesome way through a long line of cars and trucks that strung up a hillside to a little house at the top. The house was surrounded by many Apache people—all Apache people—in their errand of the early morning. Someone had an eagle feather. They were trying to give the besieged persons in the little house the feather, which would engage them in sponsoring a sunrise dance. The reason the pastor was there was because those inside the house, particularly the young son who was in the pastor's confirmation class, had called in hushed whispers on the phone to say that the people were outside their house and would he please come. The people gave way to the pastor as he walked slowly toward the door of the house. Very little eye contact was made. It was being whispered through the crowd, *"Inashood nan yah"* ("The pastor is here"). The door was locked, and it looked like no one was there. Then the people started to leave one by one, back down the hill to their parked vehicles. After a while only the pastor stood in the yard in front of the closed door. There was a slow turning of the door knob. Then a voice from the small crack between the door and the jamb said, "Is that you, Pastor?"

Probably this is one of the many reasons why cultural anthropologists vilify the missionary, the *Inashood*, as a destroyer of culture and age-old custom. It is true that there were and are things the missionary "preached" against. The *Inashood* could not support the wanton use of alcohol and its resulting misery and grief. That unbridled consumption was a tradition that stretched all the way back to the Sierra Madres in Mexico and caused the deaths of untold numbers of the people and immeasurable hurt to families and the tribe itself. Both the old warriors Geronimo and Juh died at the cold hand of alcohol. The *Inashood* could not agree to the maternal grandmother taking twins and stuffing their nostrils with sand and throwing them under mesquite trees to die. The *Inashood* would not agree that men who suspected their wives of infidelity should be able to cut off the end of their wife's nose.

Even though the speaking of English was encouraged and even enforced in reservation mission schools, there were never more fer-

---

[1] Missionary Arthur Guenther claimed that there were also Apache Code Talkers. His father Edgar Guenther, also a missionary, told him.

vent supporters of the Apache language than the *Inashood*. And what greater mentor of culture is there than the spoken language? No one ever approached Dr. Francis Uplegger in his love of the language and in his skill in developing its orthography and specifying its syntax, as he did with special signs for glottal stops, nasal pronunciations and tonal designations. His multi-volume handwritten dictionary is at the Huntington College Library in California. (Arizona State University in Tempe also has a copy of it in its archives.)[2] Two Apache men on the San Carlos Reservation were once arguing about Chief Eskiminzin's name. The one said, "It means, 'The brave stand with him.'" The other said, "No, it means 'He stands with the brave.'" They couldn't agree. Then the one said to the other, "Let's go ask Uplegger. He will know."[3]

It was the *Inashood* who kept records of the families and the names and the clans of people with their birthdays. The books are extant today: green ledger books and congregational membership books that often have German designations of record keeping but also list Apache names and families. One such green ledger book from East Fork Mission, compiled originally by *Inashood* Edgar Guenther, will be consulted to provide the letter and number names given to the people by the United States military that located the people and relocated them when they put them into communities along the various rivers, where the people remain yet today.

This book is about *Inashood*: his work, his life, his history, his relationships with his fellow workers, and especially his life with his people, the Apache. It is about a wonderful and unique place and country and time. It is a book of loyalty and love. It is a book about a work that transcends race and circumstance and culture. It is a book about what still continues to this day (although as a history this book's purpose is not to describe what is happening today). It is not a religious book or a book about religion. It cannot help, however, always to be looking to that greatest of all examples and lover of people and their ways—Jesus Christ. This is the Jesus of the Bible who commanded his followers and all who would carry the name *Inashood*, "Go and make disciples of all nations." So, in 1893 two Germans—George Adascheck and John Plocher—became the first two *Inashood* to come and live and stay with the people called Apache.

---

[2] It is also true that John Plocher, the first Lutheran *Inashood* to the Apache people, made a dictionary of some 200 pages that is kept by the Plocher family today.

[3] Dr. Francis Uplegger was reverently called by his people, "*Inashood Hastin*" (the gentleman or elderly missionary). His dictionary and linguistic work was quoted by writers of Apache history. Kenny Griffith, for instance, in his book *Mickey Free, Manhunter* refers to Uplegger's work on page 179 as "*Apache-English Dictionary, by Rev. Fancis Uplegger.*"

Many times the *Inashood* would die here too and be buried with his people in the hectic and cluttered little cemeteries that proliferated around the communities. Not far from Peridot Mission you will see the cemetery where the Upleggers and Rosins are buried with their little children who didn't make it to adulthood. There is Larry and Sue Pontel's little boy too. At East Fork you will find Ernie Sprengeler and Raymond Riess. You'll also find little Buddy Behn's grave; he drowned in the river as a child.

This book attempts to show how Christian men and women worked and gave their youth and strength and lives to a work from which they got no monetary gain. They didn't own property. They didn't get houses. In most cases their support came from Christians in other parts of the country. In a number of cases the only thing they asked was the narrow slit in the red or pale soil where their tired bodies could be buried. These were Lutheran Christians. That has to be said at the beginning.

Pastor Arthur Guenther remembered the first *Inashood* this way: "My life and ministry gave me the blessed opportunity to be influenced by not only my sainted father (Edgar) but also to a degree by Pastor Al and F. U. Uplegger, "Uncle" Henry Rosin, Ernie Sprengeler, "Tubby" Niemannn, Art Krueger, and Teachers Walt Huber and Art Meier. One must be very careful when naming names, but in this instance I speak only for myself and must include Field Secretary Ray Zimmermann and the venerable Edgar Hoenecke."[4]

In a way this book is a love story. Right from the beginning, the early Christians were characterized by the statement, "Behold how they love one another." You can't read this book and not be struck by the fact that there was this love on the reservation between peoples of disparate cultures and lives. It didn't come quickly, and it didn't come easily. Love never really does come quickly and easily, and certainly in our case it was not love at first sight. But love did come to the Fort Apache and San Carlos reservations in this way, and love has stayed. Love works and love gives and love endures. The Bible says that, and the story before us shows it.

This love of *Inashood* for his people (and *Inashood*'s wife for her people too) was there at the very beginning and continues to this day. Pastor Gustav Harders, the pillar figure of the work in Globe, wrote about the prejudice that existed in Globe in his experience while living and working there. He heard it often said about Apaches in sit-

---

4 The Guenthers were sometimes known to refer to Francis Uplegger as FU, pronounced that way. It wasn't a nickname to be particularly complimentary of the dignified old gentleman who for many years was superintendent of the field.

uations that developed around Globe that individual Apaches were "only an Indian." This same racial epithet is still around today, and it shouldn't even surprise us, although with dismay we still hear it said. No racial group is entirely innocent in this regard. Human beings have this penchant for putting down people of other racial groups than their own. *Inashood* said "Indian" too, but the word was much different in meaning to him than to the supercilious intruder.

Harders related the following anecdote to show us the way that it was at the beginning:

> "Under the large iron water tanks from which the loco-motives are watered, where it is shady and cool, one always finds all kinds of people gathered near the train tracks, and Indians are there also. I like to join their company. So it was recently in San Carlos, where I was waiting for my train. While I was conversing with about a dozen Indians, a single locomotive arrived; it wanted to help its sister locomotive, which was bringing the train from Bowie, to pull the train up the mountains to Globe. The locomotive stopped not far from the water tank, and its engineer climbed down and joined us. After a while he said to me: 'I wish I could talk to the people in their language as you do it. I think one would then get to know them better, and they would not be so bad as they have been decried. Just today it is ten years that I owe one a debt of gratitude for saving my life. Do you know an Indian named Nose?'
>
> "'Yes I know him,' I said.
>
> "'He's the one. At that time I was making my first trip as stoker on the locomotive. Between here and Geronimo[5] the train track had torn loose on a curve. Nose had seen that and had stood from midday to evening in the hot sun, and when the train came near seven o'clock, he brought it to a stop at the right time with his red handkerchief. If it were not for him, many people would have lost their lives, and the train company would have lost much property. And what do you think the latter gave the Indian? Five dollars— five whole dollars!' the engineer said in disgust."[6]

So *Inashood* Harders observed. He even spoke about a certain

---

[5] Geronimo is a small place on the road from Bylas to Safford. You can still see a few buildings there today.

[6] *Anniversary Booklet for the Twenty-fifth Anniversary of the Evangelical Lutheran Indian Mission*, printed by Northwestern Publish House, Milwaukee, Wisconsin, 1919, pp. 52, 53.

U.S. Marshall in Tucson who had expressed his racism disgustingly, "He did not want to see the Indians protected, rather only the whites protected from the Indians. He would have preferred to have seen all of the latter removed from the world."[7] The reader can look to the opening of this book and see the quote of the *New York Times'* review of Longfellow's *The Song of Hiawatha*. The U.S. Marshall in Tucson wasn't the only one who reacted in this racist way. But it wasn't the way of the *Inashood*. These were his people and he loved them. This book shows this.

The purpose of the book is surely not to make people angry who come at the topic from a purely secular side. Its purpose is also not to try and win a point or justify a stand. The purpose of this book is to tell a story. It is a story based on the facts of what happened. It is a story that proves its intent by what actually happened among the white missionaries and their Apache brothers and sisters. The story transcends theory. It isn't an attempt to figure out what makes Apaches Apache. Only God can do that, anyway. It does show Apaches as they were and as they to some degree still are. Culture is an ever-changing thing, which shows the people (the Apache word is *Indeh*) as human with all the struggles of human-kind present in their persona. It shows the missionaries as human beings too. Some of their ways were not complimentary. Some were. We even hope that when the story is told it will be seen that what *Inashood* did was indeed good and beneficial.

Pastor Harders worked in Globe a little after the turn of the 1900s. He really started the work in that place. He was the first major missionary player there, and he described the feelings he had for his people as "closer than brothers." That's the way he said it and felt it, as he described what happened with him and his Apache helper Oscar Davis and the little congregation of Apaches in Globe, Arizona, at that Christmas over a century ago.[8] Surely his life with his people there in Globe showed his sentiments. Harders said, "The wicked medicine men always want to say that the Bible religion is only for the white people and is not suitable for the Indians. But this is for all the world, and it seemed to me that I had to make that so clear to the people. Next to me stood our helper, Oscar Davis, who is a Christian like us. I drew him to myself, put my arm around him, and he, understanding what I wanted to say, put his arm around me, and this I said to them all: 'He is an Indian, and I am a white man, but through Jesus Christ we are brothers, and we belong much more

---

[7] *Op. cit.* p. 53.

[8] *Jubilaeumsbuechlein*, p. 66.

closely together than if we were physical brothers, and we have one and the same Father in common, God almighty, and have one and the same home in common, the blessed heaven, the house of our God, and have one and the same love in common, that is Jesus Christ, and one and the same hope in common, that is eternal salvation."[9]

Pastor Alfred Uplegger, himself the quintessential missionary, said this: "Pastor Harders spoke from his love in his heart for the Indians. He described their plight in detail. That touched many of the students (at the seminary where he was speaking at the time). He described how the Apache people were in a state of despair, dying of tuberculosis because of overexposure to wind, rain and snow, in spite of hot summer temperatures, not having enough clothing to keep warm, and then also undernourishment because of lack of money to buy proper food. So in the winter they were very miserable. And here I should insert: The Department of the Interior was still holding the Indians as prisoners of war. Anyone who will take time to read some of the Apache history will see how they surrendered against great odds, so that they would not all be killed. Some of the wise old men advised their fellow braves to give up. They had been chased and hounded for a hundred years already, especially since the Civil War. They had fled into old Mexico. But there the Mexican army was after them. So they had drifted back and forth over the boundary trying to find safety. Some ruthless, cruel and unscrupulous white people said, 'The only good Indian is a dead one!' So low the hate of unchristian people had fallen. 'Who is willing to volunteer to help these suffering Apaches?' Pastor Harders pleaded."[10]

Perhaps you will see a little of the psyche and soul of *Inashood* for his Apache people when you read the personal letter of Pastor Eugene Hartzell to his son, the writer. He was over 90 years of age when he wrote the letter. He wrote from his house in Lakeside, Arizona, just off the reservation. His meeting place to see his people at that time was the Walmart store in Lakeside, where everyone from the reservation came to shop. There he saw many of his people in the church he attended in Lakeside, just off the northern boundary of the Fort Apache Reservation. He served on the northern reservation at East Fork from 1958 until 1982. You can hear his pathos for the people and the work in his letter:

---

[9] *Anniversary Booklet for the Twenty-fifth Anniversary of the Evangelical Lutheran Indian Mission*, printed by Northwestern Publishing House, Milwaukee, Wisconsin, 1919, p. 49.

[10] Pastor Alfred Uplegger, *Reminiscing on the Lord's Mercy and Grace to Apache Indians During the Past 60 years*, Installment 1, page 2 (edited and re-recorded by Pastor Myrl Wagenknecht).

18 May 2010

Eric:

Writing may not be the first thing to go, but it goes. When you have trouble reading your own letters you know it's going.

I'm ashamed of how few letters I write. When I was Superintendent of the Nursery and was responsible for acknowledging the many gifts we received (especially in the Christmas season) I wrote upwards of 500 letters a year. Now I don't write that many in 10 years.

This brings to mind what we were like and what we did in those long-ago, happy, good days. Though you had little to do with my duty and the nursery correspondence, you were there in the background for sure. I'm glad I have those memories and that life. Every one of us had a part in those days – you boys, Maura, Mother and me.

It is unlikely we will ever see anything like those days again in this world anyway, but weren't they great? Who can match them? I'm glad you and your family got in on some of them. They were, as I can see so plainly now, precious beyond counting or knowing.

Lord, thank you for all those things we savored throughout those days and with every soul. We did not comprehend what wonders we were piling up. Thanks to our God for all he gave each one of us – and He is giving still.

I've enjoyed the trip down Memory Lane with you today.

Jesus' presence attend us all.

Dad.[11]

---

[11] Writer's personal letters.

CHAPTER ONE

Prologue

Don't urge me to leave you or to turn back from you.
Where you go I will go, and where you stay I will stay.
Your people will be my people and your God my God
(RUTH 1:16).

In Globe, Arizona, they draped Devereaux Street over the hilly canyons that came into Pinal Creek from the south. Pinal Creek came down from the big mountains that tower over Globe there to the south. There are aspen trees at their tops with cool breezes in the summer. In the winter the mountains serve as some kind of giant thermometer and measure the snow level which sometimes sinks below the town of Globe and engulfs it in chilly white. In summer monsoon days Pinal Creek, which wanders through town, sometimes turns into a rampaging monster that sends floating house

St. Peter's on Devereaux in 1917.
Photo Credit: St. Peter's Lutheran Church photos.

trailers bobbing down the main street. Boys stood at the top of one of Devereaux's hills and watched one summer in 1956 as such a thing happened. As Devereaux Street wends from south to north, it spans the little canyons of the town with bridges. There are even parallel foot bridges from whose underpinnings boys fastened long ropes and with the help of a tied tire swung across the canyon from one side to the other. (Their mothers did not know about this.)

There along Devereaux Street some of the houses are one-story at the entrance and three-stories at the back; they threaten to slide down into the bridged canyons. For a boy bicyclist with a yellow bike, the streets provided alternately scary fast travel downhill and painstaking pushing uphill. On that same Devereaux Street stands the little church today that is called St. Peter's Lutheran Church. The institution has been there since the before-mentioned Pastor Gustav Harders was there. He bolstered the work of *Inashood* at this

Mrs. Harders with Chinese confirmands, early 1900s.
Photo Credit: St. Peter's Lutheran Church photos. (There was a time when the Harders served a congregation of 60 Chinese people who met at the church on Wednesday evenings. In appreciation, the Chinese people living nearby had the buildings on the property wired for electricity.)

place and lived there and purchased the notch in the hillside that would provide St. Peter's Lutheran Church a little lasting presence on the slope. Pastor Alfred Uplegger was there with his people, and from Devereaux street Noftsger Hill School looms in the distance. It is on the horizon of the next hill. It isn't a school any more but a bed and breakfast establishment, but the building and the silhouette are the same. On the front of the old school building it says, "Noftsger Hill - 1917." Some of those boy bridge swingers mentioned before went to school there, walking up and down the steep streets and crossing the bridge to get to school. This school building with its corner domed roof has stood there and looked across the canyon and surveyed the work done by *Inashood* at St. Peter's Lutheran Church for 125 years now.

Right over the hill from St. Peter's Church on Devereaux Street, almost straight down to Pinal Creek below, still stand remnants of the adobe ruins of former Chinese people who lived in Globe in the early 1900s when Pastor Gustav Harders was there. Some of them clambered and climbed up to the little church place when Pastor Harders was on Devereaux Street. They frequented his classes and services. And, of course, he being the missionary that he was, slid down that same hill to meet with these "foreigners" and talk to them about Jesus. He also spoke from the courthouse steps in the middle of town. He spoke to anyone and everyone who would stop and listen to him with his heavy German accent. The courthouse building and steps were just up Pinal Creek from where the Chinese people had their adobes. The Apache people were there too. They worked in the mines. They worked at construction jobs and on the roads. There was a little school for their children there on the hillside, and Pastor Harders' daughters taught them. They fed the children there too and when they gave them rice sometimes, the reply was, "I don't want rice. I'm not a Chinaman."

Alfred Uplegger reminisced about the first time he saw Globe and stepped down from the train there: "The brakeman had set my suitcase down, and the boys (Harder's sons) put it into a buggy or a double buckboard. So they took me up the hill to the Mission and after eating supper and visiting they took me to one of two rooms added to the school building, which had been used as a room for Ernest Brown, the first Mission School boarding student, who was kept there because he had no other place to stay. The room for me had a single cot, a commode with a wash basin and towel and soap. Having slept well I was surprised in the morning to see snow on the Pinal Mountains and that the town nestled like Rome on seven hills. Pinal Creek flowed at the bottom in the canyon. Well, what a happy

Inside New Jerusalem church on Devereaux in Globe.
Photo Credit: St. Peter's Lutheran Church photos.

surprise to see the trees, mostly cottonwoods without leaves in January, but also the evergreens. From my geography book in school in Wisconsin we gained the impression that Arizona was all desert, more like the Sahara in Africa. And here we were in mountain country with all kinds of trees and cacti. This is more like a beautiful garden framed with pine trees; even Douglas fir up on the higher mountain slopes, visible from twenty miles away, even though they appear to be only seven miles away! The air is so clear, very little humidity, which accounts for nights getting very cold in the winter because of the rapid evaporation."[12]

It was from this place on Devereaux Street on a day in April in 1958 that the family of Pastor Eugene Hartzell, along with their dog Sandy, got into a yellow 1955 Ford station wagon and headed for a new place to live and work and be: East Fork on the Fort Apache Indian Reservation! East Fork Mission! It is still there, and to this

---

[12] Pastor Alfred Uplegger, *Reminiscing on the Lord's Mercy and Grace to Apache Indians During the Last 60 Years,* Installment 1, page 3 (edited and re-recorded by Pastor Myrl Wagenknecht).

day the name East Fork means home to the family who traveled in the yellow Ford station wagon. You can read the above letter and hear this family's feeling for the place. All the way up U.S. 60 toward East Fork that day in 1958, they passed things and crossed things that were Apache and would connect with them and their lives.

There was the archeological dig on the outskirts of Globe for the people there long before the Apaches got there. It is called *Besh Ba Gowah*. Those words come from the Apache language, which when translated literally say, "The metal, his house." The ruins speak of the Salado culture that came into the Tonto Basin after the Hohokam and the Anasazi peoples. Even though Apache leaders at election time like to speak about the Apaches being in the mountains of Arizona from time immemorial, the ruins and broken pottery on many sliding hillsides speak otherwise. Even on the sacred mountain *Tzilq Ligai*, the White Mountain which is Mt. Baldy today, there are obsidian arrow points and quartz and even some turquoise beads that point to these earlier cultures.

The yellow Ford station wagon usually followed the road (U.S. 70) out of Globe that went to Peridot and San Carlos on the San Carlos Reservation about 20 miles to the east. That is where the family had gone many times to sit in the evenings in the tufa stone houses of Henry Rosin and Alfred Uplegger and in the mud brick adobe house of Reuben Stock and his wife Erna. Those were pleasant evenings spent in talk about the work and the past. The veteran missionary, our *Inashood Hastin* (Francis Uplegger), was often there too. His family affectionately called him Old Papa, but we children didn't because his kindly and dignified demeanor didn't allow for this kind of childish familiarity. When the evening visit by our family was over, we were loaded back into the car and fell asleep in the back seat on the way back home to Devereaux Street. In fact, on one evening after the new parsonage was built, there was a disturbance on the front porch in the dark. All of a sudden, the Upleggers and Rosins and Stocks all started singing a hymn. They had come to warm the new parsonage and welcome our family.

But this time the Ford with the children and parents and dog veered to the left at the edge of town and went up over the hill on present day U.S. 60 and headed north and east toward Salt River Canyon. Not far out of town they crossed Seven Mile Wash. Some of their future classmates at East Fork Mission School would come from families who had lived in the Seven Mile Wash area, downstream from the bridge on U.S. 60. These future friends and acquaintances would attend East Fork High School, which Pastor Ernie Sprengeler especially worked hard to build.

One of the girls who came to school from the Seven Mile Wash area was Inez. She and Puzhy Sprengeler, son of Pastor Sprengeler, became sweethearts at East Fork Mission as they went to school there. One day they showed up at the same St. Peter's Church on Devereaux Street in the presence of Puzhy's father and were married by Pastor Hartzell. Puzhy's real name was Orville Sprengeler. He was born and grew up in Bylas on the San Carlos Reservation when his father was missionary there. He spoke excellent Apache. Probably no one among the *Inashood* ever spoke Apache as well as Puzhy did. He learned the Apache language as the Apaches did, when he played as a child and lived among them in Bylas at the mission station there. In fact, when Puzhy later stood up to speak at wakes he would begin his memorial talk, *"Nowhii Ndee..."* In colloquial English that would be, "Us Apaches..." His Apache was flawless and his vocabulary was much richer than the later generations of Apaches who were and are in the process of losing their language. Those who heard him say, *"Nowhii Ndee..."* smiled and nudged each other. And it was Puzhy who felt compelled one Sunday after church in Canyon Day to stand up and tell everyone what the Apache word for a dust devil was. Everyone had seen that mini-tornado stirring up the country side and sending tumbleweeds bounding here and there. Puzhy first asked the Apache people if they knew what the name of the dust devil was. They didn't so he told them: "In Apache, and he said the word for us all to hear, this word means 'the wind that pushes and pulls.' "

The yellow Ford station wagon worked its way uphill from Seven Mile Wash to the top of what is now called the Nantanes Plateau. Just before topping out on the last steep grade, there is a place where for an instant if you look between the cuts of the mountain to the south you can see San Carlos and the buildings and houses far below and away. The missionaries had to coax their Model T and Model A Fords up these same Nantans, as they called the mountains.[13] And then the road passed Seneca where the San Carlos people would later put an earthen dam on one of the canyons going down into Salt River Canyon and stock the small resulting lake with bass and bluegills and even trout sometimes and also try unsuccessfully to have a golf course and restaurant and service station. The buildings from that failed endeavor stand hollow-eyed and stare forlornly at the passersby today.

Salt River Canyon came next with the marvel of road making its displays. It is more spectacular than the Grand Canyon in some

---

13 The word *Nantan* comes from the Apache which means chief, so these were the Chief Mountains.

ways because you can actually drive through it. The shadows and coloring of the cliffs and canyons are always awash in different colors depending on the time of day and the season. Don't try and drive it in icy times. One time in a winter ice storm all the traffic was stopped in a multi-car fender-bender pileup. Everyone cheered when a police car came skidding helplessly along on the ice and plowed into one of the parked cars. But on good days with no ice, stop at Becker's Butte lookout and see the river snaking and sneaking through the divides below. Downstream from the bridge you can find the place the Apaches called "singing rocks." These were salt crystals hanging in profusion that if you hit them with a stick, they tinked and clinked and sounded musical somehow as they fell to the ground. The two reservations—San Carlos and Fort Apache—meet at the river. Highway 60 skirts along their joined edges through the canyon drive.

The Salt River is an impressive river now and was then that first time in April when we went to our new home at East Fork.[14] East Fork and North Fork join at Fort Apache to become the White River, and White River and Black River join to make the Salt River. There are many rivers in Apache country. They run, coerced by canyons to follow the same paths of the millennia. They have their starts in the mountains in some grassy meadow where they meander confused this way and that until they find a way down and make the green serpents lined with cottonwood and black walnut and sycamore trees that finger all the way down to the deserts. From the mountains you can see them too. White River. Black River. Carrizo Creek. Cibecue Creek that cascades into Salt River Canyon. There is the Gila River and the San Francisco River that merge and go by Peridot and San Carlos and Bylas. This Gila River, spawned in Geronimo's birthplace in western New Mexico, has been impounded now in Coolidge Dam. Its waters inched up over what used to be old San Carlos. That happened at the time of the first missionaries in the early 1930s. The resulting San Carlos Lake covered the place and the graveyard of ancient Apaches. Some said the white man's lake was cursed because of its temerity to cover the people's graves like that, but the curse was weak and the waters inched up to overflow the spillway on a few wet years.

Al Sieber, the charmed scout for the cavalry during the Apache wars, was killed in the building of Roosevelt Dam on the Salt River. He escaped the intentional death of Apache arrows and bullets to

---

[14] The Salt River drains 1,900 square miles in the White Mountains and can flow 143,000 cubic feet of water per second in flood times. For comparison, in normal times 186,000 cubic feet of water per second flow in the Mississippi through St. Louis, Missouri.

The Apache Dam Builder.
Photo Credit: Picture from Globe Historical Society.

succumb to the accidental death of concrete and stone.[15] Many of those barrel-chested warriors who actually ran after the war chiefs on their forays and raids ended up taming the rivers of Arizona. It was the white man's way because he needed a reliable supply of water for his desert intrusions. He hired his former enemy to do it.

The rivers got into the politics of the land distribution. *Inashood* understood that water wrongs had been perpetrated on the Apaches—and on other Indians of Arizona too, for that matter. In 1929 Guenther said about the rising flood of the murky Gila River water behind the impoundment of Coolidge Dam, "Fifty years ago the white man came in. He settled above the Indians' homes. The river got lower; many ditches dried up. The white man above was violating the very principles of "prior rights" that he had himself established. Many Indian farms dried up. Extreme poverty was the result. What a pity when a man wants to work for his living and is robbed of the means of doing so! Then one began to hear of a great dam to be built. This dam should hold back the flood waters of the Gila River for the "poor Pimas." If the Pima Indians were the only

---

[15] Maybe it was accidental. Some believe that Apache workmen orchestrated Sieber's demise in an accident that happened when a big boulder he was inspecting rolled on him and crushed him.

ones to benefit from this dam then you and I would never live to see it built. The white man wanted the dam to irrigate the many additional acres of land waiting for water. But the story of the "poor Pima" was a good lever for prying a concession out of Congress, and the dam was built."[16]

Cibecue turnoff goes to the left as you leave the Salt River Canyon. From there U.S. 60 goes on toward Carizzo and then turns toward Fort Apache on present Highway 77. The paved road to Cibecue goes thirty miles into the mountains to the west and stops. At one time, Cibecue was the farthest settlement from a United States Post Office in the whole United States. It was that way in the old days too, of course. Missionaries got marooned in Cibecue in rainy and snowy and red mud days. Cars would slither sideways up Cibecue Mountain when the road was not paved—and it was not paved at the time the yellow Ford went by in 1958. Missionary Paul Mayerhoff rode to Cibecue fairly soon after he got to the area in 1895. He visited the groups and clans that lived here and there, isolated from the rest of the world and even from the rest of the reservation. Missionary Guenther said he wore a hole in Sunday suit trousers when he rode a horse there from Whiteriver. In 1881 the soldiers from the Cibecue Massacre trying in the dark to get back to the relative safety of Fort Apache crossed by there. Just before Fort Apache there was the mesa on the left, and from its summit Signal Corps Sergeant Will C. Barnes saw returning soldiers from the deadly altercation on Cibecue Creek. He was awarded the Congressional Medal of Honor for his bravery in leaving the safety of the fort to see the returning soldiers. At that time Chief Alchesay himself was not very far away, as the soldiers straggled back to Fort Apache from the so-called massacre. Some people were killed up Seven Mile Canyon, and Alchesay was said by some to have been part of it. He was implicated but never was indicted.

As the yellow Ford with the Hartzells in it got closer to Fort Apache there was the big red dirt cut in the road called Geronimo Pass. Years later, someone painted out the "P" in the sign, and it stood there with its coarse suggestion for a long time. A little farther down the road toward Canyon Day and the flat there with the

---

[16] Edgar Guenther, *The Apache Scout,* February, 1929, p. 2.

ancient Kanishba ruin, was the peak of rock called *"Mboo b'elah."*[17] It was visible from the Mission to the west. It was a landmark there, along with Sawtooth which stood nearby on the horizon in the flaming setting sun. We are embarrassed to say what *Mboo b'elah* means. That is apparently what someone saw when he looked at that little peak. So we in the yellow Ford ended up calling it that too. There were some English words that approximated the sound of certain other delicate Apache words, words for certain body parts. Our classmates would laugh and snicker when our teachers unknowingly said these suggestive sounding English words. We were all soon masters of all the vulgar words that Apache boys had at their disposal. That is the perversity of foreign language acquisition. The parts of the language that come easily and can be remembered are not useful in polite conversation.

Early Canyon Day wickiups.
Photo Credit: Paul Behn. From the Hartzell photo collection.

How were we in the yellow Ford to have known that in 1943 Pastor Edgar Guenther had been driving on the same road we were as we neared Fort Apache? How were we to have known that he looked

---

[17] The name *Mboo b'elah* literally means "the owl's penis." Missionary Uplegger called Apace a vulgar language. If not vulgar it was certainly frank and straightforward. Everyone who saw the peak there by the White River got the point. There are fortifications at the top of it, an old stone wall that would have made defending the peak an easy thing. From its summit you can see down to the crossing of White River on the road that winds through the mountains and the Nantans and goes down by Cassadore Springs to San Carlos. Mayerhoff wrote an article for the *Beatrice Daily Sun* newspaper that appeared reprinted Wednesday May 9, 1984. The title was, "The Legend of Kelly's Butte." It was about the Irish character who supposedly met his end at the top of Kelly's Butte, or our *"Mboo b' elah."*

at those same mountains and thought thoughts we too would have? At that time *Inashood* Guenther personified the mountains to his Apache readers in warfare in Europe:

"Saturday— Drove to Fort Apache this morning. After all these years I still look for Mount Baldy whenever I near Guy Sisson's place. This morning Mount Baldy was looking down on Apacheland as majestically as ever. Only a short time ago he was still crowned with snow. I hope you have mountains wherever you are. They are such good friends. I imagine each of you had your particular mountain friend when you were at home. If it was not Baldy himself it must have been one of his younger brothers, depending on where your home was: Chiricahua Butte where the acorns grow, for Turkey Creek; RimRock for East Fork; Kelly's Butte for Canyon Day; McKay's Peak for North Fork; Sugar Loaf for Cedar Creek; and stately Blue House for Cibecue. No doubt you have been homesick for one or the other, but they will be waiting for you when you return. They will still be standing when the Lord Jesus himself returns.

"God himself appears to love greatly the mountains that are his own handiwork. He likes to mention them as symbols of his power and of his unchanging and everlasting love for those who are truly his children. In Isaiah he tells us, "For the mountains shall depart, and the hills be removed; but my kindness shall not depart from thee, neither shall the covenant of my peace be removed, saith the LORD that hath mercy on thee" (54:10).

"And now it is evening twilight. The sun which rose so beautifully this morning to light up the open grave for us is bidding us good night as it lights up Rim Rock with lavender hue before dropping off into the west. When it rises wherever you are, may it be a reminder of the presence of your risen Lord and of the warmth of his love and mercy, just individually for **you**!

"This rambling letter has tried to bring you back in spirit on a short furlough to the homeland. I hope it has not altogether failed."[18]

We in the yellow Ford didn't at that time know how the Apache people there felt about the mountains, but they surely did treasure mountain company. Mountains were always dear to the Apache. They traveled on their peaks and on their spines. No one could get them there. They could scurry along the summits for a hundred miles in forced marches before they stopped to rest. Cavalry soldiers on horses simply could not keep up and follow. Cochise hid out in the Chiricahua Mountains in southeastern Arizona. From Fort Huachuca in southern Arizona you could see mountains called the "sky

---

[18] Submitted by Ruth Kessel, *The Apache Scout*, May, 1943.

island" Huachuca Mountains rising to 9,466 feet. Those mountains alone harbor nearly 1,000 species of plants, 365 types of birds, 200 kinds of butterflies, 80 species of mammals and 70 different reptile species. There is Turret Mountain where white soldiers snuck up on sleeping Apaches who thought they were safe there. There are the Sierra Ancha Mountains, the Nantans, the White Mountains, the Superstition Mountains by Phoenix with Four Peaks, and the Grahams toward Safford. These mountains were home to high mountain meadows with clear streams where trout lay in dappled pools along dripping cliffs and strewn boulders. The trout surfaced in gold and blue water to snatch a floating fly off the eddy of the darkening stream. In these high mountain meadows in the evenings Merriam elk stepped cautiously out from soft blue shadows to graze.[19]

In 1897 Mayerhoff on a solo trip to Cibecue described the breathtaking views he had along the way. From the top of Cibecue Mountain he saw to the east the snow-covered White Mountains of "home." Then from Canyon Creek he described the same White Mountains to the east, the Pinals of Globe to the southwest, Mount Turnbull to the southeast with the Grahams farther off in the distance. Alfred Uplegger talked about Blue House Mountain and the view of mountains—even to mountains hundreds of miles in the distance—and he knew the elevations of these mountains and the straight-line distance to them all.

And the yellow Ford passed by the Cibecue turnoff that day as it headed for East Fork with the new missionary and his family.

In Apache country there are mountains everywhere. There are mountains where even today you can finger among the pebbles on the very summits and find remnants of the Old Ones. Pottery lies there broken. Once in a while there is an obsidian point from some ancient hunter's arrow. The Old Ones—the Hohokam and the Anasazi and the Mogollon peoples—were there once long ago. From the summits of the mountains you can imagine and dream about what it was these people saw as they stood on the peaks and looked down into the haze of distance. And down below along the dry creek beds in canyons and tucked away in cliffs you can still see where these Old Ones lived. In some places the cedar door thresholds still show the stone ax marks, and the bouldered ceiling still is dusted with the black of evening cooking fires. Even today some hiker or climber will occasionally stumble into a little cave or niche in a cliff and see

---

[19] Our friends and their families wouldn't eat elk meat. They said it would make you itch if you ate it. The Merriam elk are all gone now, but their cousins the Rocky Mountain elk, brought in from other places, still abound.

the clay pots still sitting there and the stone *metate*, as if the inhabitant had just stepped out for a minute—and it was seven hundred years ago or a thousand! All that time no clock ticked. No noise came, except the storm of silence and the sounds of the wind and the rain and the bird songs and an occasional lion squall and coyote yap at night. These dusty and deserted openings in the rocks and cliffs saw the flickering of the light and of the seasons and of the decades. The dust settled and covered the little corn cobs and the tufts of string and burlap like material left behind by the Old Ones in the mountains. We didn't know all this about the mountains that first day, but we would learn.

Just before we got to the turnoff on the corner there at Fort Apache where Guy Sisson had operated his garage many years before and had done mechanical work for everyone (the early missionaries included), our father stopped the car and we got out to look down at the White River, which had just joined hands with the North Fork and the East Fork to make the stout arm of river that would go on down twenty miles or so and join with Black River to make the Salt River. That same Puzhy Sprengeler who spoke Apache so well would take us duck hunting down there on Christmas Eve day in 1961 when we were in high school. We saw and felt the hot water springs and saw the watercress and the flocks of mallards and green-winged teal. We jumped all day on the cliffy bends of the river. On one long bend there were black and white Canadian geese that departed honking and complaining around the river canyon corner. The sycamore trees down there exuded an odor that got into our clothes, and we could later smell the flora of "the River" in our closet and think of the good times we'd had hunting ducks that day. We went down there to "the River" many more times over the years. Every time was an adventure of walking and being in wild and unspoiled country accessible only on foot. We later saw pictures of Apache men on horses on one of the steep hillsides of one of those rivers, pictures taken before we got there. The pictures showed them gambling there by their tethered horses.

As we looked down that day and saw White River that first time, we also saw a donkey in a corn field across the river. When we were in Globe we had been told about the donkeys that would be at East Fork. They ran free, there were many of them, and to boys like us what better prospect could there be than to be able to catch our own donkey and ride it? The donkeys were more or less public transportation, an original Uber arrangement. The women used the donkeys to haul firewood down from the mountains around. (You can still see the old scars left by double-bit axes on ancient gray juniper stumps high up on the hills jutting upward from the river bottoms.) Sometimes the donkeys were loaded down with so much wood you could hardly see the staggering critter beneath.

The Seven Mile boys rode donkeys in galloping groups of twenty or so. Sometimes there were three passengers on a single donkey. The one in front was hanging onto several loops of rope tied tightly behind the front legs and shoulders. A stick was the way to get the donkey to run. Poke him along the backbone and he would swish his tail and put his ears back—and run! Sometimes he would run under a tree and brush his tormentor off or cut too close to a fence post and bruise his rider's shins. To turn the donkey right, you clubbed the left side of his head and ears with the stick. To go left, club the right side. From our beds at night we could hear the donkeys braying—one way off there, and another over there answering.

The donkeys all had names and personalities. There was Naa-do.[20] He belonged to the Forrest Family, Y-28's family. He was good. He would run without too much provocation. He had that dark stripe across his shoulders that many of the donkeys had. The Adays had

Apache boys on donkeys.
Photo Credit: Hartzell photo collection

---

[20] The name was the same for the father of the Forrest clan. It maybe was an example of Apache humor that the donkey's appellation was the master's name.

28

one too, much like Naado, but theirs was always working, and we couldn't find it unemployed very often so that we could ride it. The Nash Family donkey had a slit nostril from some previous mishap, and it liked to run faster and faster downhill, and then when properly positioned propel his rider off over his head with a short sidestep maneuver. There was Morris. He belonged to the Moodys up at East Fork. He had been hit by a log truck, and his ear flopped down and was askew. One early spring day they found Morris in a snowbank up the river by Geronimo's Cave. Morris' old bones didn't make it to warmer weather and grass. There was Boots from Seven Mile, a female donkey with deformed back feet. Kino Edwards had a white stud donkey called Y-6. No one could ever really ride him. We couldn't, anyway, because he bucked too hard. He was one of the perpetrators of midnight braying, and from our beds at night we could identify him. The Wycliffs across the river had a brown and white pinto donkey that fought a lot with Y-6.

Our means of reservation travel were all anatomically correct. We all learned soon enough what Ezekiel 23:20 was talking about when it described God's wanton people in these words: *"There she lusted after her lovers, whose genitals were like those of donkeys."*

Eric Hartzell on black donkey.
Photo Credit: Hartzell photo collection

The Way Water Was Carried.
Photo Credit: The Apache Lutheran, *June 1967*

Across the river stood that lone donkey in the cornfield on our very first trip to Fort Apache in our yellow Ford. Our first glimpse of the donkey in the corn field by Fort Apache would signify many adventures with our Apache friends, just being boys and enjoying life.

As we got closer to our home at East Fork we took the very road that first missionary Paul Mayerhoff had taken when he had left Fort Apache and started up the East Fork of the White River in 1895. He had been given a tent, bed and mess-box until his own things could be brought from San Carlos.[21] The post commander there at Fort Apache had been kind to him. As he went along the trail from Fort Apache up the river to East Fork he was in the company of a one-eyed man who took him up there to the big cedar tree that is across the cattle guard at East Fork Mission. It was under this big cedar tree that Paul Mayerhoff had pitched his tent. We didn't know it at the time, but a very big man had come that first evening Mayerhoff was there. He came on a swaybacked horse and said that this was his land and that Mayerhoff should pay two dollars to camp there for five days. Later Mayerhoff paid the two dollars and remarked later that it was the best land deal anyone had ever made because he stayed there without further charge for the next 8 years.

There is a picture of the Apache scouts' wickiups taken from Fort Apache looking east toward Rimrock on the horizon. Col. H. B. Wharfield wrote about these Apache scouts in his book *With Scouts and Cavalry at Fort Apache*. Some of them had been active in the war and had chased Geronimo. The scouts' names would be the names of our classmates at school at East Fork. There was Sergeant Chow Big (Chowbick), and his family became the Adleys.[22] They all lived across the river from the mission. It could well have been that this was the very man who had come across the river with his swaybacked horse that first evening Mayerhoff was there. Private Askeldelinny also carried the name Major and was buried later in the Whiteriver Lutheran Church. Charles Bones was born May 10, 1878, and enlisted July 2, 1891, a few years before Mayerhoff would make his way up the river toward East Fork Mission in his borrowed wagon. There are Lutherans today who are related to Charles Bones. Broadus Bones was a good linguist and helped Pastor Arthur Guenther in the mission work in Whiteriver. There was scout Billy C F. The writer worked in the NYC program (Neighborhood Youth Corps) with a boy whose last name was Billy. Some of the other scouts in the picture with their wickiups east of Fort Apache were: Chissay, Cody, DeKlay (Declay), Jesse Palmer, George Pope, Alejo Quintero, Sye Thomas, Tehnehjeheh (Tenijieth). There

---

[21] Paul Mayerhoff, *Beatrice Daily Sun*, "In Days of Apaches, Chapter IV," August 15, 1933.

[22] There was a green ledger book with old Apache names in it. Edgar Guenther had procured it from Milwaukee, Wisconsin, and it had these German directions inside the front cover, "*Gebrauchsanweisung für die Seelen und Kommunikantenregister-Deckel* (Directions for the use of this soul and communicant record). Many of the Apaches listed in it were born well before 1900, some going back to the time of the Civil War. The Adleys were from the Y band. Most of the people living by East Fork Mission and on up the river from there were Y band Apaches. The green ledger book registering the members of the Lutheran church there told the story.

was also Lambert Stone, who was a scout with Alchesay. He is the one who came riding into the mission on Thanksgiving Day in 1929 with turkeys hanging over the pommel of his saddle for the nursery children. The green Mission ledger recorded that he was born on May 20, 1867, and that his number was Y-19. He lived up the river from the mission, and the riders in the yellow Ford station wagon would go by his place often in company of some of Lambert's relatives, the Rileys, who were good fishing and donkey riding partners. The handwritten note came to school one day from Lambert Stone regarding his grandson: "Daniel is sick and threw out all night. I hope you approve of this condition."

Over the years most of these names were carried through the doors of the school and church at East Fork. There even was a scout with the name Grasshopper, who would give his name to the area by Cibecue that the ASU archeology department excavated. There in the picture was the place where the wickiups of these scouts were and where we would live.[23] And the yellow Ford went by with its family, looking for the first time up the East Fork River valley at home.

Stone landmarks stood all around the mission. Rimrock was on the horizon, blue and gray with its sheer face. When the last Apaches of the Apache wars finally surrendered, they did it in the mountains east of Fort Apache in that very vicinity of Rimrock which was visible from the mission.[24] When we later hiked around up there and looked for shed elk antlers we occasionally saw heaps of rocks with mature ponderosa pines in them. The piles looked suspiciously like graves. There was nothing natural around the places that would have caused these heaps of stones. We would never know if they were in fact graves, but there were places where we could see old camps with ancient enameled cups and cooking implements lying around. Chief Alchesay's grave up on the North Fork of the White River in its solitary place looked a lot like the places we occasionally saw by Rimrock. Red Rock stood there too, much lower in the valley and closer to the Mission. We looked for arrowheads on Red Rock. We went up there and sat and watched the river valley beneath us.

---

[23] Col. H. B. Wharfield, *With Scouts and Cavalry at Fort Apache,* Edited by John Alexander Carroll Professor of History at The University of Arizona. Arizona Pioneers' Historical Society: Tucson, Arizona. 1965, pp. 21, 22.

[24] It was at Rimrock that the very last free Apaches had given up. They were Mangus and Daklugie, Juh's son. Daklugie told how it was there at the end: "We wandered north for several days without being bothered by the army. By traveling at night, following the ridges and building no fires, we managed to get into the mountains east of Fort Apache" (Eve Ball, *An Apache Odyssey, Indeh,* Provo Utah: Brigham Young University Press, 1980, p. 117).

The school kids would hike up there on outings. One Christmas the boarding school students cut a Christmas tree at the base of Red Rock and dragged it in the snow back to the mission. And there was "Gan B'sedia." That name had something to do with mountain spirit *gan* dancers.[25] That was what stood to the north of the mission, across the East Fork River that we heard from our nighttime beds in the springtime when the flooded river ran high and fast.

When the tires of the yellow Ford rumbled across the cattle guard at the Mission and we turned in that very first time in 1958, there before us was *Gad N'chah*, the big cedar tree. *Inashood* Edgar Guenther (*Inashood Ndasin*—the tall missionary) had used that name to immortalize the very tree under which the first missionary, Paul Mayerhoff, had pitched his tent. Every year sees a few more limbs drying up. The days of the old patriarch are limited now, but it is still there and has been the witness of *Inashood* and his comings and goings for 120 years.

We got out of our car and went into our new home. Pastor Paul Behn had specially designed the ceilings in the house with what was called a "bevel devil." Visitors often commented on his artwork. And the last bedroom in the house down the hall was where Pastor Ernst Sprengeler had gone to bed that night a year earlier and had told his wife Erna before going to sleep, "I feel real tired tonight." He fell asleep then and never woke up again. He is buried in the cemetery at the upper end of the mission where so many of the Apache children from the Nursery are also buried.

We saw *Gan B'sedia* standing there in the distance outside the north bedroom window of our house on that first day at East Fork Mission. It was 1958. *Gan B'sedia* stood in its mute and mesa-like way outside our bedroom window at East Fork Mission. It saw us, and we saw it on that first day when our family arrived in the yellow Ford station wagon. Coronado saw the same thing in 1540 when he came through that part of the country. He came from southern Arizona on his way toward the area of present-day Zuni, New Mexico. He must have come down Seven Mile Canyon and crossed the East Fork of the White River and proceeded on up through the pine forests of Apache territory as he and his men traveled. Apache runners later went that same way carrying news and messages from Fort Apache to the military presence in San Carlos and Bylas (Fort Thomas).

---

[25] The name *Gan B'sedia* is the English rendition of the Apache. To this day Apaches who were our schoolmates and lived in the valley with us know this name and still refer to the mesa by this name.

The parsonage from the east, farthest window on the right is where
Pastor Sprengeler died.

Painting by Eric Hartzell

Geronimo had been right about the Apache claim on the land—
and he had been wrong. The Apaches had laid claim to the land, but
they were latecomers. Spain also had coveted Arizona land for a
long, long time. The first Lutheran *Inashood* came in 1893. The first
Jesuits from Spain had come already in the late 1600s. Father Kino
wended his way into the landscape and the hearts of many early
inhabitants of Arizona. He came on horseback. He had dreams
of establishing missions on the San Pedro and Gila and Colorado
Rivers. It didn't happen, but his horse left tracks all over that Arizona country for a quarter of a century. During the 1700s Spain
sent others to ride horses among those who lived along these rivers. They were German men too, Jesuits recruited from German
states, including Padres Grazhoffer, Middendorf, Pauer, Sedel-
mayr, Segesser, Keller, Pfefferkorn and Stiger. In 1893 the German
Lutheran *Inashoods* Plocher and Adascheck, were not the first Germans the saguaro and mesquite had heard and seen. Nor was the
Lutheran *Inashood* the very first to tangle with the medicine men.

Grazhoffer criticized early Native American polygamy and drinking orgies. Someone put poison in his food—and that was in 1733.[26]

Now it was 1958, exactly 225 years later. The yellow Ford station wagon had arrived.

[26] Marshall Trimble, *Arizona, A Cavalcade of History,* Treasure Chest Publications: Tucson, Arizona, 1989, p. 65.

CHAPTER TWO

The Place and the People

God only knows. God makes his plan. The
information's unavailable to the mortal man
(PAUL SIMON, "SLIP SLIDIN' AWAY").

Even though the Apaches claimed the land as theirs, the ruins of many who had been there before proved that it just wasn't so. At least it proved that their land had not been theirs from time immemorial, as they later claimed. There is in fact an ancient Mogollon ruin not far from Fort Apache that had perhaps 1,000 inhabitants and was abandoned in 1400. It is called Kanishba and can be visited even today. Paul Mayerhoff, the first Lutheran missionary on the Fort Apache Reservation, wrote about places he saw and knew within walking distance of present-day East Fork Mission. "The other (ruin) a mile farther down the valley, was more pretentious, an eight room pueblo, evidently two story high with the upper story stepped back so the roof of the lower suite of rooms served as a court for the upper tier. The wall of the lower rooms to a height of six or more feet still stood undamaged in 1904, the year I left there."[27] The Anasazi and Hohokam peoples seemed to have left the area about the time Columbus discovered America.[28] It is surmised that those early peoples left because of a terrible and widespread drought. They left the ruins of their lives behind, and we don't know where they went to continue living in more hospitable climes.

Some of the Warm Springs Apaches who were forced to live at San Carlos credited it and its environs as the reason why defection took place in bands that went off raiding and living off the land again. They couldn't stand the place. Apart from the inhospitality of some of the other bands who had also been placed there by the government, the place itself was just not a nice place to consider as home for the

---

[27] Paul Mayerhoff, *Beatrice Daily Sun*, "Ruins Left by Prehistoric Extinct Race," June 17, 1934.

[28] Columbus Day is not celebrated on the reservations. The reader is left to guess why that might be.

next lifetime or so. General Crook's adjutant John Bourke said about the place that it was "stinking malarial flats along the Gila River." Lieutenant Britton Davis described his first night in San Carlos: "Our first night in San Carlos we slept on the ground without tents. When I started to roll up my bedding in the morning, I found that I had for a bedfellow a ten-inch centipede. I registered a complaint with (Captain Emmet) Crawford but got scant sympathy. 'You were lucky,' he said, 'I found a young rattler in mine.' "[29] Imagine if you were Naiche and your band of Chiricahuas were commanded to stay there, and you saw one after the next get sick and die until you had half the people you had before. Would you be inclined to stay, or might you too bolt for freedom and a better place? Daklugie was Apache war chief Juh's son. He said about the area around San Carlos and Peridot, "That was a terrible place, the worst in all of our vast territory." Perhaps in the summer it is. August is hot. Thunderclouds tease off in the distance but sometimes the rain doesn't come. The white alkali swelters in its own mirage. Creosote bush and cat claw scratch each other and wait thinly for night to fall and rain to come, and it seems like neither will ever happen again. But some of the missionaries would see it as a wonderful place. If you talked to the Rosins or the Upleggers, you would have thought Peridot and San Carlos were heaven on earth. They had personally and painfully experienced months in a row of swelter and sweat at San Carlos and Peridot and Bylas. They knew the drought and they knew the flood. They knew and saw the vistas of burned up alkaline soil, but still they got a reverential tone in their voices when they talked about their adopted homeland.

In spring, mats of golden poppies and lupine stretch for miles between the mesas and the mountains. Quail dart and tilt among the blooming and fragrant mesquite bushes. Blue and sacred, Mount Turnbull towers in the sunny sky. Rivulets talk in the washes. It is beautiful. People have fallen in love with the place, so that its very name tugs at their hearts and lures them back that way again. It was that way for the early missionaries. They spoke lovingly of the place. It was their home. They liked it. They— loved it! But it wasn't an easy thing or a thing likely to happen that they would love it.

The consummate Lutheran seminary professor, C. F. W. Walther identified why the *Inashood* felt the way he did for this place called Apacheland. This is what Walther said, "When a Lutheran candidate of theology is assigned to a parish where he is to discharge the office of a Lutheran preacher, for him that place ought to be the dear-

---

[29] Davis, Britton, *The Truth about Geronimo*, 1929, p. 30 (quoted in *The Smoke Signal*, December 2009, p. 203).

est, most beautiful, and most precious spot on earth. He should be unwilling to exchange it for a kingdom. Whether it is in a metropolis or in a small town, on a bleak prairie or in a clearing in the forest, in a flourishing settlement or in a desert—for him that place should be a miniature paradise. Do not the blessed angels descend from heaven with great joy whenever the Father in heaven sends them to minister to those who are to be heirs of salvation? Why, then, should we poor sinners be unwilling to hurry after them with great joy to a place where we can lead other people—fellow sinners—to salvation?"[30] *Inashood* learned to love the place and the people. It took some longer to learn the lesson than others—and some never did learn it, if the truth is told. Hundreds did love the work though in places akin to "a clearing in the forest" and "in a desert." To many it did become "a miniature paradise," and you will hear it in their words and lives.

The reader must know that Christianity is a causative force on the earth. There is no question that in this world there has never been a force like Christianity to move people to do things: hard things and self-sacrificing things. Christianity has been the inspiration for people to leave father and mother and cling to a work in a strange and hard place. Nestorian Christians took Christ to China in 635 A.D. That is remarkable when you know that these were Assyrians, the very people who had taken the ten tribes of Israel into mideastern captivity, from which they would never return. Their kin had perfected the tender art of crucifixion, but some of them—the Christians among them—felt compelled to take their belief east to China. The Apostle Paul felt this terrible dislodging force of the gospel when he said, "Woe to me if I do not preach the gospel." And so did the *Inashood* who came to this land and this Apache people. They would spend their youth and their energy and their lives. That is the place where they would have their own children and bury some of them next to the mesas. That is where they would grow old and finally drive on paved roads and risk traffic accidents with inebriated drivers that would leave them crippled and bent. They didn't come for pay, although they earned salaries that took care of their needs. They didn't come for fine accommodations. Many of them built their own houses from materials they could get on hand. They didn't come for personal advancement. Some even came with that awful stigma hanging over their heads: *Er taugt nichts als für die Indianer Mission.*[31]

---

[30] *Law and Gospel: How to Read and Apply the Bible*, St. Louis: Concordia Publishing House, 2010, p. 225.

[31] "He is only worth being sent to the Indian Mission."

The first *Inashoods* got on trains to make the trip to Apacheland. They climbed up into buckboards. They swung their legs over shying, sideways-stepping horses. They walked. And after a while they climbed up on the running boards of Model T Fords and actually backed them up the steep hills because it was a gravity-fed fuel system, and steep inclines caused the flow to dwindle to a sputter and a cough. There got to be more sophisticated cars with roll-up glass windows and heaters and fuel pumps that would get the gas to the cylinders even on a strong uphill. Travel in this mountainous land was hard and vehicles failed. *Inashood* Eric LaHaine had his Star automobile washed away in a cloudburst on the East Fork of the White River, and the roaring red surge of angry water took it away. They found it way downstream after the storm, beached and crooked and ruined.

Peridot and San Carlos were the Arizona places where many of the Apaches ended up after the wars. This was the place where the U.S. Government decreed that many of them stay. This place was determined (no doubt) by the likes of General Miles, the man who gets the credit for subjugating the Apaches. And then you have the short little man who escaped the clutches of the Civil War and ended up thereafter with Native Americans and thought out loud, "The only good Indian is a dead Indian." That was Phil Sheridan. Maybe his kind of animus poisoned the pot of Indian land distribution. Maybe the ones who said the Apaches live in Peridot and San Carlos thought they were doing them hurt and were glad. But in spite of the malicious machinations of mean men, Peridot and San Carlos and Bylas remained beautiful places, and the triplet peaks and Mt. Turnbull towering over the landscape express that beauty in desert colors and shapes. Peridot is literally a gem of a place. This is where the gemstone is found.[32] The mountains up Point of Pines way wait in the distance with their blankets of snow in the winter and their cool breezes in the summer. The desert plays its temperate trump card in December and January.

The whole southern reservation is called San Carlos. Present day San Carlos is the capital city of the San Carlos Apaches. But San Carlos wasn't always San Carlos. Present-day San Carlos was originally called Rice, after one of the Anglo government leaders of the time. The first San Carlos is no more. It stood on the shores of present-day

---

[32] There are very few places on earth where this semi precious birthstone is found. One of the best places to look for it, and perhaps even the best place to look for the beautiful pale green gems, is Peridot on the San Carlos Reservation. Emory Goseyun, former East Fork student and present Peridot Lutheran Mission member, gives tours to some who are interested in his peridot mine.

San Carlos Lake, whose waters are impounded by Coolidge Dam. Listen as Edgar Guenther describes this first San Carlos and you will understand how it was, almost in cinematic terms.

"There is no more interesting place than an army post. It is a little world all by itself. A visitor at San Carlos on February 16, 1876, or thereabouts, would readily agree to that. San Carlos lay before him like a giant 'U'. The officers' row formed the one prong, the troop and Q.M. stables the other, with the shops, house, canteen, etc. completing the curve. Between the two prongs of the 'U' lay the parade ground.

"On the hospital porch sat troopers, some recovering from sickness, others from wounds. On the porch of the officers' row fine ladies whiled away the hours, while their husbands strutted to and fro. In the restaurant the Chinese cook was being tormented by hungry troopers, while from behind the bars of the guardhouse white and Apache prisoners looked longingly to the freedom which was not theirs.

"The post carpenter was building a cabinet, the wheelwright shrinking a tire on a wheel of a lumbering Q.M. wagon, and the blacksmith was brandishing his hammer at a mule that resented the style of shoe being fitted to his windward hoof. In the canteen, soldiers were buying the necessities of life and some things that were not so necessary. At the barracks, troopers were mending trousers or writing letters, while at the stable others were greasing their saddles. They sang lustily while they worked, glad that it did not happen to be their turn to be sweltering in the heat of the parade ground under the command of some conceited little second lieutenant just out of West Point.

"At headquarters a grizzled old colonel was growling over some recent order from Washington, while in the Q.M. office an equally grizzled captain was fretting because the pay train due overland from Wilcox had not yet arrived.

"In the lowlands, sloping towards the river, camps were clustered under the spreading cottonwoods by the hundreds. Warm Spring Apaches from New Mexico, White Mountain Apaches, San Carlos Apaches, Caderas, Chiricahua Apaches and others were herded and guarded here like cattle at a round-up. Forcibly they had been herded thither from crops and homes in the distance while some official in the war office in Washington boasted how easily he had solved the Apache 'problem.' Yes, San Carlos was an interesting place on that day in 1876 or thereabouts.

"On February 16, 1930, it was no longer the same San Carlos. People were there by the score, but they had arrived in cars and did not belong there. They had come to see the large two-story stone recitation building of the Indian school blown up, the last building that had not yet been torn to the ground by the man who had bought San Carlos and agreed to have it out of the way before the waters behind Coolidge Dam should creep over them.

"Hospital, officers' row, barns, shops, all had already been razed, and in the wreckage of the old guard house brightly colored lizards flitted in and out. The waters of Coolidge Lake had already covered the Indian homes, and wild ducks were swimming on its glassy waters.

"We brought back our old church at San Carlos, and the tufa stone went into the walls of our new school at Peridot. Water may soon blot out the place where the church once stood but the stones will continue to form the walls of a building where Apache children will be brought up in the 'nurture and admonition of the Lord' long after you and I have passed on. These stones were quarried to serve in a house of God, and in spite of a change of location they will continue to serve the same cause."[33]

If anything, the land on the reservations is going back to its wilder state today. Roads and trails that were frequented in the 1960s are no longer passable in many places today. People just do not travel the old roads and learn the back ways because life has shifted its gaze to reservation gaming and computers and cell phones and gainful employment elsewhere. The cattle industry of the old years is gone. No more big lumber trucks and dozers rumble in the mountains harvesting some of the world's best timber. Arizona holds the largest ponderosa pine forests in the world, and wonderful expanses of that forest are on reservation land, but because of politics and green philosophy and spotted owls and maybe because of forest fires, the piney patriarchs stand unmolested.

This pristine nature was hard to live with when *Inashood* first came. He suffered with the rustic and rough in his travel and in his living. One describes how it was for him and the others: "For many years the road from Whiteriver to Rice has been known as the worst road in the country. How many a horse shoe, spoke, tire, crankcase, entire wagons and cars, yes tempers and vocabularies have been strewn by the wayside as luckless victims of that burly giant, Bronco Canyon, stretching one rocky arm down to Black River and the other up towards the sawmill. It seems as though he were constantly trying to push the two reservations further and further apart and render friendly visiting between the two more and more difficult. The writer has been at his mercy on foot, horseback, on two-wheeled cart, buck-

---

[33] Edgar Guenther, *The Apache Scout*, "The Passing of San Carlos," February 1930.

board and flivver. At every trip the desire became stronger to stay in the country if for no other reason than to see this monster subdued and to have the privilege of spinning smoothly over his leveled back. His wish will soon be realized. An energetic and honest road gang (yes there are such) is diligently hewing away at the giant's rocky muscles with picks, shovels and T.N.T. Before many moons they will have him down and out. Then even an asthmatic Ford will be able to make the return trip in a day if necessary. The road is being built primarily to give tourists an opportunity of driving through and viewing one of the most beautiful regions in Arizona. Let us not forget that man proposes and God disposes. Is it not highly probable that God incidentally wishes this highway to serve the gospel by bringing the two reservations closer together at a saving of missionaries' time and energy?"[34]

The Apaches knew something in their mythology of the old days and their coming from the cold north and Siberia to this place in Arizona of the Southwest. Mayerhoff records the following: "Then today, I will relate the tale of the Apaches' past and take you with me to the mist-enshrouded days of myth, fable and tradition. Chief Moseby,[35] one of the last great war chiefs of the White Mountain bands of Apaches, was a close neighbor and staunch friend of the *Inashood*, and here is the story from his lips: 'In the long ago our people were not here, but in a cold land covered with ice and snow, many many days travel to the north and west, until you come to *"to-entale,"* the sea. All living things there were covered with long hair. They walked on four feet. But one kind had feet like a man and could raise up and walk on their hind feet and use their front feet like hands to grab or dig or strike. They would catch their food or defend themselves. They could grunt and growl and even talk like men to express their feelings. They were very strong and quick and wild, for in them lived the spirits of dead warriors. They were *Shush*, the bear. One day *Jay-go-na-ai,* the Sun, our god in the old homeland, came up to see how our lost people were doing in the ice and snow land. Then came *Shush* to our people and said: 'Now you must make ready to go with *Jay-go-na-ai*, for he will go away again and cold and dark will come back. So they took boats and floated down the waters following the Sun. *Shush* was their leader until they were far away from the ice land. When he left them, he directed our people to follow *Jay-go-na-ai*, for he would lead them to a new home land and teach them new

---

[34] Edgar Guenther, *The Apache Scout,* October 1924.

[35] There are still people with the last name of Moseby today on the Fort Apache Reservation.

42

ways. Here is the land to which *Jay-go-na-ai* took our people and made them live there. High up in the hills he had planted trees and bushes and grass; he had made springs of water and streams came from the hills; he had made roots and fruits that were good to eat and many animals whose meat we could eat and whose skins made shoes and dresses and covers. But our people were much afraid, for they found everywhere dead houses and villages made of stones and mud, but no living people in them and they feared the spirits of the dead ones. *Jay-go-na-ai* said: Do not fear them, but do not touch the dead houses and villages. You must live in *"gowah"* made of boughs and covered with bear grass and skins. I will teach you many things. I will give you fire. Then he raised his hand and threw the lightning bolt and set fire to a tree.' "[36]

Francis Uplegger noted that the languages of the Indians near the Great Slave Lake and the Great Bear Lake in Canada had languages very similar to the Apaches.[37] They had come down from the far north, from Siberia and Mongolia. Whether this fact was his original observation or not, he mentioned it and was aware of it. Some of the babies at the East Fork Lutheran Nursery on the Fort Apache Reservation carried the "Mongolian spot" at the base of their little spines. The language of the Apaches was Athabascan. Eugene Nida, the brilliant linguist who among other things wrote language learning manuals for missionaries, said that this Athabascan language group was one of the very most difficult languages to learn. Very few white men would master it or even be able to muddle through it. Geronimo in Oklahoma spoke about George Wratten, a white man who learned to speak Apache, and said that he could speak the best Apache he heard any white man speak.

Dr. William Kessel writes: "Among all the Indians of the Southwest, the Apaches were regarded as the most successful hunters and raiders. Between 1750 and 1900 the Western and Chiricahua Apaches were unanimously respected and feared by Anglos, Mexicans, and other Indians for their cunning, speed and endurance on the trail. The difficulties which the U.S. Army had in capturing Geronimo, Victorio and other Apache chiefs provides testimony to a rich tradition of physical and mental training.

"From childhood on, Apache boys underwent rigorous training.

---

[36] Paul Mayerhoff, *Beatrice Daily Sun*, "An Apache's Story of Origin of Their Red-skinned Race," February 13, 1933.

[37] On page 3 of his book *Apache Indians*, Lockwood quotes Uplegger's description of Apache speech as one of explodent sounds, final breathings, breath checks, aspirates, and glottal stops—all of which makes it extremely difficult for Europeans to learn or understand."

Young boys were given small bows and arrows. (Pastor Arthur Guenther spoke of little boys shooting grasshoppers with their bows and makeshift arrows that used cactus spines for points.) Arrow games included shooting an arrow for distance and shooting for accuracy. The participants also learned strategy. For example, a boy had to decide whether it was better to shoot first or last in a contest. Other games for boys included dodge ball, hide-and-seek, tag, foot races, tug-of-war, and wrestling. Such activities produced quickness, speed, strength and agility.

"As the boys matured, by ages 10-12, the games became more serious. Horsemanship and hunting small game were encouraged. Above all, physical fitness was stressed along with responsibility. One Apache man who grew up in the late 1800s remembered the words of his father: 'My son, you know no one will help you in this world. You must do something. You run to that mountain and come back. That will make you strong. Your legs are your friends; your brain is your friend; your eyesight is your friend; your hair is your friend; your hands are your friends; you must do something with them. Someday you will be with people who are starving. You will have to get something for them. If you go somewhere, you must beat the enemy who are attacking you before they get over the hill (escape). Then all the people will be proud of you.'

"As the boys entered their teen years the training escalated. Running, running, and more running was emphasized. The fathers would say, 'Take a mouthful (of water), but don't swallow it; hold it in your mouth. You are going to run four miles with this water in your mouth.' At the end of the run they would spit out the water. If they had swallowed some they would have to repeat the run. Finally teams of teen-aged boys would form two lines and sling rocks at each other. In another game the lines would be about 50 feet apart, and the contestants would shoot small arrows at one another. Such 'games' promoted offensive skills (throwing and shooting) and defensive skills (ducking and dodging)." Daklugie, son of Chiricahua war chief Juh, said that some archers could shoot seven arrows into the air before their first arrow came to ground.[38]

In 1886 when the Apache scouts squared off against the Mexicans in the rugged country between the Satachi and Aros Rivers just west of the Chihuahua line, their opponents were the Tarahumara Indians of the Sierra Madre in Mexico. The Tarahumara were their avowed enemies and had been responsible for the killing of Victo-

---

[38] Eve Ball with Nora Henn and Lynda Sancez, *An Apache Odyssey Indeh,* Provo Utah: Brigham Young University Press, 1980, p. 15.

rio and many of his followers at Tres Castillos in Mexico. The Tarahumara are there in the Sierra Madre still today. They live in many ways just like they have for the last 500 years. They are still great runners, and for many it is their only way of locomotion. They live in caves and canyons in that remotest of places in Mexico—and in the world. This was the very place the old Apaches also frequented and loved. It suited their lifestyle too because it hid them and protected them. They went there to regroup and re-gather. The Tarahumara Indians today are at the top of extreme and endurance running. The running record they have set is 425 miles in just over two days of non-stop running. That is sixteen marathon races back to back! They run everywhere they go in this wild and remote country. Their women and old people do it too.

The Apaches were like that. They had forced marches (we would call them that today) of over a hundred miles before they stopped to rest. Women could cover the same ground as the men could as, in fact, is the case today in endurance running of 100 and 200 miles. The Tarahumara run either barefoot or use sandals they have made from discarded car tires. They do it in country that looks like eastern Arizona's Salt River Canyon on steroids. The Apache used moccasins they made from buckskin and other leather. On the front they had a "cactus kicker," which was rawhide to protect the toes from stubbing on cactus or stone. Runners jogged from Fort Apache to Bylas and San Carlos and returned in one trip of two days. The Apache man Massai (Massey by some spellings) was taken captive on the prison train that was taking the Chiricahua Apaches to Florida. He escaped close to St. Louis, Missouri, and walked and ran the 1,200 miles back to Arizona to live near Globe. War chief Nana fought with Geronimo to the end. He lived to be 96. When he was 80, lame in the left foot and suffering from rheumatism and becoming blind, he is reported to have made a raid of 1,000 miles in a month's time. That was an average of thirty miles a day! In school days in the 1960s the Apache children walked and ran the five miles to school and back from up and down the river valley. Once one of our classmates left school in the afternoon and jogged to her parents who were at the fire tower on Kinney Lookout, way up in the East Fork valley. It was 16 miles uphill to the top of the mountain, and she was alone.

The Apache people were raiders. They got their commodities from Mexico mostly. They took them as the occasion provided, and they did it for a long time. They went down the San Pedro and Aravaipa River valleys on sorties for supplies from 1690 until 1870. The Mexicans felt the brunt of most of this, but many white settlers in their area also obliged the Apaches with their horses and cattle and firearms—and occasionally with their scalps (although scalping wasn't an Apache practice). The Mexican wolf still roamed the land and howled at the moon during those days of the late 1800s. In many ways the Apaches were the human equivalent of the wolf. They were the gleaming predatorial eyes in the dark. The White Mountain Apaches even came to be called Coyotero.[39] It was Charles Gatewood's observation as he witnessed Apache warfare dying down, "Another fact seems to be well established in the history of these people, & that is, when they did appear, they proceeded to make their presence known in an exceedingly disagreeable manner. Contact with others meant war, for war, pillage, & the chase are the chief occupations on which they relied for sustenance & amusement."[40]

So today in many ways and many places the country is like it used to be. It has the names of the Old Ones as its given place names. There is Bonito Creek and Chino Springs and Navajo Bill Tank and Chiricahua Peak. The family names are the same ones that were there as the Apache wars wound down: Peaches, Gatewood, Chinche, Alchesay, Nosey, Goklish (Gokliz), Cooley, etc. The Chiricahua Apaches with Geronimo and Naiche settled on Turkey Creek and Bonito Creeks. Geronimo and Naiche traveled up and down the 2,800' elevation difference as they went from their farms on Turkey Creek to the East Fork valley. The big cedar under which the first *Inashood* pitched his tent was already a big tree when Geronimo and Naiche went by checking their fields and crops.

The fighting was far from over, and countless atrocities would still happen. Apaches were running toward Mexico, and they almost all made it too. They could stay ahead of their followers. Even the Apache scouts (and there were White Mountain Apaches in the pursuit groups) could not keep up with the fugitives. The pursuers had to spare their horses. The fugitives simply rode their horses to death and then stole others along the way. Mothers gave birth while running and threw their infants to the side of the tormented trail so they could keep up. On May 28, 1885, scouts found the bodies of two babies who had just been born. Listen to the following awful account: "During the confusion, one woman, a Chiricahua named *Chah-gah-ahshy*, a wife of Chinche, who had left the agency without her, mounted her horse with a cradleboard on her back. The strap

---

[39] Pastor Uplegger tells us that it was mostly Coyotero Apaches who went to what is now called Bylas.

[40] Charles B. Gatewood (Edited and with additional text by Louis Kraft), *Lt. Charles Gatewood & His Apache Wars Memoi,* Lincoln, Nebraska: University of Nebraska Press, 2005.

became loose, and the cradle with her nine-month-old son fell to the ground in Doubtful Canyon. The militia picked up the boy and brought him and a large herd of horses and mules to Lordsburg. Naiche and Chihuahua exited Doubtful Canyon on the west side and traveled all night through the San Simon Valley to a familiar camping place in the Chiricahua mountains southeast of Fort Bowie. All except *Chah-gah-ahshy*. She returned to look for her baby. Not finding him, she eventually returned to Fort Apache." The journey took her over a hundred miles in a straight line through rough and wild forested country crisscrossed with deep canyons that to this day has very few roads in it. 240 miles is the distance given by roads today from Lordsburg, New Mexico, to Whiteriver, Arizona.

But something else was happening in 1885 in faraway Wisconsin. In the church paper of the Wisconsin Evangelical Lutheran Synod, the *Gemeinde-Blatt*, in the very month that Geronimo and the Chiricahuas broke out from Turkey Creek, readers in the German congregations of Wisconsin and other Midwestern states read about Christian mission work among the Eskimos of Greenland. The account was prescient of the coming work of translating that the Upleggers would do with the Apache language. As translators were trying to find a word in the Eskimo language, they were at a loss because there wasn't such a word. Then one of the Eskimos present told the story of being out in a very rough sea in his kayak and would have been lost for certain had it not been for his friend who at the risk of his own life came and managed to get him safely back to land. The translators asked the man what he would have called his friend who came out and saved him. This was the word they then used for Savior (the German word *Heiland*). The June 1, 1885, issue of the *Gemeinde-Blatt* made mention of a group of Chinese women in San Francisco who were supporting a woman in China whose ministry was reading the Bible to other Chinese women. In the same issue the lament was that eighteen years had gone by since Alaska had been purchased, and no mission work to date was done there. The Presbyterians hoped to embark on such a mission when they were able to gather $6,000. Another reference mentioned that Japan had declared freedom of religion in full view of the Buddhism and Shintoism that had held sway there. This was also seen as an open door to Christian missionaries. So during that summer, when the Chiricahua Apaches were fleeing and discarding babies by the path of their flight, and the White Mountain Apaches were being enlisted to track down their own fellow Apaches into the fastness of the Sierra Madres in Mexico, German Lutherans were thinking about mission work in China and Japan and Greenland—and in Arizona among the Apaches.

It was to the descendants of these people and to this place that the yellow Ford took our family in 1958. This place became our home, and these people became our people. These two brackets encompassed forty years of combined work as *Inashood*. On the second day of September in 1980 the elder Hartzell wrote his son who was returning from Zambia, Africa, to this wonderful place and people in Arizona to be the missionary at East Fork Mission and Canyon Day. This is the way the letter went:

Eric:

How can three months seem very long? That's just about how long it will be until you come over the mountains of eastern Arizona and down into this valley that shall become your home.

Have no qualms of conscience, nor let no one even hint you are "copping out." You are not coming to a bed of roses; you are not, in fact, even getting out of World Missions. On the other hand, don't come with a heavy heart or with failure on your mind. You are in the world, but you have the Lord to help, guide, and give whatever results he may give. You can witness to your faith, but you cannot create faith in others' hearts no matter how much you might want to. You can do something for Jesus and for Apache souls—no one can really do more than that. There are so many things for you to do, and I pray for a new beginning for you and the people in your two churches. I pray too the Lord would give you love for them, for the work, and for the skills, energy, and dedication that will make your work pleasant and prosperous (at least sometimes). With my disappointments over the years, I still take good memories with me to my grave. I expect no less for you.

The disappointments and griefs have been rather limited, really: bad scenes with workers—but this has not been a problem recently. There have been disappointments with members falling away, or joining other churches. And I suppose also a lack of interest in studying God's Word (at Bible study for sure, and I suspect at home and in private also). But you tell me where these same things are not present to some degree. Besides, I think you will solve all such problems because you will work hard on all of them.

And when or if you fail—there is still work to do for the Savior. There are still many more outside the church to work on than there are in the church to worry about; and then there will be time to spend with your family. Except the time you spend five miles down the road at Canyon Day—you'll be home! Around home! In and out of home! Your children will be within gunshot even when they are in school. And you should have time on Sundays—and at least a day a week off—free to do your own thing.

And no muddy roads of Africa! Or long trips for groceries—and none available. There will be good doctors, hospital, service for vehicles, water, lights, heat and a good invigorating climate— and family close, and even the farthest of family a couple of days down the road.

But most important for you—Apacheland is a land of opportunity for the gospel.

Wish you could see it right now. We've had good rains. Had a hard shower yesterday here at East Fork Mission. In just minutes, little rivers were running into the garden. The grass is green, the sky is beautiful with big clouds, and flowers are blooming. Wish, too, you could see the apples, pears, plums. The grapes aren't much. You have your work cut out for you in getting the trees trimmed back next spring. The limbs are too long—as soon as they get fruit on them they are right down on the ground, or they break off. Pears are as big as your entire fist! Delicious red apples have never been more loaded. The grass is almost out of control. I thought someone else would mow it since we aren't there—but the thought never entered anyone's mind. So I'll have to get it mowed. (I mowed yesterday until I ran out of gas.)

The bees are hanging on the front of the hives, bulging with honey. We hope to get more taken off on Saturday.

Your Dad.

CHAPTER THREE

"The Scourge"

*Wine is a mocker and beer a brawler; whoever is led
astray by them is not wise* (PROVERBS 20:1).

*"The king and Haman sat down to drink, but the city
of Susa was bewildered"* (ESTHER 3:15).

The boys who had come that day in the yellow Ford station wagon had a friend up the river who had a female donkey that had given birth. They went up there to see the cute little character and noticed many horses saddled and tied to the fence around their friend's house. There was a drinking party going on. They sat down under a black walnut tree on the outside of the fence, not really comprehending what was happening. There was loud laughter and talk coming from the brush shelter right across from the faded frame house. The brouhaha got more and more animated and finally one man staggered off to his big buckskin horse and rode away, yelling a few angry epithets to his friends as he went. He rode away swaying on his saddle this way and that, and then he stopped and wheeled his buckskin around at a mad gallop and charged back into the line of tied horses. The charge broke the bridle straps of the horse his buckskin hit and that horse ran away shaking its head back and forth. Someone came out of the brush shelter yelling and ready to fight, and the boys went back home. They did not tell their pastor father what they had seen.

You can't speak of the work of a Christian missionary in any culture without in some way understanding the impact the wrong use of alcohol and drugs and the resultant evils alcohol and these drugs make on that culture. It is a universal maxim because it has always been the case that alcohol is something that when misused harms people and causes unhappy results and influences. The Bible's proverb says that wine is a mocker. To speak of alcohol's presence and place in the Apache culture and life is not to play the judge or critic who clucks his tongue disgustedly and speaks disparagingly. It is rather an attempt and hope to be real and to make a real difference in helping people. To help them means to first of all understand them and to understand their ways. All missionaries everywhere have to do this—want to do this—and all missionaries to the Apaches had to do this too and still do have to deal with this in work with Native Americans today. The present culture of the Midwest with its taverns on every downtown street corner and alcohol's ubiquitous presence should discourage Lutheran missionaries and people from throwing too many stones. Solomon's words of observation hold true to anyone who has wine and beer around.

Some have opined that Europeans have a systemic difference that allows them to handle alcohol better than Native Americans. That probably isn't true. The fact is that there are many Europeans and people of that cultural and hormonal extract that have trouble with alcohol. Drinking on the reservations was never concealed, as it often is in polite white society or as we are talking here, in white congregations. Drinking parties were and are public activities on the reservations. Some of the missionaries even commented that there were times when their people almost seemed to go out of their way when under the influence of alcohol to show up on pastoral porches and ring the doorbell.

If we define culture in the following simple way that describes "What people do as a people at a particular time in their history," then we can surely say that alcohol was an actual part of the Apache culture in the past. Tiswin was made in as large a supply as possible. Men used to fast for two days before a big "drink" so that they could derive the greatest effect from their homebrew when they finally drank it. The story of the Apache people is laced with alcohol. There is no question and no denying that fact for the one who reads and investigates. Major things happened as a result of intoxication. Geronimo died because of pneumonia caught while lying overnight in a drunken stupor on the ground in Oklahoma. It seems that war chief Juh's demise was linked with inebriation. More examples are to follow. Right from the beginning, the work of *Inashood* was a work that had to deal with the evils of alcohol.

It was in May of 1885 that the Chiricahua bands fled from Turkey Creek on the Fort Apache Reservation. They left mainly because they feared disciplinary measures because they insisted on having *tizwin* parties, homebrew drink from sprouted corn. This penchant for drinking would haunt and harass the work of the coming *Inashood*. Drinking had been an evil for centuries; it was as much a part of the Apache people as the landscape was. Drinking to get inebriated was there when the Catholic missionaries came in the 1600s. It would be an evil that would wreak incalculable harm to the people. Many, many times in Mexico the people were induced to drinking and provided alcohol and then murdered when they were under the influence. This is what also caused the final end of the Apache wars to go so badly for the people. Their leaders who had sympathetic and loyal supporters of them and their people were embarrassed and put in an impossible situation with the United States government authorities because the incoming groups got hooch from a shyster trader named Tribollet and ended up getting drunk and fighting among themselves and then bolting for another fling of violence. Chief Naiche shot his wife in the leg at that drunken melee because he thought she was flirting with someone else. Geronimo and the other leaders got drunk too. It was a mess. When the people finally were forced to surrender they were all sent off to Florida, where half of them would die of tuberculosis and other ills in those terrible places for them: Fort Marion in Florida and Mt. Vernon Barracks in Alabama. It is possible to lay the final bad outcome at the feet of unbridled alcohol consumption.

The very first missionary to the Fort Apache Reservation said this about a drinking party that was part and parcel of the culture of the day (and in many ways still is): "Not over a thousand feet away from my cabin was a full blown tiswin drink going on. Indians in many groups had purchased liquor from "San" the old squaw, and were socially mixing drink, cards and conversation and getting nicely stewed. Hes-to-hay had given his wife an order to do something. She failing to be quick about it, but prompt to give him the equivalent in Apache to go chase himself, put her man into mad rage. The stewed lord heaved a rock, caught her behind the ear. Stunned she falls and lacerates her face badly on sharp stones. Hes-to-hay, in his befuddled mind, thinks he killed her. Hence the events I just related. Blood revenge was the tribal law. Hes-to-hay tried to escape it. *Hastin* tried to carry it out. I stayed and cleaned the woman's face and dressed her injuries. But I was an interloper, and neither *San* nor the Indians were pleased at my presence. *San* feared arrest and punishment as being the hostess of this drinking camp. Being in a bad temper because of the interruptions and enraged at the unintentional part I played in it she jumped up, pulled a knife from her moccasin and made for me to stab me. However "Jab-tsu-yea," the chief's son, called to her a short gruff order and she growlingly subsided. I was glad to leave with a whole skin. This was the only time I felt myself in danger among my Apache neighbors. *San* got 30 days, Hes-to-hay six months, and the others just a few days at hard labor. The injured wife and her family were furious. She wanted a divorce. In a few weeks she had cooled down, her sores were healed and as her husband had free rations for the time of his sentence, she found that the two could draw more rations if she again lived with him."[41]

Missionary Francis Uplegger in describing the Mohicans in Wisconsin pointedly mentioned the evils of alcohol in their midst. He mentioned the Mohicans trying to get away from the evil influences of white men who wanted to peddle their hooch with its resultant evil and grief. Missionary Guenther wrote about the bootlegger Tribollet, the man mentioned above who with his booze messed up the peaceful surrender of Geronimo and Naiche and sent the band careening out on another fated outbreak. You can see how intently these evil bootleggers did want to have their way with the native peoples and how they wanted to foul any progress toward a truly better and more Christian life for Native Americans.

Guenther also reported in the ongoing story of missionary Zeisberger and missionary work among early Native Americans in eastern states of one instance after another where alcohol wreaked its chaos and havoc. In Zeisberger's story it seems to have been mostly rum that was brought in by peddlers lacking any scruples to the ruinations of any decent dealings between Native Americans and non-Native Americans. Much land and property were stolen from the people when they were under the influence of alcohol.

Lt. Charles Gatewood (late 1800s) wasn't just bashing the people when he talked about the evils of alcohol like he did. The people respected him and his work among them. He was fair. He put his reputation and life on the line a number of times when he defended his people on the Fort Apache Reservation. There are still to this day Apache families with the last name of Gatewood. But Charles Gatewood had to say the following about the alcohol consumption among the clans: "Except the alliance above referred to, each tribe made things lively on its own hook without regard to the doings of the others. Even when they were on their reservations, they were not peaceable. The bitterest feuds existed between families, bands, tribes & clans, & were handed down from one generation to the other. When not otherwise engaged, they would proceed to get drunk on a vile compound of their own manufacture & fight out their hereditary quarrels in a deadly manner. They called this [fiery drink] 'tiswin.' [It] was made by soaking corn or barley until the grain had sprouted, then it was 'mashed' in plenty of water, boiled to a certain consistency, allowed to cool until fermentation had begun, & drunk in large quantities after a fast of at least twenty-four hours. Pretty soon 'Rome howled' & the 'stiffs' were buried among the rocks. The wrongs

---

[41] Paul Mayerhoff, *Beatrice Daily Sun*, "Almost a Tragedy," January 2, 1934.

of a great-grandfather had been avenged & the new generation had a fresh feud to start with."[42]

Jason Betzinez, himself an Apache, lived and fought with Geronimo. He ended up a Christian in Oklahoma, and when the rest of his group got to go back to New Mexico, he and a few others stayed on in Oklahoma. He said about his own people, "The Apache never drinks in moderation. He keeps at it until the supply is exhausted or he is unconscious." It was Jason Betzinez who also said that in 1883 when Juh's people came back to San Carlos and turned themselves in, Juh wasn't with them. As the band had passed by Casas Grandes in Mexico, Juh sent a woman into town to get him some whiskey. She was good at the task and returned with the 1883 equivalent of a brown paper bag. "Juh got good and drunk. While in this condition he rode his horse along the rim of a bluff, fell over the edge, and was killed. Juh had been a good leader but whiskey brought him down just as it did many other Apaches."[43]

Missionary Arnold Sitz wrote a long letter to the people he served and he said, "But now I hear that some of you pray when you drink *tulapai* and ask God to let the *tulapai* make you very drunk so that you can sleep well! I hear that some of you pray when you gamble and ask God to let you win the game to get your friend's money? I wish every time you wanted to pray that kind of a prayer you would have to ride all the way to Tucson to that church! Then maybe you would not pray such bad prayers very many times. I say it again: If any of you pray to get drunk, or to win a gambling game, or to steal another man's wife, or to do hurt to somebody, then you are the devil's children and not God's children. And when Jesus comes in the clouds of heaven in power and great glory, and all the angels come with him, the devil's children will be thrown down into that same place of fire where *Cheen naant'an* (Chief Devil) is." He ended his letter, "Your friend, Arnold Sitz."[44]

It was *Inashood Hastin* (Elderly Gentleman Missionary Francis Uplegger) who also spoke against the scourge of alcohol. He loved the Apache people and his life and demeanor showed it in so many ways, but he would have to speak to the evil: "May they stand firm, with such courage from God, and that not only when another offers

---

[42] Charles B. Gatewood (edited and with additional text by Louis Kraft). *Lt. Charles Gatewood and His Apache Wars Memoir*, Lincoln, Nebraska: University of Nebraska Press, 2005, page 34.

[43] Jason Betzinez, *I Fought with Geronimo*, Lincoln and London: University of Nebraska Press, 1959

[44] Arnold Sitz, *The Apache Scout*, November 1927.

a drink out of a 'Can O' Heat' else only used as fuel for cooking in camp, or any such stuff that the devil only could bring men to drink. May God strengthen them to testify in general against the drink evil. For the sake of the souls of their fellowmen, for the sake of their bodies also, may they especially warn their people against the godless white men, and the misled Indians, that sell them all kinds of strong extracts for mixing with their native strong drink. The native's strong drink is bad enough. Mixed with extracts as they are brought on the reservation for that purpose it becomes rank poison. Have courage! Tell your people, warn your people! Help to save them from slow suicide, from weakening their bodies, from deadening their minds, from burdening their consciences, from ruining the health of their children,—yea, even before the children are born!" So Uplegger expressed what every missionary felt and saw. He also said, "It is so with the drinking habit and with other habits. Many a man would never again touch strong drink, and soon is again in the condition in which 'it goes around with him' as the Apache word for intoxicated says it."[45] Listen to IHS workers today and they will tell you the same. *Fetal Alcohol Syndrome* still curses those who fill their pregnancies with booze. So called camels (constantly and chronically inebriated persons) still roam the roads and communities on the reservations. Meth use is off the medical and statistical charts. Substance abuse is the way it is said today, but it is the same thing the missionaries encountered and spoke against in the old days.

Pastor Edgar Guenther was an unmistakable writer in his ability to articulate his observations and thoughts. He is also unmistakable here when he says, "We are thinking of *tulapai* as an unbalanced or rather unbalancing ration for one. It gives poison to the head and no food to the body. The drinker loses his balance. He cannot see or walk straight, neither can he do right. White mule is the latest unbalanced ration to put in its appearance on the reservation. It is even more unbalanced or unbalancing than the first named. This seems to be especially true of the stuff made on the dumps of McNary and Springerville. People say it is the kick they are after. If that is true white mule will not disappoint them. The kind that is made in coal oil cans and gas pipes is especially accommodating. It can kick you straight into the grave and beyond into hell."[46]

"This (fusel oil) is the stuff that foolish sinful man will feed to his body in every bootleg drink, regardless of what it is made. It may seem harmless at first, but is as dangerous for body and soul as dyna-

---

[45]   Francis Uplegger, *The Apache Scout*, January 1930.

[46]   Edgar Guenther, *The Apache Scout*, December 1927, pp. 6, 7.

mite would be in the sawmill boiler." He spoke in another place in his writing in *The Apache Scout* of the rich man who had gotten a "present" from an enemy in the mail that was really a bomb and killed him when he opened it. (This actually took place in 1929!) Guenther's application was to remind his listeners about an "Indian" who was found sleeping near McNary between two jugs of white lightning. Guenther said it would have been better to have named the drink "White Snake." He said the white snake in those two jugs was a present from the devil. He went on to add, "Afterthought: Are there no police officers at McNary? Are they farsighted, cross-eyed, or blind, that they cannot see the liquor that flows so freely that a one-eyed Indian could find two jugs? The *Scout* has distinct recollection that the lumbering concession was granted on this reservation with the clear understanding that evil women and liquor were not to be tolerated! What are you going to do about it?"

The Apache Jason Betzinez maintained, "Is the Indian a moderate drinker? I should say not! In all my experience I have never seen an Indian drink who didn't keep it up until the last drop was gone and he was either lying in a stupor on the prairie or was in a fighting, dangerous mood. An Indian who is drunk is a creature entirely devoid of any good desire and completely incapable of self control." (Maybe all inebriates are this way. On the other hand, missionaries would agree with this sentiment: social drinking on the reservation for anything apart from total consumption and drunkenness does not exist.)

"Alcohol is a good thing when used at the right time, in the right way, and in the right place. Alcohol is a gift of God. And when it is used according to God's will, God's blessing goes with it. (The missionaries had alcohol in the form of wine as they celebrated Holy Communion in their churches.) But the alcohol in whiskey, beer, white mule, tulapai, canned heat, and the like, is a stumbling stone to many. It makes many people fall into drunkenness, murder, adultery, quarreling, fighting, and many other sins, which separate man from God." *Inashood* H. C. Nitz made this observation.

Alcohol on the reservations exacerbated the evil of suicide. Jason Betzinez told that at the time of the Chiricahua outbreak from San Carlos that Geronimo scolded his nephew over something with the result that the young man committed suicide. Later suicide would be a terrible bane on the reservations. This very suicide with its "payback" mentality came to epidemic proportions in later years. Jilted lovers committed suicide. Young people who had been disciplined committed suicide. This propensity was made worse with alcohol in the picture, of course. Some shot themselves with their deer rifles. Some hanged themselves in wood sheds. Girls doused themselves with kerosene and jumped into the campfire. There was the slow suicide (and not so slow in some cases) of alcohol that some simply drank themselves to death. People imbibed and ended up on the frozen winter ground and lost their hands and feet. Reports came of drinking parents who hung their baby in a cradleboard in a pine tree and then forgot or neglected the infant to have it freeze to death.

The 25-year celebration booklet of the Apache mission work told of Apaches committing suicide in times of bad health. It pointed to the ongoing habit of the culture's enforced suicide of elderly people who needed to die when they were no longer productive. In times of war the Old Ones who could no longer keep up with the band had to go off by themselves and die. The article in the 25-year anniversary book pointed out that there were also those who had to live in misery within reservation boundaries with no hope that anything was going to change for the better. This condition was also fertile ground for the idea of suicide.

There was moral malaise among the Apaches too that was made worse—much worse—by alcohol. Even though first missionary Mayerhoff on the Fort Apache Reservation could say, "I have heard the statement and read it in print; no virtue in the Indian women, young and old; above the age of 8 to 10 years no pure maidens might be found. Most emphatically I disagree with such unproven views. Rather was I very much impelled to a contrary view by my observations; in other words, that little sex-immorality prevailed among the Apaches, and immoral practices were not the rule among the younger set." That referred to Mayerhoff's tenure in the late 1800s and very early 1900s. Missionary Edgar Guenther felt compelled to ask his people in 1928 at the time Chief Baha took over for Chief Alchesay, "Why so much adultery, why so many divorces, why so few good girls, why so few upright men, why so much joking about these serious things? Why so much sickness, why so many deaths of babies, why such a slight increase in population, why such a disregard for law and order, why such an appetite for idleness? Why such a willingness to follow this or that false prophet, when God warns us so plainly in Scripture and almost calls them by name? Do not these things stir your blood? Does not your tribal pride smart under them? Is it not plain that there never was greater need for a great and good chief than right now? 'But,' you will say, 'what can Chief Baha do?' That, dear friend is not the first question. The first question is: 'What are you going to do?' And this question is directed not only to the Apache reader, but to every white person working or dealing with the Indians on the reservations, as well."[47]

Inashood Guenther also wrote in the personification of a tree, "Many kinds of sinful mistletoe have fastened on the tribe and are robbing it of its strength of body, mind, and soul. The old health rules that used to keep the people strong are no longer observed. The girls no longer wear the emblem of virginity in their hair. I see too much idleness, yes in most cases I must call it laziness. There are too many idle farms. Vices like drunkenness, gambling, adultery, have fastened themselves so tightly on the tribe that no earthly power can shake them off. If conditions will not change, I fear the tribe will go under as I (the tree) am going under. White Mule is the latest parasite trying to fasten itself on the hearts of the Apaches."

Missionary Paul Behn said, "But see what the 'old timers' did with their corn. If that is right what they did, why not follow out the old ways now? Yes, corn is raised every year, but is it raised to the praise and honor of God, for life and happiness? Many know and see the idle fields where thistles and weeds are growing. Once upon a time they were cornfields. Many have been called into court because of too much 'cornwater.' *Tulapai* and beer are making people dizzy every day, so they do not know what they are doing. We hear of fighting, murder or adultery every week. The Apaches are getting fewer in number as a tribe year after year."[48]

Lutheran interpreter Jack Keyes froze to death. They found him by the road that goes from Pinetop to Whiteriver. He was stone cold drunk and dead. He was making his way back from The Dew Drop Inn in Pinetop. He didn't make it. And when they asked old Pastor Guenther if he would have the funeral, the grizzled old missionary said sadly. "Only pigs go to The Dew Drop Inn and I don't bury pigs."

The Apache religion itself with its medicine men and shaman has drawn its line in the sand. *Inashood* is looked at as the villain. Before Lutheran *Inashood* came, John Bourke quoted the following: "Like Old Men of the Sea, they (the medicine men), have clung to the neck of their nations, throttling all attempts at progress, binding them to the thralldom of superstition and profligacy, dragging them down to wretchedness and death. Christianity and civilization meet in them (the medicine men) their most determined, most implacable foes."[49] He also observed that when the medicine men ceased to be the leaders on the reservation that they had once been,

47 *The Apache Scout,* "A New Chief," EEG, Vol. 6, Number 6, p. 2.

48 Paul Behn. *The Apache Scout,* "Indian Corn of 1930," March 1930, p. 4.

49 John Gregory Bourke, *The Medicine Men of the Apaches,* Rio Grande Press. Inc.: Glorieta, New Mexico. 1983, p. 594.

in the bastion of Fort Marion, Florida, where they were imprisoned and dying, the medicine men danced and sang and proclaimed their ways and words.[50]

It was said about one shaman with his carved wooden amulet, "He prayed to it at all times when in trouble, that he could learn from it where his ponies were when stolen and which was the right direction to travel when lost, and that when drought had parched his crops this would never fail to bring rain in abundance to revive and strengthen them. The symbolism is the rain cloud and the serpent lightning, the rainbow, rain drops, and the cross of the four winds."[51]

The blue stone was present when the missionaries came, and it is still present today. Bourke said about it, "It was the Apache medicine man's badge of office, his medical diploma, so to speak, and without it he could not in olden times exercise his medical functions."[52]

There is even a resurgence of "The Old Way" today, and missionaries face the big challenge to their Christian message when Apache leaders and medicine men proclaim so-called traditional beliefs. The Old Way was never written down and the old people today who observe it say that it is not the way it used to be—at all. Medicine men still prosper and speak to this day, however, especially when someone needs a voice at a sunrise dance. They have people who follow them and support them and defend them and their ways. It has always been this way in the Apache mission work, and it will, no doubt, continue.

Missionary H. C. Nitz wrote how it was when Silas John came on the scene as Apache religious leader: "In 1920-21, Silas John introduced his snake worship in Globe. This was done so quietly that I did not learn about it until one Sunday morning not one Apache showed up for services. During the week I learned that a big snake dance had been held at Pinal. For a whole series of Sundays, I rang the bell, prayerfully waited for the worshipers, but with a heavy heart went home without conducting a service. It was a time of serious testing. Superstition seemed to have won, and the gospel seemed to have been wiped out. Then one Sunday morning, one lone worshiper came. Henry Peoria! With a guilty feeling he said, 'Snake dance no good. Just like shooting a gun. Lotsa noise. Bang, Bang! Then nothing. I want to hear the Word of God again.' With Henry Peoria and my wife as an audience, I conducted a service in the dining room of the old parsonage. Very likely due to the influence of Henry Peo-

---

50 *Op. cit.* p. 583.

51 *Op. cit.* p. 587.

52 *Op. cit.* p. 589.

ria, the Christian Apaches began to trickle back to regular worship. Hence I should like to lay this memorial tribute on the grave of my friend and brother of forty years ago: Henry Peoria. Sincerely yours, H. C. Nitz."[53]

Gambling joined these other ills and caused added grief. Jason Betzinez said, "But the rest of the time they (the people in Oklahoma) lay around their camps, gambling and, when they could get away with it, making and drinking a strong Indian beer made out of fermented corn mash. (It was no doubt *tiswin* and *tulapai*.) Missionary Adascheck, one of the first two missionaries, saw the people playing cards as he wandered along the San Carlos River. Gambling with cards was a favorite form of recreation among the Apaches, especially among the women. It finally was prohibited and punished by tribal courts in the early 1900s. Reservation traders were barred from selling decks of cards.

Talk was also a challenge. There was Apollo and his white crow and his beautiful wife named Cora. This was the way Edgar Guenther wrote. "Even missionaries are often not spared by such tongues. Forked tongues have said that I have killed Indians by baptizing them, that I have put poison under the pillows of others, etc. etc. Forked tongues have said this or that missionary is a bad man because he has told somebody of his sins and there are always white crows with black hearts who are ready to spread such reports." [54] None of these observations of missionaries are meant to belittle the Apache people. There was no animus on the part of the pastors who spoke of the dangers of drink to their people.

Gustav Harders spoke of what could have driven the people to drink and despair. "(The Apache) wants to remain an Indian, an Apache. The Apaches want to remain a whole, a people for themselves within our nation. They want to retain their way of life, their blankets and brush huts; and they know that thereby they are in the way of the white man in this large, large land; and they cannot see why; and they know that that will never be fulfilled, that they will never get back what they had and want to have again, that without which life is no life for them. They know that quite exactly and have no hopes; they are people who have no hope for this and the future life. A few years ago I got to know a young woman. I often looked her up and had the feeling that she was beginning to trust me. And one day it came over her. With many tears, she unfolded for me a picture of her life, her inward life, of the comfortless condition in

---

[53] H. C. Nitz, *The Apache Lutheran*, December 1960, p. 90.

[54] Edgar Guenther, *The Apache Scout,* "Cor-Cor," September 1929.

which her soul existed. I thought I had gained her for Christ. But it had only been an hour of weakness. She must have quickly regretted what she had done. When I came to her the next time, everything was past. She was cold and rejecting. No word, no facial expression, nothing more betrayed anything of the comfort-desiring condition in which her heart existed. She is the same still today, when I meet her, inaccessible and rejecting toward every word which is an appeal to the condition of her heart, every word which wanted to lift up, help, comfort."[55]

A positive way honestly and fairly to sum up the persona of the *Inashood's* Apaches is represented by *Inashood* Eugene Hartzell. His general observations somewhat parallel those of Harders. Hartzell's observations also go by way of the scourge of alcohol and notice its influence.

"What sort of people are the Apache people? Who can really answer that question? Our own people[56] cannot fully answer this question, and so it is certain that no one else can answer the question for them. If someone could give a perfect answer to this question today, how long would it be a perfect answer? The Apache today is not the same person he was fifty years ago, and he is not the same today as he will be tomorrow in the outward forms of his life. Outwardly all men seem to be changing very rapidly, but inside men do not change very much.

"The real difficulty in speaking about what kind of a person someone is, is to be able to know what he is inside, not just the way he acts or looks on the outside. Not many men tell you what they are thinking in their hearts. I am simply trying to report honestly on what I think about the people now after living and working among them as a Lutheran Missionary for over nine years.

"Based upon my own experience I must say that in many ways the Apaches are a kind people. I can say this because it has been a very rare occasion when I have been treated unkindly by any of them. I do not mean just members of my own Lutheran church, but all that I have had contact with. They did not always believe what I tried to teach, some may not have liked me very well, but outwardly they almost always treated me kindly and respectfully.

"Two things have changed this kindness into unkindness a few times, and the first is alcohol. In most cases where unkindness was shown, the person had been drinking, but not all people under the

---

[55] J. F. G. Harders, *the Apaches Today*, Milwaukee, Wisconsin: Northwestern Publishing House, 1912, pp. 6, 7.

[56] Anglo/White.

influence of alcohol treated me badly. The second thing which has sparked unkindness a few times is religion. The unkindest treatment which I have received, or so it seemed to me, has come from former members of the Lutheran Church who left it and became active in another church, or simply attended no church at all. There are also some who are members of other churches who always have been most kind in their actions toward me, and so I believe that if it can be said of any one race of people that they are kind, it can be said of our Apaches.

"I believe the Apache people are a friendly people. The world pictures most Indians with a scowl on their face and blood on their hands. Are they really less friendly than other people? At first they may not seem friendly, but even so I am sure that many visitors to the Reservation have found them willing to be their friend. If, in their contacts with white men, they seem to be somewhat reserved we might ask how the white person acts towards those of other races. If we measure friendliness by the number of words spoken, back slapping, hand shaking, and other external signs, then the Apache people might not seem friendly in their contacts with outsiders. If they are slow in adopting our words 'hello' and 'goodbye,' it must be remembered that in their own tongue they did not make use of such words. They did not reduce friendship to abstract words but simply felt these things in their hearts. In fact, an Apache man once told me, 'We do not say it, we just think it in our heart.' Who can argue that that is not genuine friendship? If theirs is in their hearts what more should we demand?

"No one should get the idea from this that among themselves these people are always cold and formal in their lives. Many times I am greeted with a warm smile, a good word, and also with a firm handshake. I returned to East Fork from Synod Convention once after being gone three weeks or so, and I stopped at the home of one of my members. As far as I can remember this lady had never shaken hands with me before, nor has it become a habit since, but that day she shook my hand and told me how glad she was to see me again. Whenever I visit patients in the hospital there is usually someone there who is glad to see me and shows it.

"Among themselves there is much laughter, joking, talking, and genuine friendship, and so on the basis of what I have seen and experienced I must say that they are people who value the company and friendship of their neighbors.

"I believe the Apache are happy people. I am willing to say this on the basis of two examples (there are many more that could be mentioned). I know a little Apache boy about seven years old. I would challenge anyone to look at that little boy and tell me he comes from a tribe in which happiness does not exist. I feel better whenever I look at this boy's face. He generates happiness in my heart. His face is an eternal smile pointed at my heart. He does not smile because he is rich, or because he lives in a fine home, or because he sees no one with things he does not have. He smiles from the midst of, what seems to me to be, direst want and deepest poverty. I cannot understand why he smiles, but I thank the Father in heaven that he *does* smile. Nor is the happiness of these people a frail flower which flourishes for just a few short years in the heart of the carefree children. I am thinking of an older man who seldom leaves his smile and good humor at home. Not long ago I was at the post office in Whiteriver. This man drove up in his pickup and got out. Instantly his smile, his cheerful words to friends standing there brightened the whole scene. What a gift to make others feel good through your own joyful nature. I have seen that the Creator has given this wonderful gift to his Apache people as well as to others.

"I believe that the Apaches are a helpful people. All men are born selfish, but some outgrow it to a certain degree. There is no doubt as to whether some of our people have developed a sense of helpfulness or not. It can be seen among them. Especially at the time of a death, it has always impressed me that there never seems to be a lack of help in building windbreaks, gathering wood, making a temporary shelter for the body, cooking food for those who attend the wake, and after the funeral there is always somebody helping to take down the temporary structures and cleaning up the area. There is also some sharing of labor at planting time and harvest, in building a new wickiup or frame house, and sometimes in getting firewood. Even though these do not happen as often as they could, they do happen!

"I believe the Apache people are a gregarious people. Most people are gregarious, that is they like to be with other people of their own kind. God does not command us to be this way, neither does he forbid it, so this is not something we call good or bad. It is, however, a cultural trait and more developed in some than others. A person may live in New York City and not be a gregarious person. He may not know his neighbor, visit with anybody, or talk to those around him. Every Apache knows that he is an Apache, and he feels a real kinship for the other members of his tribe. The people build their homes in clusters or family groups. Very few of them live in some valley all by themselves far away from everybody else. It is very rare to find one of their houses or wickiups built in such a place that they cannot see another camp from their doorway or window. Even the new homes being built follow this pattern. The best days of the year for

Upper East Fork camp.
Photo Credit: Hartzell photo collection

our people seem to be those when they can get together in large numbers. They like parties, games, dances, rallies, sporting events, and
other events which bring together great numbers of their people in
one place. This may be an advantage for us in our church life, and
no doubt does help our work more than it hinders it. The Apache
people are not so much a small tribe as they are a large family with
a common history, language, customs, ideas, and heritage. Into this
tribe-family no outsider has ever fully entered, nor can he.

"And I would say that the Apaches are a diplomatic people. There have been many times when I have seen them try to conceal anger and displeasure. They are often reluctant to criticize others. They are slow to show their feelings in their faces or in their actions, especially if they believe it is to their advantage to do so. They want to be on good terms with all their brothers.

"Alcohol, of course, changes all this in them just as it does in most people, but when they are in full control of themselves their ideal seems to be to deal 'softly' with others. This can be illustrated by the way they approach a person of whom they intend to ask a favor. They will always try to say or do something good first. They will try to establish good relations by some means with those they intend to deal with.

"There are other positive attributes with which the Lord blessed these people: generosity, simplicity, power of observation in the natural realm, artistic ability, endurance, to name a few. It is more important for an accurate answer to the question of who the Apaches are to also state a few things that they aren't and to mention some things that are negative.

"The Apache people, to my knowledge, never worshipped statues, they made no likeness of anything in heaven or earth for worship purposes, and they did not worship money or property as some people do. Nevertheless, many of their troubles today do come as the result of a kind of idolatry. Their 'god' is their own people. Let me explain what I mean: It is rare to find a person willing to act on his own, to do what he himself believes is right, if his act is contrary to what the people think and say. For example, a child may know in his heart that it is right to go to school, but if he hears some of his people belittle the value of education, he may become delinquent in school attendance. Or if he does come, he may not participate as he should for fear of offending his classmates, his people, his 'god.' Adults too for the sake of peace and harmony with their people, may violate their own conscience. A man who does not want to drink will drink when it is offered to him rather than offend his 'friend.' Then the excuse is given: 'I didn't want to, but he forced me.' They did not want to take the drink, but at the same time they were not able to act as an individual, on their own, but they fell down in obedience to their people. Parents fail to correct their children for fear of offending their people. Law and order break down for fear of the people, and criminals go unpunished for fear of the people. Church members will not refuse the ministrations of a medicine man even though they do not believe in him, for fear of the relatives who secured his services for them. Some even become involved in immorality and other sins

65

by participating in events where these things happen, and do this against their own conscience because they fear their people more than they fear the God in heaven."

Inashood Hartzell ended his remarks on the character of his people with these true words: "What sort of people do I think the Apache people are? They are people for whom Jesus gave his life. They are people without whom heaven would not be complete. They are people Jesus sent his messengers to teach, make disciples of, and to baptize them. They are God's children. I ask the Lord to save them, and hope they ask the same for me."[57]

---

[57] Howard Eugene Hartzell, *The Apache Lutheran*, June 1967.

CHAPTER FOUR

The Search

A journey of a thousand miles begins with a single step
(FROM THE CHINESE PHILOSOPHER LAOZI, CIRCA AD 604).

Brenner, Brockmann, Koehler, Dowidat und Dammann are all German names. Probably Apaches in Arizona wouldn't have known the nationality of the names—or cared, for that matter. That small group of German names would have something to do with the Apaches, however. As a matter of fact, those names would have something to do with the Apaches of Arizona that would continue to the present day.

Those German names belonged to German pastors in the Wisconsin Evangelical Lutheran Synod who were looking for a place to do real mission work and teach people who had never heard about Jesus. In 1885 this committee found a first candidate to send out to these peoples, to whomever they might prove to be. This young man they finally found was still in seminary training at Watertown, Wisconsin. By 1887 there were two. Finally, in 1891, there were three: John Plocher, George Adascheck and Paul Mayerhoff. Apparently, this church of German pastors had the men for mission work; they just didn't have the place for mission work yet in 1891.

In 1892, on a Tuesday morning in November, Pastors Otto Koch and Theodore Hartwig climbed up into a train car in Milwaukee and headed west. They were German too. They were going to find a place for their three young would-be missionaries waiting in Watertown, Wisconsin. Two days later their train steamed into Colorado, and for the first time the explorers and reconnoiters saw the Rocky Mountains of their adopted country. Pikes Peak was off to the left as they chugged and climbed toward Denver. The air was fresh and cool, and it begged to be breathed.

There had been plenty of coal smoke on the train, and there wasn't a sleeper bed in sight. There was no change of clothing either. They got into Denver on Thursday morning and went looking for a Pastor Rauh. He gave them some mail from several Indian agents that had been sent to him to be forwarded to the men on their way west. That same Thursday evening their train lumbered on from Denver, finally getting to LaJunta, Colorado, on the border of New Mexico. It was Friday morning, and it was a two-hour wait until the train would get there to take them on to Tucson. As they looked around them, they saw the first "Indians" and "Mexicans" in this foreign and strange place so far from their German Wisconsin. Two Indian shepherds heard that the men were on their way to Arizona to look for a place to do mission work. These two lived close to Albuquerque and traveled on the train with the pastors. They could speak a little English. They had some money with them, but they had no understanding of spiritual matters. Our two pastors tried to talk, but the language barrier left many awkward pauses. You could only point at so many things and say the appropriate word. Miming and the other gyrations of someone trying to talk with his hands lost their point and purpose, and after a while the men fell asleep, their heads bobbing this way and that. At 3:00 in the morning, they were awakened and saw the smiling faces of the two shepherds who wanted to say goodbye. It was Koch who then observed that Indians were friendly if treated in a friendly way. That observation was to be a big part in the future approach of Lutheran missionaries. Be friendly. Treat your people in a kind and open way.

They pulled into Deming, New Mexico, that Friday afternoon and had a layover of several hours. What they perhaps didn't know was that just seven years earlier in Deming the town had soldiers bivouacked everywhere. Those soldiers were ready at a moment's notice to be deployed from the very train line the men were riding on to be the third defensive ring to stop any possible Chiricahua Apache warriors coming up out of Mexico. It was in 1885 when the Committee had identified a first possible missionary to the Apaches that the Chiricahua had made their final break from Turkey Creek in the White Mountains. There had been all sorts of depredations made, and the people of Deming knew about it. The incidents were fresh in their minds. When the men walked around town they were told alarming news by the still tender inhabitants, "Don't go among the Indians. They'll kill you. They aren't settling down like they are supposed to." The people of Deming shoved newspaper cutouts toward the pastors that proved their points. Pastor Koch mused in his diary, "We haven't come this far to be put off by such talk!" Koch and Hartwig got to Tucson at 4:00 in the morning, and it was the 6th of November, 1892. How good it felt to stretch out in a regular bed again!

On Sunday morning, the two pastors thought of their congregations back in Wisconsin and pictured their people in the worship services that they would have led had they been there. It always feels strange for a pastor to miss church on Sunday morning and realize that his faithful people are in church back home without him. That afternoon they went to see an Indian school that was a mile from Tucson. It boasted 135 students, mostly Pima Indians. It was a Christian school, and our pastors heard the Indian children singing Christian songs. It seems they were inspired.

The trip on from Tucson by buckboard was horrendous. Hartwig and Koch wanted to visit the Pima Reservation near present-day Sacaton. The mail wagon would not take them the fifteen miles from Casa Grande. A man on his way back to Florence said he would swing by with them and drop them off. Swing by, he did. The well-meaning driver bragged that his wagon was specially equipped to keep it from dumping over after they clambered in and out of worsening gullies. After six hours of bouncing and bumping and retracing crooked wheel tracks, the driver climbed up on the back of his wagon and admitted after looking everywhere he could look, that he was lost. He thought he recognized the mountains on the skyline, but he wouldn't say for sure. They were all three lost now in the desert. *Irren* is a German verb that means to lose your way and wander about. Perhaps this word came to their minds that afternoon, as they cast this way and that and tried to figure out their way in the unsympathetic and dangerous desert. Finally, they stumbled blindly across a little trading post in the desert, and the French proprietor agreed to take them on to Sacaton.

Sacaton was a neat little frontier town, replete with a church and a jail. It was here that our man Koch met Cook. Both were German and both had the same name: one the German name Koch, the other the English translated name Cook. The Presbyterian Charles H. Cook was a remarkable man. His Pimas loved him. He had worked among them for eleven years as a missionary, and he had mastered their language. He lived with his people and acquired mastery of their language and their hearts in the only way there is to do that: he lived with them and became one of them. When the men got to the place of the Pima, they learned that Cook had single-handedly built two churches and established three congregations among the Pimas. He had baptized 118 souls and had 73 regular communicants. He was by himself at this time because his wife had died two years before. After she died, he had gone back to Iowa but realized after a while that he wanted to go and live the rest of his days with his people on the reservation. In his absence, his Pimas had continued on with their own church services and the reading of Scripture. German Lutheran Koch wondered to himself how many Lutheran congregations in the Midwest would have done the same in the face of these circumstances. Some of the members of Cook's Pima congregation were traveling twenty miles to church on Sundays! Imagine that!

What especially delighted Cook with Koch and Hartwig was that his German fellow Christians were finally getting out of their narrow world view and showing interest in sharing God's Word with the "Indians." Charles Cook pointed the two pastors from Wisconsin to San Carlos and the Apaches there. No one had taken the gospel there yet in the way Cook had brought it to the Pimas there at Sacaton. So after noticing that Indians didn't paint themselves any more nor did they openly practice polygamy, the two set off. They noticed too that the Pimas had their own people policing things in the community. While they were there the Pima police had brought in five intoxicated miscreants and thrown them unceremoniously into the neat little jailhouse. This was the way it had to be: the people needed to be incorporated into the work.

The next day the two Wisconsin ministers continued on through Pima territory in the company of Pastor Cook. Koch was impressed with the friendliness the people showed their white pastor. As he penned his recollections of the day he said, "I can still remember the feeling of the firm handshakes I got from the Pimas when their pastor introduced us to them." The recollection of the little church the group had made was in his mind's eye too as it perched there on a little hill in their community. They had made it with their own hands and money. They had worked shoulder to shoulder with their white pastor. They supported him too in their contributions, and those contributions were growing apace.

On their way to Florence, they passed by Casa Grande and saw "the big house." What they saw is still there today, only it is now covered by a huge roof that protects it from the sun and the desert storms. The men marveled at the four-foot-thick walls and four-story height. They fantasized how it must have been in 1538 when Cabeza de Vaca first happened by and "discovered" the massive ruins of the "big house." The Pimas had no traditions about the big house. No one knew for sure which old disappeared people had made this wonder out in the middle of the desert, in the valley of the Gila.[58] They wandered around in the rooms of the ruin and ate their lunches there. Their driver managed to get himself partially liquored up with a big bottle he carried nearby on the buckboard bench. That made inter-

---

[58] C. W. Ceram in his book *The First American* speaks about the Hohokam being the people who built and inhabited the big house (pp. 166, 168) and maintains that these people were in the area already when Jesus walked the earth. Father Kino reportedly came by this "Big House" in 1694 (!) when he was exploring the area at that time.

esting the further ride to a little place called Riverside[59] on the Gila River. Koch wrote in his diary that night, "In the middle of the wilderness of Arizona on the Gila River, in a shack made of mud, under a roof with godless men (in the next room some shady looking characters were having a card game with a large dark bottle providing refreshments), but above this roof the unsleeping eye of our heavenly Father is watching." At 3:00 in the morning, they were awakened by the now sober driver, who told them they needed to be underway. They had read Psalm 121 the night before: *The Lord will keep you from all harm—he will watch over your life; the Lord will watch over your coming and going both now and forevermore.*"

There were times during the day's travel they had to walk behind the straining horses which were trying to haul the buckboard up the steep slopes which today are measured as 15% grades. That seemed unfair too because they both had to pay 15 cents a mile to travel with the hung-over-now-sober driver. They ate with some silver miners at a place called Pioneer and spent the night in Globe. On Saturday evening, the 12th of November, they finally got to San Carlos. This was their destination, and this would be the place that would now learn to know more of these German Lutheran men.

Behind them on the skyline that day lay "Sleeping Beauty." She was the reclining mountain figure of an amply endowed woman sleeping there on the horizon. That was where the copper mines were being worked, there and in Globe itself. The Pinal Mountains stood there blue and high with their ponderosa pine and Douglas fir. But on the road to San Carlos that day there were only mesquite trees and cactus. As the way went slowly downhill toward San Carlos, saguaro cacti stood at attention. Some of them were ancient and had witnessed the passersby during the Apache wars. It is said to take a hundred years for a saguaro cactus to get an arm, and there were many there with arms upheld in spiny support of the blue sky. Mt. Turnbull stood off to the south and east. If they were to draw a classic western mountain silhouette, they couldn't have done better than follow the shape of Mt. Turnbull with its symmetrical/asymmetrical shape. And then as they traveled through the desert country of mesquite and catclaw and yucca, the face of the Triplets presented itself, at first just two faces of jutting stone on the horizon and then three as they approached San Carlos there on the Gila River. No doubt the driver of the wagon said, "You see those mountain peaks there? Rice,

---

[59] Highway 177 goes from Superior to Kearny. Just before you get to Kearny there is a sign pointing to the right that says, "Riverside." There are just a few buildings there today, but the little place where the pastors stayed is still there.

where the train stops, is there to the left, and Peridot is in the middle. The fort and San Carlos, where we are going, are off there to the right, by the river."

These two pastors from the Midwest who were looking for a place to do mission work were not the first to show up on the reservation with an idea and a wish. There were others who had come with varying motives and ideas on how they would interact and "help" the Apaches who were now forced to live on the reservations. Lt. Charles Gatewood explained how it was with one: "(The agent) was a smooth, wizened, spectacled little old man, [who] always said grace before meals. [He] held religious services every Sabbath in the schoolhouse to as many adults as could be induced to attend, & to as many children as the police could catch & herd into the school house; [he] really tried to issue more than half rations to his protégés & claimed great credit for his endeavors in their behalf. On meeting anyone entitled to consideration, [the agent] would wash his hands with invisible soap in imperceptible water. [This was his] way of showing his great pleasure at forming the acquaintance of a gentleman so well able to understand my efforts on behalf of the poor benighted heathen."[60]

Gatewood also related, "About 1870, if I am not mistaken, our government tried its hand at granting reservations and establishing agencies. It erected the necessary buildings—quarters for agents & employees, corrals, shops, storehouses, etc. It shipped immense quantities of provisions, farming implements—in fact, all things necessary for the prosperity of the people, including missionaries, a goodly store of [religious] tracts, Bibles, & school books, etc."[61]

It was to this agency at San Carlos on ration day that Koch and Hartwig came that day. 2,200 of the 3,800 total Apaches under the jurisdiction of this agency lived within twenty miles of the fort. Many of them were there that day. There were women with babies in cradleboards and mothers tugging toddling infants. Hoop and ring games were played. Some people had cards, and some were sitting on the ground here and there in groups—talking and laughing. Outbreaks of laughter characterized Apache crowds. One-liners, usually at someone else's expense, sent up outbursts of laughter. The two men sat there on their bench and observed. No one was working here in any kind of organized way to tell these people of Jesus and the Bible. The pastors were making their plans as they watched. They

---

60 *Lt. Charles Gatewood & His Apache Wars Memoir.* Charles B. Gatewood (edited and with additional text by Louis Kraft). University of Nebraska Press, Lincoln and London, 2005, p. 31.

61 *Op. cit.* p. 29.

talked to a Colonel Johnson who had a busy day trying to answer people's questions and deal with people's problems. At the end of his day he talked with the two men. Their plan developed into some basic points: have missionaries come and live close by to visit the people in their camps; learn the language; establish a school to teach the children. While this all was happening, the missionaries could give religious instruction to the students in the government school in the evenings. The teachers there seemed to welcome any help of this kind they could get. In this setting and in this way the mission work would be done. Then after a while when things got started at San Carlos, they hoped to take the message on to the upper part of the reservation, around Fort Apache (called Camp Apache at this time). The further hope was that when the beachhead had been established there among the Apaches that the work could branch out to the north and east to the Navajos. The language was practically identical, or so they reasoned.[62]

The language challenge was something that Koch and Hartwig could not fully appreciate on this first visit to the San Carlos agency. Gatewood again: "There was no white man or red either in all the country who could interpret reliably from Indian to English. So we had to have an English-Spanish interpreter & a Spanish-Indian one. This arrangement was rather slow & tedious at times, but it was the best that could be made. The Nantan spoke & understood the Apache dialect somewhat but not to an extent that would always insure accuracy of interpretations, especially in important matters. As it was, even with great care, misunderstandings arose frequently, sometimes leading to serious complications, & again with ridiculous results."[63] George Wraten with the Chirichauas in their captivity in Florida was admired and loved because he could speak Apache so well, the best any of them had ever heard. No matter that the first missionaries spoke German. Their people couldn't have understood them if they had spoken English. Apaches spoke and understood Apache, and even then, there were different dialects. And Gatewood admitted, "In narration of facts & transactions of a purely business nature, their interpretations were as faithful as could be expected, but there were times when the original aboriginal speech was not adequately set forth in English."[64]

---

[62] *Gemeinde-Blatt*, March 1, 1893, "*Unsere Erlebnisse auf der Reise zu and unter den Indianern des Suedwestens*," p 102.

[63] *Lt. Charles Gatewood & His Apache Wars Memoir.* Charles B. Gatewood (edited and with additional text by Louis Kraft). University of Nebraska Press, Lincoln and London, 2005. p. 43.

[64] Op cit. p. 44.

This inability to understand each other was perhaps the cause for the terrible debacle at Cibecue in 1881. The chief of scouts, Al Seiber, did not think the German interpreter Charles Hurrle, who was kind of a self-proclaimed expert on the Apache language, really did know what he was talking about. Seiber said the Cibecue Creek battle "was caused by misinterpretation through ignorance, the interpreter not knowing enough of the Indian language to make a close bargain with a squaw." (He didn't explain exactly what he meant there.) You can hear the trouble when Hurrle telegraphed General Crook in response and said, "There must be a misunderstanding. I did not tell any Indians or anybody that they would be put in the guardhouse only that they would be punished if they were summoned to attend court and refused to go. Alchesay and Mose were summoned. I'll bet a thousand dollars that I did not say anything of the kind."[65]

Betzinez reported that while General Crook was in Mexico not far from the Bavispe River in search of Geronimo one lone Apache was seen approaching. The General wanted to capture the man and talk to him without firing. The scouts had missed something in translation. They fired. They also missed and the man got away. This is just another instance where communications broke down. It was into this milieu that the first *Inashood* would step and speak.

Koch and Hartwig left San Carlos that first day on the reservation accompanied by Colonel Johnson and traveled to Fort Thomas on their way to Bowie. At Fort Thomas they encountered white settlers who had been terrorized by the depredations and murders perpetrated by the Apache Kid. At least that is who the frightened people were saying had done the bad things. No one actually had seen the Apache Kid at work, but everything bad that was happening was being blamed on him. He was blamed for shooting the implacable Al Sieber, head of the Apache scouts during the wars. At the time of that debacle, the Apache Kid had been disarmed and could not have been the one who fired the crippling shot at Al Sieber's foot. The Apache Kid remained a phantom figure. As late as 1935 people were still saying that he was sneaking back onto the reservation for secret trysts with people there. Some thought he was perhaps living in the Sierra Madres of Mexico, those ancient haunts of the Apache people, and from there making his forays into southern Arizona.

The Apache Kid was the topic of conversation in the mail coach in which the men were traveling. All the lurching inhabitants had weapons strapped on in good number, except our two men. The pastors told their fellow travelers that they didn't come to fight but to

---

65 Charles Collins, *Apache Nightmare*, p. 229.

establish a mission field among the Apaches. The work of the *Inas-hood* perhaps crossed the dusty trail of the Apache Kid in the lurching stage ride that day. There would be other oblique trail crossings later. On Tuesday evening, covered with a layer of fine dust, they got to Bowie. From there they made their further trek to Albuquerque, Gallup, and Fort Defiance. The very train they traveled on went on after they had gotten out and a short distance farther lost a wheel on a smoking car—essentially rendering the whole train a smoking train, killing one man and badly injuring fourteen others. On the fifty-five mile coach ride they saw only one Indian girl off in the distance herding sheep. She was Navajo.

Fort Defiance was on a little creek. The ex-sheriff who had been in charge of their travel up to that point got them there safely. Fort Defiance was surrounded on three sides by towering mountains of stone. Kit Carson had something to do with the fort being there. His heavy-handed approach had wrested the good grazing land from the Navajo to place the fort there. The Lutheran men were invited into the quarters of a Mr. Shipley, who was the agent. He was very knowledgeable regarding the Navajo and told them many things about the customs and people. He mentioned that they yearly sold many tons of wool. He showed them many astounding examples of woven blankets and rugs that the Navajo had made. The weaving process was simple but laborious. A woman weaver spent months working on a single item. One blanket there in Shipley's collection cost $100—a huge amount in those days. Shipley also told the men of his experience with Black Horse. He had gone to collect students from Black Horse's village and was attacked. The Navajo people like the Apache people didn't want their children taken from them and shipped off to schools off the reservation.[66] Shipley carried on his body the scar marks of their displeasure. This reluctance of the Navajo to send their children off to distant boarding schools would show up in the developing philosophy of the Lutheran missionaries to have schools on the reservation that would teach the children in their home communities. In fact, that first fall in 1894 when first missionary Plocher started off with his twelve students, he observed, "The people always want to know if their children who attend here will later be sent back East. When I reassure them that the 'chief' of schools has no jurisdiction here and that in fact I am

---

[66] A total of 106 Chiricahua students were sent to Carlisle, Pennsylvania, in 1886-1887. By 1895, 112 Chiricahuas had attended the school. Of this number, thirty-seven, or one-third, died there and remain buried on the former school grounds. In nearly every instance, the cause of death was communicable tuberculosis. (Quoted from *Images of America: Old San Carlos.* Paul and Kathleen Nickens. Arcadia Publishing, 2008, p. 110.)

the 'chief' of this school, they are satisfied and tell me they will bring their children."[67]

In the April 1, 1893, issue of the church paper to which Koch was submitting his written remembrances, you can hear him grappling with the big issues facing his church. How could they *not* bring God's good news to these people who didn't have it? How could they allow these people to be taken in by unorthodox churches? How could they not go and go soon? On the other hand (and you can hear the opposition to the work in these words), how could they disregard the great mission possibilities in the Midwest? How would they be able to take care of their two worker training schools? The seminary in Wisconsin was not yet completed. It would require much money and attention. Wouldn't it be irresponsible to neglect these important and foundational parts of the church's work and launch out into this brand-new work that promised to be very labor intensive and probably slow in showing results?

It was a daunting task the small Wisconsin Synod was looking at. Koch was convinced though, and so were the three seminarians who were ready to go to work in Arizona. The April 1 issue of the *Gemeinde-Blatt*, the same one that carried Koch's closing remarks of his and Hartwig's mission journey, mentioned in its small print that of the twenty-eight students to graduate that spring from the seminary, three stood ready to go to Apacheland.

---

67 *Gemeinde-Blatt*, "Happy News from Our Indian Mission," 1 February 1895, p. 21.

CHAPTER FIVE

The Stage

All the world's a stage, and all the men and women
merely players; they have their exits and their entrances,
and one man in his time plays many parts, his acts being
seven ages. At first, the infant, mewling and puking in the
nurse's arms (Shakespeare's "As You Like it").

It is a religious story, but it remains also a philanthropic story played out on the highest and noblest stage. *Inashood* came to a stage set with characters and places and times, and the times they were a-changing. Many of the characters from the earlier Apache struggles would now be players in the mission work, and what had happened in those struggles would be lurking in the background of the work. Things would be remembered. The past would affect the present, as is always the case in history and time. What is today is the result of what happened yesterday; we deal now with what was done then.

Imagine the context into which the missionaries stepped. Terrible atrocities had been committed. The Aravaipa Massacre was one, and it demonstrated the keeping of payback tallies. How could it have not been so for Chief Eskiminzin? He went to sleep in his camp on Aravaipa Creek that evening of April 29, 1871. His little girl slept in the wickiup with him and other members of his family. He was trying to lead his people to peace with the white man; that's why they were there on Aravaipa Creek. The government had placed them there, saying it would be safe for them, and they should stay there for their own safety and for the safety of the citizens of Arizona. The fires in the Aravaipa Apache camp burned down, and sleep came to the people. They didn't know or sense that out in the mesquite trees 92 Papagos, 48 Mexicans and six Anglos, all from Tucson, were stalking and circling and getting ready, fingering in their hands homemade bludgeons of cow tails holding fist sized boulders. In the faint light of dawn, they struck. They beat most of their hapless victims to death—skulls broke and brains ran. When they were finished 108 corpses lay around leering blankly at their prowling and prodding and jubilant slayers. Only eight of the 108 were men; the rest were women and children. Twenty-nine little children were also kidnapped and sold as slaves, mostly into Mexico. Two escaped and got back, and five were later recovered from Arizona citizens who had them. The rest would never be seen again. And when the slaughter started with its hideous noise, Ezkiminzin himself was knocked senseless by a Papago club. He woke when the grisly work had been done and grabbed his little two-year-old daughter and made off into the dusky dawn to safety.[68] His other children were killed.

Several months later Charles McKinney, a farmer on the San Pedro River not far from where Eskiminzin's people had been slaughtered invited Eskiminzin for dinner. He killed the fattened calf. Literally, it was so. He hadn't been part of the massacre, and it had appalled him, as it had the citizenry of the nation. Perhaps by having Eskiminzin to his home he was trying to say he was a true friend and not part of the group of murderers. Perhaps he was trying to say that all white people weren't bad neighbors. The two friends, Charles

Scouts at camp of Ishkihbago, Fort Huachuca, 3 November *The Apache Scout*
Photo from Salem Lutheran Church archives, Milwaukee, Wisconsin

68 Alfred Uplegger quoted Frank Lockwood's account, page 181.

McKinney and the Apache Eskiminzin, talked and after the dinner they smoked cigars. After the cigar, Eskiminzin pulled his pistol out and shot and killed his friend Charles McKinney. Later when asked why he did it he said he had done it from strength. Anyone can kill an enemy, but it takes a strong man to be able to kill his friend. He did it to show that Apaches could never be friends with white men. They had to remain strong—and separate. He did it to say something to his people who surely were questioning his leadership and his loyalties.

Eskiminzin did become friends with perhaps the best Anglo agent the Apaches at San Carlos ever got. John P. Clum had come to San Carlos under the auspices of the Dutch Reformed Church. President Grant had assigned that willing church to befriend the Apache. The White people were doing this with the Native Americans they had subdued. John P. Clum was a young man when he came, not different from the first missionaries in this regard. It took the vigor and optimism of youth to do the work in whatever sphere you did it. Clum organized a system of Apache policemen who maintained law and justice on the reservation. It was kind of an indigenous police force. (The word "indigenous" wasn't a big word in Clum's day, but it later became a big word, in the parlance of the *Inashood* anyway. The word indigenous would later become a kind of buzz word in the playbook of Lutheran church mission work.) Clum's efforts at indigenization worked. His group was later instrumental in the capture of Geronimo in 1886. It was the Apaches themselves who were really the only ones to ever take Geronimo captive.

It was this John P. Clum who became Eskiminzin's friend, the same Ezkiminzin who had "in strength" killed his friend on the San Pedro. They took a trip together to the east in 1876, five years after the horrific Aravaipa Massacre. Ezkiminzin tried to live at peace, and he prospered. He was an honorable man and won white people's trust in spite of the horrible things these people had done to him. Maybe he saw the handwriting on the wall and like Daniel in the Old Testament could read it. He lived like a white man and was allowed a ranch on the San Pedro by his "benefactors." He worked hard and made his ranch a paying operation. Merchants in the Tucson area trusted him and gave him credit—a $5,000 credit limit at one of the stores in Tucson! But Eskiminzin was too successful. In 1888 white men from Tucson came a second time, minus the Papagos and Mexicans, and stole his crops and all his cattle and took what he had worked so hard for. He fled to San Carlos. The authorities deemed that he should move in closer to them so they could "protect" him from his prosperity. He was deeded another little place on the Gila River, and he started again from scratch.

White men came again. This time they accused him of aiding and abetting the Apache Kid. This legitimately named renegade was Eskiminzin's son-in-law. The Kid's wife was Eskiminzin's daughter, the same one he had run wild-eyed into the mountains with when the Tucson mob had killed all his people. And sure enough! The white men found proof of Eskiminzin's complicity with ne'er-do-wells like the Apache Kid. There on the ground outside the bedroom window were the footprints of the Apache Kid! The white people were sure that what they saw in the dust was what they needed to see. On the dubious basis of the footprints in the dirt outside his window, they sent Eskiminzin away to captivity in Mount Vernon Barracks in Alabama. No one ever captured the Apache Kid. They never really had proof that he actually did what they credited him with doing.

Years later John P. Clum visited the place in Alabama where they were holding Eskiminzin captive. Clum had long since quit his thankless job of being Apache agent. He had become a newspaperman in Tucson and then later in Tombstone. As Clum walked through the work yard that day in Alabama he saw an old Apache man working there. The man was working hard; he was untended and unguarded. Something about that man caught Clum's eye and then held it: It was his friend Eskiminzin! "Skimmy!" he called out.

On May 31, 1894, Clum wrote Daniel Browning, the Commissioner of Indian Affairs, and pleaded for the release of his friend. In his letter he spoke of the atrocities which the white people had perpetrated. His exact words were, "(Eskiminzin) has been persecuted, humiliated, imprisoned, ironed, and finally exiled—not only without trial but without specific charges. Though brokenhearted over his misfortunes, I found him not only orderly but industrious." Clum spoke of that one and only white man Eskiminzin had killed. He spoke of the extenuating circumstances. He spoke of the faithfulness to truth and word that his friend Eskiminzin had shown to white men. As a result of this letter the train brought Eskiminzin back to his little place on the Gila River. He was sixty-seven years old when he got back home. Two weeks later, he died.

That heartbreak happened on the Gila River not far from San Carlos. This Gila River was a stone's throw from the San Carlos where *Inashood* Plocher and *Inashood* Adascheck were. They were there somewhere because they had come in 1893. Eskiminzin died there in 1894. What an unlikely place in the world for a preaching of forgiveness to succeed! It was a Sunday morning when almost a hundred of Eskiminzin's people had been slaughtered. Imagine how it would feel for the survivors when these white people came claiming to be friends and claiming their Sunday God would be able to help

Apaches. Imagine walking to a stone church on a bright spring Sunday morning and remembering back to that other spring morning when all your people had died. Imagine being seen in the company of white people and listening to them and following them and being friends with them after what had happened. Imagine it if you can, but you really can't.

You can hear the indignation of *Inashood* Alfred Uplegger when he said about the massacre, "This fearful, shameful massacre was an outrage against defenseless women and children. Men who knew the situation of the Indians and that the Aravaipas were not guilty of what they were accused, branded the massacre as 'one of the saddest and most terrible incidents in history.' The deep damnation of the dead cried out trumpet-tongued to the people throughout the nation. President Grant demanded that all those who took part in the raid be brought to trial before a federal judge in Tucson. One hundred four were indicted and tried, but all were exonerated by the jury!!!"[69] One strand of the Lutheran story of *Inashood* runs right through the massacred camp of Chief Ezkiminzin because there was one man there that night who escaped. He was Chief Chiquito, and he would become the father of Alonzo S. Bullis, who would be born eleven years after the massacre. This Lon (*Alonzo*) Bullis would be a very important Lutheran leader and example to his people. He became a special friend and co-worker of Alfred Uplegger. You will hear more of him in the account of Uplegger's life and ministry to follow. The important family name of Bullis came into the Lutheran church in this way, and this name is still there.

The missionaries came with the knowledge that there was an awful antagonist to their ministrations: the memory of the past with its atrocities and dishonesties. The missionaries referred to it and referenced it many times. Francis Uplegger tells how it was in April of 1877[70] in Ojo Caliente in New Mexico when John Clum and his Apache scouts encircled Geronimo and his band. "A few of Geronimo's men turned so as to break through a gap in the encircling line of scouts; the scout captain aimed his gun at one of them. There—a wild yell! A woman of the Apache threw herself upon the captain, knocking down his gun. She was braver than many a brave, risking her life for the man's life. No life then was lost; Geronimo and all his companions there were at that time made captives for some time.

---

[69] Pastor Alfred Uplegger, *Reminiscing on the Lord's Mercy and Grace to Apache Indians During the Last 60 Years,* Installment IV, page 2 (edited and re-recorded by Pastor Myrl Wagenknecht).

[70] This was six years after the massacre on Aravaipa Creek.

But readers of Mr. Clum's account of the whole affair are probably with nothing else in it so much impressed as with what the Apache woman did. And how it may have affected the man for whose life she risked her own." [71]

John Clum and the two military men, General Crook and Lieutenant Gatewood, tried to do militarily and politically among the Apache what the missionaries would try to do spiritually. From the beginning there was the effort to get the Apaches themselves engaged in the work. With Clum and Crook and Gatewood it was just this ability of theirs to enlist Apaches to fight and deal with Apaches that guaranteed and brought their success. This would be slow going with the Apache Christian mission work. It was not easy to enlist Apaches to champion something like this. It had been demoralizing and defeating to the Apaches when they realized that their own people were against them and had tracked them back to their lairs in the mountains. How could you resist the foe when the foe was yourself? It proved easier to enlist a scout like Alchesay or Peaches to serve against Apaches and to serve with white men than it would be to enlist an Apache to serve spiritually shoulder to shoulder with a white man and lead him to spiritual haunts and fortresses which the Apache frequented. This all was made very difficult in those first years especially when there just weren't any Christian Apaches out there.

At the time of the Apache wars Lieutenant Charles B. Gatewood lived with the Apaches in the same place where later missionaries would live. He was perhaps even more knowledgeable of the Apaches than was General George Crook. The Apaches respected him highly for his friendship and fairness. Louis Kraft in his biography closes his book with the following comment on Gatewood, "Without a doubt, the underlying root of his success stems from his ability to accept the Apaches as fellow humans, gaining their trust, respect, and in their own way, love."[72] It was this Lieutenant Gatewood who said, "The hatred, which each tribe bears to all the others, & which was engendered at their separation after the great battle referred to, has not to this day been materially lessened. This bitter hatred thus engendered has been the trump card in the hands of the white man."[73]

---

[71] Francis Uplegger, *The Apache Scout*, February 1929, p. 4.

[72] As a matter of fact, there are still some Apaches living on the Fort Apache Reservation in this twenty-first century who have the last name Gatewood. At Christmas time 1926 in the Lutheran church in Whiteriver, it was Chester Gatewood who used the New Testament story of Zaccheus to address his fellow Apaches. Imitation is the sincerest form of flattery.

[73] Lt. Charles Gatewood & His Apache Wars Memoir. Charles B. Gatewood (Edited and with additional text by Louis Kraft). Lincoln and London: University of Nebraska Press, 2005, p. 24.

It was Gatewood too who explained the practice and success of Apache scouts. The scouts worked well with men like Gatewood and Crook of the United States Army, not because they felt like helping out the white man who had forced them onto the narrow confines of a reservation. They had their own scores to settle with the Apaches they ran into the ground in their relentless and unswerving way. Raging vendettas among the Apaches themselves made them relentless on the trail of hated brothers. Jason Betzinez talked about an incident that happened in his band while they were in Mexico. Jason Betzinez was Geronimo's cousin and had fought with him. "A man named She-neah suddenly decided to shoot the lone Navajo who had been with Geronimo all this time. The Navajo, while previously serving as a U.S. scout, had killed one of She-neah's relatives. As usual the Apache never forgot nor forgave, so without warning She-neah killed the Navajo. We were all sorry that this happened but no one did anything about it."[74]

Missionaries learned of this smoldering lust for revenge. Apaches were not unique in this human penchant to want to pay back evil with evil. Listen to Alfred Uplegger: "The missionary was welcomed in every camp, but very rarely was he called, because he was white and the natural custom was not to ask any favors of a white man, except for their own advantage. It took a long time for them to overcome an inborn hate. Some admitted that if it were possible for them, then they would drive out every white man, or kill him, and the unconverted would do so even today."[75] The Christian virtue of forgiving your enemies seemed like a very bad idea. It no doubt seemed like letting the white man get away with doing what he was going to do anyway. A spirit of forgiveness would come hard and slow, and every human being with a pulse knows why. Geronimo in his confinement at Fort Sill, Oklahoma, would later say to the interviewer through clenched teeth, "Every day my hearts aches for vengeance against Mexico." Gatewood's observation was, "To the Apaches, a wrong always had to be righted. Josanie's violence against the White Mountains had to be revenged, and Alchesay and Sanchez would both play leading roles in their people's quest to even the score." Alchesay is mentioned in this connection. Alchesay's anger and reason for bitterness would later have its rendezvous

[74] Jason Betzinez, *I Fought with Geronimo,* Lincoln and London: University of Nebraska Press, 1959, p. 92.

[75] Alfred Uplegger, *Reminiscing on the Lord's Mercy and Grace to Apache Indians During the Last 60 Years,* Installment III, page 1 (edited and re-recorded by Pastor Myrl Wagenknecht).

with Lutheran missionary Edgar Guenther, *Inashood Ndasin* (the tall *Inashood*).

Carl Guenther (not related to Edgar Guenther) spoke of the insatiable desire for revenge the Apaches felt for those who had wronged them. He said that his people told him that the reason the whites had the upper hand and were causing them such misery by their dishonest dealings and perpetrated wrongs was that they had sinned against *Ussen*[76] and he was punishing them for not listening to the medicine men in the first place. When they got that right again, *Ussen* would once again give them supremacy and they would repay evil with evil, and even repay it with greater evil if they could. According to Guenther, the Apache could not be thankful for anything a white man did for him. *Ussen* forced him to do it. *Ussen* would also lead them to the opportunity to rid themselves of the white men. In Bible times the Lord had to remind the Jewish people and us, "Vengeance is mine, I will repay." Before Christianity could come and grow, the Lord would have to convince the Apache of this too. Guenther saw this propensity toward vengeance as aggravated by the medicine men, who were allegedly having these direct connections with *Ussen* in dreams and things and were then telling them to the people. In July of 1902 the monthly and weekly rations were supposed to end. The missionary knew of countless examples of white wrong, of lying and deceiving and taking advantage of the people. In view of all these things, how in the world would a missionary be able to lead his people to forgive and to forget? Surely only God could cause that to be.

There was fear on the stage set for mission work in those early years. Geronomo's own chief Naiche said about those times, "We were afraid. It was war. Anybody who saw us would kill us, and we did the same thing. We had to if we wanted to live." Virtually every person the new missionaries saw had terror and tragedy gnawing at his or her life. Everyone had enough enmity and impossible hurt to doom any work of mercy and trust. The Aravaipa Massacre was just one of many horror stories that festered in the people's minds and ate at their insides. The desert place where the Inashood came bristled with more than cactus. It bristled with the sharp and painful barbs of countless atrocities suffered by the people forced to live there.

Listen to Apache Chief Manuel tell his grievances after the Cibecue affair. The so-called massacre there in 1881 took place just a short distance from the later mission station where later *Inashoods* lived. Chief Manuel was talking to General Crook: "The agent gave us permission to plant on the Cibecue and gave us hoes and spades

---

[76] One Apache word for God.

to work with. Our crops were fine. I don't know why the soldiers were sent up there unless our fine crops made the agent mad. All Mexicans and Americans raise corn; take pleasure in raising it. After he had found out that we were raising corn, why did that fat agent send out soldiers after us? What had we done? We had an abundance of everything; had planted corn, watermelons, muskmelons, beans, everything. We couldn't understand why the agent should always be sending men to see what we were doing; their horses always trampled down our fields of corn. Up where we planted was an open road; no stolen horses ever found their way in there; we never did anything wrong; then why did the agent send soldiers in there? I told the agent I hadn't done anything wrong. I hadn't gone on the warpath. I hadn't stolen anything. I wanted to stay here where I belonged. But he took me, tied me all up, tied my hair, put irons on my feet and hands and put me in the calaboose. I haven't done anything wrong, at least, I don't think I have.[77]

Regarding the Cibecue Massacre and the subsequent hanging of the three Apache scouts, the Apache people back home were of the opinion that the trial had gone bad and was in fact wrong. Skippy Joe, Deadshot and Dandy Jim—all scouts for the white man's soldiers—had been lynched, as far as the Apaches saw it. General Crook understood their feelings when he wrote, "The Apaches insist that one of the young men hanged last spring at Fort Grant had taken no active part in the troubles—that he hadn't fired a shot and that his life was sworn away by heated, ignorant and mendacious witnesses."

Arthur Alchesay Guenther, Edgar's son who got his middle name from the famed chief who would play a big part in the early Lutheran Church on the Fort Apache Reservation, said, "It also must be remembered that the white men who came before the missionaries were men not interested in the souls of the Apache. They were miners, trappers, farmers, cowboys and soldiers. All wanting to take, dig, till, graze, trap and if necessary, kill. This period of push, takeover, round-up, kill and deport lasted for 40 years and only ended in a shaky 'peace' in 1886, just seven years before the first Lutheran missionary began his work. Oh, there was 'peace'—if you could call it that. Deportation, round-up and resettle, rations and robbery, subjection and whiskey. Does this all make for a happy interaction between conqueror and the conquered? Robbed of land, robbed of freedom to roam, robbed of a way of life and offered a strange combination of the open hand of friendship and then the closed fist of domination. Because of this paradox which caused so much confu-

[77] Collins, *Apache Nightmare*, pp. 219, 220.

sion, there had to follow a natural mistrust of all white men. This last condition to me was one of the major obstacles that had to be overcome by the early men. One had to gain the confidence of the Apache before it would be possible to offer a substitution for the native religion. Without this trust the situation would be hopeless. Too often the Apache had been lied to. Too often he had received the short end of the deal. History tells us that the success or failure of the early men rested upon, to a great degree, their ability to exhibit a combination of love and patience. Some possessed these two traits, and again others just did not have the ability to wait out a situation. This is something maybe we all should think about in our work even today. Gustav Harders, Al Uplegger, Art Krueger, Uncle Henry, my father are examples of this type of love and patient ministry. They were instrumental to a great degree in overcoming the mistrust that had become part of the Apache culture as a result of the treatment they had received at the hands of others."[78]

The Apaches were not even citizens of the country when the *Inashood* came. Edgar Guenther tells in 1923 that Apaches were given the right to vote if they were able to read the Constitution.

Alfred Uplegger observed a number of times that when the work started the Apaches were still considered prisoners of war. Remember that in 1893, when the first missionaries came, the place and people were only seven years distant from 1886, when Geronimo and his band made their sad and forced way to Fort Marion in Florida, in United States-provided transportation. You can see the picture of the last holdout band on the railroad embankment. You can see that little remnant of the force that had bedeviled the whole United States military for all those years. There is enigmatic Geronimo, who bridged the gap between folk hero and hardened criminal. There is Naiche, the actual leader, who would become a Christian himself in Oklahoma later. It was this Naiche who helped his captors and was sent into exile for his efforts. We may understand why he became a bitter man.

The relatives of the remnant bound for exile were the very people John Plocher and George Adascheck were going to try and convert to Christianity. If not actual relatives, the people had all been connected in some way to that railroad trestle band. Years later a wizened and wrinkled Alice Taipa (A-100's wife) at Seven Mile on the Fort Apache reservation would tell the visiting *Inashood* that she

---

[78] Alchesay Arthur Guenther, *The Ministry among the Apaches after 100 Years.* Arizona Pastors' Conference at Grace Evangelical Lutheran Church, San Carlos, Arizona, May 4-5, 1993.

and all her band had been taken captive by Geronimo and forced to march toward Mexico. Alice didn't much like Geronimo, and her family didn't either.

Alfred Uplegger later remarked in his reminiscences of the early work that there was a great suspicion on the part of the people against the white missionaries. Edgar Guenther also made this statement regarding Chief Alchesay. That suspicion was never completely overcome in the case of some. It was the nature of the Apache to remember grievances and tally them for future repayment. Forgiveness was not an Apache custom, as it really is not any culture's custom. When you think of all the boundary whittling and broken bargains and foundered treaties and agreements, it is a great testimony to the people and the men called missionaries that they ever got together at all. The sweat was almost still on the war ponies when Plocher and Adascheck got there. Reservation life as it existed then was hardly a decade old.

Loco Jim died in 1927 at about 85 years of age. He became a Christian friend of the missionaries in the Whiteriver area. He had his picture taken on the church steps of the Church of the Open Bible. He, like many of the people, had lived through the wars and the resettling. He carried many things in his mind. He spoke of the part he had played in various skirmishes. He told how he had once saved the life of a white girl, the daughter of an army officer. He had gotten some kind of reward for that. He was also commended by an army officer for his honesty in returning a large sum of money he had found. Loco Jim knew many things about the people and the place. He struggled with the native religion too. His wife was one of the few women in the tribe who was involved in "medicine" work. Jim had been a medicine man himself, so it had been a slow road in getting to know Loco Jim.

You would have to say it was because of God's power and working that this irreconcilable difference was overcome. The observation of Koch about the Pima Indians on that very first reconnaissance run in 1892 was, "The Pima (and Indians in general) keep to themselves and are generally and rightfully suspicious of the whites. Any kind of success among them is not going to happen until a missionary has their confidence." He went on, "And to establish this confidence, it is necessary for the messenger of peace to speak their language, live among them, not make rash and unkeepable promises, and be consistent in his demeanor and dealings. If a missionary does these things then by God's grace and help he will have success." Many years later, these Apaches and their children and grandchildren would come in droves to stand in stony-faced respect or weep unabashedly at the graves for these *Inashood* when they died and were buried in grave-yards with their own Apache brothers and sisters. They would gently lower the caskets into the graves with the lariats from their saddles. They would take their turns in shoveling the graves in.

There are many anthropologists and Kevin Costner Native American expert types who claim that Native Americans were just fine as they were, and the intrusions of Anglo missionaries just messed things up. They look at the before and after pictures of the Apache young people at Carlisle Indian School in Pennsylvania, for instance, in the late 1800s and cluck their tongues at the badness of it all. On the other hand—and everyone who studies must know it—the culture wasn't something that anyone could happily live with, including the Apaches themselves. They were warriors by occupation and avocation. They were the best guerrilla warfare soldiers the world has ever seen. A handful of their men kept the United States military in turmoil for thirty years, and actually it was longer than that. Those who fought them and stared for days at their empty tracks in forlorn and wild country respected their abilities to fight and strike and run and regroup and fight again. They knew the country like no one else. They knew the natural forts and fastness of it. They came and went like the wind, a sound and a stirring here and there, and then quiet. Crook said about the Cibecue affair when the cavalry of General Carr limped back to Fort Apache under cover of darkness, "Without wishing to express an opinion upon that affair, I have no doubt from what I know of the Indians and the country in question that, if the Indians had been in earnest, not one of our soldiers could have gotten away from there alive."[79]

The reality was that the Apaches were raiders.[80] They got their commodities from Mexico, mostly. They took them as the occasion provided, and they did it for a long time. They went down the San Pedro and Aravaipa River valleys on sorties for supplies from 1690 until 1870. The Mexicans felt the brunt of most of this, but many white settlers in their area also obliged the Apaches with their horses and cattle and firearms—and occasionally with their scalps. The Mexican wolf still roamed the land and howled at the moon during those days of the late 1800s. The Apaches were the human equivalent of the wolf. They were the gleaming predatorial eyes in the dark.

---

[79] Collins, *Apache Nightmare*, p. 221.

[80] Consider that Oswalt in speaking of the demise of the Hopi culture said, "It is possible, too, that the nomadic Navajo and Apache raided these settled peoples and contributed to their downfall" (p. 351).

The White Mountain Apaches even came to be called Coyotero.[81] It was Charles Gatewood's observation as he witnessed Apache warfare dying down, "Another fact seems to be well established in the history of these people, & that is, when they did appear, they proceeded to make their presence known in an exceedingly disagreeable manner. Contact with others meant war, for war, pillage, & the chase are the chief occupations on which they relied for sustenance & amusement."[82]

It really wasn't nice at all. People today speak in idyllic terms about how great it must have been to have lived like Native Americans did and Apaches in particular. There were some noble things about the culture, to be sure. It wasn't a promiscuous culture, even though polygamy was practiced. Polygamy became almost a necessity for the race because with war and fighting the *pièce de résistance*, there weren't that many men around. This culture cut the noses off of women who were suspected of unfaithfulness by jealous husbands. One or both of twins were thrown under mesquite trees by maternal grandmothers who maybe also stuffed their baby nostrils with sand to aid the miserable death that came quickly or not so quickly. In this culture, twin babies signified two fathers, and the babies paid for the supposed indiscretion. Polydactylism was in the genes of some of the clans.[83] Edgar Guenther once excised one such finger with a quick snip of his pocket knife and saved a baby's life. Babies with cleft palates were also discarded, as were babies with other visible abnormalities. The old were encouraged to wander off and die when they became too decrepit to keep up and thereby endangered the safety of the band. This unlovely practice of euthanasia is described by Harders in his book *Dohashtida* and by Edgar Guenther in his writings about the work.

Even though they were raiders and were good at it, they could also farm—and did. Geronimo wasn't a bad farmer. He farmed up on the headwaters of Turkey Creek on the Fort Apache Indian Reservation before he made his last outbreak in the spring of 1885. His underling Jason Betzinez and he had started a good field of barley

81 Gatewood in his memoirs said, "[The Apaches in Alchesay's group] regard themselves as wolves, coyotes—coyotero, man-wolf—& the Yumas & Mojaves, a company of whom they knew I commanded in the recent campaign against them, as sheep."

82 *Lt. Charles Gatewood & His Apache Wars Memoir*, edited and with additional text by Louis Kraft, University of Nebraska Press, Lincoln and London, 2005, p. 15.

83 Polydactylism is having six fingers or six toes—or both. The Philistine giant in the Bible in 2 Samuel 21:20 had that connection with some of the Apache babies with polydactylism. "There was a huge man with six fingers on each hand and six toes on each foot—twenty-four in all. He also was descended from Rapha."

before Geronimo's run for Mexico. General George Crook had counseled the Apaches at Black River crossing to get to work and farm and support themselves. Jason Betzinez said he took General Crook's advice seriously for the rest of his life. Geronimo farmed later in Oklahoma. He is pictured once in his pumpkin patch with his family. This start at farming was radically different from the former life of raiding. But at the arrival of the missionaries on the reservations, there was good indication that the Apaches were doing well at farming and raising significant crops.[84] At San Carlos in 1888 and 1889 the annual reports of the Commissioner of Indian Affairs recorded the following in bushels of grain brought in by Apache farmers:

Year	Corn	Wheat	Barley
1886-87	1,760	3,404	3,002
1887-88	6,000	6,054	12,048
1888-89	8,200	9,107	16,300

Gatewood spoke of the early farming culture: "They had to travel from fifty to seventy-five miles to the agency to receive their meager rations once a week. With these short rations & with acorns, juniper berries, roots, & mescal (a species of yucca), they managed to live & labor thru' the winter & spring, until they were rewarded with a plentiful harvest of corn, melons, & pumpkins. From that time, they have been practically independent of government provisions."[85]

---

[84] Missionary children climbing up *Gan Besedia* one day in the 1960s found a rusted sickle with U.S. stamped into the blade. People had been cutting grass for hay up there and it had been left.

[85] Gatewood, p. 41.

CHAPTER SIX

Chief Alchesay, Tom Wycliffe and Lon Bullis

*There is no real sense to having a
hammer if you have no nails.*

The missionary and his family coming to East Fork Mission in the yellow Ford that day in 1958 didn't know much about Chief Alchesay. The name Alchesay became the name associated with the high school in Whiteriver. Alchesay High School became the public school athletic rival of East Fork Mission.

In the very first issue of The Apache Scout the beginning of the East Fork Lutheran Nursery is described. This is the issue that has the picture of Alchesay as scout on the front. He is a young man and his rifle is across his knees. The one looking at the picture has no doubt that this Apache knew how to use that rifle—and had! This is our first view of this Apache leader who would play such a big part in the Lutheran church on the Fort Apache Reservation. This same Alchesay had proclaimed his allegiance to the Lutheran Church by marching up to the front of the church with his people on the church's dedication day. Alchesay said about this Church of the Open Bible that it was the only one to which he had ever given his thumb print of approval.[86]

In fact, if you were to pry open his dead hand right now from that lonesome grave overlooking the North Fork of the White River you would find the keys to the Whiteriver Lutheran Church. Chief Alchesay wanted to be buried this way. And there on the cover of the October, 1928, *The Apache Scout*, Alchesay appears again. He's an old man now, standing in front of his wickiup. The Lutherans had come and stayed, and he was one of them.

---

[86] *The Apache Scout*, "Chief Alchesay," October 1928, p. 2. This issue was dedicated to Alchesay. He had died in the summer of 1928.

Alchesay on right and Crook on mule in center.
Photo Credit: (National Archives, image courtesy Paul and Kathleen Nickens)

Inashood Edgar Guenther observed, "Before he came in contact with the gospel the Apache made no efforts to hide his suspicions of the missionaries and his disinclination to have anything to do with them. His suspicions have given way to trust and instead of avoiding the missionaries he treats them now with positive affection." Guenther described his Christmas cheer in 1927 by saying, "A few Apaches brought Christmas cheer to the missionaries' homes with gifts of their own choice. There is none that came as near to the writer's heart and stomach as the large hind quarter of venison presented to him by Chief Alchesay."

This turnaround from animosity to acceptance and even to friendship and love happened through the likes of Chief Alchesay, who over time became a staunch member of the Lutheran Church in Whiteriver. It didn't happen quickly, and it didn't happen easily. How could it have with the things in play on the Fort Apache Reservation when the missionaries, particularly Edgar Guenther, got there? When the shots were fired that killed men on Seven Mile Hill just after the time of the Cibecue massacre, it seems Alchesay was there someplace. Years later a wizened and wrinkled Alice Taipa lived at

Seven Mile[87] on the Fort Apache reservation, where she talked with the missionary through Alfred Burdette's interpreting. She lived where Alchesay most certainly passed by in his early history among the whites. He was implicated in the Cibecue goings-on, that is for sure. Alchesay said to Crook as to what his part in the Cibecue Massacre had been, "Uclenni and I were doing all we could to help the whites, but we were both taken off by General Carr and put in the guardhouse. All that I have ever done has been honest. I have always been true and obeyed orders. I made campaigns against Apache-Yumas, Apache-Tontos, Pinalenos and all kinds of people, and even went against my own people. These Indians are not to blame; they have been forced into this thing by the way in which they have been treated. I have given you my hand, and you have given me yours. If you knew everything as well as the Indians do I don't think that you would blame them."[88]

Crook, in replying to the Cibecue Massacre and its aftermath, justified the reluctance of the Apaches (Alchesay included) to admit guilt. "They were constantly told that they were to be disarmed and then they were to be attacked, as at Cibecue; the interpreters were incompetent and some of them prejudiced, and probably as a consequence of this incompetency and prejudice innocent Indians had been ironed and put in the guardhouse. No one knew when his turn would come, and they were fast arriving at the conclusion that they were all to be killed anyhow, and that they might as well die fighting as in any other way."[89]

"He was a fine specimen of manhood. Straight as an arrow, six feet in height, about twenty-eight years old, [he was] slender in build though muscular. [Alchesay had the] piercing black eyes & the high cheek bones & heavy jaw of his race. Graceful in all his movements, [he was] noted for his powers of endurance, his fleetness of foot, his skill as a hunter, & his bravery in battle. Such was the leader of this small party that looked with scorn & contempt upon the rest of the Apache nation."[90] His very name Alchesay meant "Shorty." In fact, he was tall, but that is the way with Apache nicknames, even for

---

[87] Three Mormons, two soldiers who ran the crossing at Black River and a courier, were killed not far from her place during the Cibecue Massacre of 1881, when the Apache attacked the nearby Fort Apache.

[88] Charles Collins, *Apache Nightmare*, pp. 214, 218.

[89] *Op. cit.* pp. 221, 222.

[90] Charles B. Gatewood, *Lt. Charles Gatewood & His Apache Wars Memoir*, (Edited and with additional text by Louis Kraft), University of Nebraska Press, Lincoln and London, 2005, p. 38.

their chiefs, even for a man of the stature of Alchesay. It was also Gatewood who spoke about the time right after Alchesay returned to Fort Apache after helping General Crook and the soldiers to meet Geronimo in Skeleton Canyon. "On their return to the neighborhood of Fort Apache, tags were to be issued & full descriptions recorded. All of them had served as scouts at one time or another under my command, & Alchesay had been first sergeant of my company. Consequently, there was much hand-shaking & not a little joking. For instance: "Hello, *Bay-chen-daysen* (Long Nose), your nose has grown since we saw you last."[91]

Alchesay was real. He was a chief and he was an Apache. He knew firsthand and personally what the old Apache ways were. It was he who told John Bourke, adjutant to General George Crook, the following about *hoddentin* (sacred powder) and how it was sprinkled in the direction of the full moon: "The name of the full moon in the Apache language is '*klego-na-ay,*' but the crescent moon is called '*tzontzose*' and *hoddentin* is always offered to it." Bourke credited Alchesay with this information.[92] It was also Bourke in his book *An Apache Campaign in the Sierra Madre* who wrote about Alchesay and the Apache scouts in general: "The two great points of superiority of the native soldier over the representative of civilized discipline are his absolute knowledge of the country and his perfect ability to take care of himself at all times and under all circumstances. He finds food, and pretty good food too, where the Caucasian would starve."

The following is an account given to Paul Behn by Slim Jim Reed, a contemporary and compadre of Alchesay. It sounds right. The one with the story was remembering back to the year 1884 and his time as a scout with Alchesay:

"My good friend Alchesay is gone. Many days were we together, and often we crossed the mountains together. That was in the days when we were still young men. But I have not forgotten my good friend even now when he is gone. Sometimes I sit for a long time and think about my good friend Alchesay and about my good friend General Crook—when we were together and fighting against the outlaws. Let me tell you a story about them:

"One time General Crook said to Alchesay, 'Don't think that I am over you, or that you are over me; we are going into Mexico.' About

---

[91] *Op. cit.* p. 38.

[92] John Gregory Bourke, *The Medicine Men of the Apache,* Glorietta, New Mexico: The Rio Grande Press. Inc., 1983, p. 502. It is interesting to note that Bourke's work was included in the *Ninth Annual Report of the Bureau of Ethnology to the Secretary of the Smithsonian Institution 1887-88* by J.W. Powell, director.

this time a brother-in-law of Geronimo and an outlaw, was captured and put in chains. He was taken at San Carlos and brought to Wilcox. General Crook was at this time absent on business at Chihuahua City. But in the days following, he returned to Wilcox, and there he found Geronimo's brother-in-law. On the same day that he returned he wanted to hold court. And so court was called and Alchesay said to General Crook, 'Take off those "shoe-strings" from this man. They are too tough to wear; they will last too long. Also take off those "bracelets" (handcuffs) from him; I want my brother to wear shoe strings the same as I wear. Whoever owns the shoe-strings that he has on now had better come and get them. This man has done many things; he has taken horses and cows from the Whites, even killed some Whites, but let these chains be taken off. Let me stay here with him. If he runs away, in whichever way you want to punish him, punish me instead.'

"Another time General Crook said to Alchesay, 'All the armies are under me; you are the same over scouts and soldiers. We are the same. The only one ahead of us is in Washington. Now we (General Crook and Alchesay) are going into Mexico for forty days. I was in Chihuahua City to get permission from the Mexican official to fix what we want to fix in forty days, and he told me to do it in that time.'

"In those forty days the Scouts captured some Chiricahua Indians in Mexico and passed the line into the U.S. These Indians had captured six Mexican women. The scouts brought all of them to Wilcox. Alchesay told the Mexican women to return to their homes in Chiricahua, and in that way set them free. Alchesay and his outfit brought the Chiricahua Indians to San Carlos and gave them plenty of rations, canned goods, clothing and blankets. These Indians were to be placed there.

"The scouts' time was now out, so they came home to Whiteriver. But a short time afterwards General Crook sent a letter to Alchesay and told him to come to San Carlos and bring with him Mike Alchesay, Slim Jim (the one telling this story) and Manuel (M-1). After getting rations at Fort Apache they went to San Carlos. When they arrived in San Carlos General Crook had a tent ready for them, also wood, food, and beds. General Crook said to them, 'You came today: tomorrow you must rest, and the day after that we must hold court.'

"On the day set, they held court, and General Crook gave guns, belts and two boxes of ammunition to Alchesay and his friends, and in that way they became scouts again. This was done in the presence of Geronimo and the Chiricahuas. When the court began Geronimo spoke first. He wanted land on Turkey Creek on the White Mountain Reservation. General Crook asked Alchesay, 'Do you want these people to go over there? If you want them they may go. I want you to say so, and that is why I had you come here.' Alchesay answered, 'All right, send them over there. We will live with them.' Alchesay turned to Geronimo and said, 'Are you done with your being outlaws? I don't think that you will ever straighten out. There are soldiers and scouts thick as the trees at Fort Apache, and you will never get away from them.' Geronimo answered, 'If the Whites alone were after us, they would not chase us very long; you, Alchesay, are the one who is keeping it up all the time.' Alchesay said, 'I want you to stay and be good; I'm the one that stands in front of you and keeps you from being destroyed. If they take a notion to clean you out they can if it were not for General Crook and me. We are soldiers, and we want to protect you all we can. The citizens want you destroyed, but we want to straighten out things without any trouble.' Then Alchesay turned to General Crook, 'You talk to Geronimo and his people. I'm through with them. I have given them a piece of my homeland to live on. Now I must go and shoe my horses, and I'm going to shoe my horses now.' But the general said, 'Alchesay, the captain never works.' Alchesay answered, 'Our soldiers and scouts have done everything for us, but now, come, you hold my horse while I shoe him. Let them watch us.' This was said as a joke, and General Crook knew it. The general wrote a note and gave it to a soldier. He led the horses to the blacksmith and in that way the horses were shod. The next day Alchesay and his friends returned to their Whiteriver homes."[93]

The article that Paul Behn wrote was entitled, "In the Days of 1884." It was in that same year that Gatewood wrote the following about Alchesay and his leadership of his people. He was a chief. He had the natural ability and presence to lead his people and it was recognized by the occupying soldiers on the reservation. Gatewood wrote in 1884, "Monday I am going to Forest Dale (Forestdale) to depose old Pedro as chief and put in someone else, probably Alchesay. As it is now, no one is really responsible. Pedro is old and deaf and feeble that he can do nothing with them (his band members). They sneak off the reservation and buy arms and whiskey from the Mormons, and it is almost impossible to get them to report on each other. But if there is a chief with get-up, he can be calaboosed for not reporting those who do wrong, which will have a tendency to check their going off." And history tells us, "Alchesay did indeed succeed Pedro, probably as a result of Gatewood's trip. Eventually Alchesay became a principal spokesperson for the Cibecue and White Mountain Apaches. As such, he made several trips to Washington, D.C., to

---

93   Paul Behn, *The Apache Scout,* "In the Days of 1884," October, 1928, pp. 3,4.

Chief Cassadore seated.

Photo Credit: (Smithsonian Institution, National Anthropological Archives; image courtesy Paul and Kathleen Nickens)

confer with the president and Indian Bureau officials."[94] Alchesay's friend *Inashood* Guenther said, "Alchesay was also a good chief. Many people did not think so because he would not demand of the

---

[94] Collins, *Apache Nightmare*, p. 225.

government everything that they wanted. He tried to be fair to both. He was far-sighted. He could see what would be of benefit to his people and what would be harmful. Then he would step up for what is right, regardless of what others thought about it. A man who can do that is a real chief."

When Paul Mayerhoff made his first excruciating ride from San Carlos to Fort Apache, it was to Alchesay's camp that he came. He was at that time in the presence of Missionary John Plocher and the Apache guide who had gotten them the eighty-some miles from San Carlos to Fort Apache. Chief Cassadore at Peridot had sent the men to Alchesay, who was his friend and had been a scout for General Crook with him. Mayerhoff said that Cassadore had sent them to "his friend and brother." And as Mayerhoff remembered it, "As such we were received and enjoyed his hospitality for our night's stop. His wives cooked us a meal consisting of freshly made tortillas and beef cubes fried in suet and coffee which we supplied. This was really the first meal I ate at an Indian camp and relished. I never forgot it, so outstanding was it to me."[95] A couple of days later Mayerhoff got back to Fort Apache from a trip to Cibecue for the Fourth of July celebration and again saw Chief Alchesay, who was participating in the celebrations. He mentioned that even though he was a stranger in the crowd, it comforted him being able to see Chief Alchesay and be recognized by him. Mayerhoff made his residence up the East Fork, and Chief Alchesay had his on the North Fork of the White River.

It was on this same North Fork some years later that we learn, "During the first winter of the flu epidemic, Pastor Guenther and Dr. Loe helped hundreds of Apaches including Chief Alchesay. One particular day Dr. Loe stayed at home to rest his horse and himself. That day the missionary rode a trail about 10 miles beyond Whiteriver when a plume of campfire smoke up a remote canyon caught his attention. He followed it and came to the camp of Chief Alchesay who lay dying from the flu. Guenther provided a pallet of building paper and administered some medicines which he was carrying in his saddle bags. He spoke but briefly to Alchesay. The next day the missionary told Dr. Loe where to find the ailing chief. Alchesay, however, insisted on seeing Pastor Guenther.

Not long thereafter Alchesay was converted to Christianity and became like a brother to Pastor Guenther. In 1922, Alchesay and 100 other Apaches were baptized at the dedication of the Whiteriver Lutheran Church. "He (Alchesay) wanted his heart to be made right. Therefore he was the first one to step forward for baptism at the ded-

---

95 Paul Mayerhoff, *Beatrice Daily Sun*, "The Tenderfoot on Apache Trails," August 15, 1933.

ication of our Whiteriver church. Then he had turned to all who were gathered there to remind them that his name was now on the muster roll of the Highest Chief. Then he had asked them to imitate him in this way also."[96] That was the way Guenther remembered it.

An article in *The Apache Scout* recorded: "Chief John Taylay, Chief Baha, Hoke Smith and Superintendent Charles Davis returned recently from a trip to Washington. They made the trip in the interest of the Apaches of this reservation. Chief Alchesay, the father of Baha, was afraid to risk the trip on account of his age.[97] Hoke Smith also said in the same issue of *The Apache Scout*, "In conclusion, the real honest efforts of men and women instructors in our Lutheran Missions on this reservation are bringing home to our Apache boys and girls numerous essential facts that are necessary for their spiritual and moral development. We earnestly hope that these Missions continue to display faithful administration, with capable instructors, entitling its institutions to the necessary support, confidence of the government, and the good opinions of an intelligent public."[98] This same sentiment of Hoke Smith has been repeated many times by leadership of the two reservations, the San Carlos and the Fort Apache. Many Apaches point out the educational help and excellence of the mission schools in the leadership of the Apache tribe. This was already happening at the time of Alchesay and at his own encouragement.

Hoke Smith wrote other things pertinent to the education of Apache children. He wrote an article entitled "Can the Apache Children in Arizona Receive Higher Education without the Consent of Parents?" He was of the opinion that they should be able to do this. He quoted the June 30, 1914, census as: 2,485 (population of Fort Apache Reservation) reflecting an increase of 88 over the previous year, 826 school population with 217 attending boarding schools, 116 attending day schools, 7 at non-reservation schools, 231 not physically able to attend any school, and 255 who should have been in schools but weren't.

---

[96] At the time of this writing at the Haven Home in Globe, Arizona, the granddaughter of Chief Alchesay gathers every week with a Lutheran *Inashood* to sing Christian hymns and hear about the Good Shepherd and pray The Lord's Prayer. She knows the words from memory, as do her eight fellow Apache ladies who faithfully wait at the nurses' station on Saturday afternoons. Some of the nine ladies have trouble remembering their own names today, but they all can still sing, "Jesus loves me this I know for the Bible tells me so. Little ones to him belong, they are weak but he is strong. Yes, Jesus loves me! Yes! Jesus loves me! Yes, Jesus loves me. The Bible tells me so." They sing from memory and from their hearts, and they are not alone.

[97] *The Apache Scout*, February, 1926.

[98] This was signed: "Hoke Smith, graduate of Phoenix Indian School, class of 1905.

Alchesay and wife in front of wickiup.
Photo Credit: photo from Salem Lutheran Church in Milwaukee, Wisconsin, archives

But chiefs get old too, and so did Alchesay. The picture of him in front of his wickiup does not lie. He is different from the young man we see on the cover of the first *The Apache Scout*. *Inashood* Guenther tells us of the end: "On returning home from a trip this summer I was told that Chief Alchesay had died. "Too bad that you could not have been here to say a last good-bye to your good friend," the Indians said. I was sorry for that reason too, because he had been my good friend. He had proved that in many ways. But I was not sorry for any other reason. I did not have to feel concerned about his soul. It is true, Alchesay was not a great talker. He was not always speaking of himself as a good man. He was very modest. But he had full confidence in his Heavenly Chief. When I visited him during his last illness he told me that he was ready to report in heaven anytime that his Chief saw fit to call him. Yes, Alchesay was a good scout because the Lord Jesus made him such."[99]

---

[99] Edgar Guenther, *The Apache Scout*, October 1928, "Chief Alchesay," p. 2.

It was late April to early May of 1921. Ten Wisconsin Synod pastors and missionaries met at the annual Arizona pastors' conference which that year was being held at Globe. Attending were the Rev. H. C. Nitz from Globe, Pastor Henry Rosin from Peridot, Missionary Francis Uplegger representing San Carlos, home missionary Roy Gose (formerly from Globe), Rev. Immanuel Frey from Phoenix, and others. During the four-day conference the pastors conducted worship services and presented papers. They discussed the synod's opportunity to purchase the government day school which adjoined the mission at East Fork, the souls to be won in Prescott and Whipple Barracks, and the fertile mission field known as Casa Grande. During the breaks and in the evenings, however, one topic always preempted all others: the spread of the gospel among the Apaches. One Apache man in particular was mentioned: Tom Wycliffe.

H. C. Nitz later wrote about him: "When he was young he was a bad man. He drank much, gambled and did many evil things." About 1918, however, he changed. He asked to be baptized, and his pastor gladly consented. This Apache then shared the message of Jesus with his own family and saw to it that they were baptized. In time he became an interpreter for the missionary at East Fork and even taught for a time in the school. In 1922 when the Church of the Open Bible at Whiteriver was dedicated, he was one of three Apaches who addressed the Indians in their own language. He was a strong evangelist, but his body was weak. He had tuberculosis, and because of his disease he moved his camp to the East Fork Mission ground, where he could be attended. A medicine man came uninvited with an eagle feather to Tom, and Tom took the feather and burned it in the fire. "There! What kind of a god do you have if I can burn it in the fire?" he asked. One summer day he asked to take the Lord's Supper with his mother and wife. He told the missionary, "I know that Communion is no medicine for my body. But I know that it will make my soul strong, so that the devil will have no power over me." Six days later, on August 27, 1923, his pastor and an Apache interpreter, Lon Bullis, visited his bedside and prayed with him. Between strained breaths he told them, "I think I am going to heaven today."

The missionary described what happened next: "He wanted to hear the Christian Creed and Psalm 23 over and over, and he wanted to hear Christian songs. We sang one after another of his favorites. The last song we sang was 'I Love to Tell the Story,' and just as the sun went down, Tom Wycliffe breathed his last."

That is how H. C. Nitz wrote about Tom Wycliffe. Nitz was one of the first missionaries, and Wycliffe was one of the first converts. Many came to Tom Wycliffe's funeral, and his brother-in-law, Jack Keyes, interpreted the message spoken by the missionary. This was the first church funeral at East Fork, and according to his earlier wishes, the body of Tom Wycliffe was buried in the new East Fork cemetery.[100]

It was also H. C. Nitz who wrote, "A medicine man said to Tom one day, 'See how long the missionaries have had our children in school, and they have not taken away their belief in medicine worship,' and Tom replied, 'Well, you let them work another five hundred years and there will be a change, then there will be no more medicine men on the reservation.' "

There was another historical connection made that day in April of 1958 when the yellow Ford pulled up in front of the parsonage at East Fork with its white picket fence and bridal wreath bushes in bloom. The young boys who walked alongside the house that day did not realize that in 1923 an Apache man named Lon Bullis spent the last summer of his life resting and thinking and writing in the same place where Tom Wycliffe had died. He too had tuberculosis and would die from it, but during that previous summer he and Tom Wycliffe[101] had comforted each other under the shade of those big oak trees that still stand there today. It was at East Fork that Lon spent his time trying to escape the heat. He went to the mountains from San Carlos to be at East Fork in the summer because in the evenings the cool air flowed by East Fork Mission from 11,409 foot high Mt. Baldy just up the river valley. Lon then returned to the desert in San Carlos when the cold came to the mountains. It was the same mission compound that nestled there at the foot of Rimrock and Red Rock, along the clear East Fork of the White River, the same compound close to the big cedar (*Gad Nchaa*) where Mayerhoff had first pitched his tent. It was there where the grass between the old employees' building and the parsonage sloped down to the dirt road that went by the mission, in the shade of those big live oak trees where Tom Wycliffe and Lon Bullis met and spent time together.

The two men made an unlikely alliance: Lon Bullis from the San Carlos Reservation and Tom Wycliffe from the Fort Apache Reservation. Being from different reservations would have made it improbable that they would even have wanted to be friends. But a common faith and a common fate united them like brothers. Both had tuberculosis and both would die from it. Both had been struck by the same fatal arrow, the deadly one from the white man's quiver, the arrow called tuberculosis. Both were arrow makers, and Lon ministered to

---

100 *The Apache Lutheran,* October 1994.

101 The great-granddaughter of Tom Wycliffe attended services at St. Peter's Lutheran Church in Globe in 2017 while she lived nearby.

Tom Wycliffe his brother arrow maker. Both had faith in Jesus Christ as their Savior and were unabashed about it.

The circumstances around Lon Bullis' conversion made it miraculous. Lon's father was war chief Chiquito, who was there in the camp of Eskiminzin that horrible night of massacre. Lon's father had escaped with his life that early morning, but he couldn't have escaped the yells and screams of his family and friends being murdered with cow tail bludgeons by the thugs from Tucson. It was Francis Uplegger who wrote about Lon's life and recorded his history. Uplegger loved the people who spoke the Apache language and he loved their language, and it was he who wrote of *"Dajida"* the arrow maker. Lon Bullis knew how to use the arrows he made too, no doubt. Remember what Daklugie, war chief Juh's son, said about Apache archery and arrows and that Apache archers could shoot seven arrows into the air before the first came to ground. It was Uplegger who recorded that tuberculosis came to *Dajida.*

Lon Bullis, the son of war chief Chiquito, became a Christian. He lived and talked like a Christian, and he wrote like a Christian too. Consider his words on the Sunrise Dance: *"Nayenesgani* (he who kills monsters) is a false god. It is a name that the devil himself hides behind—that the Indians may worship him. And the Indian medicine men are working for the devil even if they do not know it but are deceived. The snake-painted cross, and the eagle feathers and the blue stones used for signs of worship—are signs of idolatry and false worship. Therefore every one that goes to worship with the Indian medicine men takes part in worship of the devil. For many years in the past, we Apaches believed that the rattlesnake has power to heal the sick. Even today many still have the same belief. The evidence of it we see at San Carlos—and at other places—when on Sundays many gather near the river bank for worship. At such gatherings at first the real live rattlesnakes were used; later the medicine men set up for the people a snake-painted cross with eagle feathers and blue stones tied to it. With the name of *Nayenesgani* the medicine man commands the Indians to look upon the cross."[102] This was not the Christian cross but the cross that Silas John had stolen from the Scriptural account of Moses raising the bronze serpent over the heads of smitten and stricken Israel.

In Lon's final days, his interest was in Christian words and how they might best be put into Apache. He worked and made his own translations in his last days, and Uplegger then used Lon's work in his own linguistic work. Francis Uplegger was there when Lon Bullis

---

[102] Lon Bullis, *The Apache Scout,* August 1924.

left this world. He was summoned with a letter from the old arrow maker and it pined, "Come! I want to have you with me once more here below, and by the sacrament of the Lord's Supper to be strengthened for the going to the home beyond."[103] His wish was the same as his friend Tom Wycliffe's final wish. He died at the sanitarium in Phoenix on Friday, July 11, 1924.

At this same time there was a young man named Alfred Burdette who would leave his print on the work of both reservations. Candidate Gustav Schlegel had come to Bylas and had opened a small mission school in the annex of his church. The government finally closed its plant at Bylas and sent its pupils by bus to a white school just off the reservation. In 1926 Pastor Schlegel was called away on account of ill health and replaced by Candidate A. C. Hillmer, who served until 1929. The work languished until Pastor Ernie Sprengeler came and built up the school and its reputation. Pastor Sprengeler had a camp field of some 600 souls, and Alfred Burdette was his dedicated assistant and teacher.[104]

Sprengeler moved to East Fork, where he was very active and instrumental in the formation of East Fork Lutheran High School, and Alfred moved to the Fort Apache reservation too. Eventually he became the evangelist at Canyon Day and Cedar Creek congregations. He served in that capacity for years. At the end of the 1950s and early 1960s Alfred Burdette was interpreter at East Fork Mission. He was regularly recorded and was on Show Low radio station KVWM, The Voice of the White Mountains, with an Apache language religious program. That work was translated in the office of the parsonage across from the church at East Fork Mission.

Alfred lived nearby with his family on the ground floor of the east half of the old nursery and employees' building. He drove a stake-bed Studebaker truck and in the fall of the year would drive the mountain roads up toward Maverick and shoot deer for meat. In those days the hunting regulations were much more lax than they are today. The boys who issued from the yellow Ford that day in 1958 and who lived next to him would see him early in the morning backing up to the oak trees there along the road, the same trees where Tom Wycliffe and Lon Bullis had visited together in their last days. One time the boys even got to ride along in the back of the truck on a hunting outing that got nothing but a long and bumpy and cold ride. Alfred's boys and the pastor's boys hung out together and swam in the swimming hole and hunted together with their slingshots. One little tidbit of native

---

103 *The Apache Scout*, "Dajida the Ancient Arrowmaker," April 1930.

104 *The Apache Lutheran*, April 1990.

The first building at East Fork Mission, author's collection

wisdom that Alfred left with the boys was telling them, "Don't say anything to Indian. Indian might say something to you."

The pictures of the joint work of the Lutheran pastors in the Arizona-California District include Alfred Burdette. He worked faithfully for many years, but after all the years of work the dark day came where he was publicly involved in activity that disqualified him from the ministry. He returned to Peridot and lived there not far from the river. His hearing failed him, but he lived there in a house with its shade made outside until he was almost 100 years old. He remained a Lutheran until his death. He liked it when mission people would stop by and visit him.

There were many Apache laymen who were part and parcel of the work right from the beginning. Arthur Guenther reminds all who study *Inashood*, "We dare never forget Rankin Rogers, Lon Bullis, Tom Friday, Walter Williams, John Williams, A-1, H-8, B-3, Coyote, A-4, Y-24, Alfred Burdette, and the list could go on."[105] Oscar Davis was interpreter at Harder's time, and it was he who became the

---

[105] Alchesay Arthur Guenther, "The Ministry among the Apaches after 100 Years," Arizona Pastors' Conference at Grace Evangelical Lutheran Church, San Carlos, Arizona, May 4-5, 1993.

105

main character in Harder's novel *Dohashtida*. Rankin Rogers was at
Peridot with Rosin. Daniel Victor was teacher at East Fork. The first
missionaries got Carlisle students who knew some English and of
course knew Apache and who did their best. There were many interpreters: Jack Keyes, Tom Wycliffe, Lon Bullis, and Timothy Victor[106]
to name a few besides Alfred Burdette. Mark Hopkins interpreted
for Carl Guenther, Rosin and both of the Upleggers. Alfred Uplegger spoke of the Victor Family in connection with interpreters: "The
baptism of the family of Leis Victor was the happy fulfillment of a
wish and a hope and prayer for many years. It was at Leis' shanty
that Bible reading hours were conducted for a long time in 1922 and
1923, but he was holding back, although deeply interested, and has
been one of the leading and most influential Indians here. His brothers, Manuel and Timothy, interpreters, influenced him doubtlessly,
but Leis' association with medicine men and with followers of the
Nayenesgani worship and the Silas John Edwards ceremonies kept
him back for many years. But Christ won his heart. Thanks to him!"[107]
The danger with interpreters was the same in the church work as it
had been in the military conflicts: the message was only as good as
the understanding and ability of the interpreter to get what was said
and get it across accurately to the people who were being spoken to.

---

[106] Timothy Victor served as interpreter for the Upleggers at San Carlos for thirty years.

[107] From Alfred Uplegger's quarterly report, dated September 30, 1928. Quoted by Paul and
Kathy Nickens in their history: *Terrell Victor, Sr. Apache Cattleman, Soldier, Councilman,
and Tribal Elder*, October 21, 2010, p. 61.

CHAPTER SEVEN

John Plocher and George Adascheck

The beginning is the most important part of the work
(PLATO, THE REPUBLIC).

A very good introduction to the circumstances the early missionaries rode into comes from Arthur Guenther's observations on
the 100th anniversary of the work. He wrote, "The early men who
stepped off the Southern Pacific at San Carlos or the Santa Fe in
Holbrook were absolutely untrained and unprepared for what they
were about to undertake.[108] This is not said to discredit them or point
a finger. This is a fact of history. We, the Synod, were new at this.
There were no textbooks or manuals to study to prepare the men for
their work. The only job description was simple: 'We need a man in
Arizona—will you go?' No special training. No linguistic studies. No
philosophy of Indian Missions. Just 'Go,' and prayerfully do the best
you can. Some went, failed and got back on the train as soon as the
opportunity presented itself. Some went and tried, gave their best
and [still] failed. Others tried, failed, tried again, improvised, gave
of time, talent, love, patience, health and even life, and succeeded. It
was 'on-the-job training,' then pass on the results of your trial and
error. To be untrained was bad enough, but there was a progression of problems. One of the basic problems that led to others was
the isolation, and this led to loneliness. Think back to those early
days. No town, no roads, just paths following the game trails on the
way to the water holes or the contour of the land. No neighbors, no
phone, no hospital, no big stores. Shortages always of even the staple
goods. I think of Mrs. Plocher, a dainty, slim, china doll of a lady
living in a half-cave with an ocotillo fence for a door. No running
water and no sanitary facilities. All this and many other factors must

---

[108] David Plocher writes: "Mayerhoff indeed wrote that he got to San Carlos and Peridot
by stagecoach from Thomas in 1896. Plocher's letters (John Plocher) also mention Fort
Thomas as the end of the railroad when he and Adascheck came in the fall of 1893.
Plocher then wrote in April 1898 that work on the railroad from Thomas began in the
spring of 1898 with protests from the Indians. Understandably, Arthur Guenther may not
have known this at the time he wrote the article from which his quote comes."

have been a heavy burden on the early men. This affected their wives and thus became a vicious circle. Then add to this the illness that struck pastors, wives and children. The graveyards on both reservations bear mute testimony to the ravages of illness, malnutrition and accidents that could and often did break the best. These points must be remembered and taken into consideration when we discuss the ministry among the Apaches during this Centennial Year. The men and women who left so much, traveled so far, and gave so much were truly pioneers. Even those who for personal or physical reasons left to return to more comfortable and familiar surroundings gave of their best. They also must be judged only in the light of the facts prevalent. In their own way they contributed what they could. They may never be remembered as we remember the giants, but they must be remembered fondly."[109]

Indeed. In this book let us remember them all fondly. And so we go to those first men: John Plocher and George Adascheck. On the fourth day of October, 1893, their service of installation and ordination took place in Watertown, Wisconsin, at St. Mark Church. The service marked the pastoral beginning of Apache mission work for the young Wisconsin Evangelical Lutheran Synod. This date would play a part in forever changing the life of the Apache Indians.

Candidates Plocher and Adascheck sat and looked into the familiar faces of President Ernst and their own Professor Hoenecke and wondered how it was going to be for them in the "Wild West."

The service began with the singing of Martin Luther's hymn of Pentecost:

> Come, Holy Ghost, God and Lord!
> May all your graces be outpoured
> On each believer's mind and heart;
> Your fervent love to them impart.
> Lord, by the brightness of your light
> In holy faith your church unite
> From ev'ry land and ev'ry tongue;
> This to your praise, O Lord our God, be sung:
> Alleluia! Alleluia!
>
> Come, holy Light, Guide divine,
> And cause the Word of life to shine.
> Teach us to know our God aright
> And call him Father with delight.

---

109 Alchesay Arthur Guenther, "The Ministry among the Apaches after 100 Years," Arizona Pastors' Conference at Grace Evangelical Lutheran Church, San Carlos, Arizona, May 4-5, 1993.

From ev'ry error keep us free;
Let none but Christ our Master be,
That we in living faith abide,
In him, our Lord, with all our might confide.
Alleluia! Alleluia!

Come holy Fire, Comfort true;
Grant us the will your work to do
And in your service to abide;
And trials turn us not aside.
Lord, by your pow'r prepare each heart,
And to our weakness strength impart
That bravely here we may contend,
Through life and death to you, our Lord, ascend.
Alleluia! Alleluia!

What a fitting hymn this was and almost prophetic when we think of what lay ahead and what happened and what is still happening on the San Carlos and Fort Apache reservations! "And trials turn us not aside. Lord, by your power prepare each heart and to our weakness strength impart, that bravely here we may contend, through life and death to you, our Lord, ascend." The first missionaries heard and sang those words in 1893, on the fourth day of October.

And the service went on: the pastor said to the congregation and especially to the two young men, "The Lord be with you!" And everyone responded, "And with your spirit." The pastor again: "The Gentiles will walk in your light. Hallelujah!" And the congregation again responded, "And kings in the brilliance that comes from you!" The choir sang, "Praise the Lord, all nations, praise him all peoples! Because his grace and truth roll over us into eternity." The people all rose at the direction of the pastor, who spoke these words to them, "Let us now with the whole Christian Church on earth unite to confess our most holy faith with sincere voices," and considering the occasion, what more appropriate words could have been spoken?

We do not know the text or the words, but President Ernst rose to give the sermon for the day. He spoke to his students, his boys. The reading just before his sermon was Isaiah 42:1-8. "Here is my servant, whom I uphold, my chosen one in whom I delight; I will put my Spirit on him and he will bring justice to the nations, to open eyes that are blind, to free captives from prison and to release from the dungeon those who sit in darkness. I am the LORD; that is my name!"

During the singing of a hymn the offering was taken, and the offering was designated for the new Indian Mission. The familiar Professor Hoenecke rose to address the congregation and especially the two young men in the front chairs. And then a children's choir sang, and some of the words were: "Left to ourselves, we shall but stray; oh, lead us on the narrow way, with wisest counsel guide us, and give us steadfastness that we may ever faithful prove to Thee whatever woes betide us." Then the two young men went to the front and were installed into their ministries and into this special work that up until that time the Wisconsin Synod had not done in this way.

The Apache adventure had embarked, and Plocher and Adascheck left the next morning at 8:00 for San Carlos. Their baggage and tent didn't make it as quickly as they did, but the same reservation officials who had encouraged Hartwig and Koch the year before gave the two young men shelter and sustenance. They went first to the government-run school. They noticed that religion wasn't part of the curriculum, but Plocher was able to address the students on a number of occasions, and the result was that several Apache students showed up who had learned to speak some English at Carlisle School in Pennsylvania. Several waved their baptismal certificates, obtained through the Episcopal Church. Every day the men visited the camps of the Apaches along the San Carlos River and tried to put down the words they learned in their notebooks. Some days they reported getting twenty new words. They also reported back how difficult the language was in its pronunciation. Theological Greek and Latin and Hebrew wouldn't work here. Conversational German was out too. English was all right for those who could speak it, but it was Apache they were after, and it was Apache they needed if their work was going to succeed and prosper.

They cast about for a place to stay and put their roots down. Adascheck looked up and down the valleys. Plocher stayed and worked some with the school children. First they were on the Gila River, then they moved back up to an area along the San Carlos River. In his looking around, Adascheck discovered several villages of wickiups. On one occasion everyone was busy playing card games for money. The Apache women were involved too. One woman had a crucifix around her neck but was so engrossed in the game at hand that she made poor conversation, if she knew any English at all. Adascheck himself didn't know much English. So after observing the intense games of chance going on, Adascheck wandered disgustedly off. It didn't look to him like the people welcomed him or his message. He wasn't even invited to enjoy the card game.

These first missionaries lived in a canvas tent. In the winter they had a half-inch of ice on their water basin in the mornings. They had no stove to warm the inside of the tent. The only thing they could do to stay warm when it got dark was to burrow into their beds and wait for the dawn to come and break through that crust of ice to get something to wash their faces with and maybe try to shave. As the winter made its slow way across the landscape and left, summer also challenged and tormented them. The tent was even worse in the heat than it was in the cold. It was a blast furnace by day. Not to count the bugs and things that could crawl into it. They just had to have some kind of house to live in and to establish their presence there and let the people know, "We're here to stay." So the men of the Committee responsible for this floundering and fledgling work said to their constituents, "Men, we have work to do." They needed money and money was scarce. They figured that with $1,600.00 they could build a residence for the men and a school for their work with the children. This was resolved in June of 1894.

George Adascheck left the work and the place, and it didn't take him long. He'd had enough. He wasn't getting the Apache language, and he wasn't happy with the circumstances. He had come to the rather hasty conclusion that reservation life wasn't for him. Some who knew him later said he hated it there in Arizona. The powers that were gave him a congregation in Wisconsin. His German was good, but his knowledge of English was deficient, and, as you might expect, he had little aptitude for Apache[110] He wasn't the brightest man either; at least his grade card from the seminary didn't betray a shining intellect.

In the process of leaving, Adascheck left Plocher to work by himself. Plocher had a number of things on his plate. He was asked by the Committee to check out Fort Apache to the north as a possible second place to begin doing mission work. The Committee wanted him to survey things and then make the trip back to Wisconsin to relate his findings to them in person. And of course, the most pressing thing Plocher had to do was to get the house built. He was still living in his tent. The Committee suggested that he get the adobe bricks made and then wait until after his return from the debriefing in Wisconsin and build the house in the fall. But that wouldn't do. The rainy season came in August. The adobe had to be constructed into walls before that rain came. The drying adobe bricks would then be protected by the roof. If the rain caught the drying bricks in the open it would ruin the work of weeks.

It was also an easy matter for the men sitting in Wisconsin to tell the one in Arizona to make the trip to Fort Apache. It wasn't so easy for Plocher. It was 75 miles of wilderness travel. He would have to go through two jagged river canyons. There were no roads.

---

[110] *To Every Nation, Tribe, Language and People*, pp. 27, 28

Someone would have to take him. If he tried to go in a wagon—if indeed the wagon could even make the trip—he would have to rent a wagon. Otherwise he would have to rent horses and have someone to go with him who knew the way. That "someone" turned out to be Chief Cassadore. Cassadore had some crops he had to take care of first, but he said he would go when they were safely gathered. Plocher was entirely at ease leaving his possessions and the work project on the house in the care of his newly acquired Apache friends. He said in his correspondence that he trusted them more than he would have trusted a white man. There was no problem with his possessions, and he wasn't losing one bit of sleep over their safety. That September in Manitowoc and Reedsville, Wisconsin, Plocher told the people that Chief Cassadore called him brother.

The school building got built. It was a simple four-walled adobe building. There were no benches or desks. There was no blackboard. There were no books. There were some students. The hope was to teach the students in English, so they could have some ability to be taught Bible stories in English. They were being taught some hymns. There were also some Bible passages they were learning from memory. The hope was that when they got to the stage where they knew what baptism was and would desire it, they could also be baptized.

The perception of the committee in Wisconsin was that even though there were just twelve students in the school (the number varied from day to day), this was the proof of a great moral and spiritual breakthrough. Just to think! These Apaches were sending their children to a school that existed for just one reason: to make Christians of the children. It perhaps was more likely that the parents were glad to send their children to learn the white man's ways because the writing seemed to be already on the wall. If you wanted to get ahead in a white man's world, you had to learn some things, and schools did that for you and your children. For those who labored in the Lutheran schools for the next hundred plus years, the thought would show up often, "Why are the people sending their children to our school?" Quite a few seemed to be doing it because the mission school offered a superior and more personal education than the public school did. Already at the beginning this thought was spooking around.

Plocher got married. He managed this on his first return to Wisconsin in September of 1894. He wouldn't be the last bachelor missionary to realize that life would be a whole lot better with a wife than it was living in a bachelor state. It would be better for the work too. Mrs. Anna Plocher loved the people, and it showed in their reciprocal love to her. She got sick when she got to Peridot, and it was bad. Things were so different from what she had known. The "parsonage" was a

JOHN PLOCHER AND GEORGE ADASCHECK

Anna Plocher, wife of John Plocher, and child in 1897 at Peridot.
Photo Credit: Rev. David J. Plocher, Waterloo, Wisconsin

three-room adobe affair with a dog trot between the two rooms and the one. It was a good day for everyone when Plocher was able to report that his dear wife was getting better and showed it by being able to assume some of the household chores again.

Pastor Brenner in Wisconsin often talked about "the old, evil foe" in his descriptions of the work. Indeed, there was a foe to the work that Plocher was trying to do. He was able to teach close to a hundred children on Saturdays in the government school, but in his own school, he was having trouble getting students to come regularly and faithfully. One of the chiefs demanded remuneration for the students he sent. This of course wasn't going to happen and couldn't

113

happen. Something was backward about that. Another leader promised to send children but didn't follow through. Plocher found out that the reason was that an Apache student in Pennsylvania told this leader that he shouldn't send any student to the mission school, that it wasn't the way to go. There was the pervading thought too that children taken into tow by white men ended up spoiled and ruined. They came back home after years away in the East and seduced the good girls who were there. They brought back diseases with them. Some didn't come home at all. There was something akin to the kiss of death with the white man's school. This awful reluctance on the part of the Apaches made Plocher's life hard.

Then the weather itself caused misery. The fall of 1895 was terrible. In the recorded history of Arizona weather, September of 1895 held records. In Phoenix at that time the record low was 47 degrees in that month of September, and the record of the lowest high was 66 degrees. The rain came for days and in downpours. Large sections of the railroad line to the south along the Gila River were washed out. Mail service was interrupted for over two weeks. Plocher went out to milk his cow and returned wet to the skin in spite of his raincoat. The whole 18' by 24' school building was a mess. There wasn't a dry square inch. It had an earthen roof, and that would do in a regular rain, but this wasn't a regular rain. Everything in the building was dripping. Walls, floor, ceiling were wet. A neighbor with such a roof sat up nights moving from one dripless place to another until finally, the drips won out. He got soaked. Plocher and his wife had a metal roof on their three room house, and they thanked God for it. At least in their home they were dry. The people needed to get their corn from the fields. Because of the moisture, everything was sprouting. The small garden spot was being washed full of sterile sand. There would be no planting there next year. It was hopeless.

In this sad state Plocher's mental outlook on his work and people darkened too. He tried to get his chicken pen roof fixed. It meant getting dirt up on the roof because the previous had all washed away. In the straining to get the dirt up there, an Apache man came by who offered to help—for wages. When there was no ability to pay wages, the helper left. People were using the wet and sprouting corn to brew *tulapai*. (The Germans at large did the same thing with barley and malt.) Plocher said that if he wanted to find someone sober from Peridot to San Carlos, he would have to look very hard indeed.

The out-of-control drinking was a big problem and would remain one. But there was a bigger problem, as far as Plocher was concerned. It was the miserable lives of the white people with whom he had to work in San Carlos when he went there to have services with the 300

Deed to Peridot Land, United States Indian Service.
Photo Credit (Arizona Historical Society; image courtesy Paul and Kathleen Nickens)

students. Having to deal with "the shameful and godless" lives of the white people in charge of the school there made his life and work a misery and made it so that he went the long distance there every Sunday "with extreme reluctance."[111]

But the report of woe ended on a happy note. The storm passed. Arizona's beautiful blue sky reappeared. The grass started to grow. And even though people in Wisconsin had to prepare for autumn's

---

[111] *Gemeinde-Blatt.*, "From Arizona," Jan. 1, 1896, p. 6.

ice and snow, in Arizona Plocher's cow could contemplate a royal pasture. And in Arizona the Lutherans could contemplate new work to do among the Apaches besides that of Plocher in San Carlos and Peridot.

The Presbyterian Charles Cook who had befriended Pastors Koch and Hartwig on their initial reconnaissance work in Sacaton got in touch with them by mail. Cook had heard about Plocher in Peridot. He told of visiting Fort Apache initially in 1872 in the company of a General Howard. General O. O. Howard was a great benefactor of Christian missions among the native peoples. Since that time Cook had gotten occupied with the Pima, as was related earlier. They had built a new church 35 miles to the west of where he was located in Sacaton and had enlarged the other church, which was 11 miles to the east. He had visited Fort Apache a year or so earlier and had preached there five times. There were more than 1,700 Apaches living in the area. Some of his hearers who seemed attentive to what he said told him they didn't even know there was an eternal life. They had never been told of this. Even though there was a society of Christian women who were interested in starting some kind of Christian work among the Apaches of Camp Apache, Cook wondered if his Lutheran friend could go there. As an aside, he said that Germans had been at the forefront of mission work in Arizona among the Indians at the present time. Among the Laguna Indians a German Presbyterian was working. This man was of Jewish descent. A German Mennonite worked among the Mocquies. Among the Apaches of San Carlos there was Plocher, a German Lutheran. And among the Pima and Papago, our man Cook was working, and we remember that he was German too.

Plocher visited Presbyterian Cook in February of 1896. The purpose of his journey from Peridot to Sacaton was to give a soldier the Lord's Supper in Phoenix. The soldier had requested the visit. The first day from Peridot Plocher's horse pulled the two-wheeled wagon 49 miles. He spent the night with a rancher and continued on the next day hoping to get to Sacaton. He ended up in the dark sixteen miles short and had to camp in the open. At two in the morning with the stars sparkling above and his horse standing dumbly there, he stumbled around looking for some dry firewood, so he could get a fire going and warm up. He hitched up in the dark and got started again. He actually met Cook on the way into Sacaton when the sun came up. This gave him the chance to visit the mission station and see the good work that was done and the appreciative people who traveled long distances to attend worship services. He heard Pastor Cook preach in the Pima language. He saw the churches the Pima had built. He noticed the people's cleanliness and clothing, and Pastor Cook informed him that the medicine dances and gambling and betting had almost died out. What impressed Plocher the most was the fact that these Pima took care of themselves. They weren't given rations, and Plocher wondered out loud if his people in San Carlos weren't given rations and were expected to grow more, if they wouldn't also do more to be more self-sufficient.

Mrs. Plocher's description of a normal Sunday went like this: At 1:30 p.m. her husband returned from his Sunday service with the public-school children in San Carlos. They gathered in the school for Sunday school with the students first. The Ten Commandments

John and Anna Plocher, first missionaries at Peridot.
Photo Credit: Rev. David J. Plocher, Waterloo, Wisconsin

were gone over one by one and explained. There was the lusty singing of some hymns, followed by a sermon which Pastor Plocher presented and which was interpreted by the interpreter. In Mrs. Plocher's description of her husband's Sunday she mentioned that among the adults, Chief Cassadore was present with his wives. The evil of polygamy was not the topic of Plocher's first sermon to his people. Nor would it be the theme for his second sermon. "Please come back again next Sunday and I'll tell you more about Jesus. Won't you come back?" And some said, "Yes!" By September of 1896 Plocher could relate that on Sundays he started off with Sunday school and a worship service. Then he saddled his horse and made his way up and down the rivers, the San Carlos and the Gila. He preached with his interpreter three or four times in this way to the people he met along the way. In the evenings he came back to the mission station and had another service. 150 people were in attendance. By the end of those strenuous Sundays, over 200 people had heard the gospel. This was a remarkable accomplishment after three years of work had been logged.

The language remained a problem. There were no linguistic aids, no dictionary, no grammar. There was also the "problem" that the Apache didn't like abstract ideas and didn't have many in his language. So abstract things got concrete applications. The word "dare" ended up "do-I-na-de-go-ilch-ta-a-na-da-leh." Ink was "black water." School was "the house in which paper is counted." The word for "deaf" was "he has no ears."

Christmas came in 1896. Some congregations in Wisconsin (Watertown, Fort Atkinson, Columbus and Oshkosh) sent Christmas tree ornaments, pictures, a manger, some toys, some items of clothing. Five miles away on the north side of some hill a little cedar tree was growing; it would succumb to the pastor's ax and be carried triumphantly back on horseback to be decorated. In the mud school house there was the culture of Christmas. The people came for the simple program. The students sang "Oh Lord, How Shall I Meet Thee?" in English. The story of Jesus' birth was spoken in Apache by the students. There was a devotion. The gifts were distributed, and a good time was had by all. In relating all this Pastor Plocher did mention that he was having to pay from 10 to 15 cents a pound extra to claim his packages because of the difficulty in getting the things to San Carlos over the last hundred miles of the journey.

In the summer of 1897 Plocher returned to Wisconsin for several months to regroup and rest. He had to leave the fledgling station untended, but when he returned, everything was in order. He was there in 1898, working faithfully. He kept trying. His daughter had another of her bad spells. It was bad but not quite as bad as earlier bouts had been. Reports in the *Gemeinde-Blatt* about his work almost always referenced the Lord's promise that work for the Lord would not be in vain. The reader of these reports gets the idea that the only reason why the missionaries knew their work was not in vain was because the Bible said so. There were plenty of things happening and not happening that seemed to indicate that it was for nothing. Plocher lamented the fact that he couldn't teach religion to the children at the government school one-on-one. He lamented also the unscrupulous white people who were pilfering and plundering his people. They snuck thousands of their cattle onto the reservation to feed there and denude the land. When the train track right-of-way monies of $8,000 came among the people, these charlatans and cheats and interlopers set up gambling and booze opportunities, and *tizwin* and *tulapai* were being brewed and consumed in large quantities by the people themselves on the reservation.

It took five years of work before the first people stepped forward and asked to be baptized. The first were four school girls: Sadie, Bessie, Irene and Joy.[112] On the baptismal roles, they were the first. Five years of work and four school girls baptized! Actually, Plocher wasn't entirely happy with the instruction that had preceded the baptisms, and he wasn't entirely happy at the prospects for continuing faithfulness, but few pastors are satisfied with the prospects in any time and in any culture. The happy event took place on Easter afternoon in San Carlos. It was Plocher's hope that maybe some young men would come soon too.

The summer of 1899 loomed dauntingly on the horizon. Plocher made a porch along the south side of his adobe home to keep driving rain from eroding his adobe and for supplying some shade and a few degrees cooler temperature for his wife and baby during the brutal summer months. Mayerhoff on the upper reservation was going to be going back to the synodical convention in Wisconsin. It would be nice for the Plochers to get to the upper reservation and find some respite from the heat for the hottest time at San Carlos, but the rough wagon trip up there made that impossible with children in the picture. As he had time, he worked on the property there at Peridot. There had been some rearrangement of property due to the train right-of-way passing through the property.

But his continuing on as *Inashood* wasn't to be. His little girl wasn't doing well. It had been a hard five years. It was murderously hot in the summer, and the sterile pale soil blazed and burned around them. Perspiration was their constant companion. Then one day they

---

[112] *Gemeinde-Blatt*, 15 May 1899, p. 76

119

came to the conclusion, "We can't do this anymore." They weathered the worst of the summer, but when Mayerhoff came on September 30 the adobe house was empty. Plochers had the chance to move to the community of St. Peter, Minnesota, and they took it. It had taken five years to get from Peridot, Arizona, to St. Peter, Minnesota. They were four days gone when Mayerhoff's boots stood in front of their Peridot door and he knocked.

The mission board had hoped that Plocher's replacement could have gotten there before he left, but that wasn't to be either. Mayerhoff rode to San Carlos to see the agent there. The government people spoke highly of Plocher's near martyr-like life and work. There was panic because the agent and government authorities realized the beneficence of having dedicated missionaries working among the people, and they were anxious to have someone get there soon, even if it was from another church. Agreement of church teaching was a part that didn't disturb the government agent. The mission board issued two calls for Plocher's replacement at Peridot and they were returned. "Thanks—but no thanks!" the recipients seemed to say. Wouldn't there be anyone to do this good work and continue? Who would minister to Sadie, Bessie, Irene and Joy? Five years was surely an awful thing to waste.

It took four calls before Carl Guenther accepted and went to work. It was a lot easier to sing in mission festivals in the Midwest, "Here am I, send me, send me" than it was to actually get up and go, especially to a place like San Carlos or Peridot.

One of the Apache girls had died. Now there were three left.

CHAPTER EIGHT

Carl Guenther, Jens and J. P. Koehler

How good and pleasant it is when brothers
live together in unity (Psalm 133:1).

It was hard to replace John Plocher. Many calls were extended. As many were returned with reasons why the man called could not go. Finally, Carl Guenther was found.[113] He was the son of Pastor F. Guenther from Oconomowoc, Wisconsin. He was a student at the seminary in Wauwatosa, Wisconsin. In fact, he was a student of the first class at the new seminary in Wauwatosa. His parents were in agreement with his going to Arizona, and he accepted the challenge extended to him. He was up for it. The faculty agreed to his finishing up his schooling hastily so that he could be on his way. He was ordained on the 31st of January in the hopeless cold of Oconomowoc in Wisconsin. The Wednesday evening service was in his father's church. The president of the Synod, Professor Ernst, preached the sermon. Pastor Brenner, the president of the mission committee spoke. Carl's parents were in the crowd, and a number of his fellow students came to sing in the choir there that day.

The next day, February 1, he left for Arizona. Mayerhoff was laboring alone there in San Carlos, waiting for young Guenther to come. East Fork and work around Fort Apache were standing empty and idle since September of 1899. On the 5th of February the train pulled into Rice, and Mayerhoff was there waiting. He even had a horse, worth all of $25.00, waiting for Guenther. Mayerhoff took his new charge to the place where he would be living. There was Plocher's adobe house with its south-facing porch.[114] Mayerhoff took Guenther to see some of the Apache people in the area. The Apaches shook his hand and looked him in the eye. They remembered Plocher, and they wondered what this new man would be like. He was so young!

---

[113] Not to be confused with Edgar Guenther on the Fort Apache Reservation.

[114] The foundation of the school house is still visible in the parking area in front of Peridot Lutheran Church. The foundation blocks show the shape of that first building, and they are embedded in the parking surface.

Guenther wrote the authorities: "Brother Mayerhoff is helping me out a lot. He helped me get set up here in my place, and he has even taught me how to cook my food and bake my bread. I'm going to miss him when he has to go, but I won't think about that right now."[115] It reminds the reader of what Elisha said about his master Elijah in 2 Kings chapter 2 when Elisha was waiting for the fiery chariot and the whirlwind to whisk his mentor away. Elisha said peevishly when reminded of his master's departure, *"Yes, I know, but do not speak of it!"* [2 Kings 2:3].

Not far away from the residence of the new missionary were the twenty-some students Plocher had so painstakingly gathered and taught. The adobe school room was there too, with its ability to leak buckets in heavy rain. Not far from Guenther trying to find his way there were those students who could now read a little English and count. And in recitation as a group they could speak the words of the Lord's Prayer, the Apostles Creed and the Ten Commandments. In addition, they were able to sing a dozen hymns from memory. These students were the raw material Guenther would be working with. The school was his focus because this was the decided-upon way to reach and teach the people. By March there were 23 students on the roster, again but the attendance was from six to ten a day, and the learning was hard and slow. Sunday mornings Guenther went to San Carlos[116] and taught Bible stories and catechism lessons to the government school children there. The people were friendly. They came by with little things: one elderly man brought three small fig trees to plant in the garden. *Inashood* Guenther had some of the people eat with him in the evenings, and they could talk one on one. A fine four-building school was being built by the government in Rice. The people were resisting it. They didn't want it, and several attempts to set the buildings on fire had been made.

In June of 1900 Carl Guenther reported that an elderly man had told him, "Look, you are like my own family. I want to help you in any way I can. You are teaching my four children. I want them to stay with you here at Peridot in this school. I don't want them to go to Rice Station to the new government school." This was one of those times when what was happening overwhelmed the pastor. Here was an Apache man who on his own was trusting the *Inashood* with the most sacred of things: his family. He was calling Guenther one of his own. He loved Guenther, and Guenther was quickly learning to love him back. This was truly something wonderful! These were Guen-

---

115 *Gemeinde-Blatt*, March 1, 1900. p. 36

116 The reader should remember that this is Old San Carlos where the present-day lake is.

Peridot church and first school.
Photo Credit: Rev. David J. Plocher, Waterloo, Wisconsin

ther's people, and in the realm of human relationships it didn't get better than this and it still doesn't. Mayerhoff had said it would be this way because he had felt it himself. After Guenther had gotten a smattering of initiation, Mayerhoff left to go back to his people in the valley upstream from Fort Apache in the high country. Guenther got two weeks of shoulder-to-shoulder work and then was on his own. He felt sad and empty when he saw Mayerhoff ride off. Mayerhoff's work and people on the northern reservation had been without him since September of the previous year. He needed and wanted to get back home. He realized his people looked past his skin and saw him as *Shikissin* (my close relative).[117]

In March Guenther wrote about the four girls who had been baptized by Plocher. One had died. One had sunk back into her former way of life. Not much was known of her other than that. One had moved seventy miles away, and contact had been lost with her. But one was continuing in her Christian instruction! One was! The work was slow. Carl Guenther was studying the catechism with the young ones, and when he preached his sermons, his words were directed toward these young students.

Guenther wanted to get to Sacaton to visit Presbyterian Cook but it was dry, and water and feed for the horse on the journey were

---

[117] Once in the 1990s the pastor was talking to one of his Apache parishioners who was being free in his criticism of white people and how they weren't acting correctly and how bad they were. The pastor reminded the parishioner, "But I'm a white person too." The parishioner's jaw went slack. His mouth sagged open. He looked at the pastor for a moment and blurted out, "Pastor, I'm not talking about you. I'm talking about white people!"

123

scarce. It was the Arizona desert that he was dealing with, and he had heard about Plocher's midnight ride and the first missionaries' buckboard travel.

Then came Guenther's first Christmas. When he made his quarterly reports, he didn't translate into German what some of the Apache people had said to him, "When Christmas? How many days? When Christmas comes you give me pants!"[118] He rode 28 miles one way on horseback to get the Christmas tree (probably to the Pinal Mountains by Globe), and he worked hard. His reputation stayed. The people spoke of him and his wife fondly. His labor hadn't been in vain in terms of making this beachhead in the mission work. Around Peridot the people remembered Plocher. In fact, even in their absence from Peridot the Plochers continued to minister to the people. When the presents were distributed at Christmas time in 1901, there were bright articles of clothing for Chief Cassadore's widows. Mrs. Plocher had sent them by mail. While she had lived at Peridot in those hard years for her, she had made friends and was befriended by Cassadore's wives. They were the closest neighbors she had, and they were her friends.

On the second day of October, 1900, in Two Rivers, Wisconsin, there was another evening service. This time Rudolf Jens sat in his father's church. He was a teacher who had studied at New Ulm, Minnesota, to become a teacher. His parents supported him in his desire to teach on the reservation and free up Carl Guenther to do missionary work and learn the language. There were reported to be 900 Apaches living on the upper Gila River. They needed to hear the gospel. It wouldn't happen if Guenther had to tend the government schools and mission school and do all the chores that needed to be done just to live there. Jens came to share the work with Guenther. It was a good day when he came, in the evening on the sixth day of October. He came with the violin he liked to play. Guenther and Jens worked together, taking turns with the work and with the duties of living. There was wood to split, and there were eggs to gather. They had to tend the horses. Plocher's adobe house needed mending. Simple food needed to be cooked. And school needed to be taught. That was Jens' work mostly. There were 30 students on the roster, but the actual average attendance was 15. That seemed good to them as they struggled with their lessons and with the endeavor. The government school at Rice stole six of their students. The superintendent of the school wasn't particularly nice about it either, but the six were retrieved. Then it happened again that this time the agent himself

---

[118] *Gemeinde-Blatt*, 1 February 1901, p. 20

had taken a dozen students away, and these were some of the best students the fledgling school had. But after visiting at the site and being in their adobe house looking at the list they had of students they claimed as their students, the agent said he would help them out and support them in their work. He promised to do so, and he was good on this promise too and even provided lumber for benches. The blackboard was not good, though. It had holes in it. They tried painting over it, but it was for nothing. It really would be good to have a blackboard on which to write. On Tuesdays and Fridays in the afternoon, the superintendent of the government school said it would be all right to come and teach catechism classes to the students in the government school at San Carlos: on Tuesdays the boys and on Fridays the girls. So as the century opened its temporal doors to *Inashood* Guenther, he resolved to teach his boys on Tuesday and girls on Fridays and then with the help of an interpreter make his pastoral rounds until Friday and then return home. He would sleep out in the open or perhaps turn in at an Apache farmer's house and stay. He got back home Friday afternoon and the next Tuesday started his rounds all over again. During the winter of 1900 and early part of 1901 bouts of sickness stalked the Apaches. Guenther got medicine and took it to their camps. He showed sincere interest in them as people. He helped them, and they responded with special thanks and appreciation. Many of them thought he would be leaving them soon, but he was there working and helping them, and gradually this perception they had of his possible quick turn-around return to Wisconsin faded. The fact that in December he rode his horse 28 miles one way to get a Christmas tree for them had surely shown them that his interest in them was genuine.

The first boy to be baptized was Harry Tcheeten. He was a fine student at Carlisle at the government school. Guenther found him there. Harry had the approval and esteem of the white ladies who taught at the government school. Guenther met with him in private, so that baptism could be explained. In a special service in February he was baptized, and he confessed his faith in the Apostles' Creed. Many attended this special service, and Guenther hoped it would make a favorable impression on others, so that they would desire baptism. Myron Sippi was the first young adult man to be baptized, and that happened on Pentecost Sunday. Five more girls in the public school were also taking instruction, and then there were ten. Ten girls in ages from ten to sixteen. And they had names too: Lizzie, Mollie, Lula, Claire, Belle, Effie, Jaunita, Nina, Sophie and Ola.[119] On the

---

[119] *Gemeinde-Blatt.* 15 May 1901, p. 77

twenty-eighth day of April they were all ten baptized. In the mission school with its 22 students, none had as yet been baptized, but the students were doing well. They were taking their hymns home to their parents and singing them there. Jens was teaching them five days a week, and they seemed happy to come to school. Things were good.

The hot summer came. The three hottest months of the summer Guenther spent in Wisconsin. He spoke at the Wisconsin Synod's national convention and told the participants in the Midwest about the work. In this way he paved the way for the deputation duties that fell on later missionaries who traveled around during their furlough time while they were with their loved ones and spoke in churches and gatherings about the work they were doing. Guenther got back to San Carlos in early September. His route back had been through Topeka, Kansas, and he spoke to the Nebraska District Convention about his work and then left a day behind schedule because his baggage had gone missing. Both Mayerhoff and Jens were waiting for him at San Carlos. He had a little layover in Albuquerque, but other than that it was a direct trip to Rice. In his letter of 11 September, 1901, he dispelled the nonsense of there being unrest among the Apaches. Evidently this had gotten back to the Midwest and caused concern there. The "wild" Apaches he served knew nothing of any renewed hostilities. They were just happy to have him back in their midst again, and at 7:30 the morning after his arrival he and Jens were on their horses heading the nine miles to old San Carlos for a class with the school children there.

Christmas of 1901 had a special treat for Jens and Guenther. One of their professors from Wisconsin had been forced to go to Colorado for his health. Doctors' orders said J. P. Koehler needed the clear dry air of Colorado. Christmas was coming, and Colorado in December isn't much different from Wisconsin in December, so with the blessings of his doctor, Koehler got in touch with his former students at Peridot and asked if he could come to visit them. You can take the professor out of the classroom, but you cannot take the classroom out of the professor. This is clear from the careful documentation Koehler gave of his journey to Peridot.[120] He told how the train was late because of the increased traffic and baggage due to the Christmas season. At each stop, it got later and later: LaJunta, Col-

---

120 We are told that back at Northwestern Alumni Society in Watertown, Wisconsin, the "versatile" Professor Koehler gave a series of lectures on "Egyptian, Greek, and Roman Architecture" and it was "with the aid of a stereoscope" no less! These lectures were tangential to his theological classes taught at the seminary in Watertown. In 1884 he had addressed the assembly on the theme, "The Importance of the Study of Secular Poets for the So-called Learned Professions."

orado; Deming, New Mexico; Bowie, Arizona. The Gila/Globe train waited an hour and a half, so that it could take the passengers from the laboring Southern Pacific line. Koehler asked if there would be accommodations at Rice because it would be the middle of the night when they got there. The conductor "comforted" him in saying that not only was there no hotel, there really wasn't a station. Just a tank to take on water for the train. The brakeman wandered by at that moment and overheard the lament of Koehler over his lateness and the certain lack of accommodations. "Are you going to be met by Jens and Guenther?" the brakeman asked. "They are good boys. They'll be there. My sister is a teacher at the government Indian school in Rice, and she knows them. They'll be there."

And it was so. The train pulled into the "station" at Rice, and there in the moonlight was Jens with two ponies. They got the bags out of the baggage car and started for Peridot. In the narrative of his experiences, the professor could not here refrain himself. He had to launch into the description of this new and interesting place. He described the mesas he saw. He wrote that they were called *mesa* because of the Latin word for table. He described how it seemed these mesas had once formed one flat surface that had been chiseled and cut through with running water. The valley of the San Carlos River was a mile wide. The soil was alkaline with sand mixed in. Volcanic hills and lava slides dotted the landscape here and there. The vegetation was scruffy and tough. He mentioned the mesquite, the greasewood, and the sage. He spoke of catclaw. He described the towering saguaros. He mentioned that he had noted eight different kinds of cactus since he had been there. He even described the galloping gait of the horses as they made their three-mile journey in the moonlight, and how the heavy saddles were taken off the horses before they were turned out to graze. Guenther was there by the gate, waiting for them in his shirt sleeves, even though it was Christmas and December in Wisconsin. They made their way into the adobe house, where a blazing fire was cracking and popping in the fireplace, and they talked until late into the night.

Next morning before sunrise Jens and Guenther were out in their shirt sleeves again, getting the horses ready for the nine-mile ride to San Carlos for the Christmas service with the students at the school. There was a wonderful red sunrise for Koehler on this first day among the Apaches. Most of the way to the military base and school they could ride abreast, but once in a while they had to go single file—which Koehler called "according to Indian fashion." The young men shouted "hallo!" to the passing camps. The women and the children shouted back, *"Inashood!"*

They got to San Carlos in good time. The government buildings stood there on that floodplain bareness along the Gila River, the place John Bourke called "stinking malarial flats." No trees or bushes were in sight. There was a rowdy ball game going on when they got to San Carlos. Koehler thought it was noisier than ball games in Wisconsin would have been. They stopped dustily at the headmaster's house and were received warmly by his wife, Mrs. Wilson, and mother-in-law. It was Christmas morning, after all. The headmaster wasn't there, though. He was 50 miles away with the ball team in Safford. 100 years later, this same attention to sports would consume even the missionaries, as teachers in the mission schools scheduled basketball tournaments over the Christmas holidays.

The worship service had been overlooked somehow. The students weren't ready when the three *Inashood* got there. The matrons saw to it—and very quickly—that the students were clothed in their gray uniforms, and in military marching order they entered the hall that was their church for the day. To Koehler's ear, the voices of the children in Wisconsin and in Colorado—the white children—ended up sounding more like a scream than a song. The Apache children sang the Christmas songs in a more melodic and soft way. The girls sang especially beautifully. They even sang the *Gloria Patri* and the Doxology. Guenther gave a simple Christmas sermon delivered in English. All the English-speaking staff that could come were also there, and then they had to get back the nine miles to Peridot for their Christmas service there.

The white farmer at Peridot, a Mr. McMurren, had gone twelve miles to get a fir tree. It was there by the mission school, planted in the ground. Pastor Brockmann of the executive board in Wisconsin had sent clothing, scarfs, handkerchiefs, mirrors, combs, barrettes, harmonicas and dolls. Even Montgomery Ward in Chicago had gotten in on the act. Because of their business connections with the fledgling mission they wanted to do something too, so they sent balls and play knives and other toys. The whole celebration was presided over by Norman. Norman had formerly been a student of Carlisle, Pennsylvania. He was back home again on the reservation sporting a smattering of English that vaulted him into his leadership position. He was the self-appointed translator. He had bluejeans on and a shirt tucked into his pants with a big leather belt slung around the outfit. He had a cowboy hat on too. It was big, not to count the boots and the jangling spurs protruding off the back of the boots. Koehler spotted him through the window of the adobe schoolhouse. He was told after the service that one of the visitors that day was a medicine man who nodded his head once in a while in approval. The students were sitting on new wooden benches constructed by Guenther just days before. The five white people took their places in the front. Guenther rose and introduced Koehler. Several times that word, *Inashood*, appeared. Koehler's ear picked it up, and his mind knew what it meant. Then the children rose and sang some Christmas carols accompanied by Jens' violin. The children told the Christmas story in English. Bessie, the baptized Apache girl, recited the 23rd Psalm from memory. The children said the Lord's Prayer and the Apostles' Creed together. One little girl of eight years was wearing her mother's shoes. They were way too big for her, and she had to drag them across the floor behind her—but at least she had shoes! And the rest did too, along with blue jeans and clean clothing. The girls had their beautiful hair braided in long braids.

The adults gathered too. They came from the road nearby. There was a mixture of garments. The men often had what looked like long underwear on with a breechcloth. You see this arrangement in many of the old photographs. The women had their camp dresses on, mostly made of red cotton cloth. The skirt was big (sometimes eight yards of cloth) and over that they had a loose fitting blouse. Some of the color combinations were impossible for Caucasian taste, but to the wearer they were just fine. Two mothers had their babies in cradleboards. Some noise issued from that quarter, but the people paid attention to the preacher and to Norman and the children answering the questions. Then the joyous time came to distribute the gifts and the candy in the little packets. The men dived in with both hands. The women were more subdued and even looked slightly embarrassed as they tended to their acquired culinary treasure in the ample laps of their camp dresses. Norman got a special packet in view of his services as translator, and he received it with the decorum due his high office. Chief Cassadore's two widows were there, and they received a special gift that Mrs. Plocher had sent to them. It was they who had been her closest neighbors in her trying time there with her husband at the beginning of the work, and from Wisconsin Mrs. Plocher was thankful.

Afterwards Chief Taruschgan and his wife came up to talk to *Inashood* Guenther. The chief wanted to vent about the mistreatment he had experienced in getting proper tools to work the land. Seeing Koehler there he supposed he had someone in hearing range who could right the wrongs he had experienced. Some of the elderly women came back and said they'd had to guard their camps and hadn't been able to come. Couldn't they have some candy too? They sat there in the middle of the goings-on until the Chief had said his words. Guenther gave them some nuts and candy, and they were on their happy ways back home. Professor Koehler and the two young men spent the evening with Mr. McMurren. He had been in the area for 20 years and had even served as a scout during the conflict years. He had many interesting stories to tell. The sunlight was touching the Triplets when they left. Jens and Guenther had to do their evening chores. The horses needed tending, and the day was over. December 25, 1901, had been a far different day for all of them from any in their previous experience—Apaches, missionaries, and visiting professor alike.

When the 13th of February came, young Jens stood up as the godfather for the little orphaned Apache girl, Bertha Francis. The wife of the school superintendent at San Carlos was asked to be godmother. The school children sang, and the Scripture was read where Jesus said, "Let the little children come to me." This was the first infant baptism in the work at Peridot.

The good professor stayed on, and in March he and Guenther made the trip to the mountains to visit Mayerhoff. Professor Koehler stayed with Mayerhoff to return at Easter, and Guenther made the trip back alone to the southern reservation. This solitary return trip was no small feat in itself. The snow had been deep but had receded enough to allow the mountain traveler safe passage through White River and Black River canyons and on to San Carlos.

School started up again. The children came back with their new Christmas clothes on. The girls especially took care of their dresses. Some changed when they got home to keep their clothes from getting dirty. They came to school and went to wash up at a washing station the missionaries had established. Lots of good-natured joking and talking went on. The girls braided each other's hair. One day Guenther held up a sponge he had gotten to wipe the black board clean. It was a new thing. "This is a sponge," he said slowly. "This is a sponge," the children said back again. Throughout the day you could hear the phrase said by someone contemplating the English, "This is a sponge." Some of the boys commandeered the sponge at recess and ran to the well with it and after filling it full of water commenced to sprinkle each other with their newfound toy. That of course necessitated the law, "The sponge stays in the school room." It was school as usual. The one-room schools in Wisconsin and Minnesota had the same innocent drama going on in them, too. Professor Koehler was amazed at how quickly the Apache children learned to write. After only a year of writing they could have put a number of their white counterparts in Wisconsin to shame. Professor Koehler observed that the children were good at imitation. That is the way we all learn anyway, and even across cultures imitation remained the sincerest flattery. The girls were so shy. They had their heads buried at the elbows of their bent arms when asked to say something. But it was the girls who won their teachers' hearts. Perhaps that was so because they were so dependent on their teachers and so willing and able to learn. The missionaries were the only connection the children had with the outside world that was looming on the borders of their reservation.

As the professor observed the two young men at their work with their children, he saw the incredible need and the amazing progress and success of the effort. The work with the parents was hard. They were considered wards and minions of the state. Incentives to get established and work and get ahead were just not in the works in those days in the early 1900s. Many of the people still nursed wounds from the war years. They lived with the unfairness that had been dealt them. Some were bitter. The men were stripped of their leadership roles, and they went easily and quickly to drinking. Drinking seemed like the most fun thing to do, and no doubt it was. It did nothing to promote strong families and upright examples of fathers leading their children in industry and hard work. And the church people "back home" who were footing the bill for the effort among the Apaches were known to say, "There isn't much happening out there with the Apaches."

It was in April that Koehler finally left to go back to Colorado by way of California. Mayerhoff came down from the upper reservation, and together they had a service and received the Lord's Supper. On the same day Mayerhoff rode off to the north to return to his place at East Fork, and Guenther and Koehler rode south for twenty-five miles along the Gila. They were able to see the little settlements stretching out that way toward Mormon country in Safford. They passed by the settlement of Geronimo. They noticed once more the lassitude of the Apaches, particularly the men. They were forbidden from hunting and cutting firewood and doing much other than waiting for their rations to be distributed. There wasn't much they could do for gainful employment other than work on the irrigation ditch that fed the fields of the white farmers. There were government-sanctioned farmers who were supposed to be helping them, but most of them were charlatans. Some were as intractable as the worst-behaved Apaches themselves. Koehler noticed the sullen atmosphere among the Apache people at the prospect of the government stopping their rations, so they would get to independence and self-sufficiency in one big hop. The supposed cut-off date was July, and as the missionaries rode by to catch the train it was April.

Koehler went on and spent some days with Pastor Cook of the Presbyterian Church. It was the same Pastor Cook who years before had befriended the mission scouts of the Wisconsin Synod, Hartwig and Koch, and sent them initially to check out the Apaches as a place to begin mission work. Koehler was much impressed with Cook. The Pima were almost all Christian. They had built a number of nice churches which rivaled the rural Lutheran churches of Wisconsin in size and organization and even in architecture. What especially impressed Koehler was the camaraderie and respect that existed between Cook and his Pima Indians. They loved him, and it was evident. He had been with them since 1870. This was 1902. They knew he was there to stay. From the old chief Azul to the youngest person, they came in a steady stream day and night to talk to him and ask his help and advice. The Pimas had suffered under years of drought. Koehler thought that this perhaps helped the people look to this white man who cared enough about them to live with them and talk to them about spiritual things and to speak also of their physical lives. The wheat fields they used to tend were now lying fallow. There was no water. The Gila River dried up when it was needed most. Politics was being played, and the proposed hope of a reservoir to retain water for dry times was always on hold. Let's not forget that there were white farmers upstream too, and the political entity that would recommend and build a storage reservoir that would help the Pima also had to reckon with their own electorate that lived upstream and wanted the water for their own farms. There was a huge disconnect too between the people in Washington responsible for allocations of funds and the little starving group of Pima Indians—or Apache Indians for that matter.

Koehler wrote the men at San Carlos and told them that by all means they needed to get in touch with Cook. They would be encouraged in their work among the Apache if they could witness what the Pimas and their Pastor Cook had brought about. Three white pastors labored with Cook. In addition there were a number of Pima "helpers" who were enlisted in the work. This possibility of indigenous helpers would resonate with the Apache missionaries and especially with those who had sent them to labor there on the reservations in Arizona.

In August Guenther fled to the mountains of the upper reservation to be with Mayerhoff and the newly arrived teacher Otto Schoenberg on a ten-day trip to the Petrified Forest. The summer rains in 1902 didn't come until September. The biggest thing to report about the Petrified Forest trip was not the incredible sight of the petrified forest but the pleasant weather the riders enjoyed on their outing. San Carlos could be—usually was—very hot in August. The printed account for the good supporters of the mission work in Wisconsin rejoiced that their missionary could "escape" for a while and find time for regrouping and recuperation. Teacher Jens had escaped the heat by fleeing to Two Rivers in Wisconsin. There wasn't mention that the Apache people were stuck in San Carlos and environs and had to weather the heat without the respite of a trip to the cool mountains. Is it really possible to ever get used to heat that can often get to 112 degrees? What would it do to your outlook on life and your outlook on your subjugators who were responsible for forcing you to stay in such a place? But then there was this bit of good news: an Apache woman among the visited sick ones had given Guenther two watermelons. Surely those two watermelons did say many good things. Thank God for the watermelons and for their giver.

Guenther mentioned that in the few days since his return he had made four sick calls. We can read elsewhere that the heat affected the missionaries in a telling way too. The people were desiring their young pastor to come and talk to them when they were sick. Guenther rode the 30 miles upstream on the Gila River to what would be named Bylas. Sadie was sick and dying. Sadie was one of that first group of school girls who had been baptized. She was the reason for 60 miles of riding in the blazing heat of summer. She died on September 2, and two of the Peridot school girls died too: Lulu died the 29th of August and Kate on the 30th of September.

Two more things were in the wind. The first was the possibility of sending used sewing machines to the people around the mission station, so they could prepare proper clothing for their children for school. Mrs. Plocher had used her sewing machine well to take care of her family and to win friends among the Apache women. Now the idea was to send the used machines that the Wisconsin ladies replaced with newer models. Boys would have to have stout clothing because of their nature as boys. The girls could have their mothers make dresses for them of more feminine cloth and color. That was the first of pending possibilities. The second was that the men at Peridot were requesting a team of horses, so they could themselves haul the materials to the new church site and save that money. The supporters in Wisconsin read the request and agreed. It made sense to send permission for the team of horses.

Harry Chetlin moved in with Guenther and Jens. The idea was that he teach them Apache and they teach him English. They could do so much more if they could speak Apache. Their "parish" was forty miles long, and it was filled with 3,500 Apaches. They were the only ones there doing the work. There was a crying need for more workers because time was so short. They hired out the menial work, like garden tending. They needed the vegetables to eat, but the time just wasn't there to farm. No newspapers or books outside of the Bible came across their kitchen table. People needed help for necessities in their lives. Some of their people lived in abject poverty. Guenther had from the beginning set aside some of his own money to provide where he was able for the absolute necessities that some of his people had. He asked if the possibility existed for a special fund to be established for humanitarian purposes. He had been told by Presbyterian Cook in Sacaton that the Presbyterians had such a fund. It wasn't that his people were begging. They just needed help. The Bible even said, "Whoever sees his brother in need and doesn't help him, how can the love of God live in him?" The people brought of their crops for the two missionaries and gave the food to the pastors: melons, squash, beans, and corn.

And the facilities needed to be brought up to speed. There were a total of 25 baptized people now, mostly children. The little mud school at Peridot couldn't hold them all. On the upper reservation they had no building at all. So the report was made to take a general collection of the Midwestern congregations and send money to build the schools. The promoters of the giving drive maintained that the reservation pastors were practical men. Mayerhoff had built his own house. Now that Schoenberg was there on the upper reservation, the work needed to progress. So steps were taken and buildings were begun. Carl Guenther salvaged tufa stone from buildings demolished at old San Carlos to build a new school building to replace the mud building. There was the church at Rice, the present day San Carlos. The government had to provide the land, and the Lutherans had to provide the building. It would be tufa stone. Then the question arose about proper desks. The government schools had them, but would the Lutheran school be doomed to having cobbled up wooden benches? Couldn't there be a way to get desks? It was Koehler who made the plea to the people in the Midwest. He had been there and had seen the need. He was an educator himself.

So life went on, summer and winter. Guenther and Jens were getting along. Things were good, and there was progress visible in the work. Chores had to be done. Sometimes it took an inordinate amount of time and effort just to accomplish things that needed to be done to physically live there. The men found that there was good hay for their horses in the Safford area, and that the train would bring a load of hay bales to Rice, and they could get it there for their horses. The load came, and Guenther took the wagon that they had acquired in the building project to get the first load. Later in the day Jens took his turn and went with the horses and wagon to get the remaining hay and bring it back to Peridot and home. As he came down to cross the arroyo that had to be crossed, it was a steep slope down to the wash. As the horses held the wagon back on their way down the slope, the load of hay shifted and slid and in the process knocked Jens off his seat. He fell under the wagon. It was narrow there in the chute the wagons had cut in the bank. He couldn't roll out of the way, and the iron wagon wheel ran over his chest. Someone saw it happen and raced to get Guenther. "Come quick! The teacher is hurt!"

Jens was lying there on the ground when they got there. He was in a lot of pain, but he seemed all right to them. They got him loaded into the wagon and took him carefully back to their home, as carefully as you can take a mortally wounded man with internal wounds and a crushed rib cage on a springless iron-wheeled wagon. They got him back to their adobe house and to his bed. Guenther sat with the candle by his friend, but sometime that night Rudolph Jens' labored breathing stopped.

Guenther got his friend ready to go home to Two Rivers, Wisconsin. The government folks provided a box. The violin was there too, and it went back with its meister. Its voice had been stilled. Rudolph Jens would play it no more nor lead his children in singing with it at a Christmas service. Guenther went on the train to Two Rivers, too. When they got there to Two Rivers, Wisconsin, the two parents were waiting for the son they had been proud to send to tell the Apaches at Peridot about Jesus.

After the funeral Guenther went back to his work. He got married too. On Pentecost Day that year of 1904, seventeen girls and ten boys were baptized at Peridot. A teacher Kutz followed Jens, but because of the intense summer heat he soon left the field. Then for a while the mission school at Peridot closed. Things seemed to be dying. People were dying. One of their baptized girls, Mollie Foster, was dying. They watched at the deathbed, and they sang to Mollie. Carl Guenther's wife broke down in crying with the mother as Mollie breathed her last, even though up to this time she had told the mother not to cry. They made the coffin, and they put up the board fence around Mollie's grave.

How could this kind of love and care not have been a great force and power for good? How is this same kind of love and care still not a great power for good?

CHAPTER NINE

Paul Mayerhoff

The Christian ideal has not been tried and found wanting.
It has been found difficult, and left untried.
G.K. CHESTERTON

At the parsonage in Ripon, Wisconsin, Paul Mayerhoff's mother would put him and his five-year-old sister at the garden gate to give boiled potatoes to passing Winnebago Indian children. That was in 1872. Then a little later in West Bend, Wisconsin, where his family lived, he remembered watching Native Americans with their bows and arrows knock big copper cents from cracks on the hitching post. When he afterward went to school in Watertown, Wisconsin, he worked with a farmer, and as he plowed he picked up arrow points and tomahawks as they were uncovered by the plow. This portended the archeologist in him as he sniffed around the ancient places he later discovered in Arizona. Right from the beginning it seemed he would be an interested pioneering party in the mission work of the Lutherans among the Apaches.

That life began for him when he was 26 years old. One day in May of 1896 the Southern Pacific train dropped him off at Bowie, Arizona. He caught the stage and bounced and careened off the hard interior with the rest of his fellow travelers all night long. It was dusty and dry and hot. One thermometer unabashedly said "114 degrees." It hadn't rained in months, and he ended his reminiscences of the day by saying about the stark and unfriendly landscape, "Why rob the Apaches of such a country?" At Fort Thomas he saw the little adobe railroad shack of the agent with a tiny little garden watered by the overflowing trestle tank. Sunrise saw them all at San Carlos: "San Carlos School, agency, trader's store, officers' quarters and soldier barracks on four sides of a quadrangle."

After a brief time of acquiring a few Apache words and learning how to ride a horse (actually he learned how to get back on a horse after he had fallen off), he was off to Fort Apache in the company of an Apache guide and John Plocher, the first missionary at San Carlos. Fort Apache started as Camp Ord in 1868. General Edward

Ord had one of the tallest mountains in the White Mountains named after him. There was the following metamorphosis of names: Camp Mogollon (August 1870) and Camp Thomas (September 1870) and Camp Apache (February 2, 1871). It was finally Fort Apache in 1879. This was the destination of the first Lutheran missionary to the Fort Apache Reservation. Fort Apache is of course still there today, along with a number of original buildings still standing.

The sixty-mile trip to Fort Apache was an agony of bouncing and chafing and—pain! When they camped that evening the only position he could assume without excruciating pain was flat on his back looking up at a brilliant star-struck sky until the wee hours in the morning, when just before dawn he finally fell asleep. They finally got to Chief Alchesay's camp on the North Fork of the White River. Chief Cassadore was the missionary's friend in Peridot. Chief Cassadore and Alchesay had been together in the war times and had worked and ridden with General Crook. Chief Cassadore sent his greetings and approval of the pair of missionaries who showed up on Alchesay's doorstep. (Wickiups don't actually have doorsteps.) Chief Alchesay fed them a wonderful meal of tortillas and meat and coffee. Mayerhoff never forgot how delicious it was, and it strengthened him to complete his *Via Dolorosa*, his "way of sorrows," as he character- ized it, as they rode on toward Cibecue the next day. At Cibecue they met with another of Chief Cassadore's "brothers-in-arms." This was Chief Cooley. After seeing the place, they made it back to Fort Apache for the Fourth of July festivities.[121]

Pastor E. Edgar Guenther writes: "The following year (1896) Candidate Paul Mayerhoff was called to the upper reservation and began his work in the government school at Whiteriver, which con- sisted of two groups of buildings, the one housing the Agency and the other a combined boarding and day school. His residence Mayer- hoff established in a tent under a huge spreading juniper at a spot at East Fork some four miles away. Whiteriver Agency and our mission at East Fork form the two points of an equilateral triangle, with Ft. Apache forming the other point."

He camped under a cedar tree that still stands today. When May- erhoff got to Fort Apache that day, there stood the mesa top directly to the west that shaded the fort in the evenings. On this mesa top a soldier had climbed and risked his life to see what had become of Captain Carr's soldiers who had been in the fight at Cibecue. He won a medal of honor for his bravery. From that place he finally saw the forlorn band coming from the west across the flats where Canyon

---

121 Paul Mayerhoff, *Beatrice Daily Sun*, "In Days of Apaches," August 15, 1933.

What Mayerhoff saw. *Gan B'sedia.*
Photo Credit: Edgar Guenther and Arthur Guenther. The author's collection.

Day School would one day stand and where missionaries would serve in a reconstructed white church made from the previous reading room of the black soldiers at Fort Apache. On that 5th of July in 1896, Mayerhoff borrowed a tent and mess-box from the post commander. With his limited Apache vocabulary and appropriate arm motions he beckoned to some nearby Apaches. "I wanted to hire one of them to haul my stuff to a certain location on the East Fork of White River; that I wanted to stay there, get acquainted, learn their language and later help them," Mayerhoff wrote, but the Apaches did not understand. Finally a one-eyed man (Kessel thinks it was perhaps Martini) hauled the tent and mess-box four miles up the East Fork, received two pesos for his labors, and left. Mayerhoff had arrived. He had his work cut out for him. His mission field covered 1,664,872 acres. His task was to share the message of Jesus Christ with more than five thousand White Mountain Apaches.

Mayerhoff pitched his tent there by a big cedar tree that Edgar Guenther later dubbed *"Gad N'chah."* When Mayerhoff came out of his tent that next morning, if he hadn't noticed it when he went in, there stood the big mesa that dominates and rules the skyline across the river to the north, *Gan B'sedia.* You can't miss it. Missionary children sixty years later would clamber around on its steep sides and reach the top and see the whole scene below: Whiteriver, East Fork, upper East Fork by "Dove Salt Flats" (*hawoo b'ischii*). You could see Fort Apache and beyond it, Canyon Day and the peaks below. There was Saw Tooth and Sugar Loaf and the little diminutive peak, Kelley's Butte. There was the White River, running in the gray and rosa canyons to meet with the Black River to form Salt River. On the slopes of *Gan B'sedia* a rusty sickle of government issue was left when its hay gatherer had tired or lost interest in her hard work of gathering hay for sale at Fort Apache.

The fall of 1897 was more pleasant than the fall of '96 had been. The days were warm and sunny, the nights crisp and cool. Mayerhoff was in his little house. The house was actually colder the second fall and winter because the cracks had increased in size due to the shrinking of the lumber used. But it was all right. Apart from a few sniffles, he was well and could do his work. Those who wrote about him in the *Gemeinde-Blatt* rejoiced that he had been kept safe in his harrowing travels and dangerous experiences. Those experiences weren't over, however.

That fall at 8:30 on the morning of November 8, Mayerhoff set off with his two horses for San Carlos. Ninety-five miles of rough wilderness riding lay ahead of him. It was a trail that he had never been on, and he traveled alone. He worked his way up Seven Mile Canyon. Back at the time of the Cibecue Massacre Chief Alchesay, living up on North Fork. had been accused of having something to do with the murder of some white people in this very canyon. Where the trail crossed and crisscrossed the dry stream bed, the walnut trees still clung to a few of their yellow leaves. The sumac red lay in scattered profusion on the ground. There was a bite in the air as the sun rose over gray Rimrock. You could look back down and see the river with its cottonwoods. As he climbed up out of Seven Mile Canyon he could see Fort Apache where the North Fork and East Fork came together downstream and the White River went on alone through red and gray cliffed canyons. His eye drifted toward the place where his tent was pitched, standing there empty now and silent across from *Gan B'sedia*. His things were there. He hoped they would still be there when he got back. Once up on top of the rim, the going south was level through prairie-like grassland. Chiricahua Butte was over the Black River to the west. In early afternoon he followed the trail's switchbacks down into Black River canyon. He was making good time. He unsaddled and let his horses graze for a while, eyeing the steep slope to the south that would take him up over the mountains and straight down the other side toward the Gila River, still two days of hard riding away. When the sun was setting he happened on a pool of water and camped there. He gathered firewood. That bite he had felt when he left in the morning was resurging, coming from the blueing mountains where the big moon was rising. All night that moon journeyed over his smoky campfire of pine knots. It was cold, very cold. Sleep was fitful and spoiled by the need to have more wood on the fire for light and for one-sided heat. *"My soul waits for the Lord more than watchmen wait for the morning, more than watchmen wait for the morning"* (Psalm 130:5). Finally the inky blue began in the east, the moon set in the west, and another day of riding began.

That day brought him to solid rock declines where the saddle and pack worked its way forward onto his horses' withers. He had to lead the horses down the steep and precipitous declines. No wonder he hadn't been able to find anyone who wanted to take his chest of belongings from San Carlos to Fort Apache! How would they have gotten it up the side of this mountain? The thought of having one or both of his animals plunge to their death down the decline occurred to him. That sort of thing happened regularly when the soldiers pursued their Apache quarry in the rough mountains. That night with the full moon he slept better. It wasn't so cold. The lower altitude had taken some of the cold's bite away. He didn't even tend a night fire. One more day of riding and he came to the Gila River. The last two hours he led his horses by the reins. At nine in the evening in the moonlight he got to the Gila. It was such a steep bank down to the water that he couldn't get his thirsty horses to the water, so he clambered down with his water-boiling can and fetched the water up the cliff to his waiting horses.

When he finally got to San Carlos, Plocher wasn't there. Just his empty adobe abode was there. Mayerhoff put his horses up in the shed and after he had talked with some Apaches working in a nearby field, stretched out to sleep in Plocher's wagon. *"Grüss Gott, Plocher!"*[122] he was finally able to say, sitting up in the wagon. His unknowing host had finally come home. For twelve days they visited and talked and compared notes on the work. Two single and lonely white men awash in a sea of strange people and places. They shared Apache words garnered in their makeshift vocabularies. Mayerhoff noticed quickly enough that there was a big difference between the Apache language of East Fork and the Apache of San Carlos. The dialect was different. It was so different that the younger people on the upper reservation couldn't understand some of what was said on the lower reservation. The older people

---

[122] God's greetings, Plocher!

were better at deciphering the dialects because they had lived in closer contact in the old days with the different bands of the people. So the linguistic plot thickened.

In June of 1897 Mayerhoff reported a twelve-day missionary trip to Cibecue. They got there at two o'clock and were received by Chief Cooley on the Cibecue River. These were the same accommodations offered to him the year before when Plocher had taken him to Cibecue to survey the prospects of mission work there. Mayerhoff preached a sermon to Cooley and his band. He taught Bible stories to the children around the area. He ministered to two dying men who were extremely malnourished. He shared some of his provisions with the men. One died shortly after the visit. He talked to Chief Sandazen who had lost four children to sickness in the last several months. Twelve days he had been at it and each day cost him an average of twenty-five miles of saddle leather. He froze at night but the days were pleasant.

He continued this kind of work on the upper reservation. He visited twenty different headmen representing 632 families in their leadership. The smallest band had eleven families and the largest had 88. He went north along the North Fork of the White River. He had to cross by Fort Apache because the river was swollen. It was springtime, and he noticed that at the lower elevation, things were getting green. Twenty-eight miles away at Cooley's Ranch[123] the snow lay deep. He went on the trip to find people and reconnoiter. He also wanted to break in his pack horse. Nothing amiss happened on this trip, but on the next trip to Cibecue, the pack animal bucked everything to oblivion three times before they made it to Cedar Creek. When they finally got there they found that everyone was gone. They were tending little farms here and there in the fertile gullies around and getting some of their crops planted. That is what had happened on the trip north too. Alchesay and his band were all away to Forestdale to do their planting there.

By 1898 Mayerhoff was fully involved in mission work. On occasion he preached to the officers, soldiers, medical staff, postmistress, and other personnel at Fort Apache. If the reader peruses the state marriage records of that time and place, he will see that Mayerhoff performed a number of civilian marriages at the military base and environs. Every week he taught and preached to the sixty children in the Whiteriver agency boarding school. He rode his horse from Apache camp to Apache camp telling simple Bible stories to anyone who would listen.

---

[123] Just a quarter of a mile south of the casino at Hondah today.

He got his house built at East Fork. This was a real house with three rooms. He managed to get some furniture and appointments for his house from Fort Apache from departing soldiers. He got these things at a quarter of the worth of the items. One of his Apache friends came and gaped at it all: "You have a big house. You have four houses (four rooms). You have many things. But for all of your possessions, you are still alone." That Mayerhoff was still single surprised his Apache friends, and there was no wife in sight. The 12x12 one-room shack he converted into a storage barn, with the possible future option of using it as a school building if he could come across the materials for desks and things. After two years of work the people were approaching him about the school for their children. They feared sending their children away. They wanted him instead to teach them so their children could stay with them.

His mission station had been appointed to him by the authorities, and he worked to get it enclosed. He had wrested a garden plot out of the tangled undergrowth along the river. He had pried the stumps out and leveled the ground. The three-quarters of an acre plot was lassoed with a fence of posts and wire. He figured he would be able to beat the extravagant prices of the "traders" with their wilted assortments of vegetables. He had potatoes and turnips growing. Life was good. He had been there two years.

Since July of 1896 Pastor Mayerhoff had labored among the Apaches by himself. Finally, in 1902 the Wisconsin Synod sent a teacher named Otto Schoenberg to assist him at East Fork. Soon the preacher, the teacher, and two Apaches built a 20x20 foot building which served as a school and church building. The next year Schoenberg opened the East Fork day school, which eventually enrolled twenty students.

Paul Mayerhoff was faithful to his calling as a missionary of the gospel. He also developed a sincere love and deep respect for the people he came to serve. By the turn of the twentieth century many white authors had negative opinions about the Apaches. They pictured the Indians as murdering, immoral, bloodthirsty people, who lacked all milk of human kindness. This is what Koch and Hartwig had been told in graphic terms at the train stop in Deming, New Mexico. People showed them cut-outs from newspapers that they thought made their point. These were dangerous people, they were told. You don't want to go there, they were warned. Mayerhoff, on the other hand, relied on first-hand observations rather than such stereotypes. For example, in 1936 he wrote an article in the Beatrice, Nebraska, newspaper about Mickey Free, an Anglo boy who was captured and raised by Apaches and who as an adult was Mayerhoff's neighbor at East

Fork. Mayerhoff mentioned reading about Mickey Free: "Still more grew my attention, when to me well known characters he had contacted in his time (the author of the book Mayerhoff was reading), stood out in print before me. Imagine my pleasure when one of my valley neighbors was mentioned, Mickey Free, erstwhile Irish captive. Mickey Free had a history. May I give it as I piece it together from Apache sources?" And this is what makes what Mayerhoff has to say so interesting and worthwhile because he had that close contact with the people themselves and built the bridges from the secular history and characters to the Lutheran mission work.

He speaks of the terrible massacre that took place somewhere around Mt. Turnbull, when every single member of the group that included Mickey Free was killed—massacred. Mickey Free was just a small boy and was taken captive and then raised among the people. Mayerhoff said, "Thus it came about that a little Irish boy was captured and brought up as an Indian and became an Apache in everything but complexion." Because of the totality of the massacre, no one thought to ask about the little "Irish" boy, and it wasn't until years later when the band was brought to the San Carlos Reservation that questions were asked about the little boy, who now lived with the band as a man and warrior. It was Mayerhoff's opinion and observation that the Apache people showed "great love of children and kindly, tolerant treatment of them." He opined that his belief was that Mickey Free had received the same. "You may ask: how was he treated by his foster parents? Did a jealous shrewish hag beat him, starve him, force him to do her menial labors for her in every kind of weather and begrudge him a place to warm by her fire? Did a brutal husband take his ill nature out on him, because he was of the hated pale-faced race that were robbing the Indians of their hunting ground, streams, hills and valleys? I would say: no! Never have I seen an Apache or his wife strike or abuse a child. Rather their great love of children and kindly, tolerant treatment of them, would assure me that the little Irish captive slave received the same consideration."

Mayerhoff spoke further in his newspaper article to whomever would listen, "When I first met Mickey Free, he was a man of about 40 years of age. He had seen service with Crook and Miles in the Apache scout troops that helped to settle the last Indian difficulties in 1885-1886. Now he was a member of H Band on the White Mountain reservation. Incidentally, he and I had our homes in the same valley. So, we met often and my business as a missionary was to win him back to Christianity. One of the last things I did for him was to photograph him with his youngest daughter. Mickey Free as I knew him was a good Indian, a good provider for his family, orderly, willing to bring his children to school (not so with most other Indian parents), more industrious than the Apache braves generally." He ended the article with the following words of summary and hope, "Should he (Mickey Free) still be living I feel confident he became a devoted leader in our mission church."[124]

The historical record of the soldiers and politicians regarding Mickey Free was somewhat different from what Mayerhoff observed and believed. Jason Betzinez related how officer Bascom falsely accused Cochise and others of harboring and hiding Mickey Free, the half-Irish and half-Mexican boy. The record also states that Mickey Free interpreted with the government soldiers at Fort Apache years later and did not do a particularly good job of it. Even though Mickey Free was General Crook's interpreter in the Mexican campaign of 1883 to apprehend Geronimo, General Crook allegedly thought Free was in part responsible for the Cibecue Massacre because he had not properly relayed nuances of the heated discussion that time between the Apaches and the soldiers. In 1886 Geronimo complained in the Canyon de Embudos when Crook was trying to bring him in that he had fled the reservation because Lieutenant Britton David, Mickey Free, and others had mistreated him while he was there. General Crook considered Geronimo an inveterate liar, and some called Mickey Free an inveterate liar. Crook's adjutant John Bourke recalled whoppers that Mickey Free had said when he had maintained that a medicine man could ignite something just by holding it in his hands. Bourke discredits Free's story by saying, "This story is credible enough if we could aver that the medicine-man was supplied, as I suspect he was, with a burning glass."[125] No doubt about it though, Mickey Free and his wall-eyed appearance were around and about when the missionaries came to Fort Apache and East Fork in those early days. Mayerhoff knew Mickey Free well.

Mayerhoff studied the Apaches. He learned their traditions and customs. In February of 1899 he submitted a description of the marriage rites of the Apaches to the readership of the *Gemeinde-Blatt*. He described the visitations back and forth and the ten-day intervals in the proceedings when the young man's family met with the young woman's family. The bride-to-be had little to say about what happened. That was the doing of her family. They agreed that the bride price was right if the mother of the bride accepted the tethered

124 Paul Mayerhoff, *Beatrice Daily Sun*, "Mickey Free, Irish Apache Captive," Monday, April 23, 1934.

125 John Gregory Bourke, *The Medicine Men of the Apaches*, Glorieta, New Mexico: The Rio Grande Press. Inc., 1983, p. 458.

horse and gifts that showed up at her place before the breaking of that day. If they were unsatisfactory, she untied the horses proffered and threw the accompanying saddles and blankets to the side. That would have been the end of the deliberations. There was the final corresponding returning of the gifts too by the bride's family to the bridegroom's family, minus the horses. If as things progressed there was a problem between the bridegroom and his bride-to-be on their liking each other, religious measures were taken. The bridegroom took a rock and two spears from a yucca plant. He pointed the one spear toward his bride's wickiup and the other toward his. The rock went on top to hold the two spears in their particular orientation. The delicate arrangement between the mother-in-law and her son-in-law was discussed too. After the marriage was final, these two never would address each other again or use the other's name. They wouldn't be caught together under the same roof. The two mothers could communicate with each other and the father of the son could communicate (with restrictions) with his daughter-in-law, but the son-in-law and mother-in-law were finished. There would also be the eight-night clandestine approaches to the bridegroom's wickiup by his bride-to-be in company with her friends. They would steal away before the sun rose. The bridegroom wasn't to let on to his bride's appearance there at his wickiup. If he did, the marriage would not have happened.[126]

In the summer of 1898 Mayerhoff's neighbor woman died of tuberculosis. She told her family that the end was coming. The people had gathered when it became obvious that death was coming closer, and as the end approached the people sang more loudly. All through the night the sound of their frantic singing carried over to his house. At dawn the people slumped down, exhausted and hoarse. A few of the husband's men relatives and some medicine women remained. At his breakfast Mayerhoff heard long protracted screaming. This was kept up until death finally came. He went to watch the last. He saw the husband throw himself on the body of his dying wife crying and yelling wildly all the while. Those around joined him. After a while they grasped for a hand or a foot to hold to stave off death and to keep the dying one with them. It was almost like they were pulling her limb from limb. They forced her lips closed and put her hair over her eyes to block the departure of her spirit. Finally Mayerhoff could stand it no longer because they were strangling the woman with their ministrations. He pulled the women off and kneeling down wiped the death sweat from the woman's brow and moistened her lips with

---

[126] *Gemeinde-Blatt*, 1 February 1899, p. 21

a damp cloth. The last breath came, and she was gone. Her female relatives started taking off her shoes and clothing to prepare her for her burial. Men started to tear down the wickiup where she had died. Women came from all around and started a wild and awful keening. Her horse was tethered nearby with red and black bands tied to the mane and to the tail. A man sat behind the dead woman on the horse to hold her dead body, wrapped in her red blanket. A relative got an ax and followed to kill the horse at the grave. Cooking pans and implements and a pot of water were brought to the grave and left there. The wickiup was burned and all the things in it. Four days later the relatives cut their hair to show their grief, and the time of grieving went on for days.[127]

In another article on the Apache morality Mayerhoff wrote: "I have heard the statement and read it in print; no virtue in the Indian women, young and old; above the age of eight to ten years no pure maidens might be found. Most emphatically I disagree with such unproven views. Rather was I very much impelled to a contrary view by my observations; in other words that little sex-immorality prevailed among the Apaches and immoral practices were not the rule among the younger set." It was his opinion too that the Apache's conscience was dull. If he didn't get caught, he felt no compunction in letting his passions go. In this, he was like the Spartan whose greatest shame was not in what he did but in times when he may have gotten caught at it.[128] But if the Apache demonstrated something other than Christian character, Mayerhoff laid the big blame on the sorry examples the white people tendered in their self-imposed ruling of their charges. All the missionaries felt this way. That is why they lived and worked at a distance from the government people. They didn't want to be closely associated with those people of the same skin color. They didn't want to be polluted either by the immoral conduct they witnessed and endured from some of the whites.

It was Mayerhoff's observation that the white people were harming their charges more than helping them with their policy of rations. He compared the fact that the San Carlos Apaches got rations every week, year in and year out. The northern reservation only got rations from December to May. (Eight pounds of meat, eight pounds of flour, some ounces of coffee and some sugar.) The rest of the time the people took care of their own food. The Apache knew what had been taken from him and what he had gotten in return. The reason he appeared satisfied was that it was hopeless to resist. Actually, he just got good at being taciturn. People were able to grow things and harvest things and then sell them to the government. They got $1.24 for one hundred pounds of hay, $2.75 per cord of wood, 2-½ cents a pound for corn, five cents a pound for beans. In March of 1902 when Mayerhoff and Koehler made their rounds on horseback, most of the people were gone to the mountains. They were up there cutting firewood for the military post. It was a source of cash for the people, and they took advantage of the income.

But bad things happened in the people's efforts to raise things. Mayerhoff experienced it himself. His carefully tended garden was completely destroyed in one of the incredibly violent hailstorms the mountain monsoons spawn from time to time. The fields of the Apaches were ruined too. Literally the whole field was washed away or filled with banks of boulders. This was in the summer of 1898. There was general unrest because of the devastating storm and the troubled times. Many of the people took to the mountains and left their riddled crops in the valleys below. This hindered Mayerhoff's work because his people had scattered. Once during his stay in the East Fork Valley there was an outbreak of scarlet fever. "The following morning I was the sole inhabitant on a six mile strip of valley. Walking along from one group of huts to the next group, I found them all abandoned."[129] The people did that when there were hard times or when there were epidemics. Even today when you tramp the hillsides of the river valleys, you can see the remnants of the old camps with rock piles and an occasional ancient and weathered porcelain cup or pan.

Soldiers began to leave from Fort Apache for the Spanish-American conflict. This too affected Mayerhoff's work at the fort among the soldiers. He had services at the fort for a year. That gradually ground to a halt. The soldiers didn't come much. They had games to play and other "important" things to do, but their wives did come and so did some of the other women from the fort.[130] Mayerhoff ministered to the dying agent at Fort Apache, and he was with him the last weeks of his earthly journey. He told him of Jesus and believed him to have died in the faith. He was a faithful man. His name was Keys.[131] He

---

[129] Paul Mayerhoff, *Beatrice Daily Sun*, "Sickness, Death, Burial and Mourning, Chapter VIII," September 14, 1933.

[130] *Gemeinde-Blatt*, 15 June 1902, p. 93.

[131] You have to wonder if perhaps the family that adopted the name Keyes on the reservation got their name from this man. Remember that it happened with the name Gatewood and the good soldier who had not only given of his life to the people but had also given them his name. Among the Navajo even today a common name is Key, perhaps also derived from the family name of this soldier.

helped the fledgling work and he was missed. It wasn't like that with all the white staff at the agencies of the reservations.

During the summer of 1899 Mayerhoff returned to Wisconsin to restore body and soul with some well-deserved rest and relaxation. He spoke to the church convention about the work on the San Carlos and Fort Apache reservations. On September 4 he left Wonewoc, Wisconsin, and headed back west on the train. Three days later in the morning he arrived at Holbrook. It was still ninety-five miles of hard travel before he got home to his place at East Fork. The stage left at three in the afternoon. There off to the right, the sun set. The country looked good, because the summer rains had been good. At ten o'clock the stage pulled into Mormon Snowflake. Mayerhoff ate while the mail was gathered. Farther down the road at Taylor the horses were changed in the dark. Lightning flashed, and it poured. The roadway was washed out in places, and the going was slow. At Fools Hollow the horses were changed again. It was three o'clock in the morning and Mayerhoff's teeth rattled in his head because of the cold. The driver gave him a heavy Navajo blanket but it was stiff and soiled and didn't help all that much. One of the horses collapsed along the way and had to be replaced in the dark. At 11:30 p.m. they straggled into the next stop. There was some breakfast, and then there was some more rain. Ten miles of it. But it finally got lighter, and at 5:00 in the afternoon the words of arrival that Mayerhoff thought for twenty-six hours would never come came. There were no bad effects either, other than a little cold.

Things were good up the river too at East Fork and home. The man he had left in charge of his things was there. Everything was in order. Nothing had been stolen. He paid the man for tending his things. He had imagined everything being gone when he got there. (His cooking implements had been stolen when he had gotten there in 1895.) But everything was fine, and even the garden which had been a wash—literally—the year before was producing. It was a little overgrown, but never mind: potatoes and tomatoes, rhubarb and raspberries, onions and asparagus[132], carrots, cauliflower and cabbage. The cabbage Mayerhoff converted to sauerkraut like any self-respecting German would have done. Life was good, and the best thing was the welcome of his Apache people. They were glad to see him. They shook his hand and looked him in the eye. What a difference the three years had made in this regard. Gone were the

---

[132] A hundred years later along the river in the springtime asparagus still appeared. The children who lived on the mission at East Fork used to gather it, if they could manage to get there before Robert Perry found it all and left only bleeding asparagus stumps behind.

suspicion and distrust. Those negative things had been replaced by cordial friendship.

Three weeks after he got back home to East Fork he decided he had to go and see Plocher in San Carlos. It was a five-day trip through the mountains. When he got there, Plocher was gone back east with his family. The lady superintendent had taken over the school work and made a start. The mission board said Mayerhoff should leave Fort Apache and the upper reservation and stay and work in San Carlos. The people at Fort Apache couldn't understand this, and the government doctor lamented, "It's not right of you to leave us this way because your work here is as important as any you can do there in San Carlos."[133] The return to San Carlos was no fun either. Twenty miles out of East Fork, his horse and attached pack horse balked and then bolted and headed back to East Fork without their rider. Mayerhoff had to walk the twenty miles back. Three days later from the trip's first beginning he was back on the trail again. The first day out he made thirty miles. The second hitch was forty-eight miles which left him two miles short of San Carlos. He slept on the ground that third night too. Sunday morning found him early into San Carlos, and his work started that same day.

Since 1893 Pastor John Plocher had been conducting mission work at Peridot, but by 1899 his wife and child were in such poor health that he was forced to resign and leave Arizona. Paul Mayerhoff was then sent to fill the Peridot vacancy. He became fluent in the San Carlos dialect of Western Apache. He realized that he could not count on Plocher's gathered words from San Carlos Apaches to speak the same ideas to his Fort Apache Apaches. Finally, in February of 1900 Pastor Carl Guenther arrived at Peridot, and Mayerhoff was allowed to return to East Fork to his people there, who very much appreciated having him there again.

Once back after the hiatus in Peridot and San Carlos, he continued the work. He became chaplain for the black soldiers at Fort Apache when the chaplain who had served them left.[134] Mayerhoff baptized some of the children of white personnel on the reservation. One was a woman's daughter who was from the Missouri Lutheran Synod and was serving there on the reservation. In July Otto Schoenberg came to help the mission effort and to teach the children.

Pastor and Professor J. P. Koehler from Wisconsin got there in March of 1902. He had come Christmas Eve as we already heard

---

[133] *Gemeinde-Blatt.* Dec. 1, 1899, p. 180

[134] The lumber for the reading room for the black soldiers stationed at Fort Apache eventually found its way into the chapel at Canyon Day that Pastor Edgar Guenther built.

and spent three months with Rudolph Jens and Carl Guenther. Koehler was spoiling to get up to see Mayerhoff. The problem was the snow. Guenther couldn't find the trail if there was too much snow; besides that, the runoff from the snow would swell the Black River and the White River and make them impossible to cross. Finally, in March they set out. Cowboys and Indians were supposed to be able to make the seventy-five-mile trip in two days. (This is the way Koehler related it.) It was wilderness, and they would not see a human being along the way. They figured on the three days though, and it took them all of that. They managed on the second day to get turned around due to bad directions and only got as far as Black River. They built a huge fire in typical white man fashion and huddled in their saddle blankets. One side roasted, the other side froze. In the morning the coffee kettle had thick ice on it which had to be broken away so the new fortification for the day could be brewed. But they managed, and in the evening of the third day Guenther and Koehler came upon Mayerhoff's house by the ancient cedar tree on the East Fork of the White River. Koehler stayed with Mayerhoff past the target date. He had been commissioned by the executive board, Brenner and Dowidat, to survey the work and report back after he got back to Wisconsin. He would be the eyes and ears of the committee in their absence.

Mayerhoff's horse had absconded. It was grazing up on Seven Mile Hill someplace. The search was on for another horse and one showed up right away. The owner had traded an old violin for the horse and was willing to let it go for $16.00. Koehler was skeptical, but the horse seemed sound and made a good impression. He proved it on the trip up to Turkey Creek. That is where Mayerhoff's old derelict pinto was grazing with a bunch of other horses, some wild. Once they had the transportation back home again, a Captain Goldman from Fort Apache said he would take them to see the salt springs. It ended up being a fifty-eight-mile round trip for Koehler and Mayerhoff. They went toward Cibecue, and when they came to Carrizo Canyon they went down toward its confluence with the Salt River. There, a short distance from the river, which in the dry season went underground for a good part of its distance, the salt spring spread out, leaving salty residue all over. Mayerhoff's "wild" horse didn't mind drinking the water. They actually made their coffee from the water and got by. The water smelled of sulphate of soda,[135] and Koehler knew the smell and the substance. There were other springs on the White River that had the same smell. It wasn't a surprise that the river these salty springs

---

[135] The word was *Glaubersalz* in German.

flowed into got the name Salt River. It was early spring, and a hefty snow storm made life miserable for them on their way back to Fort Apache. Captain Goldmann and Mayerhoff spent an hour talking about hunting, and then our pair rode on back up the river where they were able to be fortified by Captain Goldmann's hospitality." Their horses found their way in the dark, and they got home late that night.

So whatever Koehler's health ailment was that caused him to leave Wisconsin for Colorado's solace in the first place, he was a stout man to have made such an outing. He was a good horseman. In fact, in Watertown, Wisconsin, on at least one occasion he had led the parade through town, decked out in his military uniform and astride his prancing horse. The next mission adventure he related described the mettle of their newly-acquired horses. Their horses proved much peppier than the military horses on their salt spring trip. They headed north, up the North Fork of the White River. They stayed the first night at a Mormon family's place. They had been Mayerhoff's neighbors before. The Mormon hosts fed them and housed them and kept their pack horse the next day, when they rode on up toward present day McNary and stopped at Cooley's place. Cooley lived there on the edge of a pretty meadow with his two Apache wives.[136] Cooley had served in the military and had been a scout. He had a "hotel" that he operated for passersby. He invited Mayerhoff and Koehler in for the midday meal. He regaled them with stories of his dealings with the Apaches and soldiers from the last thirty-five years. They headed back down the mountain and got to Mayerhoff's place on the Saturday before Easter.

Before Koehler went back to Colorado, he wanted to see Cibecue to the west, so they ventured out and had trouble right away. The saddle cinch had galled their pack horse, and they had to tend to it and go very slowly. It was torturous going up and down the canyons. Carizzo Canyon, where they had gone to see the salt springs, proved especially daunting. After two days of hard riding they got to Cibecue. A wild-looking young girl with even wilder hair flew by them on a galloping horse. She was the hectic herald of their coming to that remote community, a veritable Valkyrie. White people didn't get to Cibecue often then and they still don't. This herald on horseback promised the best show in town. They got to Chief Cooley's place and set up their tent, and Mayerhoff went off on his horse looking for better poles to secure the tent. Koehler stayed behind and dignitar-

---

[136] Just south of the present day Casino at Hondah, you can still see the chimney of Cooley's house. Vandals burned it down in the 1960s. There are still Cooleys living on the Fort Apache Reservation. This is not the same Cooley who lived in Cibecue and was a chief there.

ies arrived to talk to him. The man was chief-like, like James Fennimore Cooper's stories described! It was difficult to communicate. The translator wasn't sober, and that made it even more interesting. Koehler steered the conversation toward more factual things like the San Carlos work, and the inebriated wordsmith got along better until Mayerhoff got back. The Apache leaders the white missionaries talked to that day asked them to send men to live and work among them. They would give them a place to live.

This was to be the case. There would be two churches built in Cibecue: one at lower Cibecue not far from the site of the Cibecue Massacre and the other at upper Cibecue where it still is today. Lower Cibecue started the school that would serve the Apache people in this remote part of the reservation. There was an adobe church made and the teacherage/parsonage was adobe too. Guests came in the 1950s and stayed at the house in the absence of the teachers who were away on vacation. There was no electricity other than that coming from a generator that had to be hand cranked into action by the side of the house. There was an orchard of apple trees nearby and a long fenced walkway that went to the river crossing several hundred yards away. This is where Delores Cassadore remembered her teaching time with Pastor Arthur Krueger and his wife. He's the one who would later lament to the missionaries at East Fork Mission that the stones on the road to East Fork were round and smooth whereas the stones on the road to Cibecue were sharp and jagged. Delores Cassadore remembers the delicious home cooking Mrs. Krueger provided the school children at Cibecue and how Pastor Krueger would get up when it was still dark to start the wood stove in the school and then go around with his vehicle to bring the outlying children to school. Cibecue was also the place where former scout Peaches was, who would become a Lutheran under the instruction of Pastor Niemannn. But all these things lay in the future when Pastor Mayerhoff and his guests from Wisconsin visited Cibecue that day. He wouldn't see these things happen.

"In 1904, after laboring for eight years among the White Mountain Apaches, Pastor Paul Mayerhoff left East Fork and the Apaches, never to return to the reservation. He had worked alone until 1902 when Otto Schoenberg was sent as a teacher and helper. With the help of Apache workers they built the core part of the present chapel at East Fork. In 1904 Mayerhoff left and it was too bad. He was irreplaceable, really. He knew the language and he knew the work and he loved the people, but he went to Nebraska. Maybe it was loneliness or maybe it was ill health. Whatever caused him to leave the Apaches, they remained in his thoughts constantly. During the 1930s while he was a pastor in Beatrice, Nebraska, he wrote a series of twenty-seven newspaper articles outlining his experiences among the Apaches. In 1954, fifty years after he left Apacheland, he wrote a letter to Pastor Edgar Guenther. "One thing is sure and clear in my mind, that I always feel homesick for my Apache friends and neighbors." His one desire was to visit Whiteriver, East Fork, Cibecue, and Peridot where he had spent eight years of discomfort and enjoyment among these dear people. Yet the death of his wife, old age, and ill health prevented him from ever making the trip. Instead, he gave talks and raised money for the Apache missions.[137]

In October of 1957 Pastor Paul Mayerhoff wrote his former coworker Pastor Edgar Guenther a letter:

Well, I am 87 and 8 months along, hope to live to my next birthday February 20, 1958.

My best wishes to you and mother (Mrs. Minnie Guenther) and all other missionaries. God bless and keep you all in health and successful labor for the Lord and the Apaches.

God be with you all, body and soul, disposition and reason since through God alone you can be shielded and protected!

Inashood Hastiin *(elderly missionary)*

Paul S. Mayerhoff

He did not make it to his birthday. Two days before Thanksgiving in 1957 he died. His niece wrote to tell Pastor Guenther the news. She noted that Mayerhoff's eyesight and hearing failed but his mind had still been sharp. She regretted that he was unable to see the reservation one last time, and then concluded, "But all his love was for the Apache Mission."

In that Paul Mayerhoff was not unique. There were many missionaries down through the decades who wished nostalgically and perhaps also sadly to return to their place and their people on the reservations. It was even so that some managed to do that very thing. Paul Mayerhoff's special monetary gifts to the mission work went in part to buy a house trailer that was set up on the East Fork Mission property. The trailer sat by the present-day playground, up by the irrigation ditch. Mrs. Norma Mansell, the girls' dormitory matron at the end of the 1950s, lived there with her two children, Charles and Sandra. Then, for a while, Orville Sprengeler, the son of Missionary Ernie Sprengeler, lived there with his wife Inez and their children.

[137] Pastor Mayerhoff's story is continued here with the account written by Dr. William Kessel who is Pastor Edgar Guenther's grandson.

But the trailer meant for the shelter and accommodation of the visitors and guests of East Fork Mission is gone now, and so is Paul Mayerhoff. The footprints and fingerprints remain though, and so do vestiges of hard work and sacrifice and love for Apache people these misionary heroes called "their" people.

CHAPTER TEN

Gustav Harders

"I am give out" (Back-country Texas saying
for someone who is very tired).

Pastor Gustav Harders stepped off the train in Globe in 1905. This was his first trip to Arizona. He came to find relief from his failing health. His congregation in Milwaukee, Wisconsin, (Jerusalem Congregation) had given him a year's leave of absence. In this regard he was like Professor J. P. Koehler mentioned above because Koehler had been there for health reasons too. Harders returned to Globe to labor from 1907 until 1917. Like Hezekiah in the Old Testament, the Lord gave him extra years of life. It was he who organized the mission work into a conference with regular meetings and a unified approach. He was the first superintendent of the work, and he had a good knowledge of it. Already in the fall of 1907 he and his daughter Irmgard taught five Apache students in a little makeshift school in Globe at the little church he called The New Jerusalem.

The Apostle Paul suffered from some kind of a physical problem. So did Gustav Harders. He had a degenerative throat problem (some suspect that it was tuberculosis) that forced him from his beloved Jerusalem congregation in Milwaukee. Perhaps Arizona's dry climate would cure the problem. Harders chose Peridot on the San Carlos reservation for his retreat, and here he gave much-needed assistance to Missionary Carl Guenther, bunking in the vacant adobe schoolhouse. The year passed quickly, but when Harders attempted to resume his duties in Milwaukee it soon became obvious he would have to return to Arizona. It was now 1907, and this time the General Mission Board called him to be superintendent of the Apache Mission and also to do mission work in and around Globe.

The people on the San Carlos Reservation had been hit with a devastating flood that ruined many of their farms. At this time large copper mines were opening in Globe and the neighboring town of Miami, and many who were discouraged at the prospects of farming were lured to Globe and its environs by the prospect of good wages in the mines. Some traveled even farther west to work on the irrigation projects on the Salt River. Mission work in Globe continued even into the 1929 depression, which caused the economy to grind to a halt, and then the Apaches began to drift back to the reservation.

Globe was the third oldest place of work for *Inashood*. Pastor Haase, who came from East Fork, had started it off, but kind of like his name (which means "rabbit" in German) he scurried off again to the Midwest and left the place empty. Harders was called to Globe to reach out to the Apache people, particularly to those who lived in Bylas, Globe, Copper Hill, Miami, Wheatfields, Roosevelt, Gisela, Fort Huachuca, Clarkdale and Jerome. He arrived there to stay with his wife and seven children in September of 1907. At that time Globe had 12,000 inhabitants, perhaps more than it has today. Globe was the gathering place for people of all sorts of ethnic backgrounds. This caused H. C. Nitz to write in recollection, "On its streets swaggering cowboys rubbed shoulders with grimy copperminers, or 'muckers,' as they are called. Chinese truck gardeners sold their vegetables from house to house. Jews conducted clothing stores. Germans sold meat and milk. Swarthy Syrians conducted grocery stores. 'Cousin Jacks' from the Cornish Coast in England descended into the hot bowels of the earth to mine the precious copper; and many of them spent their earnings in the numerous saloons, gambling dens, and pool halls flanking the walls of the canyon that formed the main street of the city. English and German, Italians and Polish, Russian and Spanish, Syrian and Turkish, French and Apache, Greek and Ethiopian, these and other languages could be heard on the streets of this bustling city, justly called the 'crossroads of the world.' "[138]

In appearance it looked in some respects similar to one of the little towns in the hill country of the Holy Land. House rentals were bringing ridiculous sums in 1907, but Harders was able to procure a sizable lot with a four-room house. With personal funds he managed to build a small church and another building that served as a school, and he shingled his buildings with tin cans smashed flat to shed the runoff from the usually sparse rain that fell. The church he built with linerboards from railroad box cars and mine timber scraps. His older daughter, Irmgard, proved to be a devoted teacher, and Hilda, the other daughter, prepared noon meals for the school. Hilda also conducted a weekly evening class for some appreciative young Chinese, instructing them in the basics of English and the Christian faith. They met and studied by lamplight until ten o'clock in the evenings. In addition, other teachers would come and help

[138] *The Apache Scout,* December 1939, p. 82

the school effort: Klara Hinderer, Maria Kieckbusch (first sent to Peridot), Teacher Gurgel, and student Henry Nitz.

Harders set out full-time to the big work of being a missionary. His contemporaries called him a true *Inashood*, body and soul. In addition to Globe and Miami already mentioned, he served Fish Creek, Wheatland, Ray, Winkelman, and other little mining towns in the area. He wasn't against traveling to other parts of the state either, looking for his people and following them. He made it to Tucson, to the Verde Valley and Jerome, and to Prescott, places which in some cases were several hundred miles away. Because he was also superintendent of the Apache field he had to go by horseback and buckboard to San Carlos and Peridot and on up to East Fork and Cibecue. He was involved in some of the squabbles that came, and he had to try and mediate them. In this way he was like Martin Luther, who spent his last days trying to remediate quarrels too. On the 13th day of April, 1917, Harders died. He was 53 years old. He had worn himself out and had finished his race. They buried him in the little cemetery on the hill across the canyon from his hillside house and chapel in Globe, and the grave is still there to this day.[139]

It was just before Christmas 1916 that seminarian Alfred Uplegger was called to help Harders in the school and congregation work in Globe. Uplegger remembered how the end was: "Pastor Harder's health deteriorated. In February he had even gone to Phoenix for treatments. When he came back he was ready to stay in bed. He had been held in great esteem as a theologian. But now he could not help me at all. He grew steadily worse and one evening, when he believed that he was about to be called Home, he called all the family together for a devotion with prayer and hymn verses and requested me to pray with them and that we conclude with singing 'O Christ, Thou Lamb of God, that takest away the sin of the world, have mercy upon us.' He closed his eyes, but the sleep into death of the body evaded him. After three or four days we repeated the prayer at his request. This time the Lord in His grace relieved him, taking him to his eternal rest. Then I telephoned to Professor August Pieper, an intimate friend of Harders, to come to the funeral service to be held on the 18th of April, 1917."

Isabella Harders died October 24, 1930. She was buried in Globe with her husband, Gustav Harders. She never was in the limelight, but she shared the deprivations of missionary life with her husband in the early years. Part of her heroism was to leave her home for the mining

---

[139] There are present-day Lutheran pastors who once a year go and have a toast at the grave of Gustav Harders.

Miss Marie Kiekbush, teacher at the mission school in 1916, and Nellie Burr of Calva, Arizona.
Photo Credit: From photographs from St. Peter's Congregation in Globe, Arizona

town of Globe, Arizona. Globe was totally different from Milwaukee, Wisconsin. After her husband died, Isabella stayed in Arizona with some of her children, first in Miami and then later in Glendale.

Pastor Harders died on April 13, 1917, and Missionary E. Edgar Guenther of East Fork was called to succeed him as superintendent of the mission field on both reservations. Harders was a multi-talented man who did much to establish the early Apache mission work on both reservations. He understood the circumstances of the people he came to serve. "Anyone who gets to know the Apache as he really is, anyone who gets to see and know him without the deterring mask, gets to know a nature about which he cannot think without heartfelt sympathy and bitter sorrow. Sympathy since he would so much like to help him; sorrow because he sees no way how he could help him. I will attempt to describe to the reader the true Apache, as a couple, very few, have deemed me worthy to be permitted to get to know them and to let me look into the interior of their hearts. Only a very few have I gotten to know in their true form, but also through these few I know that also all their brothers and sisters are basically no different than they are. Briefly stated: the Apache is a person who has lost the joy of existence, for whom life—whether we say having to live or being permitted to live—has been embittered; the Apache is a person who has no hope."[140]

The minutes taken at the early pastors' meetings with Harders in charge show the progress and challenges and developing philosophy of the work that the first missionaries established and practiced. The meetings were held at Globe and Peridot and East Fork and at the other fledgling mission stations.[141] The very first meeting of this group of missionaries took place at the home and church of Missionary Harders and his family on Devereaux Street in Globe. It was May of 1908. One of the first things done after Harders had preached at the opening service was that the members of the conference organized and chose Pastor Harders for chairman and Pastor Carl Guenther from Peridot as secretary. At this first meeting, newly elected President Harders presented assigned prayers he had written for special occasions in the church year. He was encouraged by the conference to put these prayers into print with the possible inclusion of illustrations. In this regard an observer can see that the meeting was of a practical nature. There were no extant materials to use or to disseminate. Sunday school materials, educational efforts, charts, pamphlets, etc. had to all be written. In line with this perception of need, the minutes say, "The next matter of business was the presentation of Pastor Recknagel's work: 'What Is Baptism?' This was followed by Pastor Carl Guenther's treatment of the question: 'Who Should Be Baptized?' Both presentations were received with thanks, and it was also decided consequently to work out an Apache translation of the baptismal formula.

---

[140] J.F.G. Harders, *The Apaches Today*, Milwaukee, Wisconsin: Northwestern Publishing House, 1912, p. 5.

[141] The minutes were kept in a notebook. The secretary wrote in the old German script. Deciphering the old script was impossible for the author. The solution came through an acquaintance, who lived in Germany and grew up with German script. She transferred the German script into translatable German.

The first men were also unable to study and consult someone else's work in ethnology or cultural things. There were no linguistic learning aids. In regard to written materials that would help them in their work, there was nothing available. So again, those who had some facility to understand and articulate these things set to work. It was Pastor Schoenberg who undertook the work of explaining the Lutheran pastor's relationship to medicine men and what would and should be the relationship to witchcraft on the basis of Holy Scripture. The following questions were dealt with in his presentation:

1. What are examples from the Scripture of wizards and witches and their corresponding witchcraft?
2. What is the essence of witchcraft and superstition according to Scripture?
3. What judgment does Holy Scripture give regarding witchcraft?
4. How should we as missionaries respond to the likes of magicians, medicine men, fortune tellers, exorcists, etc.?

It was even contemplated that Schoenberg's work could be written in Apache for the benefit and input of the people themselves.

There were other papers and presentations assigned regarding religious instruction and study. The theme established at this first meeting was, "God our Father." The missionaries would write about that and study their efforts at the next meeting. It was also pointed out and discussed that there had to be a concentrated effort to deal with the distrust that existed between the Apache people and the missionaries. Bad things had happened, and the Apache members of the future churches would be looking at the same color of skin when they saw the missionary and when they saw some unscrupulous charlatan in some kind of government authority. It was also pointed out at this first meeting that the trust and confidence of the people would only be won through a show of love, the kind of love that God demonstrated in his Word.

One item of discussion that would have later importance and value and which would also provide fertile ground for frustration was the reporting and accounting procedures that needed to be established between those working on the field and those who were in charge of seeing to it that allocated funds in the Midwest were finding their proper expenditures on the field. At this first meeting there was a discussion about the quarterly reports and the joint mission reports. Missionaries in the Wisconsin Synod mission work would live with report forms and expectations from their leaders from this time on. Sometimes it would seem to a beleaguered missionary that the only thing that really mattered in the minds of the prevailing powers was getting the reports submitted in a timely and consistent way to the proper people.

This accounting concern and reporting of goings-on in the work came to a head several years later with the following terse statement of the missionaries in conference, "Because our reporting is not being understood by the Commission, evidently painting too rosy a picture to them that they do not understand the true nature of things here, it was our decision to have each think of a form of reporting that would present a true and realistic picture of our work here and to report on such ideas at our next meeting."

Another question that right from the beginning was challenging and would need to be answered was the proper apportionment of time to educating the children in the schools and in doing the actual pastoral work in the camps with the adults. It was expressed in this first meeting that work in the schools only had worth if there was a corresponding intensive effort and work done in the camps.

Four o'clock came to this first meeting of missionaries, and it was time for the meeting to end, but first there were two final items the minutes recorded: 1) "It is the agreement that we as a conference express our opinion of the great need and advantage of having a ministry in the Phoenix, Tempe, and Tucson areas, and that we as Apache missionaries are willing to help in whatever way we can to support this ministry." And 2) "Keep your eyes open for the arrival of the Baptists!"[142] The other churches were coming!

The second meeting was held at San Carlos on the Gila River on September 25, 1908. Today when the water in the lake is at normal levels, the old fort and accompanying buildings are under the water impounded by Coolidge Dam, but at the time of these first missionaries, things were still high and dry here. It was at this second meeting at this San Carlos, as a last matter of business, that Pastor Carl Guenther demonstrated how important it would be to establish a mission station in San Carlos where the agent was. The conference then determined to recommend to the General Synod by means of the executive committee their strong feeling that such a station should be begun. It, of course, would happen that way and when the water started rising behind Coolidge Dam, the tufa stone that made the church would be transported to Rice (present day San Carlos) and the church would be rebuilt there.

Present for the second meeting were Pastor Harders—Globe, Pastor Carl Guenther—San Carlos, and Pastor Schoenberg—Fort Apache. It was the agreement that officers of the conference be re-elected

---

142 *The Apache Lutheran*, November 1990.

Apache mothers that Harders visited about enrolling their children in his school in Globe.
Photo Credit: St. Peter's Lutheran Church photos

each year and keep their offices for one year. Pastor Recknagel had excused due to sickness.[143] Pastor Harders began the meeting with a sermon on the theme: "God works in you both to will and to do of his good pleasure" (Philippians 2:13). After he finished he read two more of his prepared sermons, which were intended to be published in a book of sermons to be used devotionally on the reservations. Regarding the printing of the prayer book that was announced at the previous meeting, Pastor Harders reported that the work had already been turned in to the printer and could soon be expected in printed form. In order to get some of the Lutheran hymns into the Apache language, it was decided that both Schoenberg and Guenther should translate six hymns apiece and have them ready for the next conference. This would of course be done through untrained and in some

---

[143] Sometimes missionaries were incapacitated for months at a time because of illness. It was only for extreme emergencies that the government hospital or medical staff on the reservation were able to help the missionaries. Otherwise, they just had to endure their illness or leave the work for off-reservation medical help and recuperation.

cases inept Apache interpreters. The question was then discussed: How do we help our interpreters be better helpers in the work? It was decided to send the interpreters out every Saturday with pertinent devotions given them by the missionaries and carefully worked through with them. The interpreters could then invite the people to church and in general serve in the camps, for instance, by making sick calls. The men warned each other: "Be careful that the presentations are previously carefully worked out."

In this second meeting, the translation of the words of the formula of baptism was begun. The group finally reached consensus on the words: "I baptize you in the name of the Father and of the Son and of the Holy Spirit." The word *Ussen* was chosen as the word to be used for God; the word *yaaka'yu* as the word for heaven.[144] Pastor Schoenberg then presented the parallel study and translation of the Lord's Prayer to the conference.[145] The question of sick visits came up and it was agreed that missionaries should make the most of visiting the sick because it was at just such times that people were most receptive to the gospel. It was then discussed in detail how difficult and how apparently incapable we appear to be when we step up to the individual sick person to try and win his soul for Jesus. It was also mentioned that with the present small number of workers—just four—how impossible it was to do all the work that needs to be done.

The Saturday afternoon session was attended by Pastor Recknagel to the joy of the others attending the conference. He had rallied from the illness that had kept him from the first two days of meetings.[146] The session began with the singing of a hymn and the reading of a portion of Scripture.

Each member present had prepared an outline for a mission festival sermon on the parable of The Good Samaritan. Matters regarding mission work in the boarding school outside the reservation at Globe, home missions in Phoenix, Tucson and Bisbee, and the matter of a raise in pay were mentioned. Pastor Harders reported that the Executive Committee had expressed itself as no longer ready to pay travel costs for missionaries to return to Wisconsin. To this both Schoenberg and Guenther protested, having been assured by word

---

[144] In the German script of the minutes, the handwritten word for "kingdom" is indecipherable.

[145] The Lord's Prayer was written in German script to capture the sounds and words of the Apache translation. Remember, this was done before there was an agreed-upon alphabet and sound system of any kind of organized approach to the study of Apache.

[146] Recknagel was a candidate from St. Louis who had come to help Pastor Harders. He was only there several years and then took a call elsewhere.

of mouth that these traveling expenses would be paid for, making a trip possible every two years. This tight discussion would be akin to "the beginning of woes" that the book of Revelation spoke of in its chapters 8 and 9. Here at the second meeting concern about salary and support raised its ugly head.[147]

At Pastor Schoenberg's invitation, the third conference was held at Fort Apache, June 3-7, 1909. Already at this time there was a specter that was spooking around the reservations, and that was the perceived possibility that somehow the funding would stop for the work. Workers on the reservations would wonder and sometimes worry if the church at large would continue to fund their work. This concern was verbalized at this third meeting of the missionaries at Fort Apache when they recorded in their minutes: "There is presently a rumor circulating that funding for the work here is going to be cut off. Should this be a fact, the conference puts the following resolve before the commission in charge of our work: Should it be a fact that the Synod is considering stopping funding for the work here in Apacheland, we would ourselves take steps in our circles here to establish mission societies through which the work among the Apache by God's help could be carried on." Missionaries would also say that if the funding would be cut off, they would continue to work without support but would go it alone. In 125 years that eventuality never happened. Today those who labor on the reservations wonder what the ramifications are when they hear someone say, "We have worked among the Apaches for over a century now. It is time for the people to step up and bear the cost themselves so we can go elsewhere in the world." That thought was already being articulated at the very beginning and found its way into the dialogue of the novels that Harders wrote from his mission perspective in Globe.

At the third conference, Harders chaired the matter of Apache children's education: "It was determined to seek permission through the committee to allow the missionaries free hand wherever the possibility would exist in view of local circumstances and according to the means of the Synod to attack the opportunity to educate children." In Globe in the following year of 1910 the well thought-out proposal of the missionaries to the Board said, "Pastor Harders shared with us expressions from the proceedings of the General Synod with regard to the Indian Mission. In order for us to achieve the recommendation of the Synod that we get a school system going in experimental form in the next two years, we decided to gather a small group of children

---

[147] The minutes for this second meeting of the missionaries are recorded in the May 1991 *The Apache Lutheran.*

that could be constantly under our care and instruction. We would hope that these children could be kept with Lutheran families for blocks of several years. We ask the Committee to find such families that would be inclined to accept such children."

Remember that Pastor Schoenberg was doing good work on the Fort Apache Reservation. He was a gifted linguist. His fellow workers supported him in his work and recommended to the "worthy" Committee that the following steps be taken:

1. That Pastor Schoenberg be relieved of the responsibility of taking care of Cibecue, Carrizo and Cedar Creek because he does not have ready access to those areas;
2. That it is absolutely imperative that a man be sent there to work, and should this be impossible, to recruit a reliable married couple from Washington D.C. who could work in the government school there;
3. Finally, the conference considers it very important for our work here that faithful Lutheran people be found who would be willing to enter government service to help us in this way.

In this same matter the conference expressed, "It was the opinion also of our conference that Missionary Schoenberg remain in Fort Apache until another worker could be found to replace him. It was the opinion of the committee that Pastor Guenther not go to Cibecue because the cold and wet weather would be harmful to his health."[148]

It is interesting what did actually transpire with Pastor Schoenberg and Cibecue. The following is what the Twenty-Fifth Anniversary Booklet said: "Missionary Otto Schoenberg had often visited the Indian settlements at Cibecue and environs already in previous years from Fort Apache and had done mission work among the Indians there. But when the General Synod had resolved in 1911 to establish a new mission station there, the missionary was asked by the commission to move there with his family and there to pursue mission work among the Apaches. A piece of land for mission buildings and a garden was bought yet in the same year. Then Missionary Schoenberg immediately went about building a parsonage; shortly before Christmas the missionary could move into the new residence with his family; until then they had to live in tents. The parsonage, built out of clay blocks, with a wide porch and extended shingle roof, makes a very comfortable impression. In 1912, next to the house, a chapel was built which must also serve for school purposes. Later

---

[148] Carl Guenther was the appointed secretary of these first meetings, and his translated minutes are recorded in *The Apache Lutheran*, September 1991.

then a dining room for the Indian school children and the necessary stable were built. The stalls for the horses lie on the other side of the road, which passes close by the chapel."[149]

At the time when Missionary Harders was in Globe, Carl Guenther baptized a young girl named Rhoda Gordy. She had a sister named Bertha. Bertha was sixteen years old and had been a student at the school for six years. The government stepped in and took her away from the school. For eight months the government officials on the reservation had her in their clutches. Missionary Harders and Lutheran President Bergemann actually went to Washington and spoke with the President himself and with the highest official in the Indian Department of the United States Government! Think of that happening!

But Bertha got sick and Rhoda came with tear tracks on her face. "You have to baptize my sister," she said. So Harders went and crawled into the small tent. There were a dozen women there, and the mother sat next to her daughter. When Harders came in and started to talk, Bertha opened her eyes. She knew him. He looked at the mother and asked permission to talk to Bertha and to ask her some questions. The mother nodded and in a disconnected way started to wash a spoon in some hot water there in a little basin.

"Bertha, do you want to be baptized?" "*Hao, Inashood, hao!*" (Yes, pastor, yes!) "Why do you want to be baptized?" Harders asked. Clearly she answered, going into English, "Because Jesus wants me." Harders with Rhoda and Bertha read some Scripture passages that talked to them all and to this place and time. Bertha was baptized in God's name: Father, Son and Holy Spirit. Rhoda came to Harders a short time later. Bertha had died within two hours of her baptism. Before she died, she had told her sister and mother, "Tell *Inashood* to take care of my body." And he did. He took her body back to Rice with the family, and there it was laid to rest to await the resurrection in the little graveyard by the mission property at Peridot. Many years later Apache people would bring *Inashood* Uplegger and *Inashood* Rosin and bury them there too.

Besides his work as pastor and missionary, Pastor Harders was a writer, and it was in one of his books—*Dohashtida*—that he made a prophecy. The prophecy as his book stated it came in the talk between two characters in the story: Van Augustus Sims, the government school superintendent, and David Brown, a visitor to Arizona whose

[149] *Anniversary Booklet for the Twenty-fifth Anniversary of the Evangelical Lutheran Indian Mission*, printed by Northwestern Publishing House, Milwaukee, Wisconsin, 1919, page 22.

life became entangled with that of *Dohashtida*.[150] Keep in mind that the characters are fictitious, and so is the situation described in the book, but also keep in mind that these words are coming from Pastor Harder's knowledge of the work and his ability to dramatize it:

> Later that evening I asked Sims why there were no longer any missionaries among the Indians.
>
> He answered, "People got tired of trying to convert the red men."
>
> "Which people? The missionaries?"
>
> "Oh no, not they, but the people who sent them here and paid their salaries."
>
> "Why did they get tired of it?"
>
> "They came to the conclusion that the Indian mission did not pay. After supplying the salaries of the missionaries and teachers for about twenty years, they thought it was high time for the Indians to do it themselves. The missionaries were told that they should work toward that end most energetically. But when the missionaries reported that this would be impossible, and that a hundred years or more might pass before one could expect such results, the people became discouraged. The missionaries reported that laying the groundwork for the evangelization of future generations was all one could hope for now. Without this groundwork the building of the kingdom of God would not materialize. They thought they might gain an occasional convert, but the hope of building a self-sustaining congregation could not be realized for some time to come. Their real hope, they asserted, lay in the children of the present generation. Such prospects were not sufficient for the people in the East, who through their missionaries had started this mission. They declared the work of the missionaries a failure and Indian missions a lost cause. One by one the missionaries were recalled, and thus a mission among this tribe is a thing of the past."
>
> "Were the missionaries faithful in their efforts?"
>
> "Indeed, they were; everyone agrees on that," Sims replied emphatically.
>
> "And did they really achieve no results?"
>
> "No results?" repeated Sims. "They had phenomenal success: In every way they had the confidence of the Indians. We government people do not have that. They had schools.

---

150 *Dohashtida* means "I don't want to do this."

Their enrollment was small, but all the children had been enrolled at the expressed wish of the parents. When we spoke of this last evening, you held that to be the ideal practice. Instead of using the police to bring in pupils, as we do, the missionaries even had Indians attending church on Sundays."[151]

And so the narrative went from Pastor Harders' pen. There were things that were prophetic in Pastor Harders' story, in fact, some of the words about having to stand on their own today and needing to supply their own funding are words that are almost word-for-word spoken today by critics of the Apache work. Fortunately, the part about the mission closing down for lack of support did not happen, but in the former references to the early minutes the reader can understand that the prospect was real for Pastor Harders and his tiny conference of missionaries.

Harders was an impulsive and eccentric man in some ways. It is reported that one time he got on the train to Milwaukee, Wisconsin, and rode the three days to get there. When he arrived he walked down Wisconsin Avenue in Milwaukee and looked around some and then got back on the train without further ado and went back to Arizona to his family and his work. He remained a writer to the end of his life, and perhaps his missionary spirit can be appreciated in one final excerpt from his writing:

> Near Easter, this past year, we learned to know Jonnie Cook, an Apache from Gisela. He had a big red silk bandana adorning his American sombrero. From time to time we were in contact with him either by letter or personally. He had taken over the distribution of our "Apache Paper" which we sent him monthly. He also received copies of the "Young Lutheran" and "Lutheran Pioneer" from the Concordia Publishing House in St. Louis. He received a number of them in order to encourage him to place an order and distribute the same.
>
> Recently I met Jonnie in Roosevelt. I arrived there late that evening. "Oh, it's you," he said as he recognized me. "So I meet you here. I was at your house for two hours last Sunday and you did not come."
>
> "On Sunday I was at home." I told him this after a long discussion. It appears that Jonnie and another Apache sat for two hours in the chapel and they thought that at some

---

151 *The Apache Lutheran*, January 1993 (a quote from Harder's *Dohashtida*)

time I would come there. After I expressed my regrets to Jonnie that I had not seen him, he explained what it was that he had wanted to tell me. It was between 8:00 and 9:00 on a mild December evening. We sat under the starry heavens by a brightly burning camp fire. Jonnie and I were alone, and then he told me in his unique way his own life's story. He had on one visit to Globe learned to know and fall in love with a girl from Globe by the name of Dalladeene. He loved her and wanted to marry her in two months. "I must marry her," he said. "She loves me so much!" With that his genuinely sincere eyes lit up with pride and joy.

What he wanted from me in particular was this: that when he came I should marry him and Dalladeene in the chapel since he was a Christian, and that Dalladeene will go to church on Sunday and I should teach her from "God's Book." "I want it!" he said. Three times he asked me to communicate with Dalladeene and tell her what he told me.

Finally, we spoke about Christian belief and Christianity. Jonnie told me of his Christian belief, and then we prayed the Lord's Prayer together. In conclusion I asked him, "Jonnie, what is the main part of our belief?" He answered, "Jesus Christ." I asked him, "What do you believe about Jesus?" He replied, "I believe he died for my sins." I then asked him, "What do you mean when you say that Jesus died for your sins? What do you think that is? Can you tell me that?" Jonnie Cook thought about that for a while, then he said, "I guess I can. It means I won't be punished for what I have done wrong."

Then I took the young man's hand and said, "Yes, Jonnie, that is correct. With such faith we live and will one day die a blessed death." And then we left each other. He went to his wickiup, and I drove off into the night in my wagon with my oldest son who was with me and wanted to spend some time with me. My thoughts for a long time were on the answer that Jonnie Cook gave me. And all my thoughts ended in this prayer, "Lord, stay with him and bless him. Amen."[152]

Gustav Harders was only 53 when he died. He was survived by his wife Isabelle, five sons and two daughters. There were Irmgard, Hilda, Hans, Claus, Knute, Jens, and Holten, according to the 1910 U.S. Census. Gustav was interested in schools and education. It

[152] *The Apache Lutheran,* September 1994.

showed up in his work with the Apache mission and the schools there. He was the one who had begun the Lutheran High School in Milwaukee. His children went on to higher learning. Claus Harders (to be a charter member of Grace Congregation in Glendale) graduated from Globe High School in 1916 and was a student at the University of California. An older son, Hans, was also a senior at the University of California.[153]

Gustav Harders' reputation as a "missionary of missionaries" still stands to this day. He was an important gift of God to the Apache mission work. As one of his contemporaries said, "To meet Pastor Harders was to meet Christ. He had the exceptional knack of turning the most casual everyday conversation into religious channels. But he did it without embarrassing the other fellow. One did not feel buttonholed and 'preached to.' He preferred not to divulge his identity as a preacher. He talked as man to man, becoming, like Paul, all things to all men that he might gain some. Whether he was sitting on the steps of the Gila County court-house—coatless, ten-gallon hat, shirt open, smoking—talking with a group of Mexican laborers; whether he was sitting on the iron-pipe fence that used to surround the old Arizona Eastern depot, talking with the black workers who were waiting for the evening train to pull in so they might clean the coaches; whether he called on Judge Little or Judge Whitcher for legal advice or a chat on politics; whether he was squatting before the campfire in an Apache tepee and sharing a mess of indigestible frijoles with his hosts; whether he was conducting a formal service in his chapel; whether he was invited to share coffee and tamales with a Mexican family in the 'smoker'; whether he was accompanying a criminal on his way to the gallows—always he was bearing witness for the Christ he loved intensely and proclaimed with sober zeal."[154]

---

153 *The Daily Arizona Silver Belt*, April 14, 1917, p. 4 (courtesy Bullion Plaza Cultural Center and Museum, Miami, Arizona).

154 *The Apache Scout*, December 1939, pp. 84, 85.

CHAPTER ELEVEN

Wehausen, Nitz, and Sitz

We must through much tribulation enter
into the kingdom of God (Acts 14:22).

In 1969, in the early spring of the year, Dr. Martin Luther College in New Ulm, Minnesota, sent this writer to do his practice teaching in the little rural parish of Liberty, Wisconsin, out in the country just a short distance from Manitowoc on Lake Michigan. He stayed with a German widow lady named Esther Hummel. She lived in a rambling two-story farmhouse about half a mile from the grade school where this practice-teaching education was taking place. Every evening the writer studied in his classroom until ten o'clock or so, and then he switched off the light and stepped out into the dark and bracing air for the half-mile walk with the sparkling stars overhead and the crunching snow underfoot. He made his way in darkness all the way to the upstairs light switch in his bedroom in Esther Hummel's house down the county road. She was very frugal and made her way from room to room in her house carefully turning off the light in one room as she switched the light on in the room she entered.

Once when they were eating their supper—and Esther was a good cook—the conversation turned to home at East Fork Mission in Arizona. On this evening the writer mentioned Martin Wehausen's name. Martin was at that time in Phoenix, where he had an old church property in an area of town that had fallen into civil disrepute and disrepair in the sprawling growth of the big city. Pastor Wehausen's little church and parsonage served as a haven for Apache travelers and missionaries who had to be passing through that part of Phoenix and needed a place to sleep. Wehausen's hospitality went without the luxury of air conditioning or even a swamp cooler. But on this evening in Liberty, Wisconsin, when the name of Martin Wehausen was spoken, Esther Hummel's fork stopped in midair and she cried out, "Martin Wehausen was born in this very house!" The happy coincidence was true, and this would not be the last time that name would stir upon the writer's senses.

Name of Martin Wehausen on the porch wall of the East Fork Parsonage.
Photo Credit: The writer's collection

Twenty years later in 1989, the writer was remodeling the front porch of the same house he had grown up in, the one where the yellow Ford had parked that day and the family had gotten out. When he tore the dilapidated porch ceiling away, there was that same name, "MARTIN WEHAUSEN" written on the side paneling up underneath the ceiling on the porch wall of the house. And, sure enough, in the short memorial of his death in *The Apache Lutheran* of November, 1974, it says about him, "Martin John Anton Wehausen was born on March 27, 1893, in Town Liberty, Manitowoc County, Wisconsin." He was born the very year the Apache mission work started.

Martin Wehausen was one of the first missionaries sent to East Fork. He left behind a short diary of his years on the mission. It is written in the same careful handwriting as his signature by the porch door of the parsonage at East Fork. "Aaron and Florence Keyes were baptized. Their father, Jack, became a Christian and was also baptized in July of that year. They were the first, on the first of April 1921." And the handwriting continued, "We took over the government day school at East Fork, having purchased it for a sum of $4,000. The complete enrollment of that school stayed with us." At the end of 1922, the ledger read, "We can record 34 adult and 30 infant baptisms, 8 burials, 3 marriages, 46 communicants, and a record of Sunday attendance, shows an average attendance of 41, not including children under school age." So said Martin Wehausen's journal.

It was at this same time (1921) that the nursery at East Fork began. It was at first called an orphanage, and one of its first children was Arnold Platt. The green ledger record says that Arnold's father was George Platt, B-19, and that Arnold was born March 5, 1922. Pastor H. C. Nitz found Arnold Platt parentless on Good Friday, April 12, 1922. The Wehausens adopted Arnold, and he became their son, even when they moved away. His was a short life, however, and today you can go up behind East Fork Mission and look in the little cemetery where so many of the orphans were buried and see the name Arnold Wehausen and also his name Platt. If the founding of the nursery depended on adopting one of the orphans as your own son, then the Wehausens get the credit for being the movers in the establishment of the nursery. The Guenthers also claimed that it was they who started the nursery, putting the babies into renovated apple crates and tomato boxes that served as cribs. From this perspective of history, it is no longer possible to tell who was first and foremost in the formation of the nursery, but it doesn't matter. Both the Guenthers and the Wehausens worked to make it happen.

Edgar Guenther wrote about the nursery: "The only Indian orphanage in the Southwest is maintained at East Fork. It owes its existence to two factors: The one, the old Apache custom of killing one of twins because of some alleged indiscretion involved; and the other, the number of mothers dying at childbirth and others who because of tuberculosis or other illness are not able to care properly for their little ones. Since the orphanage was erected, the Indians gladly turned one of twins over to us instead of killing it. The necessity for such an institution was first emphasized to the mission superintendent by Mr. Davis and Agency physician Fred Loe, both men being truly interested in the welfare of the Indians. After some years the Synod was persuaded, and in 1921 the orphanage was called into being. A lean-to, with tomato boxes serving as cribs, was the nucleus that rapidly grew into a building housing some thirty to forty little Apache tots."

Guenther went on in his writing about his and Wehausen's work: "In our mission schools approximately 350 children are learning the one thing needful. Twice that number from government boarding schools are receiving religious instructions. The orphanage is filled to capacity with forty children. Practically all camps are visited with the gospel at regular intervals. Our entire mission force numbers twenty-seven, among whom are the following native workers: two native helpers, three male teachers, and two assistant matrons. A total of approximately two thousand Indians have been baptized since the founding of our mission."

It was to Edgar Guenther that Martin Wehausen wrote the following report:

East Fork—1922

July 5, 1922

Dear Brother Guenther,

With the beginning of the quarter just past we took over the East Fork Government Day School. Mr. Nitz came up from Globe on the 28th of March to help. On the days following we made the most necessary rearrangements, throwing two school kitchens into one, grading the children, etc. On the 3rd we were able to open school in good order with an enrollment of 75 children. Mr. Nitz took charge of the thirty-two 2nd and 3rd graders, and I took charge of the remaining number.

The day school offered a dining room about large enough to seat all the children. Lucille George, a Christian Apache girl, took charge of the work for the first month. Later when she left I had to oversee the work, which meant a constant disturbance in my school work. This will not dare to go on. Mrs. Wehausen is not able to look after the work in the school kitchen any longer. She is not at all well, and besides she is caring for an Apache orphan child.[155] The $100.00 per month that has been paid her for work in the school kitchen may be subtracted from our monthly checks by September and used as a part payment to hire someone in her place. Should the Board not decide by September to hire someone to work in the school kitchen then I shall do so and pay her whatever is right and send in the bill.

Sunday services were attended well during the past quarter, the average being about twenty-five adults per Sunday. I had nine baptisms, five burials, one marriage. My camp visits on East Fork were but few. East Fork is now so large with so much land under cultivation that it is absolutely necessary to assign a special man to take charge of the industrial work. Such a man could mean a great saving for us. Our boys and girls in school must put in one hour of industrial work per day. The government asks this of us. Under proper direction this work could be

---

155 This child was Arnold Platt.

spent where otherwise special help would have to be hired. If the land we have on East Fork would be worked well, it ought to make our school kitchen self-supporting. The Board must know that we are going into a big work in East Fork and that it must be done right to begin with. Let us not skimp. All eyes are turned on East Fork. Many people have made the claim that we cannot make it go. Should not the wonderful blessings of the Lord upon our work here encourage us all to do all we can?

If we bear in mind our plans for the boarding school and orphanage in East Fork in the near future, it is necessary that we encourage our able mission carpenter, Mr. Knoop, to stay with us. I would suggest a raise of $25.00 per month for him.

I wish to thank the worthy members of the Board for allowing me $25.00 per month for Thomas Wycliffe. He is a very faithful servant for the Mission. I am paying him $1.50 per day when he works, and in that way he can well manage to make the $25.00 per month.

Fraternally yours,

M. Wehausen.

The Wehausen and Guenther women could not get along with each other. The strife was even noticed by Arnold Sitz in his road diary of the missionaries' trip to the Grand Canyon. Alfred Uplegger and Henry Rosin were involved with that trip when the feminine discord was manifested. That would not be the last time when the women folk or the pastors themselves found each others' company tedious and chafing. This internal strife was also sometimes the cause of someone leaving the work. The Wehausens didn't stay all that long. Edgar Guenther as the superintendent of the work on the northern reservation spoke finally about *Inashood* Martin Wehausen shortly before he left the work, "He is now constantly facing the self-accusation of not doing enough work in the school room and of neglecting pastoral care of his communicants, not to mention the need of regularly bringing the gospel into the tepees."[156] The letter of resignation came on February 27, 1923. The reason for resigning? "As reasons for my leaving I gave that it would be impossible to work at East Fork under the present superintendent in charge of our Apache Mission. I however asked for a transfer within the Mission, if possible. Since this was not granted, I left East Fork on June 18, 1923, trusting that the Lord would find me worthy and assign to me a new

---

[156] E. Guenther, 1923

charge somewhere in his vineyard." That happened too, and by September 1923 he was pastor in Johnson, Minnesota.

H. C. Nitz started as a missionary in the summer of 1922. and he was a contemporary of Martin Wehausen in the work at East Fork. His name was Henry but he was known by many on the field as H. C. He had been called to Globe to teach, and it was in Globe he shingled his sleeping porch with tin cut from old coal oil cans. Edgar Guenther wrote about him: "A bachelor can dodge the leaky places in his sleeping compartments, but a woman can hardly be expected to make these lightning changes. His sleeping porch ought to be repaired." Edgar and H. C. worked closely together and knew each other's work well. Nitz worked primarily with the school at East Fork from the time there was nothing there to the time when there was an enrollment of twenty-eight in the grade school and sixty-six in the boarding school. The "girls' building," as the girls' dormitory was called, was also made during his tenure. In the minutes of the Committee in Milwaukee, Wisconsin, dated October 1, 1925, we read, "The Committee again discussed plans of a new Boarding School. More definite steps are to be taken at the next meeting. Relative to the Boarding School the Committee expressed its surprise about Nitz's silence as to where his thirty-six boarding school pupils came from and where and how they are housed."

H. C. loved the work and was engaged and enterprising. He also found it easier to ask forgiveness than to ask permission. He made a trip to St. Louis and was reprimanded for not asking permission first from the Executive Committee, and Committee reports said in 1926 that contrary to the Committee's expressed wish that only Indian hymnals be used, Nitz ordered one-hundred hymnals from Concordia Publishing House. In spite of some innocent insubordination he remained the consummate missionary. Listen to the report he gave to the Committee in 1922:

> Regardless of whether the boarding school remains at East Fork, this station is in dire need of farm implements. The visiting committee of last fall was displeased with the condition of the school garden and farm. And they had reasons to be dissatisfied. But the fault did not lie with the missionary. He did what he could. But he was alone during the summer. At planting time teaching took up most of his time; and enforced neglect of camp work was ever accusing him. In addition to that, he was handicapped by an utter lack of implements.
>
> A farm even of this size cannot be worked with a few rakes and hoes, which is in reality all the equipment there

is to this day. Other implements had to be borrowed from the government after the government employees had finished their own farm work.

We hoped that with the purchase of East Fork Government Day School we should get what few farm implements were on the place. But they were not included in the purchase. We used them for a time, but the agent has now notified me to turn all implements over to the government.

Spring will soon be upon us, and we have not even a plow, nor even a wagon with which to haul the manure out of the barnyards. We even have no horses. Wehausen has used his horses to date, but since he has a car, he does not care to feed a couple of horses. He is now making arrangements to sell his horses. If this station had a team of horses, we should not only use them for farm work, but the boys could get supplies for the day school, orphanage, and boarding school from Whiteriver. Under present conditions Wehausen and I use our cars and spend our time and money hauling, in the aggregate, tons of freight for the mission. A congregation in Wisconsin has notified Wehausen that they will buy a wagon for East Fork. A good team of work horses is offered me for the nominal sum of $125.00. May I be authorized to buy the team? I believe I can even get them on liberal time payments.

In this connection I wish to remark that when we had to cut our last crop of alfalfa in the fall we did not have a mower. The machine we therefore had to borrow from the government was hopelessly out of commission. In sheer desperation I bought a mower from the government, the agent letting me have it at cost price plus the freight. I paid down $25.00 out of *Mittagstisch* (school lunch). A balance of $61.00 is still due. Will you, please, authorize requisition for this balance?

We need, for our spring work already, the following implements: hay-rake, harrow, eight-inch plow, ten-inch plow, scraper, harrow-tooth cultivator, shovel cultivator, shovel plow, grindstone. According to prices in a mail order catalog, these implements would cost about $100.00 If we do not get these tools, the greater part of our land will have to lie idle next summer.[157]

H. C. was given orders in 1926 to get an electrician and install the light plant at East Fork, and it happened. The generator was turned on at night so there would be electricity and light for the personnel

---

[157] January 1994, *The Apache Lutheran*

and for the children in the nursery. The generator itself was bolted to a block of concrete in the "generator shed" behind the parsonage which was across from the church at East Fork. When the boys from the yellow Ford walked around there that first time in 1958 there was the concrete block. The worn-out generator had long since disappeared, but the spot where it was bolted to the concrete was where the boys would later butcher their spring pigs, fed on scraps from the school kitchen.

H. C. Nitz was a missionary. He lived and breathed mission work as his remarks show, written at the occasion of the 34th anniversary of the Apache Mission:

> October is the birthday month of the Apache Mission. October 9, 1893, the first missionaries came to the Apaches. They were Pastors Plocher and Adascheck. They opened a station at the place now known as Peridot Mission. That was thirty-four years ago. Since then the story of Jesus has been told to every Apache on the two reservations. Hundreds of children have attended the mission schools. At least a thousand Apaches have been baptized. Many sick have received comfort for soul and body. An orphanage and boarding school have been built.
>
> Thirty-four years ago the gospel light was lit in Apacheland. For thirty-four years the devil has tried many of his tricks to put it out. But every year the gospel light burns brighter and brighter. More missionaries, teachers, matrons and nurses, schools and chapels.
>
> Much has been done to take away the darkness of heathenish superstition. But when one sees how strong the powers of darkness still are in Apacheland—drunkenness, gambling, adultery, murder, divorces, laziness, disrespect of law and order—when one sees all this, one is tempted to say what God once said of his people Israel, "They ceased not from their doings, nor from their stubborn way" (Judges 2:19).
>
> But we should not become discouraged. That would be sinful. And there is no need for discouragement. We are sent to sow. The seed is good; it is the gospel of Jesus. It will grow by God's grace and power.[158]

Nitz, with all of the missionaries, had to speak out against the native Apache religion. It still has to happen today. Christianity and

---

[158] Pastor H. C. Nitz, October 1927, *The Apache Scout*

the Old Way are not and cannot be in a symbiotic relationship. They remain mutually exclusive. In December of 1926 Nitz felt compelled to say to the readers of *The Apache Scout*, "If you want to believe the medicine men, do so. If you want to be a Christian, drop the old superstitions. You cannot keep both. When you buy a new pair of shoes you do not put on only one new one and keep one old one. How would that look?"

It was in this same year at Christmas time that Nitz managed to get all the salary checks withheld from mission people until he classified and added the various items under Committee code: B – Boarding School; O – Orphanage; S. – School; F. – farm, T. – truck; W. – wood; Frt. – freight. The kerfuffle that ensued with the check withholding at Christmas time would have been tedious to an over-worked man like Nitz who was trying to keep everyone happy. That this was December and that everyone would have no paycheck because of the technicality and the transgression was not a happy move on the part of the administration, but life went on. In February of 1927 Nitz mentioned that it had been very cold at East Fork, eight degrees below zero. All the water pipes had frozen, and the boys had to go to the river to fetch water.

In January of 1929 Nitz left for Rockford, Minnesota, at the advice of several physicians that a change of altitude was imperative for his wife. As mentioned before there were insufferable tensions between the pastors' wives, and this no doubt also contributed to the Nitzs leaving when they did. H. C.'s wife, Alma, was an integral part of his work and his life. She is the one who translated Gustav Hard-er's books from German and wrote her translation on the back of used paper. Her original translated manuscript of Harders' *Yaalahn* on well-used paper is extant in the writer's library.

God gave Alma Nitz not only a long and blessed life; he also gave her a warm heart for Apache people and the work there. She stayed in contact with the work long after she and H. C. had left it. She sent pictures of the early work to *The Apache Lutheran* staff. One of the pictures was the confirmation class and Pastor Nitz standing under the windows of the church at East Fork.[159] Pastor Frederick Nitz, one of Alma and H. C.'s sons[160] who served many years as head of the Executive Committee for the Apache work, wrote in a note with the information he sent regarding his mother's death: "As far as I can tell,

---

[159] The windows and the siding on the church have since been replaced by a generous gift from Naomi and Paul Doehling of Arlington, Minnesota. But the church building itself standing there today at East Fork is the same.

[160] Three of Alma's sons entered the ministry: Marcus, Frederick and Paul.

my mother was the last of the 'old timers' in Apacheland. The older Upleggers, Rosins, Guenthers, and Behns have all passed out of the picture." In the further biography of Alma's life, we read about H. C. what was already known from mission board reports, "He had also been called back to Apacheland to help out at Peridot and Cibecue in 1916 and 1917. In the fall of 1922 Pastor Nitz was called permanently as principal and missionary at East Fork. He worked with Pastor Martin Wehausen at East Fork. Pastor Wehausen was the "camp" missionary, and Pastor Nitz was missionary on the compound."

The Lord blessed Alma Nitz in many ways. He gave her a good mind and a good memory right up to the end. He gave her good health and a strong constitution, and she lived independently in Watertown, Wisconsin. She had a little shopping cart that she used on her trips to the market in Watertown after H. C. was gone. She kept wearing out the wheels on the cart, and her sons would replace them, thinking with each new set of wheels, "Surely, these will be the last wheels this little cart will need."[161]

It was at this time of H. C. Nitz that Arnold Sitz began his ministry in Arizona by serving on the reservations as a missionary. "Sitz was named after his grandfather, Erdmann Pankow (1818-1907), longtime pastor in Lebanon, Wisconsin, and well-known in his own right. Sitz never liked that first name Erdmann and so went by E. Arnold. His father August Sitz was born in Germany, and when he came to America, he settled in the Ridgeville, Wisconsin, area before moving to New York Mills, Minnesota, where he first owned a hardware store and later became president of a bank. August is reported to have owned the first Cadillac in town, purchased in 1912. In his diary his son Arnold often mentions going to Detroit Lakes to have the car serviced.

"In 1917 E. Arnold Sitz graduated from Wisconsin Lutheran Seminary, then located in Wauwatosa, Wisconsin. He was assigned to Bethlehem Lutheran Church, Oshkosh, Wisconsin, a congregation which had broken off from the Ohio Synod and which shortly after assumed the name Martin Luther. His seminary classmates also received calls: William Beitz was assigned to Grace, Tucson, in Arizona, and Henry Rosin was assigned to the Apache mission, where he served for many years at Peridot."[162] On the last day of 1919, Sitz wrote in his diary: "This is the last day of the most eventful year of my life. It has made a man of me. In one short year I have learned

---

[161] E. Hartzell, *The Apache Lutheran*, December 1992.

[162] "Sitz Diary: 1919 Trip to the Grand Canyon," Pastor Victor H. Prange (translator), pp. 24 and 25. (From The WELS Historical Institute, Professor John M. Brenner)

to love the West, to love Arizona, so that I shall, God willing, make it my home until death takes me to a fairer place." And it did happen that way. Arizona did remain home for E. Arnold Sitz.

In 1960 he wrote about his experience in the Apache mission work: "When the Apache Mission in Globe (New Jerusalem) was reopened in the fall of 1919, it was my privilege to serve the scattered Apaches in Globe, Miami, Copper Hills, Wheatfields, Roosevelt, and also in Payson, Clarkdale, Gisela, Jerome and other places in the Tonto Basin. Since I had no car, I had to restrict my work to the Globe-Miami district. Mostly on foot, I visited the so-called Railroad Camps: Copper Hill, Claypool, Upper Miami, and Wheatfields. Slowly the faithful baptized Apaches in this area began to come to church in Globe. Among the fairly regular attendants were Clark Case, Rhoda Goody, Ruth Hosay, Ruth Gitzow, Nona Kenton, Amelia Kinney, Rhoda Case, Dan Kinney, William Mattice, Lizette and Mary Early and their sister Susan Bird, Nelson Cooper, and Maggie Bryant." Few ministers would be able to recall names like that after forty years have gone by, but E. Arnold Sitz did.

His ministry in Globe, Arizona, did not last long because in March 1920 he was asked to go to Whiteriver to help Ed Guenther, who was sick. Later he served as a missionary at Carrizo Canyon, a site which US 60 now passes. In 1920 he set up his tent under a spreading cottonwood near the junction of Corduroy and Carrizo Creeks to look after the people in the Carrizo area. After less than two years he was called away to help out elsewhere on the field, leaving the missionary of lower Cibecue to look after his ministry in Carrizo Canyon as best he could. In 1923 he was called to Grace, Tucson, to serve as teacher in the school and assistant pastor to William Beitz. The following year Beitz took a call to Rice Lake, Wisconsin, and Sitz became full-time pastor at Grace in Tucson until he retired in 1972 at age 79."

During many of those years he served as the district president of the Arizona-California District. He also was the bishop of many vicars who came to Grace for their one-year vicar experience under his tutelage. He was known to refer to his charges as "birds." "You birds," he liked to say when addressing his past charges, and some of them went on to positions of respect in the church and used the very same nomenclature when they referred to their vicars and fellow workers.[163]

On May 2, 1919, he wrote a long entry in his diary about how it was that he became a missionary on the Fort Apache Reservation.

---

[163] Pastor Vilas Glaeske in the South Central District was one of these former vicars who went on to be a supervising pastor; he knew about the birds too.

The occasion for his diary was a road trip of the missionaries and other interested parties to see the Grand Canyon. He also said that by joining up with the sight-seeing missionaries he would probably have to give up his job on the Southern Pacific railroad. He mentioned that railway workers' pay was good, from $180-$200 a month. He was aware that as a missionary on the reservation he would not get that much, but he thought to himself, "If that should be the case (that I lose my railroad job), I think I'll let my job go and trust the Lord to provide for another. He needs men in his fields right here in Arizona."[164] When he got to East Fork to hook up with the traveling group, news of his future awaited him. "Another item of personal interest is that while at Fort Apache and East Fork he talked with Wehausen about a letter H. C. Nitz had just received, in which he had been called to Globe-Miami as Indian missionary, and that Sitz himself had been called to the same towns as a white missionary. "I was glad of the news," he penned in his diary, "as I was at sea as to my future course and means of securing a livelihood since leaving the Southern Pacific."[165]

The sight-seeing missionaries of Sitz's traveling journal were interesting traveling partners. They were Ed Guenther, his wife Minnie (Knoop), and their four children: Wynonah, Edgar, Roland and Winifred. Immanuel Frey, pastor at Zion, Phoenix, was there with his wife and their three sons: Conrad, Immanuel (Dick), and Paul. Martin (Jim) Wehausen and his wife Ella, from the East Fork Mission station, were along for the ride and the sights. Henry Rosin (Raisins by nickname) was there with his mother, and he was casting sidelong glances at his sweetheart Johanna Uplegger, Alfred Uplegger's sister. Alfred was there, still in a single state too, and he was the resident mechanic. No sooner had Sitz gotten to San Carlos than car repair was necessary. Alfred rolled up his shirtsleeves and got to work: the engine was cleaned, the carburetor was cleaned, the spark plugs were replaced, and a new clutch and brake bands were put in. The work as mechanics took the major part of the day, and the diarist said in amazement, "I was surprised to see Al's knowledge and handiness with tools, and in such company I myself had to show some sort of mechanical skill. I believe myself almost capable of repairing Fords now."[166]

Sitz's diary reminiscences are fascinating and provide a clear window to see the mission work and the missionaries. He describes

---

[164] *Op. cit.* p. 26

[165] *Op. cit.* p. 33

[166] *Op. cit.* p. 27

the journey travelers could make today if they wanted to. "The trip from Rice[167]: 18 miles to Cassadore Springs. Beautiful place. Big cottonwoods. Up the Nantanes Plateau for Fort Apache. Lunched at the Sawmill, made famous by its being a place prominently mentioned in Harder's novel *Yaalahn*. 6,000 feet in elevation. Uphill until Black River Canyon is seen and then down, down into the canyon to cross at Black River Crossing. The crossing is a high bridge placed in a narrow and steep part of the canyon. You climb up and out of the Black River Canyon only to drop down once again into White River Canyon. Had to cross 12 times in the streambed of the White River, which had been wasted by a wild summer storm shortly before. The afternoon's driving was the severest I had thus far done in my life. A puncture delayed us a few minutes. What a glorious sight it was to make a turn in the road to see far away ahead of us across a great flat—Fort Apache. A neat looking group of white buildings nestled down in the valley of the White River. It makes the impression on one of being a most pleasant place to be out in the wilderness. Going through the post we headed for East Fork, four miles further on, where our friends Guenther and Wehausen were located. We arrived there just shortly before nightfall."[168]

From Sitz's diary we observe some of the social interaction of not only this mission field but all mission fields. Missionaries are not necessarily birds of a feather, nor are their wives in their interaction with the other wives on the field. Two basic philosophies seem to emerge to deal with this social issue: **1)** Realize that you are different from the other missionaries and be together when you have to be for the good of the work, but otherwise stay apart and develop your own relationships and interests; **2)** Know that you are brothers and sisters with the other workers and that you had better get along and like everyone and share socially in everything. In Sitz's diary you see vestiges of both trains of thought. He shared with his diary: "After dinner some went sightseeing to the cliffs, while the rest of us overhauled the cars. Jim's (Wehausen) wife is Ella Koske, and I was rather glad to see her again. However, my joy was somewhat saddened to learn that she and Mrs. Guenther do not live on the best of terms. The trip was to bear this out considerably. This very evening Ed Guenther came to where Bill and I lay under the stars of Arizona for the night and unburdened his heart about the matter. The trip and subsequent happenings show me that both are not a little to blame for the state of affairs: Jim's and Ed's wives."[169]

---

[167] Present day San Carlos.

[168] *Op. cit.* p. 28

[169] *Op. cit.* p. 29

183

Then the diary takes us in the antique cavalcade up by present day Hondah (then Cooley's Ranch), on to Pinetop, Lakeside and Showlow. Snowflake was all Mormon and made a good impression with its substantial brick houses. As a railroad man himself, Sitz noticed the new Apache lumber railroad that came to Cooleys from Holbrook. The group went by Meteor Crater and then Canyon Diablo and finally Canyon Padre. "Walnut Canyon was simply great!" the diary gushed. Traveling conditions were good: "Good roads, grand forest, a winding little canyon which the road follows, the snow-capped San Francisco peaks almost continually in sight and close at hand."[170] And finally, Flagstaff. "Flagstaff is a town I should like to make my home. It is snugly tucked away in the deep pine forest and to the north and east are the San Francisicos. All the beauty of the eastern pine forests is here with the grandeur of the mountains added."[171] Visitors today often come away with the same opinion, especially if the visitors come from the Midwest like Sitz did. Because of the elevation and the resulting coolness at all seasons of the year, some warm-blooded visitors have quipped about Flagstaff: "Flagstaff has two seasons: summer and winter. If summer happens on a weekend, we go fishing."

Finally, the destination of the trip came. The Grand Canyon is breathtaking and unexpected somehow, even to those who have seen pictures of it and read about it. There is nothing else like it on the whole planet. This appreciation is heard in the diary: "What a stupendous sight! What an awe-inspiring wonder of God's creation! We viewed one of the hundreds of side canyons first, catching but a glimpse of the real canyon a few minutes later when we drove down to Inspiration Point. Now what an awe-inspiring scene it is! To the right and far away a glimpse of the rushing Colorado far down. Farther around to the right, was the side canyon we had first seen with its rock sides and slides in myriad colors, mostly of reddish hue. Thirteen miles across to the northern rim, seemed but a mile. A lazy purple haze was lying in the great chasm, filling it seemingly to the brim with its richness." And a little farther down the road the travelers observed: "A fine view is had from the brink at El Tovar. About three-thousand feet down a person can see where Bright Angel trail leads down and down and then goes across the plateau along a ravine. The rest camps built where the ravine widens into a patch of green look like specks. The green which looks like a lawn is a grove of trees in fact. I did not tire of looking down on this spot of emerald from whatever place I could see

[170] *Op. cit.* p. 30

[171] *Op.* cit. p. 30

it. The changes of color every few minutes as the sun proceeded with his preparation for slumber were astonishing and in truth so rapid and detailed it was impossible to follow them. Finally, night crept up from the depths of the canyon and slowly filled the canyon with his dark mantle covering one point after the other until finally all but the boldest points were hidden from our sight. And then we also went to our rest like the sun, praising God for having shown us his might and glory in this bit of his creation."[172]

The travelers were getting tired—with the traveling and with each other. After the Grand Canyon there were evenings when they all had a song fest, and then there was an evening where after the tedium of their travel and themselves they almost had a slug fest. It was time to go back home. They went through Williams and Ash Fork and then Prescott, described by the diary as a "beautiful city of about 10,000. It is one of the oldest towns in the state." They had also passed prosperous cattle ranches in the great Chino Valley. Al Sieber, the famed leader of the government trackers and scouts mentioned these same ranches in his memoirs. It was in this same Chino Valley that marauding Apaches had made depredations as they struck and then went back up into the rim country and Tonto Basin. Night came and the diary said, "We camped last night a few miles out of Prescott. Again the cloud of gloomy, restless, ill-humor descended on the camp. Alfred Uplegger lost his equilibrium because he had had to make the bed for Bill's and Jim's wives all during the trip, and it was getting to be too much. Although his outbreak was short-lived and sudden, the others seemed to have the same smoldering kind of ill-humor."[173]

The last entry in Sitz's traveling diary ended: "Early this morning we set out for Phoenix on our last lap. We came through Humboldt and Mayer and via the Black Canyon Road to the Salt River Valley, taking lunch and rest on the banks of Agua Fria. From here on the car led the way. I drove hard, leaving the others far behind. Coming down from the cool northern plateau and mountains, the desert heat from Agua Fria into the valley was almost intolerable. We were glad when we finally reached the Salt River Valley, where the irrigation waters noticeably cooled the hot air."

That was the end of the trip but it was not the end of the Sitz story. He worked on the reservations with his classmate Henry Rosin and wrote about him, "God made Pastor Rosin a natural-born teacher. He had as one of his principles, 'A teacher must always be on his feet while teaching.' He proved so successful as a teacher that

[172] Op. cit. pages 32 and 33

[173] Op. cit. p. 33

one spring just before school closed the Apache children came to him and said, 'Mr. Rosin, will you please keep school all summer?' I recall visiting him on a hot day in August. I had ridden all day from six o'clock in the morning until four in the afternoon from Ash Flat. I had taken no water along. When we reached the San Carlos River, it was in dirty flood. My pony plunged his head in to drink. But Pastor's house was just a few hundred yards away, so I passed up the muddy flood waters. When I reached his house, he came out and I asked for water. He said, 'Don't drink. I'll give you some water.' He got a cup and a teaspoon. He gave me one teaspoonful of water, then made me wait. He added another teaspoonful. Later he gave me half a cupful. Finally, he let me drink two cupfuls. Then he said, 'Come along. I have to drive to Rice (which is now San Carlos).' He took a small watermelon along that was just ripe and sweet. I finished it all the way and it still remains the best I ever tasted."[174]

He had to leave his missionary camp on the Carrizo River because of the mother church's lack of money in Wisconsin, and he went to Tucson to serve as an assistant pastor there. He stayed for a long time, but he didn't forget his people and the work on the reservations. He later wrote back home, "Four years ago I left my missionary camp at Black Rock in Carrizo Canyon. For a few years, you remember, the writer was a missionary there. Before we had a mission on Carrizo I was at Whiteriver with Mr. Guenther. So it is that almost all the Apaches on the Fort Apache Reservation are my friends. I learned to know you who live on East Fork with my friend Jack Keyes. Those who live on North Fork with Alchesay were also friends. Many times we rode to Turkey Creek and Corn Creek to tell the Indians there about Jesus. We also visited with the Indians below the Post, where Tom Friday lived. Then we went to Bear Springs. Often I camped on Cedar Creek with R-14, and R-25 was also a good friend. Then we used to go up past *Nahsinichu* to visit our friends on East, Middle, and West Cedar Creeks. We went way out past I-19's camp to the camp of the man who always wears a Mexican straw hat. On Carrizo Creek my Apache friends were visited very often. I think many times of M-32. I wonder if A-4 still camps at *Tsae-chi*? And do his goats still climb on the high rocks? I met an old white man government scout not long ago named Gildea. He used to be at Fort Bowie and Camp Apache (Fort Apache). He remembered where Bill Gatewood lives in Limestone Canyon. He saw that pretty place fifty years ago and could not forget it. I suppose that Carrizo Mike and

---

174 E. Arnold Sitz, *The Apache Lutheran*, August 1967, p. 3 (from the edition: "Golden Anniversary in the Ministry, August 1917 to August 1967").

my old friend Vivan still live in the old place? And do some of the Apaches still live at *Toon-dae-stoosae*? Sometimes my pack horse was driven over the trail to Cibecue. That time *Hasteen* Endfield was the missionary's friend. William Cooley's father was also a friend. From there we sometimes went to Oak Creek and camped overnight. Arthur Neklineeta had his camp there and Rivers Lavender's brother and many others.

"Let me write you a few words more. I am *Inashood* to white men now in Tucson. Some of you have been here. Tucson is a big town in the desert. It is many times as big as Whiteriver and Rice and San Carlos put together. It is four times as large as '*Besh-be-gowah*.'[175] Many white men, many Mexicans, many black men, many Chinamen, and many Indians live here. The Indians are Papagoes and Yaquis. There is also an Indian school. Because there are so many people there are many chapels or churches, too.

"There is one chapel down here I want to write to you about. When I was up on the Reservation, I heard many Apaches talk about it. This church is called San Xavier Church. It is a very old one. It was built more than 200 years ago. I have been there several times, but I do not pray there. They pray to Mary and the saints there. I pray to Jesus and to God the Father. The Bible tells us to pray only to them. Somebody told you, my friends, that this church here near Tucson is the best place to be baptized because it is so old. They say it is the first church to be built here. What did your fathers think about it? They heard long ago that white men were building this church among the Papago Indians. One day they came down on the warpath and burned it up! They did not like it. But the priests built it again. Once more your fathers came down and burned that chapel. Two times they set fire to it. Two times many people were killed there. Do you believe that that is the best place to be baptized?

"Do you not believe in Jesus in your camp, in your cornfield, in your saddle, wherever you are? Is not God everywhere so you can believe in him and pray to him everywhere? Can you not pray to him on your own farm, on the mountain, on the Big Flat, in the canyon? Do you have to ride to Tucson every time you want to pray?" (And here Missionary Sitz launched into his strong words to his people about strong drink, words included with other missionaries' words under that topic in this book.) And Pastor Sitz concluded his epistle to his friends on the reservation, "I have written you a long letter. I wish God to make you all well and happy. Your friend, Arnold Sitz."[176]

---

[175] Literally "The metal his home." This was the name given to Globe.

[176] *The Apache Scout*, November 1927.

CHAPTER TWELVE

Edgar Guenther

It takes your enemy and your friend, working together,
to hurt you to the heart: the one to slander you and the
other to get the news to you (MARK TWAIN).

Hanging on the basement classroom wall in the library building at Wisconsin Lutheran Seminary in Mequon, Wisconsin, is the 1911 class picture of Edgar Guenther and his classmates.

It would not be possible to know the work among the Apaches and not know Edgar Guenther. He was *Inashood*. His life and work defined the name. Some of his people called him *Inashood Ndasan*. Some called him *Bechadndazin*.[177] One of those closest to him (perhaps) was H. C. Nitz. If you look at the graduation pictures of both men, you will find that Guenther graduated in 1911 and H. C. Nitz in 1919. They were contemporaries and fellow workers in the mission work in Arizona.

It was H. C. Nitz who wrote about Guenther in retrospect:

> E. E. G., as he is known to so many, was the only child of a South Dakota wheat farmer. After his confirmation in his home church near Watertown, South Dakota, he enrolled at Dr. Martin Luther College, New Ulm, Minnesota, and was a member of the first "Tertia" class. He transferred to Northwestern College and graduated in 1908. In the midst of his senior year at the Seminary he answered an urgent call to the Apache Mission. The trip to East Fork was their (Minnie née Knoop and Edgar's) honeymoon. It consisted mostly of distressing delays and circuitous detours. At long last they arrived at East Fork on March 11, 1911. The Guenthers were not pioneers in the strictest sense. Mayerhoff, Haase, and Schoenberg had preceded them on the Fort Apache Reservation. There was a parsonage and a chapel at East Fork when the Guenthers arrived. However, despite faithful

---

[177] The epithet seems to mean that his legs are long—or his ears.

effort, Guenther's predecessors had made but a slight dent on the tribe.

The candidate went to work with the holy enthusiasm of a disciple whose heart is on fire with love for Christ. Inexperience (on the part of the missionary and board), ignorance of the native language, racial prejudice (the Apaches were still technically prisoners of war), loneliness, isolation, homesickness, transportation difficulties, superstition, poverty, vice, a lack of funds—these were some of Guenther's trials. In time, some of these difficulties became less serious, others became worse, and new ones arose.

A full-length biography of E. E. G. should someday be written. But his biographer will have a jolly time gathering pertinent material. Some men oblige their biographer by saving every scrap they have written or received, by keeping a complete diary, by saving every sermon they have preached. Not so our hero. From the literary angle, talented writer though he is, he was anything but methodical.

But, like Paul the Apostle, his biography is largely written in the hearts of hundreds—yea, thousands—of Apaches. But not only Apaches. In the course of half a century, he has left his influence on scores of government officials, military personnel, traders, Mormon freighters, cowboys, prospectors. He had the enviable gift of becoming all things to all men to gain at least some. And what a colorful parade of guests—among them some of international fame—were entertained by the Guenthers, especially since 1922, when they moved into Whiteriver.

Pious parents, a salty Low-German 'mother-wit,' dogged patience, sanctified optimism, a healthy and vivid imagination, but above all a deep sympathy with people (especially with those in trouble), combined with a generosity that at times was culpable, not to forget his inimitable gift of down-to-earth preaching—those are some of the elements that, in the gracious economy of the Lord of missions, made the Guenthers the consecrated and colorful pair they are and will remain in the memory of those whose privilege it has been to be in some way associated with them.

Edgar Guenther was a good writer. In a way he did have a diary, and in this we would disagree with Nitz, who said he didn't leave organized writing behind. It is through his writing about all sorts of things pertinent to life on the reservation and his work that we really get to know him and get to know the challenges of the work.

He was editor of *The Apache Scout* and wrote many of the articles for that monthly publication. *The Apache Scout* told of the work of the Inashood and his people. The magazine later became known as *The Apache Lutheran*, and the missionaries took editorial turns trying to keep it going. No one had the gifts in this regard that Guenther had. Many tried after Guenther laid his pen down, but the little publication really wasn't ever the same. If one of the resident pastors managed to somehow become the editor of *The Apache Lutheran* (foisted upon him by some sleight-of-hand trick at the end of one of the worker conferences), they were constantly trying to solicit articles from fellow missionaries about their experiences. The Guenthers later lamented the name change of the little magazine from *The Apache Scout* to *The Apache Lutheran*. Apparently the impetus for the name change came at the time when the Boy Scouts were the concern, and someone thought *The Apache Scout* was too close to the Boy Scouts, so they changed the name.

Once the missionaries did manage to build or find a parsonage, it was often woefully inadequate. In 1919 Missionary Guenther moved to Whiteriver. He described the accommodations:

> The only house we could find was a small hut in which an Indian had lived for four years. After a lavish application of formaldehyde and other insect-killing means we dared to occupy the house. Mr. Knoop, in a hurry, glued (!) a little porch to the house which serves us as a bedroom. Kitchen and living room are tiny but the cracks in the roof supply the necessary fresh air[178]

The account of the early work that Guenther gave continued. He spoke of circumstances on the field that were typical and to be dealt with: "In addition, the house backed up to a river and was in jeopardy every time the river rose." Meanwhile Pastor Henry Rosin's parsonage in Peridot needed reconstructing, while Dr. Francis Uplegger in Rice had to cook his meals outside since he did not own a stove. Finally, in the hot desert of Bylas, Missionary Gustav Schlegel lived in a garage room. Because of the stifling heat inside the "house," his pregnant wife could not stay with him and had to borrow money to travel to a cooler location, where she spent several months. "At least Schlegel was married. The mission board had a history of sending single pastors onto the reservations, and this often led to problems, since few of the seminary graduates were confirmed bachelors. Living among the Apaches, the young missionaries had little opportunity to

---

[178] Quoted material is supplied by Dr. William Kessell and was identified as: E. Guenther 1922a.

meet, court and marry women of their choosing. After a few years of service among the Apaches, single missionaries were prime candidates for calls. Their turnover rate was high. Meanwhile, bachelor pastors tried to cope with culture shock and loneliness at the same time." Employing a somewhat ethereal description, Superintendent Guenther (who was married) comments on his visit to the single missionaries on the San Carlos Reservation. First, Guenther visited the two bachelor missionaries in Globe. As bedtime approached he overheard their conversation.

"Then their thoughts turn in common to the morrow, to the Chinaman who brings vegetables, to the Syrian who takes orders for groceries, to the 'Liberty' butcher whose meat they cannot afford to buy, to their last month's salary already beyond recall. At this juncture the conversation lags, follows a mutual sigh, and all is quiet at the Mission. The next morning we take the train for San Carlos. He (the local pastor) talks enthusiastically of the large mission field at his very door, of his trips to the friendly Indians at Bylas, of the services in his chapel, but—and then he sighs. Did we not hear that very sigh as a duet just the night before? On leaving we look inquiringly about. Apparently here is another who has not yet grasped the full significance of Genesis 2:18 (*"The LORD God said, 'It is not good for the man to be alone. I will make a helper suitable for him.' "*). We hasten away to Peridot only to meet a fourth of the same classification!"[179]

This same Edgar Guenther said about his above-mentioned biographer H. C. Nitz with reference to the work at East Fork, "H. C. Nitz was called to East Fork as the first principal of the boarding school and began his labors there under the most primitive conditions. The first boys were housed in an ennobled chicken coop, while the girls found shelter in hastily constructed barracks. In the course of time these made way for modern dormitories." Right there with "ennobled chicken coop" you get an idea of Guenther's colorful writing and Nitz's idea of "a salty Low German 'mother-wit.' "

So it was that in 1911 Candidate E. Edgar Guenther replaced Missionary Schoenberg. Indian Agent Davis, a sincere friend of the mission at East Fork, disapproved of two schools being in such close proximity to each other. He made the missionary an offer of the entire government plant including forty acres of irrigated land and pasture land for a nominal sum, which was readily accepted. H. C. Nitz referred to this new school in his report mentioned ear-

---

[179] Quoted material is supplied by Dr. William Kessell and was identified as: E. Guenther 1920d:72. Other references were identified from 1920a – 1922a. Dr. Kessell provided these quotes in several articles he wrote for *The Apache Lutheran* over a span of a number of months in 1995 and 1996.

lier. Since that time the school drew an average yearly enrollment of ninety pupils from the camps of the people up and down the river. In addition, the mission station at East Fork embraced a camp district of some five hundred souls, with an additional seventy-five living at Turkey Creek, twelve miles up Seven Mile Canyon near the present Chino Springs.[180]

Dr. William Kessel wrote of his grandfather Edgar Guenther's life: "During the winter of 1918 and 1919, a flu epidemic raged worldwide. About 20 million people died, including more than 500,000 Americans. The flu claimed more than 200 Apaches living on the San Carlos Reservation. At the same time reports came in from the northern Apaches. The lowest number of dead from the places that reported was ten. The next winter the flu returned and more died."

Pastor Meyerhoff mentioned it happening during his stay too: when the epidemic hit, the people scattered to the mountains, leaving their places deserted in the river valleys. During the first outbreak of the flu epidemic, Superintendent Charles Davis closed the day schools. He also issued horses to Rev. Edgar Guenther and Dr. Fred Loe. Guenther, knowing that he would soon come in contact with the disease and not wanting to infect his family or those living near him in East Fork, left home and took up residence with Dr. Loe in Whiteriver. Rev. Guenther's autobiography describes their work together:

> Snow had fallen on unfrozen ground, with the result that road and trail conditions were so bad that it was only humane to let our mounts rest on alternate days. The good Doctor's saddle bags were filled with medicines, while my contribution was a roll of building paper tied behind me to the saddle. At each camp we found, the procedure was the same: first insulate the pallet of the sick against the dampness of the ground with several layers of my building paper; and the doctor followed with advice and medicine. Then with an atmosphere of gratitude prevailing there would be willing ears to listen to the Gospel of him who wished to 'forgive all iniquities of our friends, heal all their diseases, redeem their lives from destruction and crown them with loving kindness and tender mercies.'
>
> The Indians were scattered so widely in all directions that hardly anyone knew where his neighbors had gone. Part of every day was spent in looking for families we had not yet found. Dr. Loe is a very conscientious man, and we

---

180 This information came from an article written by Edgar Guenther for *The Concordia Historical Institute Quarterly*. It was quoted in the June 1991 *The Apache Lutheran*.

rarely got started on the cold ride homeward before sunset. I remember one evening in particular. We were within half a mile of Whiteriver when we met a man trudging wearily homeward. We asked him if he knew of someone we might have missed, and he mentioned a family hiding out near Bear Springs. Without another word the doctor swung his horse to the right for the two-mile climb up the mountain and down again to the spring. When we finally left the camp, it was so dark that we let the horses find their way home by instinct.

Arthur Guenther described his father's regimen when he visited the camps in the mountains. He cut a piece of tar paper for each bed, adequate to keep the blankets off the ground and dry. And Edgar himself reminisced, "Having no medicine of any kind I trapped skunks, rendered the fat and mixed it with turpentine and coal oil. To give the concoction a pleasant odor, my wife added some of her precious perfume. For chest pads, our long winter underwear was dedicated to the cause."[181] Guenther and Loe followed the progression of the epidemic from North Fork to Cedar Creed and ministered to the people as they went. During the three and a half months of the flu epidemic that winter, Pastor Guenther saw his wife only once, when she rode to Whiteriver to give him a new pair of pants. He had worn the seat out of his pants by hours of riding horseback.

The next winter the flu returned. By this time the Guenthers had moved to Whiteriver. Over 300 of the 400 boarding school children in Whiteriver contracted the illness. Guenther and Loe worked among them, and, once again, rode into the hills. Pastor Guenther's eldest son remembers one night in particular. Guenther and Loe rode home from making camp visits. The two literally fell out of their saddles and had to be carried inside. Eventually Guenther caught the flu, and Dr. Loe confined him to bed for six weeks. Then, hearing that some of his close Apache friends were ill, the pastor went to their camp hoping to be of assistance. Exposed to the cold wind, Rev. Guenther had a relapse and was in bed for an additional six weeks.[182]

The cooperation and friendship of Dr. Loe and Pastor Guenther continued. "With the flu behind him and the orphans being cared for by the Lutherans, Dr. Loe turned his attention to trachoma, a disease blinding scores of Apaches. From his work among the Apaches

---

[181] Comes from E. Guenther's autobiography in 1956.

[182] This material on the work of Edgar Guenther during the epidemics was in large part supplied by Dr. William Kessell in several articles he wrote for *The Apache Lutheran* over a span of a number of months in 1995 and 1996.

in Arizona, the Navajos at Shiprock in New Mexico, and the Sioux of Rosebud in South Dakota, Dr. Loe invented and perfected the sulfanilamide treatment for trachoma. When his method and treatment were introduced among the Apaches of the Fort Apache Reservation it met with instant success. Mrs. Guenther reported that the first volunteer was Bland Tessay, who had been a friend of the doctor during the early days at Cibecue. Bland reported, "When I came to the hospital I could not see the things on my plate; after the first week I could see my food; after the second week I could look across the room; after the third week I could look out of the window and clearly see the buildings of the Agency; and after the fourth week I returned home cured, thanks to my good friend Dr. Loe."[183]

During these years Edgar Guenther was put into leadership and supervision of the whole work on both reservations. He wrote about Rice which is the present-day San Carlos and tribal center for the San Carlos Reservation:

When the rich copper mines of the Globe-Miami district were opened, a railroad was built from Bowie to this point through the San Carlos Reservation. For granting a right-of-way through their land the Indians received permission to ride free for a period of thirty years, not however, on the plush seats of the passenger trains, but in the empty flat and box cars of the lumbering freights. A railroad station was established on the reservation and called Talkalai in honor of an old Indian chief by that name. The government opened a boarding and day school here. A presumptuous government school principal named Rice, so tradition has it, had his name substituted for that of the old chief. In 1920 Pastor Francis Uplegger established himself in an abandoned shack hidden in the mesquite brush on Sycamore Wash near the school. A parsonage and church of tufa stone construction was hurried to completion. Pastor Uplegger has charge of the religious instruction at this school of those pupils that have been assigned to him by their parents, and a large camp population is also under his spiritual care. In 1936 Uplegger was appointed Superintendent of our Indian Mission to succeed Guenther,[184] and his son Alfred was given him as assistant.

---

183 William Kessel in the November 1993 *The Apache Lutheran.*

184 Guenther resigned over the grievance of, as he described it, "the encumbrances of remote control." In this regard he was another fatality of mission philosophy and the rift between the administration and the actual workers on the field.

Apache is not a written language. It wasn't when the first missionaries came and it still isn't. Pastor Uplegger, a talented linguist, set up an alphabet of the numerous and difficult Apache language sounds in such simplicity that the language could be written on the ordinary keyboard of a typewriter, and he rendered large portions of the Scriptures in print. In 1929 the Agency was moved from vanishing Old San Carlos to Rice into a compound of beautiful tufa stone buildings recently constructed, and the name of the railroad station and Government plant were changed to San Carlos.

Guenther's same recording also mentioned the mission station of Bylas on the southern reservation. Grenville Goodwin also spoke of Bylas in his diary, and when we hear what he said we realize how inextricably the missionary work was connected with the former Apache struggles and life, even as late as 1920. Goodwin said about the Bylas people, "About 1919 the Bylas Indians found the tracks of four Chiricahua men, who had come up from old Mexico and passed along the north side of Mountain Turnbull, right back of Bylas. Shortly after, these same Chiricahua were seen by an Indian man, near Cibecue, with whom they talked at a distance. They said they had come, not to make any trouble, but only to get girls to take back to Mexico with them; that they had lots of young men down there, but no wives for them. The Cibecue man of course warned all the camps, and no girls were allowed off alone, so the Chiricahuas went back to Mexico no better off than they first started."[185]

Inashood Schlegel started the work in Bylas. Before 1920, the people in Bylas were served by visiting missionaries and traveling missionaries from Globe. Starting in 1900 and then regularly and weekly from 1917 until September 1920, the following missionaries began and continued the work in Bylas: Carl Guenther, Karl Toepel and Alfred Uplegger. In September of 1920 Gustav Schlegel was ordained in St. Matthew's church in Milwaukee and arrived in Bylas the same month and was installed as the first resident pastor of Our Savior's. Guenther goes on to speak of this early work at Bylas: "The Apaches at Bylas, near the southern boundary of the San Carlos Reservation, had for years been the most tractable of all the Apaches, owing to their being so far removed from the Agency and government control. For years the government had urged us to open a school there, but since the Synod could not see its way clear to do so, it opened a large, well-equipped plant of its own. Finally in 1922 a house and church was erected for Candidate Gustav Schlegel.

---

[185] Grenville Goodwin and Neil Goodwin, *The Apache Diaries: A Father-Son Journey*, Lincoln and London: University of Nebraska Press, 1993, p. 120.

He immediately opened a small mission school in the annex of his church. The Government finally closed its plant and sent its pupils by bus to a white school just off the reservation. In 1926 Pastor Schlegel was called away on account of ill health and replaced by Candidate A.C. Hillmer, who served until 1929."[186]

The Lutherans were disciplining, educating, clothing, and feeding the Apache children. Pastor Guenther wanted the synod to go one step further. He wanted to help the Apaches who were constantly victimized by disease. The epidemiological history of the Apaches during the early decades of the 20th century reads like a horror story. Whooping cough, measles, influenza, tuberculosis, spinal meningitis, trachoma, cholera infantum, and waves of other diseases decimated the Apache population. In fact, the Apache death rate was four times greater than that of the United States as a whole. Babies were particularly vulnerable. Thus Guenther begged the mission board and the synod for medical help. This was a particularly sensitive topic for him. In 1913 he watched helplessly while "whooping cough, leading pneumonia by the hand, swept several hundred babies and young children off the reservation." The next year he watched measles and lung inflammation claim another forty lives in East Fork. Weeks later Guenther reported that a "choking cough" and pneumonia had arrived. "The misery of these poor people cannot be described," Guenther wrote. "Sometimes three, four small children died on one and the same day; in many individual families as many as three or four were taken away by death. For instance, our Sadie lost two small brothers and two small sisters, and a third sister is not out of danger."[187]

Guenther wanted the Wisconsin Synod at large to provide medical help and personnel who could turn the tide in some of these awful epidemics. But it didn't happen that way. It was even the substantiated belief that if the church were to provide telling aid to turning these epidemics, the Apache people would see and be encouraged to follow the further message of the missionaries. It actually happened that during some of the epidemics a number of medicine men themselves were treated and helped by the missionaries. No doubt the words in the Committee report of 1927 rankled him a lot when we read, "Executive Committee is not for erection of hospital. Government should do this

---

[186] "The Continuing Saga of Early Mission Work," from an article Pastor Edgar Guenther wrote for *The Concordia Historical Institute Quarterly,* Recorded in the April, 1990, *The Apache Lutheran.*

[187] Dr. William Kessel, from the September 1995 *The Apache Lutheran.* Kessel related this information from his grandfather's records.

as Indians are wards of the state." Those words sound bad to us too. There was some kind of disconnect here. Perhaps it couldn't be helped. Guenther saw the Apaches as his people, as a Chief Alchesay who sent him a haunch of venison for Christmas. It is disconcerting to hear of these same people referred to as "wards of the state."

And then came the matter of the Milk Ranch. This was a property and opportunity to relocate the nursery and school at the higher elevation, not far from the present day casino at what used to be called Indian Pines. A number of reasons were given for having this be the center of the humanitarian work of the missionaries. The higher elevation would be more pleasant in the summer months. The down side was that it was considerably colder, with more snow in the winter than the East Fork and White River Valleys were. Those who wanted this to happen spoke about pernicious influences in the river valleys that impeded the work and negatively affected the people spiritually. Guenther's records show that the missionaries came up with the following good reasons to move the work to the Milk Ranch and not have it at East Fork where Mayerhoff had started things:

They lacked adequate space at East Fork.

1. There were inevitable clashes of authority between the East Fork day school and boarding school personnel. A move would eliminate such difficulties.
2. The Apaches around East Fork were notorious for their immorality, gambling and drinking. Thus they presented constant temptations to the school children.[188]
3. At Milk Ranch many of the children would be away from such unsavory influences.
4. The East Fork boarding school and day school children mixed together, and their different statuses made the situation awkward.
5. There was a sufficient wood supply at Milk Ranch for the school.
6. At Milk Ranch the Lutherans could procure their own supplies from nearby stores and avoid freight costs.
7. Milk Ranch was suitable for farming and dairy ranching, which would supply food for the children.
8. Cooley (McNary) had a burgeoning Apache population and could be served by the pastor from the nearby Milk Ranch.

---

[188] The writer was told (2019) by a former high school boarding student at East Fork Mission that the high school boys used to catch trout in the East Fork until they got to the area upriver around the Quintero camp, where the women would give them *tulapai* for the trout. But it was only for "social drinking" the former student said.

9. The purchase of Milk Ranch would cost little more than the needed work at East Fork, but in the end the Lutherans would end up with better facilities, equipment and land.

But, alas, the deal fell through. The missionaries were successful at doing all the preliminary work with the government and the church, but in the end it was the Apache people themselves who nixed things. Reasons they gave for not wanting the work to continue in the higher climes of McNary and environs was that the children wouldn't do well in the higher and cooler (colder) elevation. Some think that Chief Alchesay himself didn't want the resultant population surge to be near his dwelling. There also seems to have been a superstitious belief that disease came from the area where the Milk Ranch was and a reluctance then to put the nursery and school there.

The early to mid 1920s were hard years for the mission. There was so much work to do by so few. Salaries were low. Other religious groups like the Roman Catholics were making inroads. The missionaries themselves weren't physically well. There was infighting and unhappy drama in the personal relationships of pastors with pastors, and the wives often got involved too.

In 1923 Missionary Paul Albrecht complained bitterly when the seminary and mission board sent candidate Erich LaHaine to Fort Apache to replace him.[189] Notice that it is "candidate" Erich LaHaine. That was the procedure and maybe part of the problem. The young men were new, not only to the work of being missionary but to the work of being a pastor. In many cases their graduations were speeded up so they could go and fill in for some crisis of manpower or personality conflict. Guenther reported this circumstance and lamented that the men sent were so young and inexperienced. Professor J. P. Koehler had the same observation earlier when he had visited Rudolph Jens and Carl Guenther. In 1985 Pastor Paul Schulz mentioned in his listing of workers at Bylas that all of the pastors who served Bylas were assigned to service through the seminary assignment committee. Every single one. There just was no shortcut to maturity and experience, and it could be that there was some validity in Paul Albrecht's complaint in 1923. About all we know of Erich LaHaine, who was himself young when he came, was that he managed to have his Star automobile swept away and ruined in an ill-advised flash-flood river crossing.

And it was at this time in the early part of the 1920s, as infighting and unhappy drama happened on the field, that Melvin Croll and his wife arrived. They arrived July 18, 1923. They made the trip from

---

[189] Paul Albrecht served from 1920-1923.

Wisconsin in an automobile in sixteen days.[190] One of the first reimbursements from the Synod to Croll was $193 to repair the chapel at East Fork. Things were almost always in a state of disrepair on the mission stations, and part of being *Inashood* was also being a handyman, carpenter, and shade-tree mechanic. Most of the young men were not those three. They were pastors. That is what their training had been and their desire. If you had asked them in Wisconsin if they would like to go and be carpenters on a reservation and repair a chapel for $193, doing much of the work themselves, they would probably have said no. To top it off, both Nitz and Guenther were convinced that Croll was a completely ineffective teacher. So not only was Croll a substandard carpenter but also a substandard teacher as well. At least it was so in the minds and perhaps mouths of the veterans on the field. Then the inevitable happened: Croll and Nitz got into it. Supposedly the differences were settled amiably. That is what Guenther's telegram said anyway. After months of being mentioned in the minutes of Committee meetings, Croll resigned and said he could no longer continue. The rupture between him and Nitz was too great, he said, and two years later Croll accepted a call to Wisconsin.

Croll worked hard in his years at East Fork. Mention is made of him a number of times in the 1925 *The Apache Scout*. In February he reminded his hearers that Christmas had come and gone but that they should not forget the kindness of people who had given them gifts. In May of the year the Crolls had to go to Wisconsin because Missionary Croll's father was very sick. Finally, at Christmas he worked alongside Thelma Davids and H. C. Nitz to teach Christmas carols to the school children and to participate in the Christmas program. He told the Christmas story to everyone and the children sang. "The chapel was full of people so that some of them could not get in and sat around outside."[191]

There is an epilogue to *Inashood* Croll's ministry. It comes as an article in a much later *The Apache Lutheran* by the author: "The Apache Mission work affected more people and lives than those of the missionaries and their families who were on the field. Each missionary had a family and relatives from other places in the country. They were impacted by the *Inashood* either positively or negatively. If there was something ignominious it touched the families abroad. Almost always, however, children and grandchildren were happy to do work in the synod archives and by visiting the various stations where their loved ones served to find out more about their family

---

190 *The Apache Scout*, August 1923, H. C. Nitz reporting.

191 *The Apache Scout*, December 1925, p. 5.

member who had "served among the Apaches." Such was the case in the following:

Missionary Melvin Croll served East Fork Mission from 1923 to 1926. The following was inspired by interested relatives who followed up on their father Melvin Croll's ministry: "It was a blustery spring day. There had been snow the night before, and the folks had come from Apache Junction. Ruthele said, 'We are the Baileys—Ruthele and Ralph. Sixty-five years ago my father was a missionary here. We just wanted to see where he was all those years ago. His name is Melvin Croll.' "

Part of the present parsonage at East Fork Mission at that time was his home. There were of course additions made to it after Pastor Croll was there, but Ruthele could stand and look at the very house her father and mother had lived in. And the back part of the church at East Fork was the very same building that her father had preached in before she was even born.

The account goes on: "Wait a minute," I said. "Let's check the baptismal records. I remember that name." And there in 1925 we found it! Melvin Croll's signature in purple ink at the bottom of a baptismal record. "That's Dad's handwriting!" his daughter said. And we looked at it and felt the strange, sad feeling of seeing something from the past struggle to live again. At the time his children visited, Melvin Croll was 91 and his wife was 92, and they were living in Green Bay, Wisconsin.

When Melvin Croll left the mission there was a vacancy, and the Committee went to Northwestern College and talked to an Albert Meier. He "expressed his willingness to accept the call" and was called to serve June 8, 1926. Dozens of similar incidents occurred over the years, but the 1920s held more than their share of comings and goings.

The 1920s also marked the rise of Apache medicine man Silas John. He had met with the missionaries earlier and had stolen aspects of Christianity, which he had then tried to blend with the Old Way. He was intrigued with the account in the books of Moses in the Old Testament about the Bronze Serpent, and snakes slithered their ways into his religious machinations. He was successful and became more and more active. He gathered a large following who wanted to follow things more like their old traditional ways and religion, and this snake business had enough new in it to make the old seem even more attractive. That was a discouragement and worry for the missionaries too, and in this regard things haven't changed too much with the present-day resurgence of the Sunrise Dance and so-called traditional religion practiced by self-proclaimed medicine men and cultural devotees. The first missionaries, were they alive today, would still see this pulling and tugging of traditional Apache religion, and if you were to ask them about it, you would see them look to the ground with a sad smile on their faces. None would say that they really had been able to stem the tide of traditional religion. But they tried and they kept on trying, and stalwarts like Edgar Guenther kept their heads down and their shoulders to the work. There was and is the high tide and the low tide and the ebb and flow of mission life.

In 1939 Missionary Guenther related his experiences and travel to the Midwest for the Synod Convention. He met up with many of those who had served with him and even before him, those who had come and gone. "At these meetings the Pastors Plocher, Nitz, Wehausen, Christian Albrecht, Paul Albrecht, and also Arnold Platt (names well known to many of our Apaches), were all there too! One evening Pastor Nitz took me out to his home for supper. I was surprised to find all the little Nitzes grown up, and a fine young group they are indeed."[192] His visits also included seeing those laypeople who had been so instrumental in building the plants that now served on the reservation. "In Mayville, Wisconsin, we visited the A. K. Knoops, whom our East Fork Indians will remember as Arnold and Tante Friede who had charge of our orphanage over there in the days when our baby cribs were Del Monte tomato boxes. They made it possible also for us to call on the 'Bill' Knoops at Fox Lake. 'Bill,' as many of our East Forkers know, was one of the builders of our dormitory there. Way up on the Menominee Reservation we found the A. K. Knoops. Mr. Knoop, the builder, is affectionately known as 'Art' by our Indians from Bylas to Cibecue."[193] Edgar Guenther remained an emissary and advocate of the work in Arizona with the Apaches. He knew it and he knew the people, both those who were served, as well as those who did this work of love.

Gustav Harders in his book *Dohaschtida* had an old Apache woman who was being sidelined by the culture and eventually sent away to die. *Inashood* Guenther had a real life character like this in his work and life too, and he wrote about her:

> One day the missionary decided to visit a cluster of wickiups which formed the winter camp of a group of related

---

[192] *The Apache Scout*, September 1939, p. 59. Arnold Platt was the adopted son of the Wehausens. His grave is in the cemetery at East Fork Mission. At this time he was a young man living with his parents in Wisconsin.

[193] *Op. cit.* p.62.

Apaches. As he approached the dwellings he noticed at a distance a very small wickiup about four feet in diameter and about the same height. Motivated by curiosity he approached it. Inside he could make out the figure of a very old woman. She was clothed in rags, her hair matted and her face wrinkled with great age. With her hands she groped about, betraying the sad fact that she was blind. When the missionary touched her aged hands with a loaf of bread she immediately snatched it and hid it under a blanket.

Missionary Guenther inquired about her situation, and she gave this explanation: "A long time ago I was a little girl. Then I could see, and I was as happy as other little girls of my own age. One day when I was about 12 years old, I went up to the mountains to cut grass with a knife. Accidentally I cut into a rattlesnake and some poison flew into my eyes, and since that time I have been blind. I cannot walk but must crawl on my hands and knees."

The woman was now over a century old. She had been set aside by her people to die. Now for the first time in her life, she met a white man. Yes, he had given her some food, but he had really come to talk. His message was simple. "I am sorry to see that you are blind. You cannot guide your steps even if you were able to walk. There are many beautiful things that you have not seen; you have had many troubles and few friends. Worst of all you cannot see the way to heaven, a place where God lives, a place where there is no hunger, no cold, and no blindness. But fortunately, to find that place you do not need your eyes. There is One who can give you an eye to see better than many of your people who have their vision." Missionary Guenther proceeded to tell her of the Lord, the saving God.

Missionary Guenther was called away from the mission field for a time, but God was at work in the woman's heart. She kept waiting and wondering, "Why does the man not return who told me of the eye with which I can see heaven?" Then one day Pastor Guenther returned, and she eagerly grasped his hand. By this time she had grown deaf, and he could shout to her only the simplest of gospel truths. One of these was the assurance of adoption given us in Holy Baptism, and she asked to be baptized.

One cold night the old woman died. Missionary Guenther made a coffin and went to her small wickiup. Most of her possessions had been removed, and the place was nearly deserted. In a remote little canyon off the beaten path someone had dug a grave at the foot of a bluff. As Guenther reported, "Here the little centenarian was buried, 'unwept, unhonored, and unsung,' and received in heaven with honors to see the Son and the Father who sent Him."[194]

On the occasion of twenty-five years of missionary work, two Apache men reported on Edgar and Minnie's work as missionaries. Jack Keyes had this to say:

When they first came out here Mr. Guenther and his wife used to go six or seven miles on foot to visit the sick Indians and sick babies and then walk home again. They helped the Indians and they talked to them about Jesus because they liked the Indians and the Indians liked them and often asked them to come to their camps for help in sickness and trouble. Many years they traveled all over to see every Indian on horseback, and they carried their first baby in Indian cradle on horseback for over a year, too. They came to us alone and stayed with us because they liked us. That is the kind of people Mr. and Mrs. Guenther and his family are, and we are all happy over them. We like to have them with us." And Chester Gatewood added concerning the twenty-five-year anniversary celebration, "So an all-Apache committee arranged the divine services, barbecue and jollifications, purchased a Morris chair, stool, and side table as the Apaches' gift to Mr. and Mrs. Guenther. When the date arrived and everything was set, Guenther was sent off on a futile errand to a fairly distant Indian camp. Returning he found every Indian and white person on the reservation ready to do him honor for work well done. And from his place in Beatrice, Nebraska, the former missionary Paul Mayerhoff wrote about the work of Edgar Guenther in addition to his submission of the two men, "But the finest testimony is that of the convert Apaches themselves praising God for his mercy and salvation planted among them, who were once a benighted people but now have come to the light."[195]

Guenther reported that Whiteriver was becoming the tribal center for the Fort Apache Reservation, like San Carlos was for the San

---

[194] The story of the blind woman was reported by Pastor E.E. Guenther in *The Northwestern Lutheran*, 1923, Vol. 10, No. 24, p. 379. The article was entitled "'The Lord Openeth the Eyes of the Blind' Psalm 146:8."

[195] Paul Mayerhoff, *Beatrice Daily Sun*, January 21, 1937.

Carlos Reservation. Whiteriver mission field included North Fork up to the lumbering town of McNary twenty-four miles away, Canyon Day, and Cedar Creek. He didn't say it, but he was laboring as superintendent of the work on both reservations, a position he held until 1936 when he resigned, dissatisfied with "the encumbrances of remote control." He also reported that Fort Apache had been fitted to help Navajo and Apache school children who were afflicted by trachoma. Sulphanilamide helped with the trachoma but was miserable stuff for the eyes. A drop in each eye in the morning left things smeary and cloudy, until the afternoon renewed the experience for the journey home. The religious work of the Lutheran Church at Fort Apache was done under the auspices of the Church of the Open Bible in Whiteriver.

In retrospect Edgar Guenther had this to say about the school at East Fork. "The quondam superintendent of Missions visualized a more advanced institution, for which our elementary day schools might serve as feeders with its most promising pupils—an institution in which young Apache men and women might be withdrawn from the degrading influence of heathen camps and be developed into mission workers or, at any rate, into firmer Christians who would serve as a nucleus for future congregations in the various fields. The school has not succeeded in doing that with the rank and file of its students, partly because it is situated in the heart of a large Apache population with its accompanying detracting influences, and partly because the money and equipment for giving pupils a well-balanced and practical education has been lacking. In spite of all this, a number of fine Apache Christian men and women have been graduated from East Fork."[196]

It is almost 100 years ago that he describes Christmas 1922 and the goings-on of the time. His comment on the culture is surely to the point too, and his humorous way of writing makes us smile:

> Work on the chapel is progressing satisfactorily. Considerable time was lost owing to the inability of the little sawmill at Lakeside to furnish the lumber as fast as we needed it. The plastering is being finished today.
>
> On Christmas Day we closed up the window openings on the shady side, set up two stoves leaving the smoke to find its way out through the ventilators, made seats of the lumber piles and bade the people enter. Someone counted five hundred and fifty and overlooked probably fifty more. Of course, most of them came merely for a handout. They got it

---

[196] *The Apache Lutheran,* July 1990.

and not one left the chapel dissatisfied, thanks to the generosity of mission friends. Mr. Davis attended our services and brought along a large pail full of things to eat, fearing that, owing to the immense crowd, we might be placed in a predicament similar to that of the bridegroom at Cana. I do not consider Christmas giving as something contradictory to what I have just stated above.

Very few Apaches are straight on Bible chronology, which makes it so easy for them to identify Jesus with their Monster-killer, who according to tradition was the first one born after the flood. The crowd that had assembled came from all quarters of the reservation, for which reason I made it my object in my sermon to show them with the help of a large chart drawn on some boards that Christ the Savior of all mankind was born 3,000 years after the flood. The audience was unusually attentive."

He pointed out later that in 1926 there were over three hundred in attendance for Christmas services at the Church of the Open Bible in Whiteriver.

In 1928 he said,

Christmas has come and gone. The forenoon of Christmas Day was given over to the Whiteriver pupils who worship in the Church of the Open Bible, some 300 in number.

The Christmas story was told by the pupils themselves in recitations and songs hastily assigned to them by the teachers of our Wednesday evening classes. Every one of the entire number of pupils would have liked to have taken part. Gladly we would have had them do so if time had permitted.

On the afternoon of Christmas Day, Christmas services were held for the outside Indians of this field. About 600 were present. Substantial gifts of clothing were given to all whose names appeared on the ration list, and to others who seemed in need. To each of the rest we gave some little present to remind them of the good will of the white Christians back East to whom we are indebted for all the gifts received. Two of our native Christians in earnest addresses reminded their hearers that earthly presents can bring us no blessings if we do not receive the greatest gift, the true knowledge of the Christ Child and his mission.

Christmas gifts were again sent from this station this year to all of our White Mountain boys and girls attending the non-reservation schools at Riverside and Albuquerque. Several beautiful letters of thanks have already been received from these places. On the Friday before Christmas the writer had the pleasure of hearing the Christmas program prepared by Missionary Behn with the children of Canyon Day school. Here also one could see that every child was glad to take part, if not individually, then at least in letting himself be heard in the Christmas hymns. Anyone not knowing these children would hardly believe that many of them did not know a word of English just a few months ago. A few Apaches brought Christmas cheer to the missionaries' homes with gifts of their own choice. There is none that came as near to the writer's heart and stomach as the large hind quarter of venison presented to him by Chief Alchesay."[197]

There in the June issue of *The Apache Scout* the reader can see the picture of the happy faces of sixty-five boys and girls from Whiteriver Boarding School. All sixty-five had been baptized at Church of the Open Bible on Easter Sunday by *Inashood* Guenther. Incidents like this and the inclusion of Chief Alchesay and his one hundred followers on one day make a person wonder how so many could have been received at one time. How were they taught and educated, so that they knew what was happening? The answer to that question is at least partly answered by the fact that Guenther was a master teacher, and that his ministry involved much teaching, often through and with an interpreter. Superintendent Francis Uplegger wrote about Guenther's teaching in 1940 when in his superintendent report he says, "No interpreter can render pointed Biblical terms, phrases, verses, or also the preacher's own biblical expressions or allusions, at once with corresponding distincting, directness, appeal. Presentation of matter in language adapted to the environment of our Indians, wherein Guenther is a master, with popular phrasing, avoiding abstract terms to the highest possible degree, and so ably interpreted as by John Williams does a great deal to let it come to the hearers without much loss of freshness." It was also on this particular day that Superintendent Uplegger was able to hear and understand both what Guenther said in English and then how it was interpreted by his interpreter, John Williams. And on this day of reporting, Superintendent Uplegger said, "We (Guenther and Uplegger) must hasten on our way to Fort Apache, for instruction classes."[198] It was also true

---

[197] *The Apache Lutheran*, December 1995, quoting a 1928 Christmas account in *The Apache Scout*.

[198] *The Apache Scout*, June, 1940.

that when Guenther was unable because of ill health to teach the large classes he taught in Whiteriver and Fort Apache that Pastor Paul Behn from East Fork helped teach.

Edgar Guenther was interested and involved in the government leadership on the reservation. He had a close friendship with Charles Davis, who retired in 1927. He said that when he ministered to Davis and talked to him about Jesus and faith, Davis' reply was, "I have never doubted it."

Davis put his money where his mouth was. He was a strong supporter of East Fork Lutheran Nursery, and when he left he donated a substantial sum of money for the enhancement of the sun porch. Mrs. Davis was a faithful attender of services at Open Bible in Whiteriver. As a parting token of friendship and a permanent remembrance, Mr. and Mrs. Davis donated their piano to East Fork Mission. It was a Vose and Son instrument and in good condition. It was placed in the orphanage, where it offered delightful entertainment not only to the orphans but also to the pupils in the boarding school and to all mission workers and their families. At that time it was the only piano at East Fork Mission. By this gift Superintendent Davis brought to a fitting close the relationship that existed between him and East Fork Mission, a relationship of over ten years' duration.[199]

At the time of the Milk Ranch event, Guenther referred to the place as Cooley. That was the name of the former scout who lived there with his two Apache wives. The name got changed, and Pastor Guenther was not happy about it: "We regret to announce that Cooley, Arizona, is no longer on the map. The name has been changed to McNary, Arizona. Whether or not this is the name of a patron saint we do not know. We liked the name Cooley. It seemed a fitting monument to the man whose history is so inseparably linked with that of the pioneer days of the reservation. But we were not consulted when the change was made, and the damage is done. However, we still have Cooley's Mountain, and the picturesque Cooley's ranch. And, we dare say, it will be many a moon before our Apaches will permit their guttural tongues to perform the gymnastics necessary to pronounce McNary. Still, we are willing to make a slight concession. Address all freight shipments containing donations to our mission stations on this reservation to McNary—and we shall call for them at Cooley."[200]

Pastor Arthur Guenther was Edgar's son and served many years as pastor after his father died. He related this story about his father

---

[199] *The Apache Scout*, November 1927.

[200] *The Apache Scout*, April 1924.

Edgar: "About two miles up north of town lived a fine Christian Apache gentleman by the name of John Bourke. His name is a story in itself. He was our blacksmith. I loved that man as a boy and used to go down to the blacksmith shop where Alchesay Hall now stands and watch John pound the red hot metal bars into horseshoes or heat and straighten the steel rims on the wagon. Many was the time he would let me turn the crank on the blower as the coals grew red-hot and the sparks flew. When he took the heated metal out and dipped it into the water tank I would shrink back at the sound of the hissing steam.

"Father (Pastor Edgar Guenther) told me that when John was old, retired and actually dying (dying of old age and hard work and not because of alcohol or a car accident or AIDS or lung cancer gotten from smoking), he went to visit him. He had a winter home up on the bluff just exactly where the Baptist church stands today, and he had a fine 'summer shade' right near the river. He said that he loved to listen to the many different sounds that the water made as it flowed and danced over the rocks and around the roots of the big cottonwoods. 'It never hurt my ears,' he would say.

"On this occasion many of the relatives were gathered, for it was feared, and rightly so, that he was fading fast. This was not like the times when they gathered just across the river where his big farm was at harvest time. Then they were all laughing and working to gather the corn to be put into the ground to be roasted. John was a good farmer, and my father showed him how to grow some real fine big winter squash among the rows of corn.

"When Father arrived he was immediately ushered in where his friend of many years lay dying on his bed in the summer shade. After the usual warm and friendly handshake, Father opened his battered and worn Bible and read words of comfort, words of hope and words of joy to the old blacksmith. When the final words and Amen of the Lord's Prayer were spoken, it was very quiet save for the music of the river and the rustling of the oak leaves that covered the summer shade.

"As my Father looked into the tired but bright eyes of his friend, John began to speak and a smile covered his face. Father asked what he was thinking and the old man said, 'I see a very beautiful land, high mountains covered with great trees, many open areas with fat deer and deep green grass, many mountain flowers, a beautiful clear stream flowing and a sky of blue. It is the most beautiful land that I have ever seen, and I am going there soon.'

"He closed his eyes and lay back with the smile on his face and died."

All the missionaries had some vision of the work and its continuation. Edgar Guenther had a vision of the work too which the following shows: "Wallace J. Johnson, Wilson Duncan, and Earnest Victor did the interpreting for Pastor Meier since Christmas. They went with him to the camps and also interpreted the Sunday morning sermons. Wilson also daily helped Miss Davids teach the beginners' class. May this be the beginning of training native teachers and preachers."[201]

He went on, "But Jesus repeatedly gives us new hope for Apache Christian leaders. If he did not do that I would no longer be here. If I had no such hope I would be a hypocrite to our Christian people back home who support us, by staying another day on the mission. For if the Gospel will not bring forth Christian leaders in Apacheland then it is doomed here. All mission work would be in vain." He goes on to describe some charlatans that he had the displeasure of knowing. Apache Christian leaders had to be right in order to be right. There were opportunists around as Guenther said, "But we must not have the wrong idea of what a Christian leader is. A man who has received Bible instruction may tell you what a bad man he used to be and what a good man he is now. He may tell you that he no longer gambles or steals like other Indians do. Such a man may also tell you how bad the other Indians are. He may dress well and lead the conversation whenever he finds himself in a group of people. Missionaries who are new on the field often use such men for interpreters and lend them money perhaps. Sooner or later they see their mistake. They see that they have been fooled. I myself have been fooled in just that way. I ought to have known better. Yes, even limited experience should have taught me better. No, a Christian leader does not draw attention to himself." And then Guenther goes on to say, "But in Christ's Kingdom a child sitting at the feet of his teacher may by its childlike faith and trust in Jesus be a leader of that same teacher. God give us such leaders in Apacheland." And this did happen. The Apaches had these leaders. The schools prospered, and the children taught and led their parents.

In 1931 Guenther used his best Latin and reminded everyone, "*Ceterum censeo* (I further propose) Arizona must have that Lutheran Academy." He said this at the occasion of Howard Penrod, a son of a white family in Whiteriver, going to California Concordia College at Oakland. Two other young people from Arizona went too. One was his own son Roland Guenther. He added in his comments, "Whenever the Scout (himself) mentions Christian schools, he feels the pressure

---

201 *The Apache Scout* June 1927.

of a chip on his shoulder. When Howard announced his intention of going to a Christian school, well meaning friends assailed him from all sides. They advised him not to go to a school "where they do nothing but pound religion into you." He added, "It is just because parents have no Gospel gold in their own pockets, and no tickets of forgiveness for the trip to eternity in their possession, and therefore have neglected to have their children secure this wealth also, that the world has lost its balance."[202]

On March 4, 1930, there was a big celebration to commemorate Coolidge Dam and the impoundment that would be called San Carlos Lake. Guenther didn't go to the celebrations. He stayed home in protest. Something was dying, as far as he was concerned: even the graves of dead Apaches were dying. The waters were covering everything. Good fields. The old fort. People's homes. All were sinking beneath the placid water with its ducks swimming above. He was proud of the words Will Rogers tendered for the occasion and quoted from an article in *The Arizona Republican:* "A peculiar thing about the dam that you may not read in your dispatches—the dam is built on the lower side of the Apache Indian reservation, and the water is all to be used by the Pima tribe and the whites. In fact, they moved the Apaches out of the very valley where the water is backed up, and moved them 10 miles up above. The only good out of the dam is for somebody to invent a way for water to run uphill, and then they wonder why Apaches are wild. One ceremony reminded me of a blindfold tobacco ad test. Mr. Coolidge and an Apache chief and a Pima chief all took a whiff from the same pipe, the Indians didn't bat an eye, but Calvin coughed up over a carload's worth." [203]

In Minnie Guenther's *Diary of a Missionary's Wife* (1929) she said about herself and her husband Edgar, "We have had great disappointments, but fortunately, the good Lord has never let us both become discouraged at the same time." Indeed, that must have been the case. What great work was done by the two of them! How they loved the Apache people and sacrificed for them! They were neither one perfect, but neither were any of the other workers and wives and missionaries. We have mentioned Minnie Guenther in earlier writing as someone who was outspoken and was at the center of some of the tiffs that took place with various mission staff, both with the pastors and with their wives. It was that way. At the end of the 1950s this writer remembers his family at East Fork Mission across from the church there being invited to the Guenther house

---

202 *The Apache Scout,* January 1931, "Pounding Religion." EEG.

203 *The Apache Scout,* March 1930, "Lake San Carlos," EEG.

for supper one evening. Edgar was old and quiet, still tall with his shock of white hair. He didn't say much at the visit. Minnie did most of the talking. And the conversation that evening turned to the immorality present on the reservation and the number of recent rapes that there had been. Even the word "rape" was a shocking word to the fifth-grader at the table. And Mrs. Guenther had the solution: "I can fix the problem," she said. "I would use my raper scissors." Maybe she too had been endowed with a "salty Low-German mother-wit," as her husband was reported to have had.

In 1961 Edgar Guenther died. At the grave of *Inashood* Edgar Guenther an Apache man said, "Today I am the loneliest man on earth."[204] He was buried in the Whiteriver cemetery near so many of the people he had himself buried as their *Inashood*, and should you care to, you could see his grave there today.

Minnie continued to live and work among the Apaches. She did it for another twenty years. In 1967 she was chosen as Mother of the Year, in that national effort to find the mother who stands out in the whole country as exceptional and to be honored. How could they have found a better mother in this regard than Minnie Guenther? She raised nine children of her own, who all went off to become stellar citizens. She had help in this, it is true. ShiMa[205] was an Apache woman whose band had earlier run with Geronimo. Her identification number was B3. She came to the Guenther household after they had befriended her when her own daughter died. ShiMa took care of the first child, Winonah, and then helped with the others too, living all the while with the Guenthers. She died in 1945.

Minnie continued to live and work on the reservation, calling it "my reservation." It got harder and harder for her to be there for medical reasons as her health failed. Over the years she and her family had gathered many artifacts and keepsakes. People brought baskets and beadwork and things they had made with buckskin to Minnie. In some cases she gave them money so that they would have some kind of income. Many of these treasures were stored on the front porch of the parsonage at Whiteriver, and visitors used to visit to see them and admire them. On January 8, 1982, in her house at Whiteriver on "her" reservation, she died at the age of 91. People came in a snowstorm to honor her love for them all. In her will she said that her vast collection should go to the Arizona State Museum at the University of Arizona in Tucson. It is there today with the Grenville Goodwin Apache Collection, and together they

---

[204] See quotation in *Northwestern Lutheran*, XLVII (September, 1961) p. 217.

[205] *ShiMa* is the Apache for "My mother." This is what Minnie called her Apache helper.

comprise the most comprehensive record of Apache material culture in the world.

The reading of Colossians 1:3,4 is a fitting tribute also to the Guenthers, Minnie and Edgar: *"We always thank God, the Father of our Lord Jesus Christ, when we pray for you, because we have heard of your faith in Christ Jesus and of the love you have for all God's people."* It was as Jack Keyes observed above. The Guenthers surely did love God's people, the Apaches. As anniversaries of the work pass, all who love the Apache Mission and have heard of the love of those who worked can continue to thank God for the faithful Guenthers who have passed on.

CHAPTER THIRTEEN

Zuberbier and Niemann

Sometimes it is only the loose cannon that hits the target.

The history of "The 25th Anniversary of the Apache Work" was put out by the Wisconsin Synod in 1919 and includes this vignette of Cibecue: "Cibecue lies in the middle of the Arizona Wilderness, about 50 miles northwest of Fort Apache and just as far northeast of Globe in a straight line, in a wondrously beautiful, wildly romantic region, where wildlife is still to be found in abundance. There on the Cibecue River, where our mission station lies, is probably the most favorable place for mission work that we have in the broad region. Many Apaches reside there, pursuing agriculture and raising horses and cattle. Missionary Otto Schoenberg had often visited the Indian settlements at Cibecue and environs already in the previous years from Fort Apache and had done mission work there. But when the General Synod had resolved in 1911 to establish a new mission station there, the missionary was asked by the commission to move there with his family and there to pursue mission work among the Apaches. A piece of land for mission buildings and a garden were bought yet in the same year.[206] Then Missionary Schoenberg immediately went about building a parsonage, and shortly before Christmas the missionary moved into the new residence with his family. Until then they lived in tents. The parsonage, built out of adobe blocks, with a wide porch and an extended shingle roof, made a very comfortable impression." And it was in 1911 that Apache men and women assisted in building a small church at Lower Cibecue. That building is still standing today.[207]

The adobe parsonage at Lower Cibecue was there for a long while and served as home for a number of missionaries and teachers.

---

[206] The place there at lower Cibecue wasn't far from the very spot where Captain Hentig had fallen dead during the Cibecue Massacre in 1881.

[207] Pastor Arthur Guenther tried his best to get this adobe church building registered with the historical society in the state of Arizona. He had the idea that it would be protected from the elements and perhaps get some kind of restoration. Alas, this idea was not to materialize, but the building still does stand where it has stood for over a hundred years.

It was there when the Hartzell Family from Globe visited the station in the early 1950s to babysit the place while teacher Rosin and his family were away on vacation. The whole Hartzell Family came for a week with the grandparents also. They went fishing at upper Cibecue and caught a big string of nice brown trout. There was no electricity in the parsonage, except for a hand-cranked generator outside one of the bedroom windows, and the evening was spent with the smelly company of a kerosene lamp because the generator couldn't be kept running. When that was put out, except for the kerosene lamp, it was dark until the early morning light filtered through the towering cottonwood trees along Cibecue Creek.

Transportation in the Cibecue area was a big challenge at first. Pastors wore out the seats of their Sunday pants. Horseback was the way it had to go at first. Then came the Fords. Hard times made it hard to get parts—or to be able to pay for the parts. And remember, these missionaries were men who were trained theologically and not mechanically. Truth be told, missionaries are rarely very good at mechanical things. It wasn't and isn't their bent. The roads were little more than rocky trails. They choked their travelers with clouds of powdery dust in dry times. Mayerhoff mentioned that in his description of coming to the work the first time. The wheels of his stagecoach went through the pools of dust that were just the consistency of good cake flour. Then when things turned wet the dust turned to sticky and slippery clay and mud. The whole undercarriage would jam up with collected clay mud. Sometimes the wheel wells would fill, and the tire wouldn't turn any more. You had to chisel the packed mud out with a tire iron or your fingers. And then, a couple of revolutions later, you got to do the job again. It was that way when the Hartzell Family with grandparents drove out after their stay in Cibecue in the old days. It had rained and the road was slippery. The grandparents were behind the yellow Ford in a big blue DeSoto. The children watched in delight as grandma and grandpa slithered along sideways behind them on the way up Cibecue Mountain. In late December of 1930 missionaries Niemannn and Krueger were "mud marooned" from Cibecue for some time. And in the 1960s Superintendent Zimmermann had to be pulled to shore at Cibecue Crossing by two cowboys and their lariats. This condition regarding Cibecue roads would continue for thirty more years until those roads and the others were paved.

In 1912 at Lower Cibecue, next to the house, an adobe chapel was built to serve for school purposes. Later a dining room for the Indian school children and the necessary stable were built, and the stalls of the stable lay on the other side of the road, which passed close by the chapel. Delores Cassadore, who taught at lower Cibecue at the school, remembered Pastor Arthur Krueger getting up early to start the woodstove in the school to warm things up on frosty mornings. Pastor Krueger also used his vehicle to bring children to school, bringing red Cibecue mud with them on their shoes in wet weather. It was also Pastor Krueger who lamented that elsewhere on the reservation the stones on the roads were round, but in the Cibecue area they were sharp and jagged!

In November 1912, Missionary Schoenberg, who had begun the work at Cibecue, resigned and left the service of the Indian mission. In the summer of 1913, the candidate for the preaching office, Arnold Zuberbier from the seminary, was called to be his successor. After accepting the call, Missionary Zuberbier moved to Cibecue. His journey there was very difficult, but he was very happy when Superintendent Edgar Guenther greeted him at Cibecue.

Under Zuberbier's mission work, the number of pupils increased greatly. The Apaches soon gave him their full confidence. Many improvements were also made in the mission property under his administration, so that after a while it looked quite different at Cibecue than when he arrived. In the autumn of 1917 Miss Maria Kieckbusch, who had already served as teacher in the mission schools at Peridot and Globe with good success, was assigned to help Pastor Zuberbier in the school at Cibecue. She remained in this school until June of 1918, when she asked for her release from the service of the mission to care for her aged parents at home. Now Missionary Zuberbier was again alone on his large mission field. To his region also belonged Oak Creek, Carrizo, White Spring, Spring Creek, Grasshopper and Canyon Creek.

It was Zuberbier who mentioned that Luke George White, a former Apache leader, claimed to him that he fired the first shot at the Cibecue Massacre in 1881. It was also Zuberbier who wrote about Schi Kissen and how he lived and how he died. Schi Kissen (my cousin) was Z1 according to his Government identification. Of nine hundred Apaches in the Cibecue area, he was the only one who would give some of his land for the mission station. He brought his children to the school and himself attended the mission church service faithfully. When Pastor Harders asked him through an interpreter, "Why do you come?" he answered, "Because it makes me feel good inside to hear about Jesus." *Inashood* Zuberbier came to visit him when he was dying, but the missionary couldn't speak to him because of the language barrier. The family members were around him, but they were cool and aloof. They didn't want the pastor disturbing their dying relative. But Schi Kissen opened his eyes and looked at Zuberbier. The happy smile of a young person broke over Schi Kissen's face. "Schi Kissen, I'm happy to see you here," the missionary said. What to do? There was no interpreter. But with the few words he knew Zuberbier asked, "Do you know Jesus?" "Yes!" Schi Kissen said. "He's my brother." "Do you know God?" the *Inashood* asked. "I am a child of God's," came the answer, and then his eyes forever closed.

Arnold Niemann followed Zuberbier at Cibecue. We really don't know much about *Inashood* Arnold Niemann, who was affectionately (we hope!) also called Tubby Niemann. In a way, the reservation was the default setting that gave him a place to serve after his graduation from the seminary in Wisconsin. He wasn't a stellar student. There were even questions about his ability to serve in a white congregation in Wisconsin or elsewhere in the Midwest. Someone thought he could possibly serve on the reservation, and so he was sent and did serve. In some ways he represents God's amazing ability to use individuals in a wonderful way and to enable them to do wonderful things. Sometimes it is indeed true that the loose cannon is the only one that hits the target.

The adobe chapel was completed at Lower Cibecue, and immediately after the dedication Niemann was installed there by his brother missionaries. In the welcoming of the new pastor, veteran missionary Guenther said that Niemann was set aside for a special work. As Guenther said to the Apache believers and onlookers in the Cibecue valley, "This work will be of two kinds: for one thing, Missionary Niemann will be caretaker of our little fort. As such he will invite you to come in to services. Then when you do come in he will introduce you to his Captain, the Lord Jesus Christ. Missionary Niemann's other duty will be to visit you in your homes. It matters not if you live at Carrizo, Limestone, Blue Springs, or way up where Mike Rolland lives; it matters not if your home is at Salt Creek, White Springs, Spring Creek, Oak Creek, or Tsilaskai. If you live in any of these valleys Mr. Niemann will visit you regularly. If you like to read, he will supply you with the right kind of reading matter. If you are sick he will do the best he can for you. In short, he will be a true friend and a brother to you. Treat him as such when he comes."[208]

Photographer Frank Randall took the picture of Tzoe, who was also called Peaches by the soldiers. The picture was taken in 1883, while they waited for the Apaches to return to San Carlos from their flight into the fastness of the Sierra Madres. It was this Peaches who had led Crook and company into the Sierra Madres to the haunts of the breakaway Apaches there.

---

208 Edgar Guenther, *The Apache Scout*, October 1928, "Cibecue," p. 5.

Tsoe.
Photo Credit: NARA, RG 111, Signal Corps Collection, No. 82346)

This was *Tsoe* or *Tso-ay* (also Tzoe). Betzinez said he was a San Carlos Apache who went after Geronimo, even though he had been with Geronimo. It wasn't long before this time that Geronimo had given him a "peaceful release" from warpath duty because Peaches' family was back at San Carlos. Betzinez said about Peaches, "(He)

217

was chosen as guide because he had the reputation of being depend-able and besides was perfectly acquainted with the area in Mexico where the expedition was to operate."[209]

Pastor Arnold Niemann at Cibecue penned into his visitation record dated December 31, 1933, "Old man 'Peaches,' the man who played the major role in the capture of Geronimo, was baptized. This was brought about, mainly, by a visit the Rev. Guenther made a few days prior. Five sick visits were made: three to old man Peaches' camp and two to a young girl's camp who had tuberculosis." Cavalry soldier John Bourke said about Peaches, "He was one of the hand-somest men physically, to be found in the world. He never knew what it meant to be tired, cross, or out of humor." He was called Peaches by white men who could not pronounce his Apache name. Maybe the epithet had something to do with his complexion. It was this Peaches who had guided the Apache scouts and General Crook into the fast-ness of the Sierra Madres to the hideout of Geronimo, and it was this Peaches who died in his little Cibecue Creek shack one year after he became a Lutheran under the ministrations of *Inashood* Niemann.[210]

Niemann also knew chief John Taylay. This John Taylay worked with the government scouts responsible for the final capitulation of Geronimo. John Taylay and other scouts came back to Cibecue. Nie-mann wrote about him: "John Taylay and his band settled down on Cibecue Creek, where he was living at the time of his death. John was issued a few head of cattle by the government, and his sons helped him to take care of them. At the time of his death he had a herd of per-haps a hundred head. He also was receiving a pension for his services rendered to the government. He was made chief of his tribe because he was well liked and had the qualities that a chief should have. At the time the first Cibecue Day School was built (1904 I believe), he together with twelve bodyguards stood guard, so that no harm might befall the workers. He and his bodyguard were all dressed up in their regalia, with their rifles loaded ready for action, and it must have been a sight to behold. He taught his people to respect the govern-ment and to do what they were told and to keep the peace. He also told them to respect God's word. They should listen to their mission-ary and should go to church on Sunday—although he did not get into this habit himself." And then the *Inashood* Niemann spoke, "There-fore we should be wise and prepare for the life that is to come. Many

---

209 Jason Betzinez, *I Fought with Geronimo*, Lincoln and London: University of Nebraska Press, 1959, p. 118.

210 EEG later told of Peaches' daughter Ruth and that she died in the faith. She had contracted tuberculosis and before she died "saw" heaven.

people make the sad mistake of making good preparations for this life but no preparation at all for the life that is to come."[211]

Inashood Niemann also mentioned a John Cody who had not gotten a pension for his military services. He was rightfully bitter and resentful of the white men around, Missionary Niemann as well. Niemann thought that John didn't speak English and so he addressed him through an interpreter as many of the missionaries did in the early days. But one day after a few years of visiting him in his home, Niemann told the following: "But now as he (John Cody) began to gain his confidence, he made an effort to speak English with words something on this order: "What's the matter with White Man? He's no good. He lies. He soldier, he get pension. Me soldier, me get no pension." This came as quite a surprise to learn that he could speak some English and helped one come to the conclusion that there was some truth to his words. But now the question: if he was a soldier, why hadn't officials taken care of this matter for him? Had he been overlooked? After more conversation, it was learned that he had tried several times but was turned down. At that time, officials, it seems, were not as considerate of the Indian as they should have been in some cases." So Niemann was sympathetic. We do not know his contribution to John Cody's pension situation, but we do read from Niemann's pen, "Having consulted the state chairman of the V. F. W., an investigation was made by him, and it was verified that John Cody, an Apache, had served as soldier in the U.S. Army during the last part of the the last century and the first part of this century and was deserving of a pension but somehow had been overlooked. After a few months, John received the equivalent of a few years' back pay and the regular monthly pension thenceforth due a soldier at that time. Now John's confidence in the White Man, which had been disrupted for a time, was restored. The missionary was looked upon as a true friend. He was ready and willing to hear more about the religion of the missionary, the religion of the Bible."[212]

Arnold Niemann became John Cody's pastor. "After a few years it happened in the fall that some of John Cody's horses broke into his corn field by his house. While chasing them, he overtaxed his weak heart and brought about his death. While his life was coming to a close here on this earth, with some of his immediate family gathered round, some of his last words spoken were that he was not afraid to die. The missionary was notified that he should come over to conduct the funeral services the next day. And so the next morning the

---

[211] A. Niemann, *The Apache Scout,* June 1940, pp. 129-131.

[212] A. Niemann, *The Apache Lutheran,* April 1972, pp. 3,4.

missionary picked up two of his friends and John Williams, who was serving as part-time interpreter because the regular interpreter, Allan Danford, had died. It was also true that because of the Depression, the Synod was low on funds and asked the missionary to get by with as little extra help as possible. By car it was about fifteen miles from the missionary's home to the residence of the deceased. This was in the fall during the rainy season, and the wagon trail on the bank of Carrizo Creek was washed out in places. A trail for wagons was made in the creek bottom. The two Indians and the interpreter came in handy, as the car would high-center on debris and stones, which had to be rolled away at times. Finally, after a few miles of this, the camp was reached where the funeral was to take place. When the carpenters had the coffin finished, it was covered with black cloth inside and out, and a white ribbon was tacked on the cover in the form of a cross which gave the coffin the appearance of an ordinary one. Then when everything was ready, the people present, about twenty in number, were asked to march around the coffin to view the mortal remains the same as at any ordinary funeral. Then the coffin was transported by wagon to the grave not far off under some juniper trees where the graveside rites were conducted. Thus the life of one of the first Apaches to join the ranks of soldiers, came to a close here on earth to enter into the glory of the Lord."[213]

After full-time Cibecue mission work, Niemann went to East Fork to help teach there. He taught grades three through five. On weekends he tried to get back to Cibecue to preach there as well. It wasn't easy going. The river crossing claimed his car once. It didn't completely swallow the automobile, but it caused it to ingest fluid and it wouldn't run. Niemann's car wasn't the only one to be towed to dry land by Apache cowboys, who backed into the water with their horses and ropes, hooked on to a bumper, and pulled the car out of the torrent. Christian Albrecht closed his story of Niemann at the fords and said, "Now Pastor Niemann hopes that his car will again stand on all fours early enough to make the Cibecue trip next Saturday."[214]

The account has already mentioned Pastor E. Arnold Sitz's work on Upper Cibecue and Carrizo. After less than two years Sitz was called away to help out elsewhere on the field, leaving the missionary of Lower Cibecue to look after Carrizo as best he could. Finally in 1928 permanent headquarters were established at Upper Cibecue for this field, and Arnold Niemann was placed in charge. Forestdale, thus far a part of the Whiteriver field though over forty miles distant, was also

---

[213] Op. cit. pp. 4-6.

[214] Christian Albrecht, The Apache Scout, "East Fork." October 1929.

placed under Niemannn's jurisdiction. The rationale for all this was that this valley, now crossed by the new Highway 60, was more easily reached from Cibecue than from Whiteriver. Forestdale was said to have been the site of the first Mormon settlement in Arizona. When a new survey proved this fertile valley to be within the confines of the reservation, the Mormons were compelled to abandon their homes. Their old log meetinghouse still stands. It was part of Niemann's parish. In 1941 he was replaced by Pastor Paul Schliesser.[215]

---

[215] *The Apache Lutheran*, March 1990.

CHAPTER FOURTEEN

Paul Behn

And it came to pass, that in the morning watch the Lord
*looked unto the host of the Egyptians through the pillar
of fire and of the cloud, and troubled the host of the
Egyptians, and took off their chariot wheels,
that they drave them heavily* (Exodus 14:24,25).

Paul Behn got interested in the Apache Mission because he was a carpenter. In this he had something in common with Jesus, who was also a carpenter by occupation. Pastor Francis Uplegger was at San Carlos living in temporary quarters, while two men worked as carpenters building the parsonage and church. The two men were Paul Behn and his father. While he was at San Carlos (Rice) he became interested in mission work and returned to Wisconsin and the seminary to become a pastor. Upon graduation he was sent to the Apache Mission.

Paul Behn was born June 22, 1900, in Brillion, Wisconsin, the son of Herman and Wilhemina Behn. He was baptized and confirmed at Trinity Lutheran Church in Brillion and attended Northwestern Preparatory School in Watertown, Wisconsin, graduating from Wisconsin Lutheran Seminary in 1925. He served as missionary to the Apache Indians at Whiteriver, Bylas, East Fork and Cibecue from 1925 until 1940. He served as friendly counselor and instructor at the Chinese Evangelical Lutheran Church in Hong Kong and Cross of Christ Lutheran Church in Kingman, Arizona. At the end of his life he lived at the Arizona Lutheran Retirement Home in Phoenix, Arizona, and finally lived with daughters.

That is how his life went, and he also often visited and reminisced about the work on the reservations. He did it in private conversation, and he did it in his last years for *The Apache Lutheran*. He was sometimes a critic of the Wisconsin administration of the work, as you will see from the excerpts of his recollections. He said about his early work:

> I was called from the Seminary in 1926 to labor in the Apache Indian Mission in Arizona. The ground rules for such laboring were set by the Lord himself on the day of his

ascension: into all the world, teach, preach, and baptize. Yet following these ground rules is not the only thing involved in evangelizing the world. The spiritual side has the priority, of course, but there is also the material side in the life of a missionary. He must eat and drink and travel to carry out the Gospel call.

My salary was designated as $1,000 per year and 5 cents per mile for traveling to the Indian camps. However, I would have to furnish the car. Having been in training as a student, there was no income and only out-go, so father had to help with a loan to purchase my first car.

The place to which I was called was Whiteriver. Missionary E. E. Guenther, the superintendent of our Apache Field, outlined for me the area of my activity: The Indian camps around Whiteriver, then south nine miles past Fort Apache and the Canyon Day flats, then around the mesa to Bear Springs, and, following the road over Cedar Gap nineteen miles to the west, Cedar Creek, with West Cedar and Middle Cedar as offshoots, now on to Carrizo, forty miles from Whiteriver, and it always took half of a day to drive there. This was just one direction. Driving north from Whiteriver, my field of work included the Indian camps on the North Fork of the White River, continuing on to McNary, twenty-three miles from Whiteriver, on to Forestdale and those encampments about fifty miles from Whiteriver. The only way to get there was via the north road through an unimproved trail in the ponderosa pines. Visiting either Carrizo or Forestdale required staying overnight, camping on the ground near an open fire.

"I will forego camp-visiting experiences of those eight years I spent, but I do want to take my readers back into the kitchen and open some cupboard doors to let them look behind the scenes. At the end of the month we handed in our requisitions to the Mission Board, listing the salary, $83.33—⅓ in my case,[216] and give our mileage at 5 cents per mile. Provision was made if we married at $10.00 per month for the wife, and $5.00 per month for each child. President John Brenner called this "Kopfgeld" (head money), and he said it with a curl on his lip.[217]

---

[216] And Behn added in parenthesis, "Every third month not to forget that cent so books would balance!"

[217] Paul Behn, The Apache Lutheran, "Depression Days at East Fork 1934-1940," July, 1986.

Early mission work, Apache ladies reading.
Photo Credit: Paul Behn (from the author's collection of photographs)

Few missionaries did as much actual carpentry work and building as Paul Behn did. In 1939 he renovated the church at East Fork at no expense to the Mission Board, and he did it with the help of the school boys. Pastor Behn said it was at the time of the terrible hail storm in East Fork that ruined the roof on the church and almost ruined the building itself that the first offering was received from the people themselves. There was no money from the Mission Board. They had none, they said, so they asked the "Indians" to bring gifts to help. Offerings were not taken for the first decades because of the worry of being considered charlatans who were just out to fleece the people. There was an onus here that the missionaries had to overcome. That occasion came with the hail storm and a folding table that finally actually buckled under the weight of the freewill offering of Apache coins that were brought to repair their church's roof. Missionary Behn had a funny way of laughing, and after he told about the collapsing folding table he laughed and his hearers laughed with him.

There was no parsonage to live in when Paul Behn came to East Fork with his family. The epic story of how he built the parsonage at

East Fork is fascinating reading because it tells about life and relationships and off-reservation families supporting their families on the reservation. This phenomenon of self-help and mutual help in mission work has found expression in many other mission endeavors. The recollections of Paul Behn help us to remember how it was and to know, in some ways, how it still is today.

Inashood Behn wrote at the time of the building how it was with his house:

> The summer was begun with a great deal of fight and enthusiasm for heading into the work on the house, but now I must admit that it proved to be the hardest and most hectic that I have ever spent on the field. Perhaps it will always be that way when one not trained to be a carpenter and boss must make corrections, give decisions and the like that are not really in his line. But to make an appropriation stretch the limit when the odds are against one to begin with, and laboring with unskilled help day after day—that finally saps one's strength and gives the solar plexus rheumatism. (The

The parsonage at East Fork Mission that Paul Behn labored to make.
Painting by Krista Sedgeman

latter is not so far fetched, since it seemed for a time that I would have to run away from it all to get my balance again. My nervous system was pretty hard hit.)

The men on the place lent their help all they could as inexperienced men. My father came from California (with mother) and put in three solid months, granting his help to the Kingdom with no charge. The trades were handled by one and all on the roof, at plumbing, at wiring, at carpentry as if they were old hands at it.

When work was first begun, we were careful to salvage all the lumber from the rear porch wherever possible, but we found that the folks back in the good old days figured to make a good job of it by using 30-penny spikes wherever possible. We had a hard time salvaging much. We found the plates under the building in rather poor condition, which called for extras. The house itself had no sheathing, no building paper, no bracing—and we wondered why it was so cold. Later we found that the house was leaning by about two inches, which made more work for us than we ever thought. Floors were single and very poor, and the ceilings were eleven feet high. I wonder now that no one ever thought of creating an ice business. When we came to the five windows in the house we found them rotted beyond repair, so also the frames. And when we took off the outside casings the windows almost fell on us. Some construction! There was also little to salvage of plumbing goods, pipes corroded and breaking when detached. A new trench and sewer line had to be put in to run into the one leading from the boys' building. The old bricks (made locally about forty years ago) crumbled when we took the chimneys down. A few were used in the new chimney. All told, there was little to nothing to salvage.

While it really should not be, yet it is also true that one has more personal expenses than anticipated. Vacation was forfeited entirely, the garden was let go (which is a very large item to us in the sticks and far from the market), and when bargain hunting for materials for the house one always has personal expenses that would otherwise not be. Not knowing where to go with the family during moving time we stayed in the house with the little ones, the youngest born in February—and moved from room to room as required.

The enclosed list of expenditures for the house is a tale of woe, for we went past the mark. We did not want to exceed the appropriation, but all the unforeseen expenses, the condition of the house and the like, forced us into it. My father was a very conservative man, having graduated from the school of hard knocks quite early in life, and had to work hard in his days. From him I received most of my tips and advice."

And as Behn went on in the present tense of his diary and memory:

The house is not finished as yet, and if I am to do the rest myself, it will yet take many a weary day to wind it up. Mr. Knoop is at the finishing of the rooms, at the windows and doors, at the cupboard and shelves and the like. That is beyond any one of us. Mr. Krueger from Cibecue was also with us a few days, then Mr. Otto gave us a hand for a day. As for bargains, perhaps the largest one was to buy U.S. gypsum board for $35 per thousand instead of paying the regular $50, which is the board on our walls and ceilings. It is a wonderful insulator. Old wall board that was yet of value is being shifted to the service porch, hall and such places where nail holes and breaks will not be so easily seen. Then, of course, we received a 10% discount from Sears and Wards. Note that freight took practically a hundred dollars. Materials cost twice the labor. While the stucco is to be put on within a week or so, we are racing with Old Man Winter, hoping that the quarters will be at least so comfortable that we may go through the winter safely.

Would it be possible to tap in on the insurance money to supply the overshot on the house? I wrote of a possible overshot in June and pointed to this possibility at that time. The furnace was ordered from Mueller Bros. Milwaukee for $174.42. That was the best bid that I received. Kalamazoo was about fifty dollars higher. I may add here that I received a dealer's discount from them since my brothers install Mueller furnaces in northern Wisconsin, and the courtesy was extended to me. I referred them to you (the Mission Board) when I ordered. Of course, freight is extra. I will have to borrow the money to pay for the furnace until you are able to reimburse us.[218]

The house was affected further by the placement of a road that still runs through the property at East Fork. This road would necessitate moving the house to the spot where it would stand across from

---

[218] Paul Behn, *The Apache Lutheran*, June 1995.

The study at East Fork Mission parsonage.
Painting by Eric Hartzell

the church at East Fork. Missionary Behn thought back to those early days in his later rememberings too.

> One morning we received a phone call from the reservation superintendent at Whiteriver requesting a meeting. He and the Indian Mission superintendent (Missionary E. E. Guenther) would meet me at East Fork at a certain time. The reason for the meeting was that the government planned to improve the old dirt road between Fort Apache, through our property, and past the government farm station to the other side of the East Fork River. In doing so, he promised to build a fence to protect our property, and also put in an improved cattle guard.[219]

---

[219] This road-building was at the time of the early picture of the East Fork Mission compound with *Gan B'sedi*a in the background. In the picture on page 74 you can even see the initial house that eventually became the parsonage across from the church at East Fork. The cattle guard is still in place today.

Pastor Guenther and I realized that the government had no other choice but to place the road where the old road existed. But this presented a problem for us. By widening the road it would nudge our back porch. All agreed on this. We asked the superintendent if he would excavate the new location, pour the foundation walls, and move the house to this new location. He agreed to do this for us. So, all was set! But when the reservation superintendent forgot his promise to us, we appealed to a highway maintenance man, who agreed to excavate the basement (for the future parsonage). We borrowed needed equipment to pour the foundation walls and afterward hauled the house across the garden and placed it on the new foundation. Our East Fork Manpower came to the rescue, and my father also came from Pasadena, California. The latter was also a big help afterward in constructing door and window frames.

The house we were occupying was 30' by 30' in size. Previous missionaries had added a screened porch to the front, which served as a study during the warm weather. Also a screened porch was added to the rear of the house, part of what served as an entryway to the kitchen, the other as sleeping quarters when nights were comfortable. To explain about "comfortable weather": East Fork is in the White Mountains, having an altitude of about 5,300 feet. There are usually two very cold spells during a winter. There is also a wind factor, when breezes come off the hilltops every night. We lived through nights of 20 degrees below zero. The eleven-foot ceilings in the house added to our discomfort, and our family with three small children huddled in the kitchen, keeping the stove well stoked. All this was explained to our Mission Board in detail, suggesting with this move to add twenty feet to the house, necessary for growing families. The Board briefly replied, offering one thousand dollars but no further suggestions. Was the Big Depression cutting us short? We had a real problem!

During the reconstruction we learned why the old house was so uncomfortably cold during the winter months. The trouble was not just the high ceilings. When we removed the beaverboard from the walls we could see daylight. The beaverboard was all there was between us and the outdoors. The shiplap siding had shrunk, leaving cracks between the boards. Add to this: no diagonal braces in the walls; the plumb was off by four inches! We added twenty feet to the

229

house, installed a furnace and a hot water heater in the basement, and lowered all ceilings to 8' 5". The front porch was cemented, and the four posts holding up the roof of the porch were small pine trees, skinned and dried. The sides of the house were covered with tar paper and stuccoed.

The interior of the house contained a study, living room, dining room, kitchen, back hall, bathroom and three bedrooms. The living quarters received oak flooring. The walls and ceilings were covered with gypsum board, attractively patterned. All materials were purchased from a lumber company in Holbrook, a hundred miles away, which provided us with a "bevel-devil" with which we could bevel the edges of the gypsum board, so that it looked finished without the need of battens.

How was it possible to accomplish all this with only one thousand dollars? It wasn't possible! The Christmas Fund came to the rescue. We did everything to stretch the money we had. The balance was done by love's labor, offered by teachers and our maintenance man and by my father. My own work clothes were donned on Monday and rested on Saturday, not always just 48 hours each week.

We really enjoyed living in this house for the rest of our days until 1940 when we moved to Milwaukee. Since then almost fifty years have passed. Word has echoed back from people who occupied this house saying that they too enjoyed being there. In fact, only two years ago I was again approached by someone in Watertown, Wisconsin, expressing her joy in having lived in that house. She called attention especially to the attractive ceilings, like the one in the dining room with eye-catching "turkey tracks." And this parsonage has outlived a number of other buildings on the mission compound, in fact, it still stands as the parsonage for the pastor at East Fork and his family.[220]

So wrote Pastor Paul Behn about the house that stood across

---

[220] Those pine log supports on the porch were replaced by Pastor Eric Hartzell in July of 1989, when he and his family lived in the house. The posts were rotten. The very porch Behn talks about here was remodeled and enclosed with double-pane glass and was a wonderful place to sit on a blustery spring day in warm sunshine because it faced to the south. During that process of remodeling, Martin Wehausen's signature was found written on the siding up under the ceiling. It was a wonderful house, but before Pastor Hartzell had hardly gotten to Texas in his move there to be pastor in Georgetown, the powers at East Fork decreed the house to be destroyed, and they put a prefab double-wide in its place. "You take paradise, put up a parking lot," as the song goes.

from the church at East Fork. He went on to reminisce about the early days of the mission work he had been part of on the Ft. Apache Reservation:

> My dictionary says that a pioneer is one "who goes before to prepare the way for another; to open up, as a way or road; to take the lead in." When we consult our Synod's yearbook today under the heading of Arizona and of our churches on the Fort Apache Indian Reservation, it is most interesting to find congregations listed under the names: Canyon Day—served from East Fork; Cedar Creek—served from Cibecue; Fort Apache—served from Whiteriver; and McNary—having been served by various missionaries. These congregations all had beginnings. It is of these beginnings that I want to reminisce.
>
> When I was given the call in 1926 to serve as associate missionary at Whiteriver, Arizona, I soon learned why this station needed two men. Superintendent E. Edgar Guenther was the missionary of the large local congregation and Church of the Open Bible. The associate was assigned to the "field," roughly forty miles west to Carrizo and forty miles northwest to Forestdale (no highway directly between). Visiting the Apaches in their settlements along the trails was very slow and tedious work for the associate and his interpreter. It usually meant taking along lunch and water and spending the day going from tepee to tepee, or even at greater distances, sleeping under the stars. There were no congregations, no churches, no chapels. Usually we met as families, during the cold winters inside the tepee, and during the summer days under the family's home-constructed shelters nearby. The missionary took with him large books in which were mounted Bible pictures of the Old and New Testaments. His message was illustrated through the appropriate pictures.[221]
>
> The Gospel made its inroads slowly into the hearts of many who listened patiently. Many who were touched thanked for the visit and often extended their hands with a smile, adding the invitation to return soon. Such were the beginnings, the pioneerings. Little signs of growth developed especially during the warm months. With the honking of the automobile horn, people would congregate. Leaflets

---

[221] Consult the photograph that shows the women looking at materials that *Inashood* Behn had brought.

with Bible pictures were distributed, and with the help of the interpreter the Bible story was told, explained, and applied to each one. Then followed an appropriate prayer and the Lord's benediction.

In time we spoke to groups Sunday mornings at the time of their choosing, first at Canyon Day, which was about seven miles from Whiteriver. There was a government school at Canyon Day for children from kindergarten through the third grade, where the missionary held Bible classes once each week. These children were instrumental in bringing their parents to hear the missionary on Sundays. Soon things developed so that there were services of this same kind at Cedar Creek Crossing, which was nineteen miles from Whiteriver, and here we met at the back porch of R-14, with Chief Amos Altaha, about 11:00 on Sundays.

We tried something new. I purchased a stripped-down model T Ford and built a trunk at the rear of the car to accommodate a camp organ and a filmstrip projector. The projector was operated from the car's six-volt battery. I used filmstrips covering the Old and New Testaments and simple hymns and showed these at Canyon Day certain evenings. A canvas was hung under a shelter for a screen. It was surprising how many people were attracted.

Eventually a shed became available at Canyon Day near the homes of Chief Charley Shipp and Eli Opah which we used as a church. Planks were placed from applebox to applebox to serve as benches, and an old circle saw was hung outside the door as our bell. Now we could "have church" rain or shine. All our efforts were blessed. There was a swelling in attendance.

Old Fort Apache ceased to be a military post in December 1923. A new Theodore Roosevelt School was constructed by the government especially for Navajo children brought here from their reservation. Children of the upper grades of Canyon Day were also enrolled here. During the school year I drove five miles once a week to conduct Bible classes for the Apaches.

For McNary we had to drive twenty-two miles north to this sawmill town, where a number of Apache men were employed. Fortunately, we had the use of a new building built by the Cady Lumber Company on a cement slab to be used as a pool hall. Instead, it became the home of Joe and Edith Ivins. Here was where we met Thursday evenings for our informal services. Roe Clark and his wife were also pillars of this group. I will always remember a Christmas service here because of an exchange of gifts, some of which were hand-tooled. When the summer months came, we enjoyed "fishing with poles" (really wiener roasts) in the woods. In later years fire destroyed the "pool hall," and it was on that slab that Pastor E. Guenther built the present church.[222]

And it wouldn't be mission work if there weren't some drama with "the encumbrances of remote control," as Edgar Guenther called it, or "Dual Control," as General George Crook labeled it. It happened and Paul Behn wrote aggravated episodes that described it, even if humorously to us from our safe present-day position of history.

> Dear Brother R.: As yet I am unable to give a comprehensive report on the gasoline consumption, since with the statement of remittance other things entered in that I am unable to answer at this time. That will follow as soon as I receive data necessary.
>
> Perhaps the enormous gasoline purchases of October-November 1938 are partially answered by this time, after you have received the statements for the following months. May I call your attention to this fact once more that we cannot always obtain gasoline just when we want it. So it happens that the deliveries pile up during one period, while at another it strings along "catch as catch can." It has happened that the truck was expected on a day because they telephoned from Holbrook that they were coming, but when he came he had made deliveries along the way and did not have enough left for us. To tide us over we have purchased in smaller quantities. Weather has been a factor in deliveries also, since the truck cannot possibly get to our supply tank when it is muddy. We have had two deliveries in one day, one barrel hauled by ourselves in the morning, and in the afternoon the truck came. Because of such irregularities we try to order the next consignment of gasoline when we have about fifty gallons in the storage tank. Oddly enough, we have run out a number of times before the consignment reached us.
>
> Did you actually believe that 438 gallons of gasoline were consumed in October when a delivery of 208 gallons was made on

---

[222] Pastor Paul Behn, *The Apache Lutheran*, October 1990. (By the way, that original building of Edgar Guenther is still in use today, although it has been remodeled a number of times.)

the 27th? Then what did we use up to the 11th of November? Did you also believe that we used 518 gallons in November when a delivery of 163 gallons was made on the 28th? Then what do you suppose we used for fuel up to the 22nd of December? And so 266 gallons on the December bills was consumed up to Jan. 21st, and the Jan. 30th delivery was consumed in February. It is also a fact to which I have referred before, that the F-M (the light plant generator) is consuming more gas per hour this year than a year ago. The statements to the State Highway Department testify to this also. Your statement "We are convinced that the F-M did not require 406 gals. of gas during this period of 1938. Then what was it used for?" leads me to believe that you did not believe my markings on the bills, which show it was used for power, and that the statements to the Highway Department were sworn to falsely. That the average for monthly gasoline consumption from June-November 1937 is 342 gals. per month, and that from June 1938 to January 1938 averages 360 gallons per month is by no means an outrage. In fact, we held down the time of running the F-M this year, starting it 20 to 30 minutes later in the evening than we should, and have used candles instead to get along.

Oil consumption—You know how much of this there has been used during the past months. Would you believe that it is possible for a motor to suddenly quit using oil and go on a strict economy basis of less than one-fourth the former consumption? Believe it or not, the F-M did. Already last fall we used kerosene to flush the crankcase and loosen carbon in the motor—but it availed us nothing. Not so long ago Mr. Klaus gave it an overdose in the crankcase, in the combustion chambers and valves. It was enough to get into every crevice of the rings and cut the carbon that kept them from expanding properly. The rings functioning properly again, it cut down on the use of oil. We did not believe it possible without dissecting the motor and doing an overhaul job, but it did. It has, however, not cut down on the consumption of gasoline. On a test this morning, using only a one quart measure of gasoline, that quart was burned up in thirteen minutes.

The gasoline and oil report for February is enclosed. It is early, but I am enclosing it to use together with the above report.

Sincerely, P.B.[223]

The next description and writing happened in September of 1939, almost in the war years. Actually, as we discern from these let-

---

[223] Paul Behn, *The Apache Lutheran*, March 1992.

ters from Paul Behn, there were some shots being fired over the bow on the reservation at this time too.

"Some time ago I reported to you my findings on the price of diesel fuel. Union Oil Company will not handle it because it does not pay them to haul it from their distributing point at the price that Standard Oil is selling it here. Mr. Crawford explained that they can purchase it in Los Angeles for 3½ cents, but the freight on it to McNary is 4½ cents. It costs them 1¾ cents to handle it locally.

Richfield is charging 9 cents delivered from Holbrook to Sisson's garage. Standard Oil's price is 8¾ cents delivered to Whiteriver. They will not haul it to East Fork at this price. Our truck must get it. Mr. Klaus tells me that it takes a quart and a half of oil and two gallons of gasoline to make the round trip to Whiteriver.[224] The truck has no compression at all. It has a hard time propelling itself empty on a straight road, and takes low and compound low to go up a hill. Thus the tremendous consumption of gas and oil. The Standard Oil salesman told me that if we took eight barrels at once he would haul it in his pickup directly to our door, but that would not affect the unity price."

Then I explained to him our method of payment. He said he would take it up with the Phoenix office, but he doubted very much whether they would sell to us on sixty days. To date I have not heard the outcome. Judging from the local stores who have purchased from these oil companies for years, and are asked to pay cash, I doubt whether we will be treated differently. The stores have been on a cash basis of two years.

If Standard Oil asks for cash, what do you advise? Is it possible to send these bills to you at once for payment? Standard Oil delivers only to Goodman's; they ask 2 cents per gallon for handling. They are good enough to let down the bars to us if we can handle our accounts ourselves. [225]

Pastor Arthur Guenther used to object very much to people from off the reservation coming onto the reservation and saying derogatory things about the Apache people regarding the wrong use of drugs and alcohol, or mentioning living conditions and social mores—or the lack of them. This is the way all the missionaries were when it came to

---

[224] That is a total of 10 miles! (Editor).

[225] Paul Behn, *The Apache Lutheran*, May, 1992.

these imported attacks on their Apache people and their communities. There was (and is) much of this negative chatter and uncomplimentary stereotyping of the Apache people in the white communities that border the reservations. But Pastor Guenther and the other missionaries felt that the missionaries earned the right to speak about things that were impacting their work and their people in a negative way. Their work was not being done in a vacuum, and it was influenced and affected by what went on in the communities of the reservation where they were living and working and trying to help. Perhaps, to sum it up, missionaries were the insiders who were actually living with the people and trying to help them and encourage them. They earned the ability to speak against social evils and to identify them so that they could help. It was like a family member speaking, as opposed to someone who lived across the street speaking, who wanted to criticize and cluck their tongues at someone who was not related to them.

Pastor Behn spoke clearly of his feelings about the ills that were plaguing his people. Fifteen years of life and commitment gave him some right to speak the way he did. His comments were not policy, but they were personal and came from experience and observation close up. When Missionary Arthur Krueger wrote a paper entitled "Should Missionaries Take Part in the Economical and Industrial Development of the Indians?" and he presented it to the mission group, it was a trigger that caused Behn to fire off, "But why are the Apaches poor? It is because they want it that way. They choose not to work. They have their cattle, and we see they are getting less on most ranges, because they do not want to ride their ranges. They have their land for farms, but so often we see the weeds choke the corn, because they do not want to hoe the corn. So, they choose to be poor, they choose not to learn, they choose to be idle. They are the richest people in the United States. Therefore it is not our business to help this condition along with also our support. The support the government is giving is harming this condition of idleness enough." [226] As time went along, agricultural efforts on the reservation did wane. Irrigation ditches silted up and washed out. Willows grew in the fields so that the ground could not be plowed. To this day, the potential of agriculture has not been met at all.

Fifteen years of life on the Fort Apache Reservation went by, and *Inashood* Paul Behn moved on. What happened as the result of his fifteen years of work and labor? The answer to that question—which could be asked with a sigh or with a frown—is that good things happened because of the missionary's presence and work. Even at that

---

[226] Paul Behn, *The Apache Scout*, "Northern Reservation Mission Workers," June, 1931, p. 31.

time Superintendent Edgar Guenther could write, "On the Friday before Christmas this writer had the pleasure of hearing the Christmas program prepared by Missionary Behn with the children of Canyon Day School. Here also one could see that every child was glad to take part, if not individually, then at least in letting himself be heard in the Christmas hymns. Anyone not knowing these children would hardly believe that many of them did not know a word of English just a few months ago."[227]

Paul Behn really was a missionary to the end. He worked in Hong Kong for a while later in his life, and before that he developed a standard procedure for the training of Apache men in the ministry of the churches on the reservation. It was a four-step program: Interpreter/lay worker, catechist, vicar, missionary/pastor. He was almost a visionary in this regard. It would actually turn out similar to this as the Apache Christian Training School (ACTS) did its work at the end of the 1990s into the 2000s. In defining outline point "A" under his fourth step of "missionary/pastor" Behn gave his opinion about the status of this missionary/pastor and said, "He (the student) shall be considered a full-fledged pastor among his Apache people. He shall not necessarily be considered eligible for a call to other than Apache congregations, and shall have the title of 'pastor' after he as a vicar had satisfactorily passed a colloquy."

The Behns had their own personal connection with the little cemetery up behind the mission at East Fork. In May of 1928 former superintendent Edgar Guenther wrote about them: "Word has been received from Pasadena, California, of the birth of a little boy to Pastor and Mrs. Paul Behn. We welcome the young man to our corps of potential missionaries." Little "Buddy" Paul Behn would drown in the river at East Fork while his parents served there. He is buried in the cemetery above the mission alongside many little Apache children who died at the nursery and were also buried there. But missionaries were also buried in that cemetery, and "budding" missionaries were too. Pastor Ernie Sprengeler and teacher Raymond Riess also rest from their labors there.

When Chief Alchesay died August 6, 1928, it was Pastor Paul Behn who buried him on that lonely cliff face overlooking the North Fork of the White River.

---

[227] E. Guenther, *The Apache Lutheran*, December 1995.

CHAPTER FIFTEEN

Two Albrechts, Schlegel, and LaHaine

Thunder is good, thunder is impressive;
but it is lightning that does the work (MARK TWAIN).

When pastors left the reservation, more often than not, they were replaced by recent seminary graduates. Some of the missionaries began to suspect that the placement committee was not sending them the cream of the crop. In 1923 Missionary Paul Albrecht complained bitterly when the seminary and mission board sent candidate Erich LaHaine to Fort Apache. Missionary Albrecht had trouble with the authorities too, as his further account shows. As it turned out, Guenther was very pleased with LaHaine's work.[228] This polarization between the perceived "haves and have nots" happened. How could it have been avoided among human beings living and working together in close quarters as these missionaries were? People in missiology have said that the hardest thing for missionaries on a foreign field is not acclimatization or loneliness or struggling to get proficiency in the language. The hardest thing to overcome and live with is the rub of relationships with fellow missionaries. That observation and thought were supported by some of the histrionics of the Apache mission field. To deal with this phenomenon two philosophies emerged: the first was that the missionaries should do everything together to hopefully get over the differences and hopefully develop some fondness of familial feeling; the second was to have as little social contact as possible and to come together only when necessitated by the work itself.

At this time in the story of the Apache Mission even the seasoned missionaries had become embroiled in disputes. Edgar Guenther in his recording of the history that transpired provided a number of instances of the strife that was going on in the work. In 1922 he even resigned as Superintendent of the Indian Missions because of bitter remarks made against him and his wife by Francis Uplegger and

---

228 This information was from Edgar Guenther's own writings, supplied by his grandson Dr. William Kessel.

others.[229] Francis Uplegger stated that the synodical mission board refused to accept Guenther's resignation. Within a year Paul Albrecht tried to get LaHaine called to Minnesota and insinuated that Pastor Guenther was dishonest. For such remarks Albrecht was resoundingly censured. Even the administrative committee got into the fray. Paul Brockmann, chairman of the Executive Committee of Missions, wrote a letter in 1924 to his friend Pastor Guenther and confessed that he was tired and frustrated and planning to resign his position. It wasn't something that he ended up doing, but he thought about it. Pastor Nitz and Mrs. Plumb of the orphanage became involved in a disagreement, and the latter threatened to resign. Pastor Guenther intervened and drew up guidelines for the supervision of the orphanage. Meanwhile both Nitz and Guenther were convinced that Melvin Croll, who took Martin Wehausen's place at East Fork, was a totally ineffective teacher. Two years later Croll accepted a call to Wisconsin. Historian Kessel mentioned that dozens of similar incidents occurred.

When fellow missionary Paul Albrecht had his trouble in the work on the upper reservation, Rosin showed some missionary mettle in a terse letter written January 19, 1923. "Since Paul Albrecht cannot satisfy the dictates of his conscience by returning to Whiteriver, your requesting him to do so would simply force him out of the service. This cannot be your aim. To be justified in forcing him out you must necessarily be absolutely certain that Albrecht is in the wrong. I believe you have not this certainty. In the interest of the mission I write this, and I beg you not to take any other action than such as will do justice to Albrecht and be for the good of our mission. Sincerely, H. E. Rosin."

Albrecht's crime was that he had balked about being in Cibecue. It took him two days by horseback to reach the place. The isolation and hardships of just getting there had taken their toll. It took a special person to be at Cibecue. Rosin's son Rupert would be there as a teacher in later years. Even then there was no electricity, and the roads were red quagmire in any kind of rain or snow. Later missionaries almost came to grief in crossing Cibecue Creek in high water. The water was going through the cab of their panel truck, and the superintendent of the field was even there in the cab! Two Apache men lassoed the bumper and with their horses pulled the inert missionaries and their panel truck to safety. This was the place that had done Paul Albrecht in. He hid out at the U. S. Game and Fish Station

---

[229] There were others (Sitz, Wehausen, Nitz to mention a few) who had trouble peacefully coexisting with Minnie Guenther.

in Lakeside for a while to escape those who were coming after him. These were for him just plain the worst of times.

There was also Missionary Christian Albrecht who gave five years of his life to the mission at East Fork, serving from 1929 through 1934. He wrote in 1929 about life on the mission in an interesting and engaging way. Concerning the school he wrote,

> At this time there is an enrollment of 22 boys and 21 girls, a total of 43. In these figures 8 boys and 3 girls are included who make their home in the orphanage. These are regularly classed as boarding school scholars as contrasted to day school or camp scholars. No sickness beyond slight colds occurred during this period, for which we were thankful to the Lord who held his protecting hand over us.
>
> A few weeks before Christmas the matrons and the girls could at last move into the new girls' dormitory. Special credit is due the matrons in charge and the girls for taking care to preserve the inside appearance of this building so that at the end of the school year hardly any traces of wear and tear could be noticed. In the basement, however, quite a number of window panes were broken due to the fact that there were no screens. This evil has been remedied during the summer months.
>
> The attendance at the grade school has improved very much over past years. Aside from cases of sickness it has been almost perfect. This must be attributed to the tireless efforts of the teachers, Pastor Meier and Miss Albrecht. Naturally the efficiency of the classroom work has improved correspondingly. Miss Louis Ahrens who served as day school matron during the past year has again returned to her home in Tucson, Arizona. I want to acknowledge here the modest and efficient way in which she went about her many duties as day school matron and assistant boarding school matron. This year Miss Esther Prigge is again filling this position. We are thankful that she has regained her health sufficiently to take hold of these duties again. During the first weeks of school this fall, the enrollment wavered slightly, and at the close of this period the total enrollment is 64."

Missionary Albrecht goes on to speak of the orphanage at East Fork, "Since January 1, eight children were admitted into the orphanage; five died and one returned to camp. This gives us 27 children now as compared with 25 last January. Five children were in camp during the summer months but have returned for school. One of these, Cora

Suttle, fell from a horse on the way to school and broke her leg. She was then taken to the Whiteriver hospital where she still is under treatment. We hope to have her with us again in a short time. Another girl, Mary Garland, fell from the fire escape in July, breaking her left arm near the socket joint. She was taken to the Whiteriver hospital, where the arm was improperly set because the doctor thought it was merely a dislocated shoulder. When the break was finally discovered with the help of an X-ray in McNary, it was too late to bring the arm back to the correct position. The bone was, however, rebroken and placed parallel that now she can at least move the arm freely." And besides these happenings at the orphanage Albrecht reported that the new orphanage building was well under way: "The excavation under the orphanage was completed, and the foundation walls built down to about eight inches below floor level. Now there is a complete basement under this building. The additional room gained is to be used for 'stockroom' and 'root cellar.' "

And the last part of his informative report says,

> During this period our milk supply generally was good. Since we have our own bull, several cows have been bred to freshen in fall when we need the milk most. This helps much to supply our milk needs. But most of the cows are of such poor breeding that we must feed twice as many cows as would be necessary if we had good stock. A poor cow will eat as much as a good cow. A poor cow like most of ours will produce two to three gallons a day, a good cow eight to ten gallons.

> This summer we raised five calves which we are butchering now for baby beef. This should help reduce our beef bill a little. Besides these calves we also raised three pigs, fed mainly on table scraps. The goats have been a thorn in my eyes as long as I have been here. I therefore tried to dispose of them. The young ones I sold at $1.00 a piece, one old one with two kids for $12.00. Two of the younger old ones we butchered recently. Now we still have one old nanny and billy which we fear to bring to the table. We have already spoken of turning them loose in the hills.

> The apple orchard was loaded with fruit to capacity. When a little more than half of the apples were picked we had a very heavy hailstorm which damaged many of the finest apples. The hail stones were so large that they literally punctured the paper roofing in many places. So you can imagine what happened to the apples that were hit squarely. These apples are now being used first.

Because of the lack of funds to hire painters I did much of this work myself. Still the paint job could not be finished. The "Meier Place" was not touched because of the contemplated addition to this house. The chapel and my house received one coat, and as mentioned before the orphanage two coats. As soon as the field work is finished Mr. Kussow and the boys should complete this work.

Water is still our unsolved problem. My plan is to develop the spring for a drinking water supply so that we would always have pure spring water for drinking and cooking and soft river water for washing etc. When the river is muddy during spring and summer floods we could pump all water from the spring.[230]

The Sunday evening service was discontinued shortly after my arrival in East Fork. Pastor Meier and I agreed that it was superfluous, since all of our people, with the exception of one orphanage matron, attended the morning service. This evening service also deprived the children of this necessary study time and burdened the pastors, who were already tired from school work, with a sermon every Sunday. Hence we have had only one Sunday service, Pastor Meier and I taking turns in the pulpit. While Pastor Meier was in the East during the summer months, I conducted services every Sunday. On one of these Sundays I preached in Whiteriver, Pastor Guenther not having yet returned from the East after synod meeting and Pastor Behn having gone to Bylas.

Nearly all of the school children are in attendance at church every Sunday, but the camp attendance is rather meager with the number wavering. Because of Pastor Meier's absence, I officiated at five funerals, and in addition to this I officiated at four orphanage funerals.

We have pressing needs! The first of these is an immediate necessity. The hail storm mentioned in this report put the paper roofs in such deplorable condition that if they are not redressed before spring we must expect that the spring winds will finish the destruction begun by the hail. This means the roof on the chapel, the orphanage, my house, and the "Meier house."

---

[230] Missionary Albrecht did develop the spring at the bottom of the hill for water supply, replete with the "pump house" where later mission people stored government surplus butter and cheese for the school kitchen.

Then I want to call attention to the benefits we could derive from a silo. A new barn would also be very desirable for the cleanliness of the milk, the comfort of cows and horses as well as that of the farmer, the appearance of the station.

I have other suggestions for improvements in mind but the realization of these plans seems to be so far removed in the dim future that I would rather not burden your minds with them at this time.

Respectfully submitted to the Superintendent and Board of Indian Missions this sixteenth day of October, 1929. Chr. Albrecht."

Christian Albrecht also told of Lambert Stone, the former Apache scout, riding into the mission compound at Thanksgiving time in 1929 with two big wild turkeys hanging from the straps of his saddle. One went to the nursery where his granddaughter, Mary Garland, had been for several years. She carried the bird that nearly equaled her in weight into the nursery and plopped it down on the floor by the sink.

Gustav Schlegel came and worked at Bylas and did good work too. He was responsible for getting the work at Bylas off the ground. But sickness got him, and he had to leave. Acute Bright's Disease was the malady, and he went back to Benton Harbor, Michigan, and then he had a relapse. He was told by doctors that he could not go back to life and work on the reservations. He regretted it very much, and so did the mission committee, who recognized his good work among the Apaches.

It was because of Missionary Gustav Schlegel's illness that young Alfred Uplegger came to serve in Bylas. It had all started for the Schlegels in 1924. The heat was impossible for Mrs. Schlegel to stand, and then Gustav had gotten sick and had to leave. Later he wrote, "Some time ago I myself took sick, very sick, and I was on the road traveling away from home. At last I went to see a doctor. He examined me, told me to take a train and go to the home of my relatives for I was very sick, and might not get well. This was sad news, but I thought of the word of God which said, 'I am the Lord that healeth thee.' And I said: 'Lord, if thou wouldst, Thou canst heal me.' So I took the train and went to the home of my parents. Here I called another doctor, who did not say much the first time he came. But now, since I am getting better, he told my wife that when he first saw me he did not think that I would live long, perhaps another day or two. But it is not the doctor, but the Lord who has my life in his hands. Of course I take the medicine which the doctor gives me. There are many things which I am not to eat; I do what the doctor tells me to do.

I am feeling quite a bit better now. Is it the doctor that is making me well? No, it is not the doctor. It is he in whom I have placed my trust, he who says, 'I am the Lord that healeth thee.' "[231]

And finally, Erich LaHaine swings into view. He is the one whom Paul Albrecht so hoped would not come to work on the mission, and it was he also with whom Guenther was well pleased. "He began his duties as assistant missionary on the Whiteriver field on July 15. We hope this will be good news to the Indians living below the Post, and North Fork, and Cedar Creek."[232]

At Erich LaHaine's time on the mission field one of his fellow missionaries wrote, "We were on our way to the post office but were stopped at the 'wash.' It had rained hard in the mountains: down the wide bed of the 'wash' came the waters from the higher land, rolling, foaming, carrying mud and gravel, rolling boulders, tearing away shrubs at the banks. On the other side of the 'wash' people were waiting for the time when it would be possible to cross over to our side. We remembered having seen in another 'wash,' half in mud, gravel and stones the wreck of a truck the driver of which, with a companion, could just jump off in time when the rolling waters began to strike it. We thought of the two missionaries who, when their car was stuck in a 'wash' while it was raining thought to let the shower pass over before they would start the car again, but then heard and saw at once a solid mass of water rushing down toward the spot so that they barely could jump to save their lives, while the car was rolling away and wrecked among the rocks below."[233]

Pastor Erich LaHaine had the misfortune of losing his brand-new Star automobile in a flood near East Fork in August. He and Pastor Albrecht barely got out of the car in time. It seems they were the ones mentioned before as "the two missionaries." If they were indeed those two, it was ironic that with the animosity that existed between them, they had this life-changing experience together. Erich LaHaine's unlucky Star was a total loss. That's what Edgar Guenther reported. The Star was found downstream beached and beaten and worthless. Missionary Guenther goes on to report, however, that "Mr. LaHaine is happy to own another new Star with which to cover his large field."

And Missionary LaHaine got $30.00 in 1925 to build a chicken house in Whiteriver. The reader should not snicker to hear these humble facts for Missionary LaHaine. We know very little about this

---

[231] *The Apache Scout,* October, 1926.

[232] *The Apache Scout,* August 1923), EEG.

[233] *The Apache Scout,* "The Rock that Is Higher Than I." August, 1925.

man other than a wrecked Star automobile and a $30.00 chicken pen (provided it got built) and an innocent inclusion into a missionary squabble on the field. We also know that Missionary Guenther liked the work of this young missionary. Cars, chickens and personality cliques were the reality, though. Mission work was about living everyday life in a strange and different place, but mission work was about ordinary and common things, too.

CHAPTER SIXTEEN

Uplegger, Uplegger and Rosin

Always forgive your enemies.
Nothing annoys them so much (OSCAR WILDE).

Alfred Uplegger was first to the missionary work among the Apaches; his father Francis came later. He came from the seminary in Wisconsin to Globe, Arizona, in January of 1917. Pastor Gustav Harders was the pastor in charge when Alfred arrived, but it was only to be that way until April when Harders died.[234] Listen to how he described things when he came:

> A story of the determination of a missionary tells how he was warned by friends in regard to privations that he would meet there on a South Sea island far from communication with other people. But he said, "Is there bread there?" "Then I can live there also even if there are no conveniences there!!"
>
> Pastor Gustav Harders was such a man, and Pastor Carl Guenther also and those few that brought the Gospel to the Apache in those early years. When he needed a chapel for worship services, then he went around to the merchants of Globe, Arizona, and asked for help in the form of boards and roofing, and set to work with his daughters and sons to build the necessary little chapel and a very simple school building. The members of the Wisconsin Synod were not well aware of the needs of a mission among the Apache Indians who were still actually prisoners of war who had been subdued and put on the San Carlos Indian Reservation in 1873, only twenty years before our mission began at Peridot. They did not receive citizenship till 1924.
>
> Now my story: In November 1916 Pastor Harders came from Globe, Arizona, to Milwaukee, Wisconsin. Though not

---

234 There have been a number of father/son teams in the mission work: Edgar and Arthur Guenther; Henry and Frederick Nitz; Francis and Alfred Uplegger; Eugene and Eric Hartzell.

Fancis (left) and Alfred Uplegger (right) at church in San Carlos
with Apache family.

Photo Credit: Uplegger Family photo, author's collection.

well at all, suffering from a throat infection which developed into throat tuberculosis, yet out of love for the Apache
Indians and for our mission among them he braved the
three day journey to come to the Theological Seminary in
Wauwatosa, Wisconsin, in order to speak to the faculty and
address the Senior Class.

He told of the plight of the Indians suffering from overexposure and under-nourishment and of the emergency in the
mission field. We third-year students sat with faces glued to
his description of the situation. He told of the missionary,
Pastor Carl Toepel, who was stationed at Peridot and who
had accepted a call to Town Newton after four years of service. Pastor Carl Guenther had been at Peridot from 1903 to
1912, but had to leave on account of health with throat trouble and was unable to speak, whose wife died in Arizona of
tuberculosis, and who was a sister of my own aunt.

Pastor H. C. Nitz had vicared there at Peridot in 1916
giving up his second year at the seminary, though he had
already sacrificed the year before teaching in the mission
school at Globe. Now Peridot was vacant again, and a sec-

247

ond emergency arose when Miss Marie Kieckbush suffered a nervous breakdown. This caused Pastor Harders to plead for help by two students to come before graduation. He spoke from his love for the Indians. He described their plight in detail. That touched many of the students. He described how they were in a state of despair, dying of tuberculosis because of overexposure to wind, rain and snow, in spite of hot summer weather. They did not have enough clothing to keep warm, and then they were also undernourished because of lack of money to buy proper food. So, in the winter they were very miserable. And here I should insert: The Department of the Interior was still holding the Indians as prisoners of war. Anyone who will take time to read some of the Apache history will see how they surrendered against great odds, so that they would not all be killed. Some of the wise old men advised their fellow braves to give up. They had been chased and hounded for a hundred years already, especially since the Civil War. They had fled into old Mexico. But there the Mexican Army was after them. So they had drifted back and forth over the boundary trying to find safety. Some ruthless, cruel and unscrupulous white people said, "The only good Indian is a dead one!" So low the hate of unchristian people had fallen.

"Who is willing to volunteer to help these suffering Apaches?" Pastor Harders pleaded. Willing to endure their hardships with them in order to bring them hope by the Gospel of the forgiveness of sins through the Savior Christ, so that in their misery and suffering they do not all lose salvation, but lay hold on the life to come.

Four young students raised their hands. Ewald Sterz and Raymond Huth did not get the consent of their parents. Henry Rosin and Alfred Uplegger also raised their hands, and their parents gladly consented even before they were asked. We should be ready to come as quickly as possible because the emergency did not allow waiting. Gustav Harders received his call to Peridot and hurried to get there so that he was at Peridot for Christmas in 1916. After that the Mission Board members, Pastor Henry Gieschen, Sr. and O.H. Koch, came to the house of the Director of the Lutheran High School of Milwaukee, Dr. Francis Uplegger[235], the day after Christmas. I saw them come and knew at once what

---

235 Francis was Alfred's father. He was director of the school in Milwaukee at this time.

their message would be. After a few minutes I was called into my father's study. "How soon can you be on your way? We shall get a railroad pass for you." And after wishing me a safe journey and hoping that the Lord would be with me to grant a safe journey, I went. My one regret was that I could not finish the year at the Seminary. They said, "The year with Pastor Harders will be sufficient compensation. The faculty knows about it already."

There was not much to get ready. January 1, 1917, my own father ordained me after a memorable sermon on Isaiah 6:8 by my enthusiastic and dear Professor August Pieper whose expositions of the Prophet Isaiah were soul-touching to all students who sat at his feet! At 5:00 a.m. the following Sunday morning, the 7th of January, my father accompanied me to the Milwaukee Road Station, and my Rock Island and Pacific train left Chicago at 9:00 a.m. and arrived at El Paso, Texas, on Tuesday morning after two clear, moonlit nights, then proceeding on the same train over the Southern Pacific Road to Bowie, Arizona. In Bowie I had to change to the El Paso and Southwestern branch line to Globe, Arizona, arriving there about 7:00 p.m. on January 9, 1917. It was very enjoyable for me to watch the countryside peering through the window expecting to see Indians on the Reservation. But it was dark and no Indians were in sight. I waited to see the desert, but no desert came along, instead rolling foothills with lots of mesquite and scattered in between the yucca, on the narrow, elongated leaves on which the moonlight seemed to dance in hiding fashion. I noticed the train engine chugging harder. It was gaining altitude. The railroad was cut through many low hills extending down from the mountain like fingers into the valleys below. At last at the top of the long grade, before the last two miles, the brakes were tested and then the train rolled coasting down into the mining camp of Globe.

Pastor Harders and the daughter Hilde and the sons Knut and Jens were at the depot to receive me. Before my feet stepped down to the ground, Pastor Harders beckoned me to wait and to listen. I waited till I stood on the step. "Listen, you have come very quickly, but you must know that in my letter to you, which you did not receive before leaving home, I said you cannot be my assistant because you are to be in charge as missionary and teacher. If any assisting becomes necessary, then I will try to give it." Then of course

I had to assent. The brakeman had set my suitcase down and the boys put it into a buggy or a double buckboard. So they took me up the hill to the mission and after eating supper and visiting they took me to one of two rooms added to the school building, which had been used as a room for Earnest Brown, the first mission school boarding student who was kept there because he had no other place to stay. The room for me had a single cot, a commode with a wash basin and towel and soap.

I slept well and was surprised in the morning to see snow on the Pinal Mountains. The town of Globe nestled like Rome on seven hills. Pinal Creek flowed at the bottom in the canyon. What a happy surprise to see the trees, mostly cottonwoods without leaves in January, but also the evergreens. From my geography book in school in Wisconsin we gained the impression that Arizona was all desert, more like the Sahara in Africa. And here we were in mountain country with all kinds of trees and cacti. This is more like a beautiful garden framed with Pine trees; even Douglas fir up on the higher mountain slopes, visible from twenty miles away! Even though they appear to be only seven miles away. The air is so clear, very little humidity, which accounts for night getting very cold in the winter because of the rapid evaporation. The sun warms the air in a short time in the morning.[236]

You can see the interest in life and the attention to detail that Alfred Uplegger had. You can witness his missionary zeal and his willingness to go even to a Sahara Desert if necessary, but instead the place he came to was beautiful in his eyes. When he later described Peridot and San Carlos to people it was as though he were describing heaven itself. His autobiography written on sheets of paper and recorded also on tape cassettes of the old vintage tell of it all.

Pastor Edgar Hoenecke, of later missionary fame himself, wrote about Alfred, "The responsibility of the church and school in Globe now rested on Uplegger's inexperienced shoulders. However, his best friend and classmate, Henry Rosin, was also assigned to Apacheland after his graduation from the seminary. Harders' example of loving devotion and warm concern for the Indians left a life-long impres-

---

[236] This account is from Alfred Uplegger's own writing and autobiography. Pastor Myrl Wagenknecht has retyped it all.

sion on young Uplegger and, through him, also on Henry Rosin."[237]

In 1918 the mission board sent Alfred Uplegger to San Carlos. There was a little chapel there outfitted with an organ and a bell by the General Synod, made of volcanic tufa stone. Alfred was sent there to serve and to hopefully stave off the advances the Catholics were making in the work begun by the Lutherans. Peridot, where Henry Rosin would live and work and spend his life, was just up the road a few miles. Alfred's initial assignment was to serve at old San Carlos (later to be covered by the waters of Coolidge Dam). In addition, he served in Calva and in Geronimo some twenty miles farther to the east. He managed to get a house built there at San Carlos for about $2,000. The government said it was worth $3,000 ten years later when it condemned the place to the rising waters of Coolidge Dam.[238]

Alfred Uplegger was, like Gustav Harders, the consummate missionary. No doubt he learned from his missionary mentor Harders in Globe in 1917. He followed his people as they traveled and moved from place to place seeking employment and life. As an example from many years later, he followed the Hunter Family to Chicago and found them there as he traveled back to the Midwest for a visit. Around San Carlos he preached at Hilltop, Warm Springs, Ash Creek, Bear Canyon, Seneca, Regal Mine, the CCC camps, Winkleman, Bylas, Roosevelt Dam, near Payson, and in many other places. At first at San Carlos he had both a horse and a Ford. It got too expensive for both. His salary was pinched and would not reach, so the horse went and the Ford stayed. With his Ford he navigated the dusty roads and the sometimes roaring gulches and washes of the reservation. He was aided by Apache men who helped him in his work and preaching. He didn't have the gift of language his father Francis did, but Rankin Rogers, Mark Hopkins, Timothy Victor, Clarence Bullis and other Apache men interpreted for him and stood at his side.[239]

Who can imagine what it was like back in those days when Alfred Uplegger came and saw this place where he would spend his life? Globe was a rough and reckless mining camp. The church spot was on one of the brushy hills that overlooked the town. It was horribly hot in the summer time, with temperatures soaring way above

---

[237] The Fall 1984 issue of the *WELS Historical Institute Journal.* Quoted in: *To Every Nation, Tribe, Language and People,* p. 33.

[238] The money for the sale of this house would later be used to build the parsonage at Upper Cibecue on the Fort Apache Reservation.

[239] Mark Hopkins died after he was severely burned in a gasoline explosion. Timothy Victor served for thirty years as interpreter.

100 degrees, and in the winter it could get down to zero on a cold and still night after a weather front moved through. The nearby Pinals never lent their shade in the summer but did lend their snow in the winter. Henry Rosin pleaded for his friend Alfred that the mission board provide a decent place for him in San Carlos where he could live and exist. The friend up close was more compassionate than the board far away.[240] Just to end up calling San Carlos home was a feat for a young and not-so-robust man from Wisconsin. [241]

San Carlos and environs were a place of sickness and death. During the fighting days the Apaches confined there died in great numbers. In the 1880s Naiche lost half of his people to disease and malaria bred in the brackish backwater of the Gila nearby. That in itself was a big cause for the outbreaks that happened. What an awful choice the people had to make: stay and die or break out and run and be killed in the catching or be brought back to the place of contagion to start the process all over again! Uplegger wrote that in his ministrations to the sick people he used his right hand when he needed to touch the people, and he kept his left hand for himself. It didn't work completely for Alfred and the staving off of sickness. He did get sick. In 1923 he had a bout of tonsillitis and languished all summer in his sweltering cell of a room because of the intense heat. There was no air conditioning, not even a laboring and dripping swamp cooler that the later missionaries used to make it through the awful summer months. The heat got to him again in 1925 and took him out of commission for July and August.

One of the things that someone who only saw Alfred Uplegger as an older distinguished gentleman would not have guessed was that he was a pretty good shade-tree mechanic. He was kind of the resident mechanic for the motor trip to the Grand Canyon in 1919. Missionary Arnold Sitz's diary of the event tells that Alfred accomplished several fixits on the trail. When the initial travelers pulled into Alfred's place there at old San Carlos, we hear that Alfred "rolled up his shirtsleeves and got to work: the engine was cleaned, the carburetor was cleaned, the spark plugs were replaced, and a new clutch and brake bands were put in. The work took the

---

240 Today on the wall of a sublevel classroom at Wisconsin Lutheran Seminary in Mequon, Wisconsin, you can see the graduation picture of Henry Rosin and Alfred Uplegger.

241 Fort San Carlos had played a stirring part in the early days when Uncle Sam was trying to run down a few hundred renegade Apaches with some two to five thousand soldiers. During the years in question it served as Agency headquarters in the midst of a very large Indian population. In 1929 this station had to be abandoned, and the Agency moved out before the ever-rising waters behind Coolidge Dam. The Indians had to take up new homes either at Bylas or in the Rice area, and Alfred Uplegger returned to Globe.

Alfred Uplegger as a young man.
Photo Credit: Uplegger Family photos, author's collection.

major part of the day." And the diarist Sitz mused, "I was surprised to see Al's knowledge and handiness with tools, and in such company I myself had to show some sort of mechanical skill. I believed myself almost capable of repairing Fords now." [242]

That same trip showed something else of Alfred's persona that seems out of character for the later mellow missionary: "We camped last night a few miles out of Prescott. Again the cloud of gloomy, restless, ill-humor, descended on the camp. Al lost his equilibrium because he had had to make the bed for Bill's and Jim's wives all

---

[242] "Sitz Diary: 1919 Trip to the Grand Canyon," Pastor Victor H. Prange translator (From *WELS Historical Institute Journal*, Professor John M. Brenner (brennerj@wls.wels.net.) p. 27.

during the trip, and it was getting to be too much. Although his outbreak was short-lived and sudden, the others seemed to have the same smoldering kind of ill-humor."[243] This was a small manifestation of a bigger challenge for the missionaries. They had to get along with each other in close quarters. Traveling together in the way they did for that 1919 trip to the Grand Canyon threw them all together. Little idiosyncrasies became big—huge!—idiosyncrasies after a while. We all know the three-day rule for fish and company. It is said that both start to stink after three days. Missionaries who wouldn't have chosen each other's company suddenly had it for months and years at a time. They had to get along. There were rubs, in deed and in word and in thought. The surprising thing in this account of Uplegger's temper is that of all people, he was such a kind and easygoing man. Perhaps gentle patience was a necessarily acquired behavior on his part to work with all the different kinds of personalities he met.

Alfred had a wonderful memory of the past. He could tell you which year it had been that the filaree weed was knee-high in the springtime at San Carlos because the winter and spring rains had been so good. He could speak about crossing the Salt River in a buckboard and looking down into the water to see many big fish swimming resolutely by. He said that very soon there was a big flood, and he wondered if there was some kind of reptile premonition about the impending high water. In his written recollections he recorded descriptions of early travels to Cibecue and to Blue House Mountain on horseback. He always knew the mountains on the horizon and in the distance and knew how far it was to each of them: the Pinals, the Grahams, Four Peaks to the west, Mt. Baldy. On a clear day from some of the mountains you could actually see the San Francisco Peaks by Flagstaff. On one particular jaunt to Cibecue he came upon a working archeological expedition under the supervision of the Smithsonian. What he remembered about that meeting was that camp personnel showed him Teddy Roosevelt's sleeping bag—the very one! Someone had it there and was using it. At that time from Blue House Mountain by Cibecue he made his way back toward Show Low and Snowflake and then took the unattractive and tiring trip on north to Holbrook to catch the train east and leave the mountains.

Listen how his diary remembers that trip:

> So from Cibecue Rosin and Guenther took me back to Whiteriver and from there with my trunk to Show Low. There I got a bed in a farmer's brick house for the night. At eight in the morning a mail and freight carrier was ready

---

[243] *Op. cit.* p. 33.

for me and my trunk to take me to Shumway, twelve miles to the north. There I waited for the mail carrier who drove a 1916 Model A Ford, to which the fenders were held in place with bailing wire, which also served to hold the U.S. Mail sacks in place on the running board. Other sacks were beside the driver on the seat and on the floor. He delivered mail at Taylor and Snowflake. Where was my trunk? On the back seat of the Ford. Where did the passengers sit? Two Mexicans sat on the left side on top of my trunk, and I myself hung on on the right end.

The road to Holbrook was not paved, neither was it oiled, neither was it graded! Only the worst ruts and holes were covered with a hand scraper. In very many places the driver turned aside from the road, which was meant to be the road. It had not rained for two months. The road was ground to powder, most of all the chuckholes. The strong wind was blowing from the southwest. We were traveling north. At every chuckhole the wind picked up the powder sand and whirled it up from the wheels on the lee side right back onto me, so that with perspiration the powder dust stuck to me, and we finally bumped over those last 30 miles in three hours!!! Holbrook was just a little town then, a trading place for Navajo Indians, for cattlemen, for the Santa Fe Railway trains to stop. I headed for the hotel. The proprietor and manager saw me coming, and seemed to know over what kind of a road I had come. Very, very kindly he invited me into a well-kept room, saying, "Here is water in this big pitcher. Pour it into the broad washbowl. There is soap and towels." I do not know why he did not later charge me anything. With sincere thanks I started for the railway depot to catch the train east.

Just across the tracks stood a strong, tall man: the Sheriff of Navajo County. "Well, young man, how come you are walking? Where did you come from and where are you going?" "I am coming from San Carlos on the Indian reservation near Globe. And I have to get the passenger train to Chicago and Milwaukee," I said. "Would you show me your registration card?" he asked. "Certainly and gladly," I responded. "Well, you sure are the youngest preacher I have seen. Class V, eh?" the sheriff said. (Class V in the registration of draftees or enlistees was the class for students of theology and ordained ministers. At the time of World War I, it was not the class of the sickly, feeble, or incapacitated.

255

I had a very good constitution, perfect vision and strong heart and lungs.)

Two nights in a Pullman sleeping car, or in the chair car, when the Pullman berths were taken in advance, brought me to my parents' house, where my father was still director of the Lutheran High School maintained by both the Missouri and Wisconsin Synods. Father and mother and my sisters were happy to hear about the Apache Indian Mission, my reception by the people, and my wanting to go back as soon as possible because they needed us. Our Lutheran missionaries were the only ministers at that time: two on the Fort Apache Reservation (E. Edgar Guenther and Adolph Zuberbier) and two on the San Carlos Reservation (H. E. Rosin and I), plus the mission in Globe for both Indian and white members.[244]

Alfred was single for his first six years among the Apaches, and because he was single he was also lonely. He longed for companionship and a Christian wife and by his own admission prayed daily that the Lord would send him a helper and a companion. His prayer went like this, "Let the one whom Thou, O Lord, hast chosen for me, to serve Thee at my side, be one, who, like Rebekah, is willing to leave her people and to come into this strange Apacheland, and to accompany me into the Arizona desert and into its mountains. Give her health and strength to be able to endure whatever we might need to endure for Thy Name's sake. Let Thy Spirit comfort her and cheer her, so that we may serve Thee and Thy chosen children together for the glory of Thy Name and for their joy and eternal salvation."[245]

When he got to Milwaukee in the trip just described he thought about a spouse and a sweetheart who would go back with him to Arizona, but nothing happened and the time came for him to return. At the end of his Wisconsin stay, his cousins arranged a little party with fellow church members on the shores of Lake Michigan. As he recollected this in shades of Henry Wadsworth Longfellow's poem *Hiawatha*, Uplegger called the place "Gitche Gumee, the shining big sea-water." He remembered the date, September 13. And there he saw her! He knew it was she because he had had a dream and saw her in the dream before he ever laid eyes on her there by Gitshe Gumee!

244 Pastor Alfred Uplegger, *Reminiscing on the Lord's Mercy and Grace to Apache Indians During the Last 60 Years*, Installment III, pp. 4, 5 (edited and re-recorded by Pastor Myrl Wagenknecht).

245 A. Uplegger, *The Apache Lutheran*, "God's Blessings on a Missionary's Wife, Also on Him and on His People through Her," Nov. 1972.

After he returned to Arizona he wrote from the reservation and she wrote from Wisconsin. Finally, one letter carried the proposal: "Will you leave your home and come to Arizona to be my wife?" Yes, she would! The proper authorities had to be approached for a railroad pass from Arizona to Wisconsin for "future domestic happiness." The pass came with the three words written, "Here you are!" Alfred remembered fondly about the one who sent him the pass, "That was Pastor F. Brockmann, with the very heavy eyebrows."[246]

"The wedding day was bleak and dark with many intermittent showers. Yet there was a joyful sunshine of confidence in their hearts." That's the way Alfred said it and that's the way it was. For the next half century, "Aunt Irma" was there by Uncle Al's side. In spite of bad sinus attacks and migraine headaches which plagued her all her life, she was there with her husband. She held little Apache babies from the jostlings of a Model A Ford up over the mountain ranges by Black River and White River. It was she who between those two ranges once said in alarm from the back seat as she tended twins, "Al, the babies are turning blue!" They had not yet been baptized. The Upleggers were trying to get to the mission and the nursery at East Fork, twenty-five miles in the rough and rocky future. Would they make it? They still had to drop back down into the canyon where the White River was, cross it, and then go on through the twenty miles of arroyos and gullies to East Fork Mission east of Fort Apache. They couldn't take the chance of making it, so the babies received Christian baptism there on the road. The water for the ceremony came from the radiator of the Model A. The babies did live for a short time. They made it to the nursery, but later their little graves were added to the others in the cemetery behind the mission at the foot of Redrock. It was the same place where a number of missionaries would later also be buried with their people and with the little nursery babies.

The Upleggers did have the chance once to leave San Carlos and the reservation. In fact, many missionaries who served in Apacheland had the chance to leave after a while, and many took the chance and went away never to come back again. It wasn't so with Alfred and Irma however. In 1926, after almost ten years on the field, he got the call to go to Brunsville, Iowa. He left with Irma on December 6. We don't know why it was that he left. Did it just seem like the right thing for him to do for himself and his wife and his ministry? We

---

[246] Pastor Alfred Uplegger, *Reminiscing on the Lord's Mercy and Grace to Apache Indians During the Last 60 Years,* Installment VIII, pp. 7, 8 (edited and re-recorded by Pastor Myrl Wagenknecht).

don't know why he left San Carlos that one and only time, but we do know how he felt when he packed up his things to leave. He tells us in this letter:

Brunsville, Iowa

October 17, 1927

Dear Brother,

From now on it will be a greater pleasure to write to you again, because I shall be able to write as one of your co-workers again. We are very happy. We are rejoicing, filled with thanksgiving to the Lord, who has dealt graciously with us, in that he has permitted us to be called back into the Indian Mission. I am thankful to the Board for extending the call to me. I am thankful to you for your recommending me and hope to be able to show my appreciation by working with you and my father and Henry (Rosin) and the other brethren to the glory of the Lord's name and to your and our own joy in serving the Savior among the Apaches. And the cause of these words is the letter from Rev. P. T. Brockmann, which I received this morning, in which he informs me that I am called back to San Carlos, which call I shall accept in the fear of the Lord after this congregation has given me its vote to let me go. Then we shall hasten to come. And it will be a pleasurable task to pack up, which was so grievous last year when we left.

Acts 20:32. Auf Wiedersehen! Nalqli hiltse, ndi' ad'ae!

Sincerely yours,

Alfred M. Uplegger.

In writing about this to Edgar Guenther the superintendent on the field, Alfred's father Francis wrote, "The attitude of the Indians in general in the field is one of thankfulness for the services given them by their former missionary and of wishing him to come back to them. A number of them have asked directly when his health might be sufficiently improved so that he would come back to them. I have replied with expressing a possibility of his being with them again, some time. Their attachment to him acts as a barrier against endeavors of the Romanists now to break into this field of ours. Not a spark of confident expectation is brought forth in the people by telling them that perhaps soon another missionary will occupy the post among them, months having elapsed since their own missionary left (Alfred himself). The personal element, the personal contact, being of great importance particularly in the work with the Indians, it is greatly to be desired that not a man without experience be called into this field."[247]

The following was penned after the Upleggers got back to their beloved San Carlos:

San Carlos, Arizona

November 29, 1927

Dear Brother,

At this time I am able only to write that we are most thankful to the Lord for having brought us here safe and in good health. We arrived Friday evening and I have been at work since Saturday, not only at getting settled, but also in making pastoral and sick calls.

Indians are welcoming us very cordially.

As soon as possible I shall write more.

With greetings to you and best wishes to all,

Brotherly yours,

Alfred M. Uplegger.

In their love for the people and for children, Alfred and Irma often came to the nursery at East Fork. They came bringing babies. They also came to help out and support this work. On one of those times Pastor Uplegger did some painting work at the nursery. He wrote about it in 1929. His writing wasn't about the painting he and Missionary Charles Albrecht were doing. His interest was in one of the little boys in the nursery who had snuck in unnoticed at first. The portable organ was there that the missionaries used for camp work. The little boy started "finding his notes." As Alfred related it, "'From'— and having found the note, 'heaven'—another note, 'above'—another note, 'to'—and again, 'earth'—two more notes. After a few minutes of locating certain tones, he slowly began to add the words to them in a whisper. But a little later he forgot to whisper." And then Alfred concluded his account of the little nursery musician: "That is better than listening to an orchestra, better than listening to a big choir, I thought at my painting. That singing is a delight for angels. And that boy's special guardian angel surely was thanking God for the simple, trustful faith in that singing child. So did the missionary also."[248]

---

[247] From the "Indian Mission Report" March 31, 1927. (File kept at the Synod Archives.)

[248] *The Apache Scout*, "Singing to the Lord," Vol. VII., Number 8. p. 3.

Alfred and Irma loved children and wanted to have many of their own, but it wasn't meant to be. They finally had a son, Karl. He was a fine and handsome boy, and his father said he had perfect health. He wanted to become a pastor like his father, and after graduating from Globe High School in May of 1941 (because his parents were serving at Globe at that time), he attended Northwestern College at Watertown, Wisconsin. But the war came, and even though his cousin Rupert Rosin at Peridot and many other young Lutheran boys got religious deferments and didn't have to go to serve in the war, Karl didn't. He had to go and fight and did so with the 78th

Irma Uplegger with her son Karl. Uplegger
Family photo, author's collection.

Lightning Division in Germany. He was wounded in the Battle of the Bulge, March 1, 1945. He got shot through the pancreas. They brought him back to Denver, Colorado, to Fitzsimons Medical Hospital where his parents could be with him. The medical care was for nothing, however, and at the end Alfred noticed that when he gave his son a drink of water it ran out the wound in his back. Mother and father were with Karl when he died on Pentecost Sunday morning in 1945. His body was carried back to Peridot, and they buried him in the cemetery not far from their mission station and home, where both Alfred and Irma lie buried today next to their son Karl.

Aunt Irma still loved children though, even though she was unable to have children of her own. They adopted a little white girl named Rachel, and she took Karl's place and became their daughter. Aunt Irma loved every Apache child she ever saw, and she loved the missionary children as her own. She came and stayed with us in the parsonage in Globe when the pastors went to pastors' conferences. Often when she came to stay with us for several days she brought her caged canary and covered it up carefully in the evening, so it wouldn't be in a draft and get sick. Early the next morning we went there and peeked under the cover to see if it was still there. What a nice lady she was, Aunt Irma! She always made chile con carne for us when we came to visit her in San Carlos. It was good. We liked it, but we did wonder sometimes why it was always chile con carne and if she could cook anything else.

In later years, after the canary cage episodes, the Upleggers would sometimes come up from San Carlos to stay with us for several days at East Fork Mission. They usually came in the summertime, when it was cooler at our higher elevation and the afternoon monsoon showers made things green and lush. Pastor Uplegger (as we always called him) was an early riser. He got up and sat and read out on the front porch. But when it was time, he would go down to our middle bedroom and bend over and kiss Aunt Irma good morning. She told us matter-of-factly that Uncle Al always did that every morning, and when they visited us we watched it from around the corner. Because we knew Aunt Irma so well, and because we also knew about Gitche Gumee[249] and how much Pastor Uplegger loved his wife Irma, it was heartbreaking to read how Alfred described in a later article in *The Apache Lutheran* how Aunt Irma died. She was in

---

[249] On one of the times when Pastor Uplegger came to visit us, he brought our sister *The Song of Hiawatha* by Henry Wadsworth Longfellow. There we read, "By the shores of Gitche Gumee, by the Shining Big Sea Water." As adults we also found out that it said, "As of one who in a vision, Sees what is to be but is not, Stood and waited Hiawatha." That was the very way Pastor Uplegger described his "seeing" his wife Irma in a dream before he knew her.

her kitchen when the fatal attack occurred. It was the same kitchen where she had made us chile con carne.

Her husband's impeccable memory retrieved the whole day: "September 19, 1972, was our brother-in-law Pastor Henry Rosin's eightieth birthday. We celebrated it by having a light dinner together with my sisters, Johanna and Gertrude. After that 'Aunt' Irma looked at some new drapes for house windows at Penney's in Globe. We bought some groceries. Then there was still some time to visit 95-year-old grandmother Katie Rupkey, the widow of the former Trading Post operator, R. L. Rupkey, at old San Carlos. Katie was very glad that we called on her again. Aunt Irma was quietly cheerful. She set the groceries away into the refrigerator and fed the cats. Then she said: 'Now I am tired,' and sat down in her easy chair."[250] It was then that the heart attack came, and she slumped to the floor. Two doctors at the Indian Health Services hospital in San Carlos tried everything to revive her. It was no use. She was gone. Alfred related, "Within ten minutes of getting her to the hospital dozens of Indian friends, members of the congregation and many others, had gathered in the corridors of the hospital and very visibly showed their concern and most cordial sympathy with tears flowing freely. As serious as it was, so touching it was also. The proof of sincere love was so evident. The loss of a dearly loved one was deeply felt. So many kind members and friends just could not do enough to help in the days following till the memorial service.[251]

One memory we had of Pastor Uplegger was on a summer night outside the little church on Devereaux Street there in Globe. Pastor Uplegger was about to depart in his Studebaker to go back to San Carlos. The stars were shining brightly, and in those days there wasn't much light interference in Globe, Arizona, to spoil the sight of the dark sky above us. Pastor Uplegger pointed out the Dipper and Orion and the scabbard where the sword was. He pointed where the hazy light of the Pleiades was and told us that the ancient Greeks said the Pleiades were the seven daughters of Atlas, whom Zeus had placed there. He said that same group was also called "The Seven Sisters." One time he called our father on the phone and told him, "Gene, go outside and look at Venus! She's going to kiss the moon!" Apparently Venus also kisses Jupiter from time to time, but we didn't know that—and even hearing Pastor Uplegger use the word "kiss" surprised us children.

---

[250] Pastor Alfred Uplegger, *Reminiscing on the Lord's Mercy and Grace to Apache Indians During the Past 60 years,* Installment 8, page 8 (edited and re-recorded by Pastor Myrl Wagenknecht).

[251] *Op. cit.*

Alfred was a Christian missionary. He taught Christ to the people who had never heard about him before, and he ministered to those who had. That was why he went to live in San Carlos in the first place. It is what he did at first and it is what he did until he died. After Irma was gone and he lived on in San Carlos by himself, he made peanut butter sandwiches for those who came to his house asking for them. Even after he was hit by an inebriated driver and left partially paralyzed, he still made the peanut butter sandwiches for those who came to his tufa stone house and asked.

He related to *The Apache Lutheran* the story that follows from the early days of his work. The story he told was of a man whose name was Somigo. Somigo was dying of tuberculosis, as so many of his people did. Pastor Uplegger knew when he went to visit Somigo in his wickiup that he was dying. He had been going to visit Somigo on a regular basis, but as the end appeared he wanted Somigo to be able to die with the comfort and blessing of baptism. Alfred wasn't fluent in Apache, so we read his words:

> So that the father (Somigo) might also understand the meaning and blessing of baptism, *Inashood* (Uplegger himself) went to get an interpreter. After two hours he returned with the man who should repeat in Apache the words spoken in English. When everyone was ready and a warm fire was burning in the middle of the tepee (wickiup) beside the bed, *Inashood*, kneeling beside Somigo, began in the name of God: the Father and the Son and the Holy Spirit. All were in devout attention. All felt that this was a holy moment. God was near with his Spirit and blessing.
>
> First the words of the Sacrament of Baptism were explained and interpreted. The interpreter tried to put the words into good Apache. But as he interpreted and came to the name of the Son of God, Somigo suddenly raised up in bed and with a loud voice said very decidedly: "*Nayenezgani do-ani-da!*" ("Do not say *Nayenezgani!*") It was with those words that Somigo confessed that he believed in the Son of the living God, Jesus Christ, as his Savior. He would not have it that the interpreter should try to use the vernacular name of the big hero of Indian story and legend. *Nayenezgani* means Monster-killer. No, Somigo would not have a monster killer for his Savior, nor would he believe or trust in him, who never really lived, but was only told of in story handed down from mouth to mouth by old heathen Indians who did not know the true God. Somigo believed and trusted in the true living Son of God, Jesus Christ, the

Savior of the Bible, whom he learned to love and whose love and grace he was experiencing even in his sick-bed of quick tuberculosis. Had *Nayenezgani* died for him on the cross and won for him forgiveness of sins, salvation and everlasting life? No, not he. But Jesus Christ had done so. Out of love for the poor sinners Jesus had given up his own life. Somigo knew this and was glad because of it. And into the Name of this Savior, Jesus Christ, he wanted to be baptized. And in the name of the Son of God he was baptized, and in faith he put on Christ and became a new creature, whom the Lord Jesus called to him the next day, when Somigo's spirit went to heaven, into the new life of rest and peace and happiness with God.[252]

Somigo's homegoing happened on January 7, 1924.

San Carlos was Alfred Uplegger's home. It just was that. He was so like the Old Testament Ruth, who had been told by her homeward bound mother-in-law to return to her own home in Moab. But Ruth wouldn't do it. She said to Naomi, "Don't urge me to leave you or to turn back from you. Where you go I will go, and where you stay I will stay. Your people will be my people and your God my God. Where you die I will die and there I will be buried." In San Carlos, among people who weren't his own by race, Pastor Uplegger said Ruth's words and lived them.

He stayed on in the work as an old man, fragile and thin. San Carlos and the work there were his home and his life. He lived with his unmarried sister Gertrude, and then he lived by himself. He attended all the conferences for the called workers, whether they were on the San Carlos or the Fort Apache reservations. When he rose to speak at the conferences his lips quavered, and so did his voice, but his thoughts were clear and compelling. He gave his memoirs of the work in "to be continued" presentations over several years' time. These presentations came at a time when the old Apache religious way was making a resurgence on the reservations. Sunrise dances were becoming something that were being held every weekend from the earliest spring to the latest fall. Gone were the days when it was only something that was done at the Fourth of July celebrations, and there was panic and alarm in the ranks of the missionaries who watched the people of their churches get a feather and then drop from sight for six months' time until their involvement in the dance wore off, whether as a sponsor or family participant, and they felt they could once more come back to church. The old frail

---

252 From the story of "Somigo of San Carlos." *The Apache Scout*, April, 1924.

missionary would stand and speak, and his counsel was to be patient and kind and forgiving. He lived those virtues all his long life among the people, and they loved him for them.

His day came and he died. The articulate head of the World Missions was at the funeral and he spoke in his gifted way of Alfred's passing: "As is their custom, the Apaches remained at the graveside, and many helped commit his body to the bosom of the earth by actively taking part by turns in the burial. As we walked down the rocky slope it was as though we heard him speak as Eliezer, Abraham's faithful servant, did of old, his mission in life accomplished, 'Do not detain me, now that the Lord has granted success to my journey. Send me on my way so that I may go to my master' (Genesis 24:56)"[253]

Francis Uplegger was Alfred's father, but he came to Peridot and San Carlos after his son did. The biographer tells us about Francis:

> Franz John Theo Uplegger (more commonly known as Francis J. Uplegger) was born in Rostock, Germany, on October 29, 1867. He emigrated to the United States in August of 1886 and settled in St. Louis, Missouri. He studied at the Concordia Seminary but was not granted a Doctorate of Divinity until 1957. In 1891 Uplegger became pastor of St. John congregation (Wisconsin Synod) in Hermansfort, Wisconsin. He went on to hold posts in Denmark and Germany and served as director of the Lutheran high school in Milwaukee, Wisconsin, upon returning to the United States. In 1919 Uplegger followed his son Alfred to San Carlos to establish a mission to the San Carlos Apache, where he remained for the rest of his life.
>
> When Uplegger arrived in Arizona he was already familiar with German, English, Norwegian, French, Hebrew, Greek, and Latin. He learned the Apache language while at the mission and wrote a four-volume Apache-English dictionary. His works include Apache translations of most of the Lutheran Catechism, Creed, liturgy, and much of the Bible. Uplegger also assisted the San Carlos Apache in writing their constitution in 1930-1931. This document was later used as a model by many other tribes. Known fondly as "Old Man Missionary," Uplegger was officially adopted into the San Carlos tribe in 1961. He died on the reservation on June 13, 1964.

---

[253] Edgar H. Hoenecke, *The End of an Epoch in the Apache Indian Mission*, (Alfred M. Uplegger 1892-1984 and Henry E. Rosin 1892-1982).

265

Arizona State University in Tempe, Arizona, provides that good thumbnail sketch of Francis Uplegger's life. It might be said too that he married Emma Plass and that they had four children: Alfred Martin Johannes (1892-1984), Johanna (Uplegger) Rosin (1896-1983), Gertrude E. (1898-1991), and Dorothea (Uplegger) Behn (1902-1986). The reason for noting those four children is that they each spent many years working in the mission at San Carlos. Their father Francis remained their hero and example. He was the patriarch of the Uplegger clan, and together they accumulated over 200 years of time spent in service to the Apache people on the San Carlos Reservation. These four carefully and honorably tended their father in his old age. He was "father" to them all, and he often found his way into their conversations.

No one did more than Francis Uplegger in formulating the written Apache language. He preached in it and taught in it and knew it intimately. He knew the etymologies of the words themselves. Anthropologists like Keith Bassow did good work in identifying place names in Apache and giving their meanings, but in our estimation, Uplegger was better. For one thing, he was closer to classical Apache than the later anthropologists who worked with the language. Uplegger's original four-volume dictionary of the Apache language (approximately 500 pages!) is at the Huntington Library in California. Arizona State University also has a photocopy of the dictionary in its archives.

Uplegger wrote about himself: "My ancestors were farmers and fishermen at Retwisch, a village of Mecklenburg Schwerin (in Germany), close by the shore of the Baltic Sea. I was born not far from there, in the city of Rostock, on 29 October 1867, and a few days thereafter baptized in St. Nicolai church of that city.

"In 1891, upon graduating from Concordia Seminary, I followed the combined call of the St. John's congregation and of the Elias Congregation in the town of Herman, Shawano County, Wisconsin. There I came in contact with some of the very last of the Mohicans. Later, after I had for some time served the Messiah congregation in Sterling, Illinois, and followed a call from the combined parish of Gillett and Town of Howe, some Potawatomi Indians attracted my attention. Never could I forget the voice of human need which spoke to me when the Potawatomi Jack Waupaca,[254] who had lost three children in an epidemic of those days, came into my house. When shown a framed picture of the Risen Savior, and having listened to my explanation and application, in a tone of deepest sad-

---

[254] There is a town by that name in central Wisconsin today.

ness and longing, said, 'Nice! Nice! Me like it. But—me poor Indjun, me know nothing.' "

And Francis went on, "It pleased the Lord, before calling me into Indian mission work, to lead me to further learning and the joy of serving: serving, besides my two German congregations, for some time Norwegians in Town Green Valley and then a number of Danes in Town Maple Valley. In consequence thereof, through correspondence of Free Church people in Denmark with the faculty of Concordia Seminary, St. Louis, I received a call into the Lutheran Free Church of that country, and advised by the St. Louis faculty, I followed the call.

"Family considerations, however, caused me to follow the call back to my former congregation in Town of Howe, Wisconsin. Here, after four years of pastoral work, teaching the congregation's school, serving again our Danes in near-by Town Maple Valley, and not forgetting two other preaching places, I was in need of medical care. Right then there came as a Godsend a call from the Saxon Free Church congregation in Hamburg, Germany." So, off to Germany he went, but not for long.

"Back in America, I was offered the pastorate of a congregation that had been served by the Iowa Synod. It wished to be connected with that synod. So I could not serve there. My good friend, Pastor August Pieper,[255] Milwaukee, caused my being called into the Wisconsin Evangelical Lutheran Synod. So I served congregations at Sault Ste. Marie, Michigan, and in the towns of Greenville and Newton, Wisconsin.

"After four years of my pastorate at the latter place I was called to be the director of the Lutheran High School in Milwaukee. After four years of my service in that position, the medical advice from a member of my family was, for complete recovery from the effects of the influenza, the widespread contagion of that time, to go to Arizona. Just then the Mission Board of the Synod wished to send a man of some experience into the general mission work in this state and so also to have the Apache Indian Mission be served. Hence, I was called into this work late in 1919. My daughter's health was soon restored in Arizona, and as the Apache Indian Mission was especially in need for another worker, my call was specified for work in this mission.

"The Lord enabled me to preach the gospel and teach the way of salvation to Apache Indians in their own language as well as in English. Now in the thirty-seventh year of the ministry I still joy in it,

---

[255] Francis at the age of nineteen entered Concordia Theological Seminary, which was important and formative: he became a theologian of depth, having sat at the feet of such solid churchmen as C. F. W. Walther, Franz Pieper, and George Stoeckhardt. Every pastor in the Wisconsin Synod today knows who Franz Pieper is.

through the Lord's sustaining grace, in accordance with His word to Paul, 'My grace is sufficient for thee, for My strength is made perfect in weakness.' My son, Alfred, who studied theology at the seminary of the Wisconsin Synod, was called into the Apache Indian Mission a year and a half before I was called to be associated with him. My eldest daughter, Johanna, is the wife of Pastor Henry Rosin, the missionary at our station in Peridot."[256]

It was this son Alfred who described how the constitution of the San Carlos Apaches was formulated by his father Francis: "In 1931 leading Indians of the Tribe came to him for advice and help in framing a constitution for the Tribe. For weeks leading men of influence and understanding of the needs of the Tribe gathered on the lawn of the Lutheran Church. Dr. Uplegger answered the questions, explained the meanings of terms of law and of words used in constitutions, and acted as secretary. The draft of a workable constitution suitable for the needs of the Apache Tribe was sent to Washington by the Superintendent in charge. It was approved and recommended also to other tribes to use as a working model. Though the constitution has been revised, the chief elements have been retained and are in practical use. Of the men who consulted with Dr. Uplegger for advice were: Oliver Belvado, Sr., Henry Chinn, Thomas Dosela, Victor Kindelay, James Polk, Ben Randall, Fred Galson, John Rogers, John Nosie, Roy Harney, Richard Johnson, Emory Starr, Mike Nelson, Myron Sippi (see page 73), Stephen Smith, William Swift, Manuel Victor, Timothy Victor, Henry Telto, and others."[257]

In 1936 Helge Ingstad, the Norwegian traveler and writer of the book about the Caribou-Eaters of northern Canada, visited Uplegger at San Carlos.[258] They had wonderful things in common. They were both anthropologists and linguists in their own right and in their own interest. Listen to Uplegger speak to the readers of *The Apache Scout* about Apache ethnicity:

> South of the country of the Caribou-Eaters lies Lake Athabaska. We have learned that this lake has been so called by the Forest-Cree Indians who belong to the Algonquian language family. In their language, *athab* means as much as "in succession" or "extent," and *askew* is "grass,"

256 The *Concordia Historical Institute Quarterly* printed a short autobiography of Francis Uplegger, written by him in 1937. This quote comes from that article.

257 Those family names are still sprinkled richly throughout the population of the present-day San Carlos Tribe.

258 The book was: Helge Ingstad, *The Land of Feast and Famine*. Alfred Knopf, New York, 1933.

also "reeds." So *athabaska* is a stretch of "reedland." The people living near that large lake were designated as *Athabaskans* or "Reedland People." But then all Indian tribes of the same language family have been so designated (as *Athabaskan*). There are a number of tribes, mostly small tribes, in western and northern Canada, as also the Navajo and the Apache in our southwest. Just south of Lake Athabaska we have the Chipewyans; away southward, in Alberta, we find the Sarsi. Continuing southwestward, we would in Oregon come to the Umpqua, in California to the Tolowa, the Hupa, the Kato, and others that all call themselves with the same name as the Caribou-Eaters do and as the Apache also do . . . On the lower Yukon River we are among the *Kaiyuh-kho-tana*, as white people have spelled their tribal name, and up there are other *Kho-tana*. We are reminded of the Apache *Tshi-bi-ko-dndnae*,[259] our "Cibecue" people. Where are we now? We hear strange sounds of language; we also hear familiar sounds. It is as if the twigs of one branch brushed into those of another. Among the strange sounds we also hear, for instance, *tchlo*, for "grass," which the Apache calls *tql'oh*; we hear *konh*, for *"fire,"* Apache: *kov* (nasal o); *utson*, "meat," Apache: *itsiv*; *kya*, "arrow," Apache: *k'a/'*. We hear a boy called *kenne*, and we think of the Apache *eshkinn*. We hear *atta* and *imma*, for "father" and "mother" and it sounds to us as if an Apache child whispered *shi-ta/, shi-mav*, "my father, my mother.[260]

The book, *The Last of the Mohicans* by James Fennimore Cooper, is well known. Francis Uplegger knew the Mohicans. He knew their history, and he knew that mission work had proceeded among the Mohicans with translations of Luther's Small Catechism into Mohican. Efforts to get religious materials into the vernacular had happened with the first Apache missionaries, too. The minutes of the early missionary meetings in Globe, Arizona, tell it. Uplegger himself translated Luther's Small Catechism into Apache, as well as the Christian church liturgy and large sections of the Bible. Uplegger records the story of Chief Konkapot who was responsible for Christianity coming among his people, the Mohicans. The Mohicans sold a tract of their land to the colony of Massachusetts in 1724 for "460 pounds of Sterling,

---

[259] You can hear this very word used today to identify Cibecue on radio station KNNB in Whiteriver.

[260] *The Apache Scout*, October 1937.

three barrels of cider and thirty-six quarts of rum."[261] A John Sargent came to do mission work among the Mohicans in 1734 with none less than Yale College as the benefactor and instigator. When that first missionary died after having worked among the Mohicans for thirteen years, he had baptized 180 Mohicans, and 42 of them were communicants in the Christian church. Uplegger also mentions the work among the Mohicans to educate the children. The same John Sargent began a day school which also became a boarding school, attended by both Mohicans and white children. Educating the children was the mindset not only of Upleggers but of all the Lutheran missionaries from the very beginning. And there in *The Apache Scout* is the picture of Esther Miller and Alice Davids and the caption reads, "Two of the Last of the Mohicans."

A young Mohican woman named Thelma Davids (Thelma Davids Putnam) came to work in the early mission work at East Fork Mission on the Fort Apache Reservation.[262] Thelma grew up in the town of Red Springs in Wisconsin, just across the road from the Lutheran mission there. As a result, she "grew up with personal knowledge of and [was] a personal friend of many of the pastors, teachers, and employees of the Lutheran Mission."[263] As her nephew, Steve Comer, tells it, Thelma Davids was the first Stockbridge Indian he knew of that "went off the Rez and made her name in the world." When Thelma Davids was growing up it wasn't common for rural people (not just Indians but also whites) to attend high school. But Thelma attended and graduated from Milwaukee Lutheran High School and went on to serve as a missionary/teacher among the White Mountain Apache in Arizona. The writer of the Putman family history went on to say, "Thelma Davids Putnam appears to have followed in the footsteps of the German-born Rev. Francis Uplegger, who began his ministry in Shawano County, and later became the 'Director of the Lutheran High School in Milwaukee' and missionary at the White Mountain Apache Reservation.[264]

In 1919 Thelma Davids wrote a most interesting letter to Francis Uplegger. He had worked in the Lutheran High School in Milwaukee, Wisconsin, and it was in 1919 that he began his work on the Apache Reservation in Arizona. The country was not friendly toward

---

261 *The Apache Scout*, February 1926.

262 Thelma Davids (Putman) was a descendant of the Millers and Yoccums on her mother's side and David Naunauneekanuk on her father's side, according to the Davids Family Genealogy. She was born in 1901.

263 Putnam, page 2.

264 Putman, page 31.

the Native American population, whether it was in Wisconsin or in Arizona. That is what makes the story of *Inashood* so interesting and the story of Apache mission work so impressive. There were German missionaries who loved the Native Americans—or the "Indians," as people said in those days (even Thelma Davids called herself that in her letter).

Gresham, Wisconsin

October 7, 1919

Dear Professor Uplegger:

Your letter certainly was welcome to us all, but especially to me, for to hear again from someone at my dear school certainly was a pleasure. I am glad to hear there is so large an attendance there this year.

I have been thinking over what you said about going to Arizona and I will say this, that if I would receive a call there I would be happy to go. It is far from home and all my friends I know but I should not regret leaving them and I'll try not to also.

They are in need of a teacher for the upper grades at the Red Springs Mission now but they do not ask me. The people around here are always asking me why I won't apply for the position as I know they would like me, but as they don't pay the teacher they have nothing to say about hiring one. Someone even told the minister "Why don't you hire Thelma?" and he said they had a primary teacher. I don't see why I couldn't teach the upper grades as well. M. N. teaches up to 8th grade and many of the others do too. Perhaps our ministers think our High School only prepares teachers for primary grades. I believe he is a fine man and interested in our people so I don't believe he would willingly thrust me back.

But the Mission Board has hurt me very, very badly. A year ago, the next week after I left Milwaukee, I applied for a position at this mission and was quite sure I'd get it for I knew they needed two teachers but I waited all summer long for an answer and finally when the summer was gone I got an answer—a cold little note saying that they wouldn't hire me because I was an Indian and they made it a rule not to hire Indians. But that isn't true, Director, for they do hire Indians. One has a job there now for all the year, but they always give them the lower jobs. I have heard that the Board claims that there is jealousy and hard feelings existing if some Indian is given a job and thus the school wouldn't go as well if Indians were employed. This however, isn't true either and I'm sure everyone agrees with me that when our own people were employed there everything went fine side of what it does now.

Oh, Director, it makes me feel so discouraged when I think of it all. How can an Indian rise above the common level or how can they try to make use of their talents when at every turn they are rebuffed by their white brothers? Do you think these men on this Board can be true Christian men and still behave in that way?

Well, Director, I suppose you will be rather astonished at this letter but it has been on my mind for so long. I feel as if I can't bear it any longer. I would so like to do something in this world, to feel like I am really doing some good and to have special aim here on this earth. Of course my highest aim is to reach that most blessed home, heaven.

Yours sincerely,

Thelma Davids.[265]

While there was one mission church in Massachusetts in the 1700s (and it was supported by wealthy and powerful people overseas), the situation was very different in the 1900s. In the twentieth century, a number of small, scattered Indian congregations sprang up in Shawano County in Wisconsin, not far from the Menominee Reservation. The credit for preserving the history of those congregations goes to Thelma Putnam. Her book, *Christian Religion Among the Stockbridge Munsee Band of Mohican Indians,*[266] tells of the many comings and goings of ministers and their families. It also tells in detail how various church communities lacking financial resources began without the benefit of a church building and met in people's homes, the cook shack from an old logging camp, the tribal headquarters, and even in a converted saloon.[267]

So Thelma Davids did listen to her "Director" and she did go to work a work of love with the Apaches in Arizona. While Thelma Davids did her work with the Apaches in Arizona, she stayed upstairs in the employees' building at East Fork Mission. She was the pri-

---

265 This letter was typed just like it was written. The handwriting is beautiful, like the letters on a handwriting chart. This letter reposes in the archives of the WELS in Milwaukee, Wisconsin.

266 The book was written in 1978 and was self-published.

267 This comes from a blog about Algonkian church history featuring Algonkian Indian tribes who voluntarily accepted Christianity.

mary teacher in the day school. When school opened in September of 1923 at East Fork Mission, Thelma had 49 students in her class. She pleaded with the administrative committee for another teacher to help her but didn't get any help. At Christmas of that year she helped distribute the Christmas presents given by the people from "back East." In the spring of her first school year an awful measles epidemic broke out. Wallace Wesley, one of her students, died and had to be buried in the cemetery behind the mission because they couldn't get his body to his home in Bylas. The measles went up and down the East Fork valley and struck many in the camps. Miss Davids and Pastor Meier spent long days in the camps caring for the sick students and their families.

The Apache Scout in June of 1927 recorded, "We are sorry to report that Miss Thelma Davids has resigned. She has rendered four years of efficient and faithful service as primary teacher. Her resignation, we are glad to add, includes that she may be again given a position as teacher of Apaches in another year or two. She plans to rest for a year and then go to school for a year or two." In September of 1927 we read in *The Apache Scout* that Thelma Davids had gotten married and was living in Milwaukee with her husband Steve Putnam. And then it was Francis Uplegger who wrote of a trip to Red Springs Lake, Wisconsin, to again visit the Lutheran Mohican Church and work. He came away with a photo printed in that 1937 issue of *The Apache Scout*. There were six children in the photo: two Mohicans, two Oneidas, two Chippewas, and then he said, "At that flying visit we also saw a former Mohican pupil of ours who later for a time was a teacher at our East Fork Mission School, then the Miss Thelma Davids."

The linguist Francis Uplegger pointed out that the name Apache means "Enemy." That is what the Pima Indians who spun the name thought, anyway. Uplegger went on to point out that we were all enemies of God but have now been brought into sonship and citizenship with other saints in the Christian Church. The Apaches certainly did know about enemies. Their lives had been one long unhappy dealing with enemies. The missionaries had to convince them that they were not enemies, and *Inashood* did win the hearts of many of those called Apache. There were gentle and kind people like the Upleggers who went far to remove the perceived threat and the real animosity that existed.

It was Edgar Hoenecke, head of the Lutheran church's world mission effort, who referred to Uplegger being called *Inashood Hastin*. Behind the Apache title Hoenecke wrote in parentheses, "(The Venerable Missionary)." That probably was a little more complimentary than the term usually intended. In Apache the word *Hastin* could also be spoken of a man in his dotage. There was veneration though from the people, and as Hoenecke rightfully noticed, "The Apaches knew *Inashood Hastin* to be a gentle man of God who gave them understanding, hope, and life. His manners and appearance were courtly, his speech and gesturing dramatic, his carriage stately, whether he sat a horse or sat beside the people on the red earth of the San Carlos desert, urging them with earnest, kindly, and vivid words to bethink them of their sinful mortal lot and of their high destiny as the sons and daughters of God, the Lord of Life through Christ Jesus." [268]

Before beginning their practical field work on the San Carlos or Fort Apache Reservations, new missionaries were required to spend six months learning the Apache language under Uplegger's tutelage. Missionary Edgar Guenther stated the need for this: "It has been an oft-repeated question among us missionaries: 'How can those whose time is occupied with school work or a never-ending array of other duties become sufficiently rooted in the Apache language to bring the Gospel ABCs to the old in camp even when no interpreter is at hand?' Experience has proven that a hit-and-run attempt at the language will not suffice." But he went on to say, "There is one on our mission force, who because of special gifts, diligence and circumstance, has acquired a better knowledge of the language than most of the Apaches themselves." He was referring to Pastor Francis Uplegger.[269] The language was indeed a problem in the old days, even with the six-month study. Few of the pastors— very few—mastered Apache, even with the excellent teaching of Pastor Uplegger. Work had to be done with an interpreter or done using simpler English.

When the Lutheran missionaries showed up in 1893 there was no written Apache language. There was not even a guide for the proper pronunciation of the very difficult sounds. That was true until Francis Uplegger came to spend countless hours visiting camps, listening, jotting down words phonetically in his notebooks with the help of certain diacritical marks. Gradually a crude written Apache language appeared that could be taught to others. An Apache grammar followed soon after. Then he began to translate Bible texts and stories, a catechism, Scripture lessons, a Lutheran liturgy, and even a hymnbook into Apache that included twenty-five hymns he himself had composed. In recognition of his labors, Concordia Seminary

---

[268] Edgar Hoenecke, *To Every Nation, Tribe, Language and People*, Milwaukee: NPH, p. 5.

[269] *The Apache Scout*, March 1931, in an article entitled "Apache."

conferred on him an honorary Doctor of Divinity degree in 1957, and over the course of the years he completed his 500-page dictionary of the Apache language, which now resides in the Huntington Library in California.

He was indeed a linguist, *par excellence*. Here is another example of his linguistic skill:

A man interested in the Apache language must note, first of all, that Apache is to a very high degree a tone language. Tone-variation is so peculiar to it that a man listening to it with a keen ear may think of a muffled song of the mocking bird which the Apache call *zagolavni*, "the many-voiced-one." And if you give the first a in this Apache word the sound of a in the English word arm, and pronounce the av as the same a with a longer and slightly nasal quality, and the i as the i in machine, and apply the proper pitch, then you have a sample of the music in Apache. If white people do not hear its music, it is because not all speak their language carefully and the Apache very often rather hums when a white man may shout—in harmony with the noise of his civilization. The white man's ear is, as a rule, not trained to the keenness with which the Indian has in nature learned to hear. An Apache who taught the present writer, sometimes helped him in his aiming at the correct speaking of an Apache sentence, saying, "Sing it! Or hum it!" In fact, it would be helpful to write the Apache as music is written. But we have neither time nor means to write it so, nor can we have it so printed. And we cannot with a typewriter set accents and other marks above Apache vowels; so we must set auxiliary letters or marks beside those letters the peculiar quality of which is to be indicated. Thus we may mark a dozen or more different soundings of the vowel *a* in Apache, which all are only variations of the English *a* sound in the word father; about six variations of the *e* sound in the English met; twelve or more variations of the *i* sound, twelve or more of *o*, and about four of *u*. In a like manner we also indicate peculiarities of consonant sounds." [270]

In the next issue of *The Apache Scout*, he gave the word used for God in Apache: "The Personal Being according to whom there is life." And he points out that in Apache the word to believe and the word to swallow (to drink) are closely related. And, wonder of won-

---

[270] *The Apache Scout*, March 1931, "As the Apache Says It."

ders, the same is true in English! "You don't expect me to swallow that?" is the same as saying, "You don't expect me to believe that."[271] Uplegger learned to fashion theological words in the Apache that were understandable to the people.[272]

Francis Uplegger loved the people who spoke the language even more than he loved to study and know their language. He wrote of *"Dajida"* the arrow maker. This Dajida was Alonzo S. Bullis, son of war chief Chiquito. Alonzo was shortened to Lon, and Lon Bullis became a pillar of the early work. In the story Dajida was able to make arrows. He knew how to use them too, no doubt. (Remember what Daklugie, war chief Juh's son, said about Apache archery and arrows, and that men could shoot seven arrows into the air before the first came to ground.) But after Dajida became a Christian, tuberculosis came to him. He spent his time trying to escape the cold or the heat. He went to the mountains from San Carlos to be at East Fork in the summer. In the evenings the cool air flowed by East Fork Mission from 11,409 foot high Mt. Baldy. He then returned to the desert in San Carlos when the cold came to the mountains. He died at the sanitarium in Phoenix on Friday, July 11, 1924. Lon's interest in those last days was in words—Christian words and Biblical words. He worked and made his own translations which Uplegger also used in his linguistic work. Lon had ministered to another arrow maker, Tom Wycliffe, under the big oak trees there at East Fork. Tom Wycliffe and Lon Bullis (Dajida) could very well have been feuding clan members in an earlier time, but their lives both ended with them being in the same spiritual clan and band. Both had been struck by the same fatal arrow, the deadly one from the white man's quiver, the arrow called tuberculosis. Francis Uplegger was there when Lon Bullis left this world. He was summoned with a letter from the old arrow maker and it pined, "Come! I want to have you with me once more here below, and by the sacrament be strengthened for the going to the home beyond."[273]

We hear Francis Uplegger's philosophy of culture and native religion when he wrote to his Apache people,

> Who, then, is on the right trail? God gave to the very first people on earth a simple Gospel, the good word of the One who should come and save from sin and mistaken ways. The religion of all men that did not hold fast that first Gospel

271 *The Apache Scout,* April 1931, "As the Apache Says It."

272 This was the observation of Thomas E. Mails in his book *The People Called Apache.*

273 *The Apache Scout,* "Dajida the Ancient Arrowmaker," April 1930.

Dr. Francis Uplegger and his people at San Carlos Lutheran Church.

became wrong. Indians and other peoples living in a state of nature did not get so far away from the first and true religion as many peoples did in what is called civilization.

Among you Indians the word about the one Lord of Life did not altogether die although your fathers began to worship works of God and powers that God made. (Many white people have gone so far that they do not worship anything except perhaps themselves or their own reasoning.) And how is it that your fathers spoke of One great helper that was to live—and did live—as a man on earth but was and is more than a man? It was because of some knowledge of the Old Gospel which was told by the forefathers of old to their children and their children's children, but was much changed in the mouths of men, sinful and forgetful as they were. But the true old story was written down; more words of promise were added to it through men taught by God, and then the story of the true fulfillment was set down in writing, as Cecil Hauzous also, with others of your people, became convinced of by reading the Bible. Don't follow the wrong ways of men that now and again find something new for having their own will and way. In simple-heartedness, your mind simply turned toward what is true and right, use what in civilization can be used as gifts from God. But don't let your souls get tangled up in the many things that have got the minds of many people into a great tangle. Don't take a trail that is grown over with what is worse than poison ivy, poison sumac and locoweed.[274]

Francis worked hard among his people. In his ministry to the Apaches he practiced and placed great importance on what he called "the personal element, the personal contact." In 1927 he wrote to the mission board authorities:

At the dam site (Coolidge Dam), nine miles from San Carlos, evening services will be conducted by either Mr. Rosin or myself as they can be best arranged for. For holding meetings there, a "cooler," a shade roof, will soon be erected. Its place will be in the new Indian village that has sprung up on the river bank above the dam site proper. For the gathering of people living close by the dam site proper we may be permitted to use the large dining hall built for the employees of the contractors for the building of the dam. Every Tuesday I devote entirely to work in the San Carlos district. I then visit camps, six to ten, have religious conversations with the people, come in contact with others, and instruct fifty to sixty children of the San Carlos Day School. Recent activity of the Romanists have made necessary extra visits at San Carlos, the dam site, and outlying camps, also the sending of the native helper around on the field, with a sermon written out for him, when I could not myself be absent from here.[275]

---

[274] *The Apache Scout*, October 1926.

[275] *Indian Mission Report*, March 31, 1927.

He ministered to old Chief Talkalai. Chief Talkalai was 108 years old when he came to visit, hanging onto the stick his fourteen-year-old guide used to pull him. He was completely blind and came trusting in Uplegger to help him with his pension, which was validated by the fact that he had served as a scout with others who were getting their pensions from the government. Uplegger got Chief Talkalai's financial matters straightened out for him. He talked with Talkalai "face to face like a man talks with his friend." He talked to Talkalai in the language of friendship, and the chief understood.

You can hear his perceptive mind and ability in his teaching and in his drawing on nature for comparison and example as the Apaches themselves did.

The Apache call the blue lupine in their language *Ya-ai-ye-naelth-iw-ne*, that is: The one that looks toward the light-bearer. This Indian name for a flower reminds us, again and again, what a man's soul should do without ceasing. It is not to be like the gopher, burrowing in the ground. It is not to be like the hunting dog keeping his eye and nose on a trail, in search of a piece of game. But it is to look into the light around us, and listening, or remembering, thinking—to look up into the light that has come down to us from heaven, keeping the mind, the soul, turned toward this light. It is believing according to this light, thinking according to this light, gladly living according to this light. That is Godliness. That is what is to be understood by the Apache word *Big'-ego Ihidnan yitj'-iw'-ad'ae hi*, "the being toward the Lord of Life." A man's mind and soul are to be constantly turned toward God, as that blue flower has its blossoms turned toward its Creator."[276] And listen further to Dr. Uplegger's brilliance as he demonstrates the craft of linguist and translator and Bible scholar: "Having your mind's eye on Him, believing in Him, you stand right before God—you are 'justified' as the Bible calls it. A man 'justified' according to God's Word is in Apache, *n'nae nzhogo i-j'-nalti'-hi-nbi-ilthta' agod'-ae-hi-yits-aw'-zhi'-go*," which means in English, "A man well cleared of his sin." And, because it is all through Christ, one of the telling words in Apache for "the Savior," used first perhaps at East Fork, is *Bilah-yu-nzhogo-djaehikai-hih*. This is, "He under whom we well went free."

You can see that this was new and unique work in putting the truths of Scripture into the minds of the hearers. Who before or since knew so much about the workings of the

---

[276] *The Apache Scout*, "Looking toward the Light-Bearer," July 1930.

Chief Talkalai.
*Photo Credit: (Gila County Historical Society;
image courtesy Paul and Kathleen Nickens)*

Apache language as Dr. Francis Uplegger, *Inashood Hastin!*[277]

For several issues of *The Apache Scout*, Dr. Uplegger wrote about a blind man. He wrote out the name the blind man was called.

---

[277] "Several individuals have commented on the Apache language, probably one of the most extensive studies has been by Rev. F. Uplegger, a Lutheran missionary on the San Carlos Reservation since 1920. On page 3 of the Apache Indians Lockwood quotes Uplegger's description of Apache speech as one of explodent sounds, final breathings, breath checks, aspirates, and glottal stops — all of which makes it extremely difficult for Europeans to learn or understand. Cremory, Life Among the Apaches, 237-39, indicates the Apaches have a system of counting which enables them to reach 10,000 or beyond." (Leonard Brown, *The Arizona Apaches and Christianization: a Study of Lutheran Mission Activity 1893-1943*, The University of Arizona).

According to the government census list he was born in 1825. But Dr. Uplegger could talk to the man, and even after he misread the road with his blind eyes and fell twenty feet into a wash, Dr. Uplegger talked to him in the hospital. "As your writer spoke to him about the heights of light beyond the valley of the shadow of death, he raised his old and sightless head as if striving to see. The rays of the visible sun do not fall upon his bed, but there was sunshine in his wrinkled face as he listened to what the missionary said about "The Way, and the Truth, and the Life." And when he heard that the Savior said, "Behold, I make all things new," and how this would apply to him also, his inner eye looked ahead, and with a voice thrilling with joy, he said *Gosh'-iwh do.h!* "I shall see!"[278]

Francis used the Bible. It was his and the other missionaries' unchanging and unchangeable standard. Once at *Gagaedeskanne* (the Apache name for the place that has something to do with the crows someone had seen there) there was a showdown between Pastor Uplegger and the missionaries and an Apache leader who was championing the Old Way. The messages were different. The people wanted to know which way to go—right or left—and the meeting got tense. Pastor Uplegger said you could have heard one cottonwood leaf fall from the cottonwood trees there. Finally, he took the Bible and held it between him and the leader of the Old Way. "Can we agree to call this our norm and standard?" he asked in Apache. The people waited. It was quiet—it was very quiet. After a while the man raised his hand. The tension that was palpable went away with the raising of that hand. The agreement was that the man and his group would come, and they would study from the Bible, but it didn't happen that way as it turned out. "The man did not come." Those were the terse words that told it. This disparity of culture and Christianity remains the tension in the work of the missionary with his people. Which way? The standard of the Bible which is outside and above the missionary's own feelings and thoughts and culture or the standard of tradition and "the Old Way?"

The people themselves vindicated Francis Uplegger and his Christian teaching and belief. There were those cultural challenges which came and went, but the gentleman missionary's quiet and gentle way won their hearts. Medicine men came and went. The Old Way got even older and more separated from what that old way once was. The Word of God didn't change in its proclamation of Jesus, and there were many Apaches who at the end of the day said, "I am Christian." They recognized the work of *Inashood Hastin* as being true

---

278 *The Apache Scout*, "Another Word about Our *Bin'na-etdinni*," July 1930.

and what they wanted to follow. In May of 1963 the Apache people of the San Carlos Apache tribe received the elderly missionary as an honorary member of the San Carlos Apache Tribe.

Francis Uplegger was also an artist. His oil painting above the old altar in San Carlos Lutheran Church is of Apache believers on the way of life, and the medicine man is standing off there to the side beckoning like one of the classical sirens of old. There in that same desert picture of Peridot and San Carlos, emblazoned on a monsoon thundercloud, stands Jesus with his hands lifted in blessings. It is a Jewish Jesus. He isn't like the medicine man standing there. Nor is he like the Apache men, women, and children on the road. But they are his people, and he has his hands lifted above them. The Triplets stand in mountain fastness and watch in the background in the picture, as indeed they still watch what goes on below them today. The listeners at the services then and now study the picture, as their eyes still wander from the preacher to that silent scene above the altar. The picture is still there today in Grace Lutheran Church in San Carlos.

"It was four in the morning, in the city of roses, oranges and palms, Phoenix, March 13, 1925." That is how Francis wrote about the death of his beloved wife of 34 years. Emma's last word was the German word, "Ja!" She said it in dying tones when Francis read to her the 23rd Psalm about the rod and staff comforting her. He and his son and daughters were able at that hour to sing some hymns. "Jerusalem the Golden" was one. The letter he wrote went to Emma's sister in Germany. Francis described to the sister how at the funeral six Apache girls in their traditional dress had carried the coffin out of the church. His wife Emma's remains were laid in a grave next to where his daughter Johanna's one-day-old infant boy lay. It was in Peridot by a mesquite tree, on the southeastern side of the mesa by a hill. Off in the distance towered 8,000-foot Mount Turnbull. This was Apache country, and this was the home for *Inashood Hastin* and his wife. It was the home of the whole family. They are all sleeping there in that plot today, and as the poet said, "The lone and level sands stretch far away." This is where their lives and their time were spent.

There was a postscript at the end of this harbinger of death. It was a soliloquy of sorts from the old missionary at that tender hour: "Something has become clear to me in this hour that I have often thought about. Why did I have to wander so with my wife? I never wished myself away from any place where we lived. I received calls and I followed them if it seemed that the conditions warranted it and demanded it. Restless blood? Lapses in judgment? It was nothing of the sort. God willed it to be so. Everywhere we went there was some blessing in store. And this much is absolutely clear to me: God wanted the people in all these places and lands to witness this quiet, humble, private, intensely spiritual woman and to get to know her. Everywhere she went she drew people to blessings. Pastor Guenther in his funeral address said he experienced this the first time Emma shook his hand. In her the mystery of the Christian woman was revealed. It was 'unsought, unintentioned, causing a person to contemplate and think and appreciate this great worth.' "[279]

Francis Uplegger lived for many years without the company of his dear wife. He stayed on among the people he loved. Of course he got old, but it is possible to say he got more distinguished looking, with his white goatee and his quiet gentlemanly and deliberate way. He sat in the back of the room at the conferences for the called workers. Sometimes he would raise his hand to speak. Once in a while it happened when he was finally called on to speak he said, "I have long since forgotten what I was going to say."[280] Once on the way to a conference in California, when he was one of four in the back seat of Henry Rosin's laboring Chevrolet, he was heard to say, "I am reminded of the story in the Bible of the woman who overlaid her child." And the years went away and so did he finally at the age of 97. On the back of his headstone in that same cemetery plot at Peridot is the passage written in Apache, the language he worked so hard to get written and understood:

"DA(YONAS(YU K'AD) ITINN NAEL.AV:NA. DALQLIHI- HIVLTSEH'! DADVIVDNI; JESUS GOLIV-YU IHIDNA DO-GO- NAEL.AV-DA) HIH:/:" F.U.[281]

Finally, in this awesome threesome of missionaries (Uplegger, Uplegger and Rosin) there was Henry Rosin. When he came, he was a handsome young man and an athlete. Perhaps he could have fit the description of Joseph in the Bible who was described as "well built and handsome."[282] They called him Raisins. His German name meant that. It sounded the same, and the name stuck. Years later Rosin's contemporary and schoolmate Karl Schweppe in New Ulm, Minnesota, would talk about Raisins. He always chuckled when he reminisced about Raisins. This Raisins had been quite a baseball

---

[279] From the letter written from Rice, Arizona, the 16th of March, 1925 to "Elisabeth and Wilhelm" in Germany. The occasion was the death of Emma Uplegger, Francis Uplegger's faithful companion of 34 years.

[280] The writer heard him say this on several occasions.

[281] This is the inscription on the tombstone of Francis Uplegger. Bonnie Lewis translates: "The road ahead of us—As the road ahead of us is still here, respect and keep it holy—It is true—Where Jesus lives, life is eternal."

[282] Genesis 39:6.

Funeral of Francis Uplegger.
Photo Credit: St. Peter Lutheran Church photos.

player in his youth. He carried his love of baseball with him to the reservation. Many afternoons spirited baseball games were played after church. The Apache men liked to play baseball too, and in later years there were many tournaments and teams that were mustered for semi-serious competition with each other.

Henry Rosin was a contemporary of Alfred Uplegger. In fact, he came to the reservation at the same time that Alfred Uplegger did. He was in the same class as Alfred Uplegger but finished the school year and came eight months after his classmate. He would later marry Johanna Uplegger, Alfred's sister. Miss Marie Kiekbush came from Wisconsin and visited the reservation. She taught school in 1916, the year before Henry's arrival. The note on the back of the photograph said about her, "Pastor H. Rosin is happy to have had her (Marie Kiekbush) as his teacher in Wrightstown, Wisconsin."

On a particular 1919 caravan trip to the Grand Canyon, Henry Rosin scared everyone to death. Arnold Sitz, another Apache missionary at the time, described what happened at the Grand Canyon—which still squeezes our stomachs today when we hear it: "To the left, a jutting and detached rock stood out into the canyon on a pedestal.

284

A little side trail led to it. I was the first to discover it and crawl out to it. Hair-raising the look over its edge! A sheer drop of 1,000 feet! Far below could be seen pines and trees growing. It took 12 seconds for the sound of a dropped stone to reach our ears. Although the rock was but four feet wide and like distance separated it from the mainland and a misstep meant to be dashed into the abyss below, Raisins jumped it. It caused not a little talk and consequently also a little ill-feeling when he took exception to the talk. However, it soon blew over."[283]

That is one way the old people remembered Henry Rosin. Even as an old and deaf man, he ran. He ran up the hill from his house there by the salt cedar trees to get to the church or the school at Peridot. He waved his hand, and away he went up the hill at a full run.

There was another thing about Henry Rosin that all who knew him remembered too. He had a row of honey bee hives that sat down by the railroad track that went by Peridot Mission. The bees foraged on the mesquite trees and the catclaw blossoms. In the kitchen of his tufa stone house with its big screened porch he kept the amber mesquite honey in gallon glass jars. More than one visitor to Peridot left with such a jar full of honey on the back seat of his car. Pastor Rosin was impervious (almost) to bee stings. He opened the beehives without a smoker and bee suit. He just lifted up the lid and took out the frames with the crawling bees all over and those buzzing around his head. Once at East Fork when he looked into another missionary's bee hive one miscreant bee got into his pant leg. He stamped his leg. We could see him do it. And then we heard his loud voice, "Ouch! You rascal! You stung me!" And then he laughed his laugh again.

When he launched out from Peridot to visit people near and far he often took gallon jars of honey with him. It happened that way on his first visit to the Hartzell Family living in Globe at that place on Devereaux St., where St. Peter's church perched. He had his mesquite and catclaw honey with him. When Rosin came up to the Hartzell boys with his honey on that day in the 1950s, he stooped over with his hands on his knees to talk to them and promised them that if they would visit him at Peridot he would get an Apache pony to give them rides on. That promise never panned out, but the promise itself had a long shelf life which led eventually—perhaps—to the Hartzell boys getting their own horse one day.

That place in Globe on Devereaux St. knew Henry Rosin very well by the end of his life. He came there initially to do the work, about the same time his friend and future brother-in-law Alfred

---

[283] *Sitz Diary: 1919 Trip to the Grand Canyon*, translated by Pastor Victor H. Prange, p. 31.

Uplegger did. They had been classmates at the seminary in Wisconsin. Alfred Uplegger arrived in Globe in January of 1917 and worked with Pastor Harders there until the latter died in April of that year. It was in August of 1917 that Pastor Rosin came, the 11th of August to be exact, and when he came Alfred Uplegger took him around Globe and introduced Henry to the Apaches in the town who were coming to church there on Devereaux Street. They went down the steep hill to downtown Globe and got some necessary basic furniture—a bed and dresser and the like.

Henry Rosin started his work by teaching in Pastor Gustav Harder's little school there off Devereaux Street. He tried unsuccessfully to reconnoiter and find some new students for the school. On September 5 he started teaching his little group, but the attendance was discouraging. The night before novice Rosin started teaching, a dance was held among the resident Apaches, and his students were sleep-deprived and celebratorily hung over. The commotion of the sunrise dances still has this deleterious effect on students today. The roster of Rosin's school claimed to have twenty students, but there were never more than eighteen there at any one time. In those first months the average attendance was thirteen. He taught the children from the Old Testament. He got from the Creation account to the giving of the law on Mount Sinai. The students learned to say the Ten Commandments from memory and some other passages as well. From his classroom he graduated gradually to holding worship services in both Globe and Miami on Sunday afternoons.

Rosin was a practical man who worked well with his hands. His penchant for repairing things started when he painted the buildings that clung to the hillside at the little mission in Globe. This kind of work was his bent. Teaching thirteen students didn't consume the whole day. He thought he might as well tidy up the place. He could do that. In fact, he wrote that it was necessary to do maintenance on the buildings, or the whole place would physically collapse on itself. It was in this same year of 1917 that Noftsger Hill School was completed across the canyon to the north a quarter of a mile or so. You could see it there on another hillside. Rosin saw its fastness there on the hill, a stone's throw from his humble school with its Apache children. The date 1917 still stands on that same school building yet today.[284] He

---

[284] The pastor's children from that same place on Devereaux Street would in later years make the trek to that school across the canyon every day. In 1956 one would sit in the upper left-hand classroom of Noftsger Hill School and listen with his fellow classmates to Don Larsen's perfect game in the fifth game of the 1956 World Series. It remains the only perfect game in World Series history. The teacher, Miss Setka, was a devout Catholic and wanted her students to listen to her Yankees play that day.

put a roof on one of the buildings after carefully requisitioning tar paper from the "Commission." He pleaded with the Commission that they put a house up for ailing Pastor Uplegger at San Carlos, so that he could make it through the brutal summer months.

At San Carlos at this time the government school was claiming the students in the little mission school for its own. Both Uplegger and Rosin worked to get their students back. Superintendent E. E. Guenther also was involved, writing the people in Washington. The government official at the time was not a religious man (by his own admission, Rosin said). In 1918 Spanish influenza struck. Whole families died out. Rosin knew of one family of three generations where every single member died. At the government school, of the 200 students attending, 193 got sick and 22 died. Not one of his 33 students died, and the Apaches noticed this. It wasn't that Lutherans didn't get sick. They did and they died too, but in this case Rosin's Lutherans were spared, and his school attendance went to 35 students.

Besides the unbelieving school commissioner in San Carlos commandeering Lutheran students, the situation was not so good in Globe either. The mission work was 25 years in the making. Rosin noted that it was a great achievement to have come among the Apaches and single handedly to have accomplished what they had with the few men that had come. But they needed more workers. The Roman Catholics were "snooping and sniffing" around. The Catholics even built a big church in Miami, not far from the train station there. Many of the Apaches were being attracted to go there rather than to attend the ramshackle Lutheran edifice in Globe. People haven't changed: they wanted to go to the big church in Miami rather than to the one that was not big in Globe. Other Christian people were working to introduce the people to Christianity. A certain Presbyterian layman had worked in educating school children on his own. But he was going to have to leave, because his monetary support from his job in the mines had given out. As Rosin opined, at the 25 year mark of the work (1918) it was good that the Presbyterians and Catholics were working among the people too. He was the only one of the Lutheran missionaries who talked like this. In his opinion the goodness of the other churches working was that someone was telling the people about Jesus. There were so many Apache people, and the work was so big. No one man or church could do it all. After a while Rosin himself had 200 families in his congregation and work. No one person could do justice to that work. He pleaded for more workers from the Commission.

There is a picture of Rosin's school at Peridot and some school children by the tufa stone church. It was a small part of the total work, but it was a part that would grow and consume its share of time and energy. It's still there today, and the children are still being taught. Since the time of the first pictures, generations of young Apaches have been there to that place, Rosin's place. In view of the picture mentioned Pastor Rosin said, "The peridots in the picture might appear to you rather rough and unpolished. And if you should have the good fortune to meet them and live with them a time, you would be sad indeed to find some very rough corners to their souls as well. Yet each is a precious stone in God's eyes, more dear to him than all the gold in the earth."[285]

In 1925, with eight years of work under his belt, Rosin was asked by the Committee to go to the northern reservation to work there, smooth over troubles, and hopefully stave off ventures into unionism, which in the Committee's opinion were being entertained. The Committee gave Rosin the highest commendation for being a seasoned and sensible man who would be able to take on the personality challenges and get things back on the right keel. It was also said confidentially to Rosin that he was the only one Edgar Guenther recommended for the ticklish situation.[286]

Rosin and Rogers were the teachers of Peridot grade school with its 81 students when the school building was dedicated. It replaced the adobe building (probably from the first missionaries). It still stands, but barely. In 1928 Chairman Brockmann noted in his comments to Pastor Rosin that he was having 40 people in church on Sundays, of which 30 were children. Only ten adults!? He did add the caveat, "I know what it means to teach school all day and to prepare a sermon for Sunday on top of that: but would it not be possible to do camp work at least one evening a week? Please try to do this if at all possible. It is good to have the children, but we must have the parents too."[287]

There was a special church service on February 16, 1930, to commemorate the work done in Rosin's little school. Francis Uplegger wrote, "Peridot now has an enrollment of 81 pupils with practically all grades. Missionary Rosin and Rankin Rogers are the regular

285 *The Apache Scout*, August 1923.

286 Chairman Brockmann's actual quote to Rosin was, "I also wish to state that brother G. recommended you as the only one he knew would fit in at Whiteriver." (Waukesha, Wisconsin, August 7, 1925.)

287 Correspondence from Brockmann, dated March 6, 1928, Synod archives.

Peridot Mission School, (from left to right) Teachers Reuben Stock, Dorothea Uplegger, Pastor Henry Rosin, Dolores Ohlmann

teachers of the school.[288] Rankin is a young Apache. He was formerly a pupil of Pastor Rosin and under his tutelage passed from a place behind the desk to one in front of it. There are many temptations ever trying to draw him away from his place of honor and responsibility, as is the case with every faithful laborer in the Lord's vineyard. Therefore, think of Rankin in your prayers." The writer went on: "Anyone who has ever been near enough to an Indian school to hear its bell will know at once that two teachers cannot give 80 pupils the individual attention that they need. For this reason, Mrs. Rosin has been conducting a third class during this school year."[289]

Yes, there was a Mrs. Rosin. Pastor Rosin married Alfred Uplegger's sister, Johanna. Apparently, it was not love at first sight, at least on the part of Johanna. From that same Sitz diary of the 1919 Grand Canyon trip we hear the confidential information about Henry's courtship with Johanna. Sitz recollected: "At 6:00 p.m. we attended

---

[288] Rosin spoke of measles striking his children in their classrooms and emptying them all. Fevers of 104° were common. Parents tended their children at night. Some caught pneumonia too, as they struggled with measles. Even Rankin Rogers and his classroom succumbed at one point.

[289] E. E. Guenther, *The Apache Lutheran*, May 1993.

a lecture with moving pictures of a 1,400 mile trip down the Colorado and through the canyon by the Kolb brothers, who made the trip. At 9:00 p.m. we bade Mrs. Rosin (Henry's mother) goodbye to go back east to Wisconsin for the summer. It was one of the pleasures of the trip to see with what fine love and respect Raisins treated his mother. She was his first concern, and that in the face of the fact that the girl he loves with all his heart was a member of the party, Johanna Uplegger, Al's sister. Nothing was too good for her; she was never neglected or left to her own devices. The Lord never overlooks such piety; it will be rewarded. And that brings me to other shots. Henry confessed to me in conference in Tucson that he was in love with Miss Uplegger; also that she had refused his proffer. He is taking it like a man, though, and she is finding princely attention at his hand—something I could not do. At the same time, I think his cause is not at all lost; she needs but realize her regard for him. I have told him so, also. I am glad to find myself his confidant as far as he confides in anyone."

After there was a Mrs. Rosin, Henry called her "Hunchen" which was the affectionate German diminutive of Johanna. Affectionate—yes, but there wasn't one bit of affectation about Johanna. She wore dresses that may have been in style in her youth, but she was not young when we saw her. The Bible says, *"Gray hair is a crown of splendor; it is attained by a righteous life"* (Proverbs 16:31). It was true for Johanna Rosin. She who endured a three-day dust storm in a tattered and flapping tent was a survivor. She coped. We heard later that during the times of flu epidemics and contagion she went around after visitors left and wiped all the door knobs with a chloroformed rag. But a more loyal fan of Peridot and its environs couldn't be found. Maybe some snickered behind Johanna's back at her kind of prudish and old-fashioned ways, but Pastor Rosin loved her. He called her "Schatz" too. We didn't know it at the time but that nickname meant "Treasure" in German.

Pastor Rosin liked children. He would take visiting children and show them his hen house. There the more intrepid of them could reach into the lair of a broody hen and snatch her egg away. It wasn't an easy feat though. Sitting hens peck if given the chance. Pastor Rosin laughed with a kind of good-natured cackle when he saw the beady eyes of a biddy take aim. He told one such group of visiting boys about a bobcat that had gotten into his chicken pen. The thought of that tawny and tan marauder in that very place killing chickens was a scary thought to the boys standing there in the sunshine. One of Pastor Rosin's students who attended Peridot grade school said that one day Pastor Rosin "whipped" him because he accused him of shooting his chickens with a slingshot. The student maintained his innocence in the charge, but his idea of Pastor Rosin's happy and jovial nature was forever blemished by that whipping. And others have spoken about this sort of thing too. One lady remembered that Pastor Rosin slapped a niece in confirmation class for not getting her memory work done. How this slap, if it ever was even reported to them, affected the relative family we don't know. It is part of that repository of sacred information that exists when relatives labor in close quarters. It is perhaps part of the Scripture's command to "bear one another's burdens."

Once President Brockmann said to Henry in a letter, "The house for Peridot has been authorized. The amount set aside for this purpose is $5,000; however, I told the mission board and the synod that in all probability we would not use the full amount as you were a very practical man and had volunteered to help as much as you found possible."[290] Virtually every building connected to the mission work on both reservations had Rosin's handiwork on display somewhere. He built the house he lived in at Peridot. About the porch he said, "The pillar and arch construction for the front porch will be practical for ensuring a comparatively cool place on hot days and an extra sleeping place in the very hot season."[291] He asked for a cook stove. He asked for a windmill so he could make his salary reach the end of the month with a garden and vegetables he would raise himself.

He never really got into the Apache language. He talked with his hands and with his legs. He ran almost everywhere he went. He sprinted up the hill to the tufa stone church or to the tufa stone school. Then he coasted back down the hill teaming up with gravity by leaning back a little and his legs brought him back to his tufa stone house with the big screened porch and the salt cedar trees where occasional hens hid their eggs. He killed a big coiled rattlesnake on the porch step of that house one night. He used a hoe and did the job in a no-nonsense way, like a man who was good at baseball and making things with his hands.

Peridot was Pastor Rosin's life. Everything that happened there was just an extension of who he was and what he was. He struggled for over fifty years in a humble way to preach and teach Jesus to his people there. On the side he worked hard with his hands like the

---

[290] Correspondence from Paul Brockmann, dated August 24, 1923. Waukesha, Wisconsin. Synod archives.

[291] Correspondence with Paul Brockmann, 1923, Synod archives.

(left to right) Henry Rosin, Johanna Rosin (Uplegger), Francis Uplegger, Dorothea
Behn (Uplegger), Alfred Uplegger.
Photo Credit: Hartzell photograph collection

Apostle Paul did.[292] He built buildings of tufa stone and wood, causing the committee in 1925 to comment on how attractive the simple parsonage was that Rosin had built. He asked for money to put
up some canvas curtains on the sleeping porch, and they willingly
granted the request. They could see his good work, but he always
labored with the gaunt specter of monetary scarcity haunting him.
Things got old and dusty and tired at Peridot. Reclaimed tufa stone
from 9 miles away at the Coolidge Dam site found its way into his
buildings. You could always tell the missionaries who lived at Peri-

---

[292] *"Make it your ambition to lead a quiet life: You should mind your own business and
work with your hands, just as we told you"* (1 Thessalonians 4:11).

dot by their dusty shoes, and the people who worked there gradually became that way too.

When he was old and ready to retire because of hearing and health reasons and he couldn't run up the hill to the school anymore, a charlatan happened by and offered him a ready-made fortune if he would invest money in a gold mine. A gold mine! There was no guile in Pastor Rosin and he believed the man. With this "investment" he could get some needed funds to fix things yet that needed fixing for Peridot and the work. He used some church money to do this investing, and he used his own too. Charlatans are charlatans, and they don't care about the feelings of old men who trust them and who want to do something good for Apaches. It was heartbreaking the way it went after the money and the man went away. Pastor Rosin had to be called on the carpet. The visiting pastor sat with him in the car parked outside the house where he could shout the proceedings into Pastor Rosin's deaf ear. After a while ancient Johanna came out of the house and pecked on the window of the car with her finger. She wanted the story to be "right."

Pastor Rosin died in Globe in 1982. He had been at Peridot more than fifty years. Descendants of his bees still probe the mesquite blossoms there. The eroded tufa stone church still stands, his handiwork. It squats squarely on the little hill there. Bats fly out of the belfry to forage for insects. The smell of guano is overpowering sometimes—to the uninitiated anyway. Even the century had gotten old by that time and dusty. Someone got Pastor Rosin's fabled bag of peridots.[293] It was rumored that he once had a whole gunny sack full. Maybe he had just given them all away. We knew he did that sort of thing. Maybe the crook with the proffered gold mine got them.

Pastor Rosin is buried at Peridot in the cemetery where all the Upleggers are buried. It is not far from the place he spent his strength and life, just over the hill. The cemetery plot is fenced in with a no-nonsense chain linked fence. Pastor Rosin's place is on the lower left-hand corner of the little quadrant. There is also the stone by him that says, "The two infant Rosin sons." He who worked his whole life with Apache children had only one son himself. The child was not well as a youngster and caused his parents much worry. In May of 1923 he wrote to Pastor Brockmann, the President of the Board at that time, "Our baby has been failing since the month of January. At

---

[293] The peridot is a beautiful pale green semi-precious gem. It is the traditional birthstone for August, and is found only at Peridot, Arizona, and a few other places: Burma, Afghanistan, China. This was the Creator's special compensating gift to this perhaps otherwise unattractive spot of landscape, and it was said about Pastor Rosin that he had a sack full of peridots, for which he had paid the people money who had brought them to him.

first barely noticeable; now he is but skin and bones. He is 11 months old and weighs but 12 pounds. The doctors on the Reservation and at Globe did him no good. We were afraid we would lose him. Then we heard of a prominent pediatrist, Dr. E. M. Tarr, here at Phoenix, who has had wonderful success with children."

One of the last things we remember about Henry Rosin was one evening when we swung by there to visit on our way home to East Fork. He came out of his house, the same house that held the gallon jars of mesquite and catclaw honey when he was younger and could lift the full supers of honey. He was an old man this evening. His face was wrinkled. His good-natured laugh wasn't heard much anymore. It was never heard by him: he was deaf. The dust of Peridot was invasive in its quiet and relentless way, and it was there that evening. He seemed sad that evening as he stood there by the salt cedar tree at the front of his house. People were making small talk before leaving. As we were leaving, Pastor Rosin confided to our parents that one of the pillars of his church who had been his encourager and his rock of support had just taken an eagle feather for a sunrise dance. That is all he said and as we left that evening, we saw him walk slowly back into the screened porch of his house. He wasn't running anymore.

In commemoration of Rosin's ministry, Alfred Uplegger wrote about him, "In all the years that he lived at Peridot he saw it as the "cheery, bright green spot" and he made it cheerful by his cheerful spirit. In spite of all disappointments, trials, losses, hardships, the joy and peace shed into believing hearts through "the good tidings of great joy," announced by the angel of the Lord to the shepherds of Bethlehem, were reflected in his eyes, in his voice and in his manner in general. He thoroughly enjoyed the Gospel story and wanted everyone also to enjoy the beauty and blessing that it brings with it."[294]

He did enjoy it. He loved Peridot, and he is buried there not far from his home in the tufa stone house.

---

[294] *The Apache Lutheran*, August 1967, Alfred Uplegger, p. 10 (from the issue entitled, "Golden Anniversary in the Ministry, August 1917 to August 1967").

CHAPTER SEVENTEEN

The Schools

*Train a child in the way he should go, and when he is old
he will not turn from it* (Proverbs 22:6).

Carlisle Indian School in Pennsylvania was an attempt on the part of the U. S. Government to educate the Native American children and so bring them into the predominant culture of the country. There is one picture of all the students sitting side by side outside the dormitories of the school, dormitories that looked like military barracks. There was not a smile to be seen in the whole crowd of hundreds of side-by-side students. Pictures also show the before and after of Chiricahua Apache children: there is the "before" with everyone disheveled and dirty and unkempt with long hair and the same group six months later "civilized" and clean and some even sporting jaunty poses before the cameras. That was the way the pictures were meant to impress the ones who looked at them. Everyone was hoping that the students would make good citizens. It would take the same government that set up this indoctrination a long time before it actually would make the students full-fledged citizens, but it made everyone with different DNA feel better to see what looked like progress.

The training and indoctrination of the youth to fit into a new society was something that the Apaches themselves understood. Mickey Free, the half Irish and half Mexican boy[295] captured by the Apaches, was surely educated into the Apache culture and life when he was taken captive as a child and raised up by his captors. Missionary Mayerhoff was impressed with what he saw in Mickey Free at the turn of the century in East Fork. The same indoctrination and assimilation happened whenever children were taken captive from Mexico as they were from time to time. It was also sadly done by Mexico when Apache children were taken there and dispersed as slaves after the horrible Aravaipa massacre.

Right from the beginning in the Apache mission endeavor the missionaries believed in this education of the young. They could

---

[295] You read different stories as to which half of Free's ancestry was which.

imagine no better way to win the hearts of the people than by the loving education of the young. Apache parents perhaps above all else realized and appreciated this demonstrated love by the missionaries for their children. They knew what was happening to the children who were being sent off to places like Carlisle to be educated. The children caught diseases for which they had no immunities. They learned bad things. The girls came back home to the reservation and they were no longer good girls. The world was changing out there, their way of life was over, and they were confined to reservations and told what they could and couldn't do. That was all bad enough, but it was infinitely worse to have their children taken from them and brought back again forever different and changed.

So the first missionary on the San Carlos Reservation had people who brought their children to him to escape sending them off the reservation or even sending them to the government school on the reservation. And it was reported that on the Fort Apache Reservation the same dynamic was in play as Edgar Guenther gathered students: "The year was 1911. It was the first day of school at the new East Fork School, or at least it was supposed to be the first day. Pastor Edgar Guenther rang the school bell and patiently waited for students to fill the desks he had made with his own hands. No one came. Pastor Guenther was not one to give up. The next day he rang the school bell once again. This time a distinct form could be seen in the distance. It was the form of a tall, handsome, elderly Apache. In English his "name" was Y-24.[296] Y-24 walked slowly and deliberately, holding the hands of two of his grandchildren. This dignified man with the long hair walked up to Pastor Guenther and in his best English simply said, 'Teach them.' "[297]

This change of mores brought about by the education of the children was something the Apache believers hoped for too. Missionary H. C. Nitz wrote the following about the Lutheran Tom Wycliffe who lived across the river from East Fork Mission: "On the birthday of our mission it is good to have the mind of Tom Wycliffe, a faithful Apache Christian who died at East Fork four years ago. A medicine man said to Tom, 'See how long the missionaries have had our children in school, and they have not taken away their belief in medicine worship.' Tom said, 'Well, you let them work another five hundred years and there will be a change, then there will be no more medicine men on the reservation.' "

---

[296] Since many of the Apache names could not be pronounced by the English speaking soldiers, the Apaches were given letter and number names.

[297] Glen Seefeldt, *The Apache Lutheran*, February, 1993.

The government brought the philosophy of child education onto the reservation with reservation schools, and that first attempt came in 1880 and 1881 in San Carlos. Government officials and personnel came to run the schools, and there was a group that came to San Carlos. All the teachers left in haste, however, when the Cibecue Massacre happened, and they were left wondering if it was safe for them on the reservation. They reasoned that they weren't safe and fled. The school at San Carlos didn't actually start until some years after 1881, not so many years before the Lutheran missionaries came. Some of the government people in charge of reservation education of the young were good and some weren't. The first missionaries at Peridot realized that one of their greatest challenges was to overcome associations being made between them and certain of the government teachers. On the other hand, there were loyal and supportive government teachers and officials who recognized that the mission schools had special advantages to offer that the government schools often could not duplicate. There were government officials who came to be some of the best supporters of the reservation mission schools.

When Hartwig and Koch came on that first reconnaissance in 1892, they visited a school a mile outside Tucson that boasted 135 students, most of them Pima Indians. It was a Christian school, and these Lutheran pastors heard the Pima children singing Christian songs. The singing of these Christian children inspired the searching men to accomplish something similar among the people they would find. The mentality of having schools was clearly there in the beginning. The Twenty-Fifth Anniversary Booklet of the mission work among the Apache said that the hope of doing mission work among the people depended on the Christian school, and that if the school system was intact among the Apache they didn't need to fear the future or worry about the success of the venture.[298]

When Pastor Gustav Harders stepped off the train in Globe in 1905, he was already thinking of starting schools. It was he who organized the mission work into a conference with regular meetings and a unified approach. He was the first superintendent of the work and had a good knowledge of it. From the minutes of a 1906 meeting of missionaries we read, "In the afternoon after a reading and prayer Pastor Harders gave the report regarding the Synod. He reported that both the Synod and the Committee for Apache Missions were in agreement that a day school taught by Irmgard Harders should be begun in Globe. It was further agreed that the interpreters should

---

[298] *Jubilaeumsbüchlein*, p. 34.

help out with that work."[299]

Already in the fall of 1907 Harders and his daughter Irmgard taught five Apache students in a little makeshift school in Globe at the little church he called The New Jerusalem. He and his family bought a house which perched on the hill, right off present-day Devereaux Street, and he built a little chapel.[300] His daughters Irmgard and Hilda joined him in the work, and they were his teachers. In addition, other teachers would eventually come and help: Klara Hinderer, Maria Kieckbusch (first sent to Peridot), Teacher Gurgel, and student H. C. Nitz. Harders fed his school children a noon meal with food he scrounged from local hotels. This lunch program became the cited example from the authorities to the other mission stations, the trouble being perhaps that the others didn't have access to leftovers from local hotels. The wives of the missionaries helped out. They stood solidly at their husbands' sides and stitched and sewed and cooked and cared for the little children. When they had regular care and food the students showed up regularly. When these were missing, then often the students were too. In addition, the early missionaries enjoyed the favor of some of the government day school administrators and were encouraged and invited to teach classes of a religious nature in the government schools.

The missionaries met with Harders in regular meetings, and in one such meeting they issued this fiat: "Our conference presents to the honorable committee for the Apache work of the General Synod of Wisconsin, Minnesota, Michigan, Nebraska and Other States the following recommendations: We see the way to establish a Lutheran congregational system here among the Apaches in the Lutheran congregational school. In other words, we must be able to have the children in our complete care and instruction in order for the church to grow (in order for there to be sufficient leaven for the dough). In order for us to have a Lutheran school system that could stand unmolested next to the educational system of the government, it is necessary for us to remain in constant touch with the Department of the Interior."[301] In the minutes of 1909 we read under the title of "The matter of schools and education" the following: "It is determined to seek permission through the committee to allow the missionaries free

---

[299] The following tangential reporting was connected to the minutes: "Matters regarding mission work in the boarding school outside the reservation at Globe, home missions in Phoenix, Tucson and Bisbee, and the matter of a raise in pay will be discussed at the next general synodical convention."

[300] There is a picture of the inside of that little chapel.

[301] This was a quote from the transliterated German minutes in the author's collection.

hand wherever the possibility would exist in view of local circumstances and according to the means of the Synod to attack the opportunity to educate children."[302] And finally as the first missionaries looked at the schools and their relationship with the government in regard to educating Apache children, they said: "The conference holds it to be of utmost importance to maintain a good relationship with Washington, partly to defend ourselves against attacks coming from other quarters, and partly to help us in our work. For instance, there are opportunities for our Lutheran people to enter the government schools to contact our people there. And it is certainly going to happen in the immediate future that the Indians on the Fort Apache Reservation will get sizable income from selling timber. If someone would then be inclined to give something for the help of the mission, this could only happen if it comes by way of the authority of Washington. Because of this and other instances like this it is the recommendation of the conference that a representative be chosen who could represent our work here in Washington."

The fledgling work on both reservations had schools. Missionary Plocher started the school at Peridot and worked within its adobe walls to teach children hymns and Bible passages and how to read and write in English. Parents fearfully eyeing the reservation government schools and the specter of having to send their children away brought their children. It was these children who would be the first to be baptized and brought into the church. Carl Guenther and teacher Rudolph Jens continued the work of the schools begun by Plocher. Carl Guenther baptized a young girl named Rhoda Gordy. She had a sister named Bertha. Bertha was sixteen years old and had been a student at the school for six years. The government stepped in and took her away. For eight months they had her in their clutches. Missionary Harders and President Bergemann, the seventh president of the Wisconsin Synod, actually went to Washington and spoke with the President himself and with the highest official in the Indian Department of the United States Government. Think of that happening!

Besides his and his daughters' personal work in education, Harders wrote in his fictional novel *Dohashtida* the following snippet of dialogue between a skeptic and a government worker named Sims. They had this discussion: "And did they (the missionaries) really achieve no results?" "No results?" repeated Sims. "They had phenomenal success: In every way they had the confidence of the Indians. We government people do not have that. They had schools. Their enrollment was small, but all the children had been enrolled

---

[302] Conference at Fort Apache, June 3-7, 1909.

at the expressed wish of the parents. When we spoke of this last evening, you held that to be the ideal practice. Instead of using the police to bring in pupils, as we do, the missionaries even had Indians attending church on Sundays."[303]

The early mission station at Bylas had its school too. For years the government had urged the missionaries to open a school there, but since the synod could not see its way clear to do so, the government opened a large, well-equipped plant of its own. Finally, in 1922 a house and church were erected for Candidate Gustav Schlegel at Bylas. He immediately opened a small mission school in the annex of his church. The government finally closed its plant and sent its pupils by bus to a white school just off the reservation.

Paul Mayerhoff worked alone on the Fort Apache Reservation until 1902, when Otto Schoenberg was sent as teacher/helper. With the help of Apache workers they built the core part of the present chapel at East Fork. In 1903 Mayerhoff left. It was too bad because he was irreplaceable really. He knew the language. He knew the work, and he loved the people. But he went to Nebraska, and it was Teacher Otto Schoenberg who was colloquized and became a full-fledged pastor, joining Heinrich Haase to become the team to work at East Fork and to begin the school. In 1911 Schoenberg was moved by the Committee to Cibecue, where he was instructed to work and win the Apaches there. He worked hard in Cibecue too, and he built the chapel of adobe bricks that is still there today.[304]

In the fall of 1910, Edgar Guenther replaced Missionary Schoenberg. Guenther had instructions to reopen the mission school at East Fork under the most primitive and adverse conditions. The school had been closed when Schoenberg left. Then the government had established an educational plant adjoining the property, and all eligible children were enrolled there. Nevertheless, Guenther's call asked for the immediate opening of a mission school—with no equipment and barely any funds available. While the government fed and clothed the children in its school, Guenther was permitted to make no such promises. By persuading a few parents to send their children who were still under school age and admitting a few outcasts from the government school, Guenther made a start in the autumn of 1911 with sixteen pupils. Desks were improvised in imitation of the real thing. The children received a noonday meal in the missionary's

303 For a more complete reference to Harder's *Dohashtida* and its reflection on the work, refer to the section "Dual Control."

304 J. P. Koehler visited the field and said that Schoenberg had the same facility in Apache language acquisition that Missionary Mayerhoff had.

home, with the mother church in Wisconsin granting an allowance of 50 cents per child per month! Lessons sufficient for the following day were composed and duplicated on the old Oliver typewriter between sunset and sunrise. After the first year no children were solicited, the parents preferring a primitive mission school where love appeared to reign to the well-equipped government institutions where teachers' interests were controlled largely by the dollar.[305] In thinking back to the Lower Cibecue school, Guenther remembered that the school "held its own and this in spite of the fact that the government maintains a school bus line past our station to encourage pupils to attend its own spacious and up-to-the-minute equipped educational plant."

Government Agent Davis, a sincere friend of the mission at East Fork, disapproved of two schools being in such close proximity to each other. He made the missionary an offer of the entire government plant including forty acres of irrigated land and pasture land for a nominal sum, which was readily accepted. Since that time the school drew an average yearly enrollment of 90 pupils from the camps of the people up and down the river. In addition, the mission station at East Fork embraced a camp district of some 500 souls, with an additional 75 people living at Turkey Creek, twelve miles up Seven Mile Canyon near the present Chino Springs.[306]

In 1917 Mr. Gustav Gleiter came to help with the school. He lasted only a short while because he was called up to fight for his country. The draft board found a Lutheran teacher in the wilds of an Arizona reservation! It was, after all, 1917! Then Martin Wehausen came to the work in 1918. This Martin Wehausen left behind a short diary of his years on the mission. His written reporting was in the same careful handwriting that wrote his hidden signature in the parsonage at East Fork.[307] He wrote in 1921: "Aaron and Florence Keyes were baptized. Their father, Jack, became a Christian and was also baptized in July of that year. We took over the government day school on East Fork, having purchased it for a sum of $4,000. The complete enrollment of that school stayed with us." At the end of 1922, the ledger read, "We can record 34 adult and 30 infant baptisms, 8 burials, 3 marriages, 46 communicants, and an average Sunday attendance of 41, not including children under school age." So said Martin Wehau-

---

[305] Dr. William Kessel of Bethany Lutheran College wrote this history of his family and grandfather. Dr. Kessel is the grandson of Missionary Edgar Guenther.

[306] This information came from an article written by Edgar Guenther for *The Concordia Historical Institute Quarterly*. It was quoted in the June 1991 *The Apache Lutheran*.

[307] The signature was found under the ceiling cover when the porch was renovated in the 1990s. See the photo of it on page 172.

sen's journal, and Guenther added, "In our mission schools approximately 350 children are learning the One Thing Needful. Twice that number from government boarding schools are receiving religious instructions. The orphanage is filled to capacity with forty children. Practically all camps are visited with the gospel at regular intervals. Our entire mission force numbers 27, among whom are the following native workers: two native helpers, three male teachers, and two assistant matrons. A total of approximately 2,000 Indians have been baptized since the founding of our mission."

In the fall of 1921 Pastor H. C. Nitz was called to East Fork on a temporary basis to start the boarding school. The mission board planned to call a permanent principal after the school was started, and Pastor Nitz was to continue serving at Globe. But it didn't work out that way, and in the fall of 1922 Pastor Nitz was called permanently as principal and missionary at East Fork. Edgar Guenther said about Nitz, "H. C. Nitz was called to East Fork as the first principal of the boarding school and began his labors there under the most primitive conditions. The first boys were housed in an ennobled chicken coop, while the girls found shelter in hastily constructed barracks. In the course of time these made way for modern dormitories."

It was to Edgar Guenther that Martin Wehausen wrote the following report in the era of Nitz, Sitz and Wehausen:

July 5, 1922

Dear Brother Guenther,

With the beginning of the quarter just past we took over the East Fork Government Day School. Mr. Nitz came up from Globe on the 28th of March to help. On the days following we made the most necessary rearrangements, throwing two school kitchens into one, grading the children, etc. On the 3rd we were able to open school in good order with an enrollment of 75 children. Mr. Nitz took charge of the 32 second and third graders and I took charge of the remaining number.

The day school offered a dining room about large enough to seat all the children. Lucille George, a Christian Apache girl, took charge of the work for the first month. Later when she left I had to oversee the work, which meant a constant disturbance in my school work. This will not dare to go on. Mrs. Wehausen is not able to look after the work in the school kitchen any longer. She is not at all well and besides she is caring for an Apache orphan child. The $100 per month that has been paid her for work in the school kitchen may be subtracted from our monthly checks by September and used as a part payment *to hire someone in her place. Should the Board not decide by September to hire someone to work in the school kitchen then I shall do so and pay her whatever is right and send in the bill.*

After twenty-five years in the Apache mission work, the *Anniversary Booklet* records, "The government has also set up a whole number of schools among the Apaches in which the Indian children receive the usual elementary instruction in the English language. Our missionaries have free access to these government schools. Indeed, the government officials not only permit it but also mostly like to see it when our missionaries come and instruct the Indian children in religion in the free hours. To the present day our missionaries are doing mission work in the following government schools: Rice Boarding School, San Carlos Day School, East Fork Day School, Canyon Day School and Whiteriver Boarding School. These five government schools are attended by more than 600 Indian children. Our mission messengers instruct these children in the free hours in Bible history, catechism, and singing our Lutheran hymns. Oh, but what a beautiful opportunity our missionaries have also here to sow the seed of the divine Word in the tender hearts of the children and to lead them thereby to their Savior! Every Christmas, in all mission and government schools, a Christmas celebration with preaching

Children singing.
Photo Credit: "WESTERN WAYS PHOTO," Charles W. Herbert

and gift-giving was instituted for the Indian children. This is always a day of great joy for our people. Our dear Christians in the General Synod have constantly provided for it that the Indian children could be given an abundance of gifts at this festival."[308]

The education offered to the children was first-rate education. Superintendent Francis Uplegger reported in 1940: "It speaks well for the mission school teachers that also other pupils from their school here at the large government school are recognized as advanced beyond its own; mission school 6th graders, here at once in 8th grade."[309] The Superintendent noted as he observed the lower grade classroom, "Very interesting and gratifying. Excellent in method and personal disposition and manner. Model governing of children. Remarkable progress of beginners, of class in general, in reading English. Wholesome atmosphere, Christian spirit sober, not excluding a little humor. Mrs. J's quiet influence for good in her pupils' lives, in the quiet of the institution. Always active, quiet, exact, kindly, helpful. May God move her to firmly decide for further stay at East Fork."

It is impossible to talk about the schools on the reservation and not mention Arthur J. Meier, who was both teacher and principal of East Fork Mission School for fifty years. His faithful companion and helper through those years was his wife, Doris. She recalled that when she came from Sleepy Eye, Minnesota, all those years before, it was night and Arthur had to be outside the house for something. All of a sudden, she heard the awful braying of a donkey outside, but she didn't know from Sleepy Eye, Minnesota, experience that it was a donkey. It sounded like an awful monster to her. She was so glad to see her husband come back through the door, safe and sound.

Mr. Meier's work as principal of the grade school and high school at East Fork Mission was never easy. At about the time of Woodstock (1969) with young people rioting and challenging authority and education, Mr. Meier wrote, "Godliness with contentment is great gain." He wrote it in 1971, and what a simple yet profound statement it was. "Minds engrossed in disruption and violence cannot possibly reap the benefits of an education acquired through thoughtful study. Discontent is not peculiar to college campuses only. Consider the high school dropout. Somewhere among all the reasons given for dropping out, we will always find discontent. To a lesser degree this

---

308 *Anniversary Booklet for the Twenty-fifth Anniversary of the Evangelical Lutheran Indian Mission*, printed by Northwestern Publishing House, Milwaukee, Wisconsin, 1919, page 26.

309 *The Apache Scout*, April, 1940.

can be noted in the number of applications for enrollment at East Fork Mission for the second semester by students attending other schools. We don't doubt but that a certain unrest has played into the several requests for transfers by our own students. Surely there is a lack of contentment in our day and age, and even Chrsitain teenagers may be affected by such adverse influence. We can then be content to leave our entire life and the future for which we are preparing in God's hands, knowing that 'Whatever God ordains is good.' Students with such an attitude of mind have GREAT GAIN. They can pursue their studies with minds uncluttered by strife, envy, worry, and discontent. There is no question that minds freed from such evils are more ready for deeper concentration and meditation, both requisites for gaining more knowledge, greater wisdom, and a deeper satisfaction and contentment in life."[310]

An article in *The Apache Lutheran* said the following about Mr. Meier (as all his students and fellow workers knew him),

> The reason for calling attention to the fact that Mr. Meier came to church on January 9, 1994, at East Fork, is that it was fifty years to the very week when he first came to East Fork to church. He began his work of service at East Fork Mission in January of 1944.[311]
>
> The church was full for the first service in the morning. Mr. Meier recalled the way it had been fifty years earlier. It was a terrible winter that year, cold and wet. The roads were mud. The people lived in wickiups, and there was no electricity. He doubted whether there were twenty-five people at that first service he attended. As a matter of fact, the old record shows that on January 23, 1944, at 11:00 there were twelve who came to the Lord's Supper. Mr. and Mrs. Meier were listed #2 and #3 on that list. But on the Sunday he attended church fifty years later, over 300 came to church in two services with 140 people taking the Lord's Supper.
>
> And there was another important thing that happened in connection with his going to church at East Fork that day. Emma Nash was there with her husband Peter. Emma had been in the first service Mr. Meier attended fifty years before. In fact, in the Communion records that still exist from February 14, 1937, through January 23, 1944, Emma

---

[310] Arthur Meier, *The Broken Arrow*, January, 1972.

[311] There are copies of those first letters that Arthur and his wife Doris wrote to their family in Minnesota. He always began his letter, "Dear Folks," and then the description of the latest adventures at East Fork began.

(Cruz) Nash was faithful in attending the Lord's Supper. On a brown piece of paper folded into the record it says: "Confirmed: Samuel Adley, Samuel Cruz, Charles Aday, Emma Cruz, Arthur Clay, Adam Adley." On December 31, 1942, the name is Emma Cruz. On Good Friday, April 23, 1943, the record reads Mrs. Emma (Cruz) Nash. In talking about this the other day with Peter Nash at the hospital, he said, "Yes, I have been married to my wife for fifty years now!"[312]

Arthur Meier came to the mission at East Fork in 1944. We know how one of his emergency teachers saw the teaching in 1948: "I had a few days to settle in and get acquainted. The pastor and his wife seemed friendly enough but were a bit aloof. Mr. Meier, the principal at the school and his wife, on the other hand, welcomed me warmly. I took to them at once. They were in their early thirties, had three

Hilda Tessler lived upriver not far from where Peter and Emma Nash lived. Hilda was also a faithful worker in the nursery.
(Hartzell photo collection)

---

312 E. Hartzell, *The Apache Lutheran*, February 1994.

lovely, blond children, one of whom, Ruth, was going to be in my class. Mrs. Meier had me over for dinner and made me feel welcome. Mr. Meier gave me a crash course in teaching elementary school. The course consisted of showing me my classroom, handing me a stack of textbooks I would be using, giving me a sketchy outline of subjects to teach, and assuring me that he would always be there to help me. Miss Kolberg also gave me advice and suggestions, but by and large, I was on my own. The first day of school, I left my bedroom with a racing heart, scared and trembling. What was ahead of me? Mr. Meier had told me there would be thirty-nine Apache children and one white child—Ruth, his daughter."[313]

At the height of the school presence in the work, there were Lutheran grade schools at Peridot, Bylas, Cibecue (both Lower Cibecue at first and then upper Cibecue), and East Fork, and there was a high school boarding school at East Fork. The Bylas and Cibecue schools have since faded away, and the high school at East Fork did too.[314] But today Bylas Lutherans are considering reopening their grade school, and in 2015 East Fork Lutheran High School opened its doors again and is offering a Christian education today to a respectably sized student body. It used to be that it was a status symbol in tribal circles for people to be able to say, "I graduated from East Fork!" There were times in the past when virtually every family on the reservation was touched in some way by the presence of East Fork Lutheran High School.

Was the dream of the initial founders completely fulfilled and happy? No. But please consider the words of senior Loren Bush in 1989 as he spoke to 700 people in the packed gymnasium at his graduation from East Fork Lutheran High School:

> The teachers have been a tremendous influence on our lives. The school is very fortunate to have a faculty like the one we have. They made us work hard and tried to make us better prepared for what we should expect from the world.
>
> This might sound strange to some people, but the teachers' main concern was not that we knew how to write an expository paragraph, understand the judicial system, learn the volume of a sphere, or understand how friction works. Their number one priority was that we knew that Jesus Christ died for our sins and that heaven is ours through him alone.

---

[313] Barbara Laila Klaszus née Peters, *East Fork, Arizona, 1948-1949.*

[314] On May 24, 2019, the first senior class of eight students from the "new" East Fork Lutheran High School graduated at East Fork Mission.

It would be impossible to state all the things they have done for us to get us here where we are on Friday, May the 26th, 1989. So, in all sincerity and from the bottom of our hearts, we say, "Thank you, for a job well done."

And if there is one particular group of people that we owe a sense of gratitude, it would have to be our parents. They sacrificed a lot for us to make things more convenient for us. They made us who we are, what we are, and all we hope to be. Our parents not only took care of our physical needs but they especially took care of our spiritual well-being. This is evident in that they sent us to a Christian school to obtain the One Thing Needful: God's Word.[315]

It isn't a perfect world we live in, but it wouldn't be possible to represent the hopes of those who championed Lutheran education on the reservation better than Loren Bush did it in his graduation speech. There were strifes that developed in school-related matters among the workers. There was the constant and ongoing stress and strain related to budgeting and finances. There was disagreement regarding policies and practice. And there was the perceived notion that the schools were some kind of cosmic black hole that absorbed all the energy and light of the mission effort, leaving little to the actual work that was supposed to be done in the churches and congregations on the reservations. Edgar Guenther, who certainly earned his right to say it, said about himself toward the end of his ministry, "The quondam Superintendent of Missions visualized a more advanced institution, for which our more elementary day schools might serve as feeders with their most promising pupils and be developed into mission workers or, at any rate, into firmer Christians who would serve as a nucleus for future congregations in the various fields. The school has not succeeded in doing that with the rank and file of its students, partly because it is situated in the heart of a large Apache population with its accompanying detracting influences and partly because the money and equipment for giving pupils a well-balanced and practical education has been lacking. In spite of all this, a number of fine Apache Christian men and women have been graduated from East Fork."[316]

But then, harkening back to the belief of Harders and the other pioneers in the work, Guenther says what most certainly has hap-

---

315 *The Apache Lutheran,* May, 1989.

316 This is from the final installment of Pastor Edgar Guenther's historical overview of Apache mission work as he wrote it in the 1940s for publication in *The Concordia Historical Institute Quarterly.*

pened and is true: "But in Christ's Kingdom a child sitting at the feet of his teacher may by its childlike faith and trust in Jesus be a leader of that same teacher. God give us such leaders in Apacheland." And this did happen. The Apaches had these leaders. The schools prospered and were invaluable. The children taught their parents and led them.

DeAlva Rainbow Henry was Miss White Mountain Apache in 1989. She was a former East Fork Lutheran High School graduate, and at the time she was Miss White Mountain Apache she was also a member of Gethsemane Lutheran Church in Cibecue. This is what she said to the readers of *The Apache Scout*, the official newspaper of the White Mountain Apache Tribe,[317] before the coronation of the new reservation queen:

> This year I met one of the royalties who seemed to know everyone of importance except our Savior. My little brother who is nosy said to her, "You know everybody but God, don't you?" I encourage the White Mountain Apache Nation to put God first in everything. There is nothing more important to me than to share with you as Miss White Mountain that the one to know is Jesus. No matter who we know, we remain spiritual outcasts unless we know the only true God. That is why the Gospel writer implied that life is worthless for the person who gains "the world"— and that includes prestige and fame—but loses his soul in the process (Mark 8:36).
>
> Thinking to the night of August 12 when I will crown the 1989-1990 Miss White Mountain Apache, I walked outside in the early morning and I looked across at the beautiful Cibecue Mountain that I love, and I prayed to my Heavenly Father for our beautiful land. Then in the evening I looked up into the great sky where God was lighting his lamps, and I said, "I will no longer be your Queen, but people, I shall be alive in Jesus, and I pray the White Mountain Apache Nation will look unto Jesus, the author and finisher of our faith (Hebrews 12:2)."[318]

Thirty years later in 2019, still queenly in her appearance, DeAlva attended the graduation service of the first high school senior class in the re-started high school at East Fork Mission. She

---

[317] Not to be confused with the earlier Lutheran Church publication on the reservation that had the same name.

[318] This quote was reprinted by permission of *The Apache Scout*. *The Apache Scout* is the official newspaper of the White Mountain Apache Tribe.

was there with the celebrants. And all felt compelled to thank God for his goodness and kindness in preserving this good institution! Long live East Fork Lutheran High School!

If a person understands the prevailing philosophy of how the mission work was supposed to go (and that would be through the Indigenous Church philosophy of Stanley Soltau, which has been espoused by the leadership), it is easy to understand why there was so much tension and struggle connected to the schools in later years. In Soltau's recorded lecture of 1956 the commentary says with regard to Christian Education: "An educational institution which is intended to influence the heathen people is too expensive and does not constitute the right use of mission money. If it is to be thought of as an evangelizing institution it is totally inadequate."[319]

November 3, 1986, made everyone think it all through again, and lines were drawn and statements made. It was a Monday at East Fork Mission. The school children, grade school and high school, had met for their devotions, and then they had all gone back to their classrooms and classes were being held as at any other time on any other fall day. The pastor at East Fork Mission was in his study across from the church, the same study that had the signature of Martin Wehausen on the wall up above the ceiling on the front porch. At 11:15 a.m. children were seen hurrying by the church, going on up the road, and their teachers were with them with their heads down resolutely, urging their students to keep moving. Strange. What was going on?

The pastor walked outside, and there were more children coming up the road from the school and hurrying by. The teachers seemed to be herding them along. And then he saw it! Smoke was coming from the roof of the school house. Some moments before there had been a "BOOM!" but there were often sonic booms from jets that were passing over and this "BOOM!" was dismissed as that. There had been a gas explosion in the gymnasium of the school. High school boys were sweeping in the gym when the explosion happened. The heavy 2' x 12' bleachers were blown several feet away from the walls, the same bleachers that students had stood on when they had school Christmas services with Christmas trees at both ends of the gym, the same bleachers on which folks from up and down the river had squeezed together to watch the basketball games on Saturday evenings; the

319 This is from a copy of the distributed synopsis of Soltau's vision of mission work. The copy that contained this had these words underlined. This was the prevailing emphasis of those who had overall charge of running the school system on the reservation. They had inherited the school system when they came on administrative boards, and they were trying to have the school system come into compliance with Soltau's plan.

same bleachers and gym Apache Christians had filled to overflowing when the Wisconsin Seminary Choir came and Director Professor Albrecht had asked before it all began why they had put up so many folding chairs? Whom were they expecting to come? It was those bleachers that had borne the brunt of the explosion. None of the students were hurt. Everyone got to safety, but the school burned. The fire got between the rubberized flat roof and the internal structure, and the water from fire hoses wasn't effective. The school burned down one room at a time, laboriously, hideously, sadly. People from all over the reservation came and sat in their cars by the spreading elm tree nearby. People spoke in whispers and low tones. People's hands hung limply at their sides.

Frank Clarkson told the pastor that evening, as they stood there and watched the dull red flame that was still consuming their memories and hopes, that he shouldn't worry because God was going to give them a new school. That was the way of faith, but the pastor thought to himself, "Frank, how is that going to happen? We weren't even able to fix the plumbing in the sub-grade bathrooms. There wasn't money budgeted for that. How would it be possible to replace the whole school?"

The next day the charred structure of the main school was removed, so that the basement kitchen area could still be used—perhaps. Fort Apache school officials made school rooms available, so that classes could continue for the rest of the school year. (Fort Apache as a fort was the first place to aid the mission work way back in 1895 when Paul Mayerhoff had come and asked for a place to do mission work.) The addition of several classrooms to the original school was still fairly much intact, and once the rubble of the rest of the school was removed was still usable.

Then a miracle happened! It surely was that. It went against all expectations. It was totally counterintuitive and by everyone who knew and understood, it was just that: a miracle! The school was rebuilt. There were countless meetings. People came from the Navajo Reservation (former students from there) to the meetings held to determine the fate of the burned school. The Executive Committee came too. Remember Soltau's belief that education was "too expensive and does not constitute the right use of mission money. If it is to be thought of as an evangelizing institution—totally inadequate." It seemed to some that those in the leadership almost welcomed this fire: this was a way out of this big burden of the school. This was God's way of getting the albatross off the church's neck. A school like East Fork Lutheran High School was totally incompatible with the ideal of some who fostered the Indigenous Church idea.

But the people wouldn't let it happen. They rallied. The Apache people near and far came and stood up in the meetings and often began by saying, "I'm not a good speaker in public." But they were! Native Americans have a penchant for oratory. Listen to some of Chief Joseph's speeches and hear it. We heard passionate Apache speaking for the school. We all heard it, Executive Committee and *Inashood* alike. We heard it.

Hear the people speak still! The following are all comments written and recorded pertinent to the school at the time it burned:

"From experience, that school helped all my family members. When I started going to school there, I started taking instruction class. After I got confirmed my mom started taking instructions. We never really attended church regularly until me and my brother started going to school there. Then we attended church regularly, and my mom and I started to take the Lord's Supper. If my brother and I didn't go to school (EFM) I don't know where we would be. Because of that small school, we started attending church and taking the Lord's Supper. Also, it tells me, my mom and my brother where we stand with our Savior. It also helps me a lot, not just my family members. When sometimes I think about it, I cry because if that school didn't help me, I don't know where I would be. I realize the teachers care about us a lot. If someone were to ask me to go to a public school, I would say no. I would tell that person that I get God's word every day and that is important. You know something else too? It seems like we are a big family. We all go through the same things together. We also help each other lift each other up" (a student).

"The people around here think highly of our school. When they ask, 'Where do you go to school?' and we reply, 'East Fork,' they begin to show respect for us, knowing that we learn about Jesus, and that we are the chosen ones. Then the people would be very proud of whenever we see them. They say, 'He/she goes to East Fork' " (a student).

"The school helped a lot in my family. My mom went to school there; my two brothers and my two sisters. Now one of my brothers is a council member on the reservation. And he still goes to church. There are a lot of people who are successful that went to school at East Fork" (a student).

"East Fork Lutheran High School has been helping people on the reservation for over 50 years. The Wisconsin Lutheran Synod has given us the chance to study God's word. If it weren't for you good people, we probably would still be following old Apache traditions and worshiping false gods. I have been coming to East Fork Lutheran since the 2nd grade, and since then have been studying God's word.

This is the only Christian school on the reservation, and that is important to me. I could be going to a public school, but I would probably be getting drunk every day. Once, I went to a public school as a visitor with my friend and students were smoking marijuana right in the hallway. Here at EFLHS the teachers and students are close. There isn't drugs and alcohol on campus" (a student).

"I am a student here at East Fork Lutheran High School. I live off the reservation in the lower reservation. My mother and father both attended East Fork, and they sent me here so that I can continue my Christian education, learn more about the Love of God and things he did for us. God could have taken us all easy that day to be with him forever in heaven, but maybe he did this for a reason when he burned down our school. He wanted to get a new school built for us. I thought for sure that some students wouldn't be back, but they all came back. If they didn't care for their Christian education, they wouldn't have been here, but they all came back" (a student).

"That day we students stood by the side of the road looking at our school going up in flames. It made us all cry. It was like someone in our family died. A part of us was gone. I just hope there is something we can do to build the school again, raise money, to continue our Christian education" (a student).

"East Fork is special because God's word is taught here. The teachers help us in school work, but most importantly they teach us about God and his works. East Fork has helped me in my decision to become a teacher and to teach others about the importance of learning God's word" (a student).

"The way I feel can't be described by writing it down. It's something I have in my heart. When I saw the school burning, I felt so helpless. All I could do is watch as the school I went to for thirteen years was burning down to the ground. It was one of the saddest days of my life. Something inside me died as the building died. But EFM will make it because the people really have grown from the school's existence spiritually and mentally. This school just won't roll over and die because God's love and works are in it and they get stronger every day. We will do whatever it takes to get a new school if it means going to TRS (Theodore Roosevelt School at Fort Apache) for five years to make the money we need, but let's face it. Even before the fire we were in need of new facilities. We are going to get them because the school is growing. We've needed a new school for years now. We're going to get one. Many times I looked at that ugly grey building and have wondered why do I go here? And then I realize I don't go for the building; I go for what's in it, for God's Word and the friendship of fellow believers. I guess what I am trying to say and not doing a good job of it is the size of the school doesn't count. It is what is in it that counts. God says, 'Suffer the little children to come unto me and forbid them not for of such is the kingdom of heaven.' I hope the people at the top can really open up their hearts and help us because we love this school and we're ready to fight for it" (a student).

"I think East Fork High School was destroyed because God wanted to change the school and rebuild this school. We need East Fork High School because public schools around us don't allow religion to be taught in their school, and I think that's good because not everybody believes in Christ the same way as a Lutheran does. So I think we should rebuild our school and teach Christ in our own place, the right way. What I've gotten now is from what East Fork taught me in the last three years. I have received the wisdom, the knowledge and the understanding of God's Word, and it's important to me because it surely will get me to heaven. In the same way we should all help and get East Fork started soon and teach these things to others. East Fork has helped me in many ways. To get new and more friends, get closer to God, how to take care of myself, how to live a good life in the world, how to help a person when he wants to be saved and received by God. Through East Fork I've learned to pray and in the prayers God has answered many of my prayers in many thankful ways. In the same way, I know God has helped and still is helping all the other students and many family members of East Fork Lutherans, Whiteriver Lutherans and all the others" (a student).

And hear the following, a letter from an important person in the government school at Fort Apache:

To Whom It May Concern:

I came to the Fort Apache Reservation in 1968 as a young teacher just graduated from college. I have worked at the Bureau of Indian Affairs boarding school at Fort Apache ever since. In the meantime, I have received a Master's degree in elementary education and am presently working toward a Principal's certificate. I have 18 years experience in education and administration on the White Mountain Apache Reservation. My husband, a Tribal member, was born in Whiteriver and has lived most of his life here. We have two sons, ages 5 and 11. We are firmly convinced that the most precious gift a parent can make to a child is that of a good education. It is well worth the cost, both in time and in money.

For precisely that reason, my husband and I decided to send our sons to the East Fork Mission School. East Fork's reputation for academic development and achievement is excellent.

The mission school provides some advantages which the public system cannot, i.e. Christian discipline and a small pupil-teacher ratio. The former instills character and confidence while the latter insures more individual attention and assistance. All these combine to produce a well-rounded and well-grounded young person.

From our earliest days on the reservation, my husband and I have noticed a distinct difference between the young people who have attended East Fork Mission School and those from other systems. East Fork students project a quiet self-confidence and positive attitude all too often missing in their contemporaries. By word and deed they demonstrate that they value education and Christian teachings. These values are reflected in their daily lives, and so East Fork students immeasurably enrich the reservation community. It would be a terrible loss to the White Mountain Apache people if this fine institution was no longer available to their children. East Fork Mission School has served these people for more than half a century. Many Apaches look to it for guidance and inspiration. They treasure its history as their own.

Therefore, we would ask those to whom the power of decision-making is given to abandon any and all thoughts of closing any portion of the East Fork Mission School program. Every part of that system, from the nursery level all the way through the high school, is vitally important to the young people of this reservation. The young people, in turn, are vitally important to the future of the White Mountain Apache Tribe. We cannot believe that the Lord's will would be to deprive the Apache people of something so precious.

Yours truly,

(The writer and her husband both signed the letter.)

And a former student of EFLHS wrote this:

The purpose of this letter is to discover the situation involving the East Fork Lutheran Mission School and more specifically the High School. My understanding is that a fire totally destroyed the school, but that rebuilding is being planned. I intend to support this effort in whatever way I am able. Unfortunately, I do not have a great deal of financial assets to contribute, but I will do whatever I can financially, physically and spiritually.

I am a 1969 graduate of East Fork Lutheran High School and feel greatly distressed about the destruction of my alma mater. I regret that I have not been closer or more supportive of the school, previously, but I want to be of service now.

Recently, I heard what I hope is merely a rumor, but in the event that there is something to substantiate it, please read on. According to the rumor, the high school is not going to be included in the rebuilding of the school. If this is an accurate report, I would like to prevail upon all committee members involved in such a decision, to reconsider before reaching a conclusion. High School is a critical time in an adolescent's life and a solid Christian education is very important, as I am sure all will agree. Eight years of Christian training are a good beginning but, I feel, need to be followed with four more years in a Christian atmosphere. Understandably, Arizona Lutheran Academy is available in the Phoenix area, but I am convinced that there remains a need for a high school on the East Fork Mission. The East Fork Lutheran High School could serve the White Mountain area and surrounding communities, as well as the Apache Indian population.

East Fork Lutheran High School was one of the best educational and memorable experiences of my life, and it saddens me to think of this tradition coming to an end. While attending EFLHS and living in the girls' dormitory, I learned not only what prepared me for a college degree, but also how the Lord wants us to live together—Apache and White, side by side. I still thank the good Lord for granting me the extraordinary opportunity to attend East Fork Lutheran High School and pray that others will have the same chance in the years to come.

In conclusion, I hope what I heard is an unjustified rumor, but if it is not, please remember my pleas and my thanks. East Fork Mission was there when I needed it (although I did not realize it then), and I want to be there when it needs help. For the good of future generations, I hope and pray that East Fork Lutheran High School is rebuilt.

Thank you for your attention to this letter and if I can be of further assistance please let me know.

Sincerely yours.

At the top of the following letter is a name and a title under the name which says, "Attorney at Law."

Dear High School Staff:

*Enclosed you will find a check in the amount of $100 as a dona-
tion from us. We feel a great sense of loss over the destruction
of the school, but at the same time we are glad that the support
has been good.*

*My wife and I both graduated from there back in 1973. That
seems like a lifetime ago! I feel that spiritually it has done us
a lot of good and that we are able to teach our son right from
wrong. The school in itself meant a great deal to us and what it
has taught us, is the reason we are where we are today.*

*We both know that when something is destroyed and is rebuilt,
it usually is never the same, and the feelings do not always stay
the same. But in time we shall see what this school meant to the
people who went to school there, and through them we will still
have a brighter future with a new school for the generations of
children to come.*

*Remembering you all in our prayers and knowing that God
works in mysterious and wondrous ways. God bless you all.*

Sincerely,

*Both the man's and his wife's signatures are there at the bottom
right-hand corner of the page.*

The Tribal Chairman at the time, Mr. Reno Johnson, wrote:

"At this time, I would like to urge everyone to rally as a community, reservation wide, to help support the East Fork School and all
the wonderful people out there to help rebuild this fine establishment. I am looking to all of you for I know we can do this. East Fork
School, we are behind you and will do everything possible to help
you get going again real soon."

The Tribal Council itself adopted the following resolution. It
was submitted and read at the post-fire meetings to the Executive
Committee by one of the councilmen, himself a former student of
the school.

RESOLUTION OF THE WHITE MOUNTAIN APACHE TRIBE
OF THE FORT APACHE INDIAN RESERVATION:

WHEREAS, *the East Fork Mission School has recently
been destroyed by fire, and the Lutheran
Synod is in the process of making a determi-
nation concerning the future of the school;
and*

WHEREAS, *the Tribal Council is of the opinion that the*

East Fork Mission School has been and continues to be a valuable asset to the White Mountain Apache people, in that many of our professionals and tribal leaders have graduated from the school and have gone on to higher education at colleges and universities, and the Tribal Council is desirous that the tradition of academic excellence and leadership development at the East Fork School be continued; and

WHEREAS, *the East Fork School provides an alternative to state and BIA supported schools and offers students a learning environment where high academic standards are maintained and where principles of moral value intertwined with religious instruction are taught, and where the principle of strict discipline is still adhered to. Therefore be it*

RESOLVED *by the Tribal Council of the White Mountain Apache Tribe that it strongly urges the Lutheran Synod to rebuild the East Fork Mission School with elementary and high school classes, in order that the White Mountain Apache people may continue to have the opportunity to receive an education of the highest quality and thereby enable them to make the utmost contribution to the advancement of the White Mountain Apache people for generations to come.*

But perhaps the best was what the people did to show their appreciation for the school by their actions:

- E. S. saw the men working on cleanup and asked about their dinner. When told there wasn't really enough at the nursery to have lunch for them, she went to town herself and bought everything needed and brought it to the nursery at a cost to her of more than $30.
- D. and her husband in San Carlos heard about the fire, and before it was over they were there at the school.
- J. W. in Minneapolis, Minnesota, before the first day was over called and said, "I heard about the fire. I want to help. I went to school at East Fork."
- On November 9 the women worked with sticks and brooms

to pry the debris off the floor and throw it over the walls. It was dirty hard work with little purpose in it, but they wanted to do something, so they worked all afternoon. When the afternoon was over, the floors were all clean.

- Both M. S. and J. D. offered to give a beef apiece. They didn't have the money, but they could give what they had.
- Women came from Whiteriver and Canyon Day to clean and cook at the nursery for the workers.
- People came several days in a row from Cibecue to help move the high school to Fort Apache.
- 1,600 hours of volunteer labor came the first two weeks.
- Apache people spoke at their respective church services on the Sundays after the fire, impressing on their own people the need to support the school.
- With the help of the people, the upper story that had burned was completely razed, and all the blocks and debris removed at a savings of thousands of dollars.
- The men and children picked through the ruin and salvaged over 1,000 blocks, which have been stacked on the softball field for sale at $.30 apiece.
- R. C. and wife and D. V. and wife and D. came from San Carlos and attended a meeting at 8:00 on a Wednesday evening and then drove back home after the meeting at 9:30.
- D. went from door to door among the Lutherans of San Carlos and collected $500, which she brought and gave to one of the teachers.
- People donated their backs and their pickups for moving the rubbish.
- Women went over all of the desks and cleaned them all, painting some, putting contact paper in the bottoms where rust had started, repainting shelves, buying new curtains from their own funds.
- A small boy came to the pastor's study one morning. In his hand he held a coffee can full of nickels and pennies—$6.06. "It is for our school," he said.

CHAPTER EIGHTEEN

The Nursery

Whoever is kind to the needy honors God
(PROVERBS 14:31).

Those who lived at East Fork knew personally, as did all those who worked on both reservations, that there was a special force at work that had important and far reaching positive effects on the Apache people: it was the East Fork Lutheran Nursery. Its official opening was August 2, 1922. There really was no one individual who started the Nursery. The Guenthers and Wehausens were the founders, but it was a group project and process, and there were many who played a part.

Reservation Doctor Fred Loe stated the crying need for the Nursery: "Apaches love their babies. Still a very large percentage of their breast-fed and 100 percent of their not breast-fed children die."[320] The government superintendent of the field at the time said, ""The East Fork Orphanage is an oasis in the great desert life of the Apache babies. Formerly many such infants were frequently abandoned, not from lack of parental affection, but because no hope of saving them could be entertained. Now there is hope so far as this orphanage is able to care for them. Each little bed added means one or more lives saved."[321] Information from Mr. Mackey, principal of the boarding school in Whiteriver in 1930, showed that there were fifty deaths of children under the age of two from July 1 of 1928 until June 1 of 1929. This number represented a third of all the deaths on the reservation, the population being about 2,600 White Mountain Apaches. In 1927 twenty-two children died before they were one year old. Twenty-eight children died before their first birthday in 1929. It was also noted that the death rate among the Apaches was four times as great as that in the nation of forty-four states.

And without a doubt Guenther's other observation was part of the problem with infant mortality at that time: "An Apache

---

[320] Fred Loe, M.D., *The Apache Scout,* April 1923.

[321] Charles L. Davis, Superintendent, *The Apache Scout,* April 1923.

mother with an unventilated heart also leaves her home for some camp to spend the day there in gambling and drinking. She spends no time planning for her child. She does not try to find out how it should be fed and otherwise cared for. Its head and face may be crusted with dirt. It may have no other clothing but a sleeveless rag without buttons. It knows nothing of a daily bath and warm underwear. No notice is taken of it if it has a cold or cough. When the time comes for weaning, it is turned loose on white flour, gravy, tough meat and tougher tortillas, while the mother plays. Often it stumbles into the fire and is burned to death or disfigured for life while its mother plays on. Summing up, we find that the mother has often had a day of fun and lost a precious baby as her reward. If the heart of such a mother were right she would know that children are a gift of God to be guarded and cared for like the most tender flower." Earlier Guenther had also opined, "The Apaches were once a most sturdy race and are still living in one of the most healthful spots of our country. Once the Apaches were so strong and numerous that they could keep Papagos, Pimas, Hopis, Navajos, and Pueblos—and a section of old Mexico—in a state of terror. And now the Navajos alone are numerous enough to come down here and sweep us off the reservation!"[322]

In 1922 Wehausen described the beginning of the Nursery. "In this year lies the beginning of the Apache orphanage, Arnold Platt, son of George Platt, B19, was found by the missionary at the foot of Rim Rock, well nigh starved, his mother dying. This was on Good Friday, April 14. The following day Arnold found a home at the mission at East Fork. The mother died and was given a Christian burial on April 16. Milton Opah, G12, and Iona Browning were brought to us from the government hospital at Whiteriver, where they had been kept since infants, on August 20, 1922. Mrs. Eli Beardsley was called as matron of the orphanage. Priscilla Joy Stover, one of a pair of twins, born to Oliver Stover on September 30, was next to be taken in. Then followed Franklin Anderson, a twin baby born November 7. Since the orphanage quarters were not suitable, he was also taken at the mission."[323]

So what happened in 1922 was a wonderful thing, and the news appeared as an article in the very first edition of *The Apache Scout*, published in April of 1923. In that first issue the beginning of the East Fork Lutheran Nursery was described. This was the issue that had the picture of Alchesay as government scout on the front cover. This was the same Alchesay who proclaimed his allegiance to the

---

[322] Edgar Guenther, "A Study in Figures," *The Apache Scout*, January 1929.

[323] *The Apache Lutheran*, "East Fork – 1922," May 1986, p. 5.

Lutheran Church by marching into the church on that Sunday with one hundred of his people. (By the way, as has been said, he was buried with the Whiteriver church key in his dead hand.)

This is the way Martin Wehausen saw the nursery at its inception:

Only the most urgent need of an Apache orphanage could ever have forced us to consider the present temporary quarters to be used for that purpose. To the rear of the school house, which we purchased from the government a year ago, was attached a room, 16 by 16, formerly used as a sewing and industrial room for the school girls. Attached to this was a little shed, 8 by 16, which had been used as the school repair, tool and paint shop. To these two rooms a 16 by 16 addition was made, of very light construction. This addition, with the most necessary repairs to the other rooms, cost us but $165.00. This included all material and allowed but eight days of extra carpenter labor. The reader can readily figure out for himself that the new addition was no less a shack than the old. Our plan had been to have the addition serve as sleeping quarters for the orphans, but when winter set in the cold made it impossible. A warming fire kept night and day made but a small impression. Lucille George, the Indian assistant, Milton and Inona alone braved the cold sleeping quarters. Little Priscilla Joy was kept in the combined kitchen, living and dining room, and the former sewing room, as close to the cook stove as possible. Three doors enter in this little overcrowded 16 by 16 room. Can you imagine how unfit these quarters were for a little motherless, bottle-fed infant? Priscilla did so poorly that when Franklin came on November 8, we had not the heart to expose him to the same condition, so he found a home with Arnold. On the day following, Priscilla had to be taken to the hospital. After two weeks she was returned to the orphanage, only to lose what she had gained. A change had to be made, and she was taken in to live with Arnold and Franklin. In warm and quiet quarters she did well, gaining a pound in ten days. Once more Priscilla was turned back into the orphanage, December 19, now weighing five pounds. Then came a cold, which ushered in an epidemic of colds among the Indian children, of which many camp babies died. All the orphans took sick. Milton and Inona were kept in bed for three weeks, not because they were sick all this time, but because the bed was the only warm place in the orphanage. Priscilla Joy was so low during this time that no one expected her to live. The good Lord, however, knew well what effect Priscilla's death would have on the success of our orphanage, and by his grace and through his wisdom he let her live. After the epidemic had cleared away, Priscilla, now four months old, weighed less than four pounds. In the meantime, Marie and a little later "Stonie" came. Now three infants were kept in the overcrowded kitchen, close to the stove, all three packed in one crib, so as to make the most of the few blankets we had.

At present conditions are no better. The quarters are more crowded than before. Another infant has been added since Franklin was returned to the orphanage. The Knoops are forfeiting practically all home life, all home comforts and privacies, and sharing everything with the orphans and the boarding pupils.[324]

And then in his last entry Martin Wehausen said, "The work at the orphanage steadily increased. Quarters were soon too small and also unsuitable for orphanage work. Mrs. Beardsly was relieved by Mrs. Arnold Knoop, and by June she was caring for eleven infants." The work of the congregation was going on apace too: "Until June 17 the following may be noted: adult baptisms 2, infant baptisms 5, burials 3, marriages 1, communicants 31. The last burial, Priscilla Joy Stover, was on June 13. She was laid to rest on a plot of land at this time set aside for a mission cemetery." So little Priscilla didn't make it and became the first nursery baby to be buried in the cemetery that is still there and in use today.

In the fall of 1921 Pastor Nitz was called to East Fork on a temporary basis to start the boarding school. (The mission board planned to call a permanent principal after the school was started, and Pastor Nitz was to continue serving at Globe. But it didn't work out that way.) In the fall of 1922 Pastor Nitz was called permanently as principal and missionary at East Fork. He worked with Pastor Martin Wehausen at East Fork. Pastor Wehausen was the "camp" missionary, and Pastor Nitz was missionary on the compound. Pastor Nitz found Arnold Platt on Good Friday, April 12, 1922. The Wehausens took this little boy into their home and later adopted him. The Wehausens had no children of their own and were the main workers in the beginning.

As can be seen, the need for a building was realized right away, but the building of this facility languished due to a lack of lumber in 1924. In that same year the water system froze up, and water for 100-plus inhabitants on the mission had to be lugged from the East Fork river.

---

[324] Martin Wehausen, April 1923.

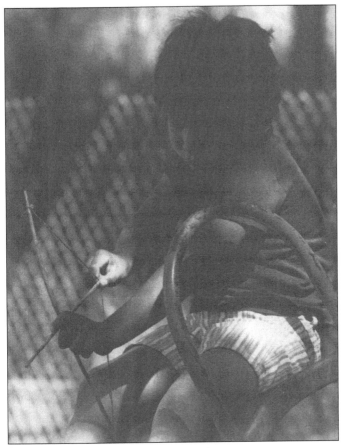

Future warrior playing at East Fork Lutheran Nursery.
Photo Credit: Mission photo, author's collection.

Krueger from Cibecue and Knoop from East Fork worked very hard, and in August of 1925 the building was completed and thirteen children had a home. It was two stories high with a basement and twelve rooms. Two matrons stayed there as well as the single lady teacher.[325] By early 1926 forty-one children had entered the nursery. Of those, eight had returned home, fifteen were living in the nursery building, and eighteen had died. In early 1927 a measles epidemic swept the reservation. Twenty-two of twenty-three children in the nursery got sick, but only one died.

Although many children did die, many hundreds of them lived to take their places later in the Apache tribe. On the cover of a

---

[325] Mrs. Eli Beardsley was the first matron.

recent tribal publication, *White Mountain Apache Tribe* (Discover the Many Amenities of the WMAT), is a picture of Edgar Perry and an accompanying article entitled, "Edgar Perry: A True Keeper of Apache Culture." Edgar Perry was brought to the Nursery as a small child in 1937. In a call-out of the article about him, Perry says, "The old people all called me by my Apache name; the young people called me 'Edgar.' The Apache name means 'one who watches the kids.'" The name Edgar[326] came from the elderly missionary who befriended the young child in the nursery.

As was reported earlier in reference to Francis Uplegger and his work as *Inashood*, in the early years of the school at East Fork, Miss Thelma Davids was a teacher, and she looked after and loved the children of the nursery. She was a Mohican from Wisconsin. Missionary Francis Uplegger had been instrumental in getting her to come and teach at East Fork. She even took a little boy, Johnnie Perry, to a Lutheran hospital in Fort Wayne, Indiana, so that he could be operated on to repair his cleft palate. At first it seemed that everything was fine. The doctors so carefully sewed up his lip that hardly anything of the ugly cleft could be seen, and he withstood the trip well. But he contracted a cold, and after a week's illness God took him to heaven. He was the Matron's favorite orphan.[327] Thelma Davids was a faithful worker in the school and in the nursery.

Pastor Uplegger did some repair and painting work at the nursery. He wrote about it in 1929. He said that while he and Charles Albrecht were painting, one of the little boys snuck in unnoticed. The portable organ was there that the missionaries used for camp work. The little boy started "finding his notes." As the old Inashood related it, "'From'—and having found the note, 'heaven'—another note, 'above'—another note, 'to'—and again, 'earth'—two more notes. After a few minutes of locating certain tones, he slowly began to add the words to them in a whisper. But a little later he forgot to whisper." And then the eavesdropping painter concluded, "That is better than listening to an orchestra, better than listening to a big choir! That singing is a delight for angels. And that boy's special guardian angel surely was thanking God for the simple, trustful faith in that singing child. So did the missionary also."[328]

Christmas came and there were observers of the miracle of the birth of God's Son who wrote, "In the orphanage the shades are drawn, and under the sparkling Christmas tree are the gifts from

---

[326] The name came, of course, from Edgar Guenther, the missionary.

[327] *The Apache Scout*, October 1923, p. 7.

[328] Alfred Uplegger, *The Apache Scout*, "Singing to the Lord," p. 3.

325

our friends all nicely arranged by the matrons. All who can spare the time have gathered in this room, mission workers as well as boarding school children. Even Mr. Priggie, at this time a bed patient, has found a place on the day bed. The little family comes in. Oh, how their little dark eyes sparkle and shine at the sight of the lighted tree! From the age of three upward they sing: "From Heaven above to Earth I Come" and "As Each Happy Christmas." The matron hands each of them their gifts of toys, dolls, etc. The solemn silence of the holy night is broken by great rejoicing and shouting for joy. Everything has been put into readiness in the chapel. One hundred and ten school children have taken their places in the front closely crowded together, some of them almost under the tree, where things "not to be seen for the present have been placed. The remainder of the chapel is filled to capacity by old and young from far and near. Quite a number of them sit on the floor, partly because of lack of room, partly by force of habit. Even a few dogs find their way in and leave again with a yelp. The program begins..."[329]

From the nursery's beginning there were patrons. Boxes and boxes of clothing and toys and supplies were sent or brought by these patrons. Storage buildings were built to house these "mission boxes," as they were called. People rented vehicles and came from Wisconsin and the Midwest. There were also those who came and lived on the mission and helped out wherever they could. The Mr. Priggie just mentioned in the account of Christmas was an example. He was ill at the time Christmas came but rallied to participate in the happy goings-on. He was a male patron saint of the East Fork Lutheran Nursery. Henry Priggie was the father of Esther Priggie, who served on the boarding school staff at East Fork in its early years. He came to help out like so many others who would come and give of their lives and time for the Apache work.

Edgar Guenther writes, "Mr. Priggie is one of those practical men who served their apprenticeship in the workshop of life as pioneer farmers before the days of milking machines, pneumatic tires, and sulky-equipped harrows. He has set ideas on conservation and order and sets our younger helpers a lively pace." And then comes the add-on, "Some time ago, while making repairs in the ceiling of the church at East Fork, Mr. Priggie had the misfortune of missing the ladder and falling a distance of sixteen feet to the floor. That he suffered no fractures, to say nothing of fatal injuries, can be attributed only to this, that the Lord 'had given his angels charge over him, to

329 Christian Albrecht, *The Apache Scout*, "Christmas at East Fork," January 1931, pp. 5 and 6.

keep him in all his ways and to bear him up in their hands.' "[330] And if you visit East Fork Mission today you will still see these mature saints of God who come and spend months and years helping and befriending Apache children.

Probably no missionary spent as much time with the actual running of the nursery as did Pastor H. E. Hartzell. He acknowledged every gift to the nursery with a handwritten letter in the return mail. Many nights he was called from his rest to sit in the hospital parking lot in Whiteriver by the big cottonwood tree and wait for Miss Louise Kutz to come out with her little sick charge.[331] Sometimes she didn't come out with the little baby, and sometimes there was a funeral up behind the mission compound. It was as it had been from the very beginning of the nursery. Missionary Hartzell was a poet and wrote many poems in the little informative nursery publication called *The Cradleboard*. Memories pulled at his heart strings, as they did to the army of saints who cared for the little babies.

> All those years and babies
> Now are only memories.
> Every one is grown or gone.
> Even so I'm not alone.
> Each of them left behind
> Some little thing in my mind:
> Name, or face, or long, long look,
> Forever in my memory's book.
> So many I baptized.
> Every soul the Father prized.
> So many that I carried,
> And not a few I buried.
> Our God remembers too,
> All those many and those few;
> And in his book we shall find
> Better memories than mine.[332]

But things don't go on the same forever, even good things and maybe especially good things. Times change. The nursery was expensive to operate, and the church had decreed that it operate outside the mission budget. In the early years it did well that way. It had a special attraction that people liked and admired. Put a picture

---

[330] Edgar Guenther, *The Apache Scout*, "A Friend in Need," January 1931.

[331] Miss Kutz in her long tenure at the Nursery was known to have rocked over one thousand Apache babies and children in her rocking chair at the Nursery.

[332] H. E. Hartzell, *The Apache Lutheran*, June 1993.

**East Fork Lutheran Nursery and Miss Louise Kutz
at mealtime with children and workers.**
Photo Credit: Mission photo, author's collection.

of a little Apache baby on your request for funding, and the money came. Tribal police trucks pulled up at all times of the day and night to bring little babies whose parents had to be incarcerated. Apache women up and down the river found employment taking care of the babies and talking to them in Apache. Every day workers walked through the mission with tots and toddlers and headed for the big elm tree's shade in the school yard. So the minutes of the advisory board to the nursery read: "In the interest of economy the question of closing the nursery at East Fork came up for thorough discussion. It was pointed out that the need for the nursery still exists. Some infant Apaches would die were it not for the nursery. The publicity value to the Wisconsin Synod was also brought out. The committee recommends keeping the nursery in operation as heretofore. A. Meier, secretary."[333] That was in 1957.

The Tribal Social Services came into its own and there were people who were trying to promote their own careers and programs.

[333] Minutes of Joint Meeting (Committee on Parish Evangelism and Advisory Board of Control) in Session at East Fork Mission, Whiteriver, Arizona, May 11, 1957.

They didn't want to place the children anymore with a Lutheran facility. Finally, February 15, 1993, came and doors that had been opened at the first of the century closed for the last time.

Pastor Eric Hartzell, the last superintendent of the nursery, wrote:

The nursery has existed for seventy-one years, one year more than three score and ten. It had a long and full life and served many well. It was officially closed February 15, 1993.

The reason for closing the Nursery was threefold. 1) The contributions from Lutheran supporters of the nursery has not kept up with rising costs and expenses. 2) The Tribal Social Services responsible for placing children at the Nursery refused to increase its subsidy of placements beyond the state foster care rate. At the best, this supplied $16.56 per child, per day. 3) The Tribal Social Services, for whatever reason over the past year, did not place children with the nursery in numbers that made it possible for the nursery to continue to be able to pay the expense of operation or to justify the continued expense.

During the past year (1992) the nursery's financial situation dipped close to $20,000 into the red. The hope was that the situation would change, that finances would make a marked improvement over the Christmas season, that the Tribal Social Services and the Tribe would change their stance with regard to placements and support. But this did not happen. The balance in the nursery account after the bulk of the Christmas support came was just over one thousand dollars. In view of this, the Executive Committee made the difficult decision to close the Nursery as of February 15.

During the last year four different correspondences with Tribal Social Service were made pleading for help and consideration of the situation with regard to the future of the nursery. In that year the chairman, the vice-chairman and members of the tribal council were individually contacted and apprised of the situation. One last effort was made with a letter dated February 4. The letter was copied and distributed to Tribal Council members. They met on the matter to discuss what the Tribe could do. In that letter the statement was made that in order for the nursery to be able to continue, $12,000 per month would have to be guaranteed by the Tribe. (Still much short of the $200,000 needed to keep the nursery open for a year's time.)

That ability and willingness did not materialize. The Tribal Social Services will now have to take care of the children on their own, and there are many questions that still remain to be answered. What do we do for workers and people who have come to depend on the nursery for their livelihood and their life? What happens to the facility? Is there any other use we can use the nursery for? What do we do with support now? How do we continue to pay the bills and expenses that will still come for a while? How do we in a good way alert the people who have so faithfully supported the nursery?

The nursery has served faithfully and well. The names of the people who have been helped would fill a large book. Lives have been saved; lives have been helped; much joy has been brought; many have been blessed. But the times have changed, and the Tribe is in a different position now than it was 71 years ago. The problems of the children are different too. The responsibilities and challenges have grown as the sword of litigation dangles more precariously over our heads like Damocles' sword, as childhood diseases and ailments have also taken on deadly aspects with AIDS and STDs rearing their ugly heads, as government regulations increase, and as charitable monies grow ever scarcer.

It remains hard though. A friend and companion has passed. God bless the children![334]

[334] E. Hartzell, *The Apache Lutheran*, March, 1993.

CHAPTER NINETEEN

Dual Control

"Dual control or anything approaching it
must be carefully avoided"
(GENERAL GEORGE CROOK, 1885).

In the summer of 1885 the United States Army on the ground in Apacheland called the phenomenon "dual control." In the parlance of our topic of *Inashood* we could almost say it was, "Too many chiefs and not enough warriors," only the Apaches didn't fall prey to this problem. The whites did, however. This dual control phenomenon was happening early on between those on the reservations in charge of making progress and between the authorities appointed from elsewhere. There were many participants in the problem: the Interior Department and the War Department and the appointed civil Indian agents and the generals and officers on the reservations and back in Washington. One player in this mix was short General Sheridan.[335] He's the one who had maintained that the only good Indian is a dead Indian. (Alfred Uplegger in his writing mentions on a number of occasions that this was the awful view of many persons in the area who peered into the reservation milieu and saw only "Indians.")

There were all sorts of authorities, all with their own ideas how to fix the problems. General George Crook didn't want his officers on the reservation to be in a role subordinate to that of the civil Indian agent.[336] Historian Sweeny says, "Crook launched into a tirade blaming the outbreak (of the Chiricahua Apaches from Turkey Creek) on the Interior Department and on the scapegoat of the day, "dual control." Historian Sweeny called it a tirade. He perhaps never lived on a reservation where he was chided for not doing what others man-

---

[335] Sweeny, *From Cochise to Geronimo*, p. 430. (General Sheridan was one who understood that General Crook needed to be making the decisions on the ground. Sheridan supported Crook and stuck with his decisions when the press and the population were pretty much against what Crook was trying to do. One of the biggest successes of General Crook was his using the Apache scouts to bring their own renegade relatives to justice and to quiet.)

[336] Sweeny, *From Cochise to Geronimo*, p. 430.

dated that he do. It is hard to take orders from someone who does not know what the local situation is. That is exactly what Sweeny admitted when he recorded: "(Crook) had had enough of Geronimo, the citizens and newspapers of Arizona, and Washington's armchair quarterbacks, who thought they knew more than the commanders on the ground."[337]

Dual control is hard. It maybe is even impossible for it to ever turn out happily. The concept is fraught with all sorts of troublesome possibilities. The problem in the 1880s was made worse because of communication overlap. Perhaps it all couldn't be helped, and perhaps it still can't be helped. Someone does have to be in control. The Proverbs say, *"For lack of guidance a nation falls, but many advisers make victory sure."*[338] Some kind of power struggle results: some of the participants in the situation turn into alpha males and some into unhappy beta males. And the rest head off for another place as soon as they can. There are the visionaries who plan and prod the work from a distance. They perhaps have never been on site or have been there very infrequently. They have plans they would like to see implemented. Their plans agree with their philosophy of the work and what the outcome of that work should be. And there are those then who have to try and implement what others see as the right way to go. Dual control isn't a bad way of describing the resulting tension of this kind of circumstance.

This problem of dual control showed up in the work of the *Inashood* too. It was there right from the beginning. The first two scouts for this new mission work, Hartwig and Koch, were themselves pastors and would be the first leaders of this group who headed up the work from Wisconsin. There was no play book for them. This was all uncharted territory. They had to act and direct according to the will of the Lutheran people in the Midwest who were supporting this mission work among the Apaches. What that ended up looking like was that those in Wisconsin were the ones to decide how the work should be carried out. They kind of listened to those who actually were trying to do the work. They mulled over the monthly reports that those on the reservations were later asked to submit. These authorities did this very conscientiously, for instance, sometimes noting a discrepancy in the "rooster roster"[339]as the following vignette shows. Those on the field at Bylas had to keep track of the number of laying hens they had and report that number. That ended up being microman-

---

[337] Ibid. p. 529.

[338] Proverbs 11:14.

[339] This is no doubt said snidely by the writer.

agement at its finest—or worst. It was a work that majored in minors. You can hear this in the dialogue that follows later. It caused grief as people tried to defend their numbers and their reasons for doing things, even with chickens.

At the very beginning of the work, J. P. Koehler visited and observed the work on both reservations. His final recommendation to the Wisconsin authorities was that if the church responsible for the work on the San Carlos and the Fort Apache reservations was serious about doing mission work, it ought to send a team of its best and most experienced men to establish and do the work and give them free rein to do what had to be done. That was, of course, pretty much the opposite of the way things were being done: single young men with not even any ministerial experience were sent to work alone and try and stay in tune with the long-distance coaching from the committee.

Pastor Edgar Guenther later shared his views on this topic: "The work accomplished between the years 1893 and 1906 can be compared with that of a prospector doing just enough of the yearly assessment work required by law to hold down his claim. This casts no reflection on the men who labored in Apacheland during this period. There could have been no more prospect of two men evangelizing either of the reservations than there would have been of Caleb and Joshua single-handedly occupying the Land of Canaan. This will become obvious to the reader if he will recall—what was just mentioned—the size of the reservations, the inaccessible terrain, the scattered homes of some five thousand souls and, by no means least, the individuality of the proud Apache, who despised anything feeble or puny—and our Gospel attack was feeble to say the least. A faint echo here and there of a God who revealed himself in a man named Jesus could hardly stir this folk to give tribal attention as did Paul's discourse in the market place within the limited area of Athens. The immediate sending in 1893 of at least three and preferably four men to each reservation, unencumbered by school work and each living on one of the main streams, would have made the Gospel a live issue and born fruits that under the initial policy were decades in materializing. Furthermore, while other denominations sent older and experienced men (very often doctors of divinity), to break the sod, we tore young men loose from the seminary apron strings.[340] And finally, while other denominations in all foreign fields granted their new men an entirely unencumbered year on the field for the study of

---

[340] Pastor Paul Schulz mentioned that every single pastor to serve at Bylas up to his time there had been sent there directly from the seminary.

the language of the land, our young men immediately had to plunge into the duties and responsibilities that are kindred to every station. Under such conditions it takes almost as long to acquire a smattering of the language as it did for a German immigrant pioneering in the Middle West to converse intelligently with his Yankee neighbor."[341]

What the young men did have going for them as they attempted to do the work of missionary was that what they lacked in experience they perhaps made up for in toughness and energy and optimism. This is still the way the Wisconsin Evangelical Lutheran Synod tries to carry out Jesus' Great Commission to go and preach the good news to every person. The church sends young men, still tied to the seminary's apron strings as Missionary Guenther supposed. We say to them, as one young seminarian was told who was being sent to Zambia, Africa, "You're going to like the oranges at Mwembezhi." The young seminarian asked fearfully, "But what about my wife and my little son? How will they manage with no electricity and no hospitals nearby?" "Don't worry, they have good hospitals in Lusaka," he was told. They didn't. But it was a young man who went and made do and ended up with twenty-five bush congregations to monitor and serve by himself.

The minutes of the early pastors' meetings show Harders and his fellow pastors meeting at Peridot and East Fork and the other fledgling mission stations.[342] The pastors said to their executive committee in Wisconsin, "Our conference presents to the honorable committee for the Apache work of the General Synod of Wisconsin, Minnesota, Michigan, Nebraska and others states the following recommendations: We see the way to establish a Lutheran congregational system here among the Apaches in the Lutheran congregational school. In other words, we must be able to have the children in our complete care and instruction in order for the church to grow (in order for there to be sufficient leaven for the dough). In order for us to have a Lutheran school system that could stand unmolested next to the educational system of the government, it is necessary for us to remain in constant touch with the Department of the Interior."[343]

---

341 Guenther reminisced often of this topic, as he looked back in his work and wrote about it.

342 The minutes were kept in a notebook. The secretary wrote in the old German script. Deciphering the old script was impossible for this writer. The solution came through an acquaintance, who lived in Germany and grew up with German script. She transferred the German script into translatable German.

343 This was a quote from the transliterated minutes at the time of Harders and his Globe ministry. These minutes are in the author's collection.

From the 2 September 1909 meeting the conversation continued, "Pastor Harders shared with us expressions from the proceedings of the General Synod with regard to the Indian Mission. In order for us to achieve the recommendation of the Synod that we get a school system going in experimental form in the next two years, we decided to gather a small group of children that could be constantly under our care and instruction. We would hope that these children could be kept with Lutheran families for blocks of several years. We ask the Committee to find such families that would be inclined to accept such children."

This discussion with the executive committee and board about the proposed best direction the work go in is reflected in the following three quotes from the early missionary meeting minutes:

> It was the opinion also of our conference that Missionary Schoenberg remain in Ft. Apache until another worker could be found to replace him. It was the opinion of the committee that Pastor Guenther not go to Cibecue because the cold and wet weather would be harmful to his health.

> Because our reporting is not being understood by the Commission, evidently painting too rosy a picture to them that they do not understand the true nature of things here, it was our decision to have each think of a form of reporting that would present a true and realistic picture of our work here and to report on such ideas at our next meeting.

> And finally, it was decided to strongly encourage the Committee to establish contact with Washington regarding our work here."[344]

Pastor Gustav Harders encapsulated the tensions of religious dual control in his novels about Apache mission work and life. The stories were written in German. Alma Nitz (wife of Missionary H. C. Nitz) translated the stories into English. She used the back side of used paper to do it, a frugal trait that the Nitz family would manifest later too. Her original translated copy is still around. Harders wove into his stories the actual tensions and challenges of the work. The fictitious characters in his stories spoke the truth about the way it was on the field.

It is in one of his books—*Dohashtida*[345]—that he made a proph-

---

[344] The meeting adjourned with prayer. Carl Guenther was the secretary. (*Apache Lutheran*, September 1991.)

[345] *Dohashtida* is the Apache word for "I don't want to!" It was the story written by Missionary Harders of one Apache man's response to the work of the missionary. The German title was "*Wille Wider Wille*" (Will against Will).

ecy. The prophecy comes in the discussion between two characters in the story: Van Augustus Sims, the government school superintendent, and David Brown, a visitor to Arizona whose life becomes entangled with that of Dohashtida. Keep in mind that the characters are fictitious, and so is the situation described in the book. But also keep in mind that these words are coming from Pastor Harder's knowledge of the work and his assessment of it:

> Later that evening I asked Sims why there were no longer any missionaries among the Indians.
>
> He answered, "People got tired of trying to convert the red men."
>
> "Which people? The missionaries?"
>
> "Oh no, not they, but the people who sent them here and paid their salaries."
>
> "Why did they get tired of it?"
>
> "They came to the conclusion that the Indian Mission did not pay. After supplying the salaries of the missionaries and teachers for about twenty years, they thought it was high time for the Indians to do it themselves. The missionaries were told that they should work toward that end most energetically. But when the missionaries reported that this would be impossible, and that a hundred years or more might pass before one could expect such results, the people became discouraged. The missionaries reported that laying the groundwork for the evangelization of future generations was all one could hope for now. Without this groundwork the building of the kingdom of God would not materialize. They thought they might gain an occasional convert, but the hope of building a self-sustaining congregation could not be realized for some time to come. Their real hope, they asserted, lay in the children of the present generation. Such prospects were not sufficient for the people in the East, who through their missionaries had started this mission. They declared the work of the missionaries a failure and Indian missions a lost cause. One by one the missionaries were recalled, and thus a mission among this tribe is a thing of the past."[346]
>
> "Were the missionaries faithful in their efforts?"
>
> "Indeed, they were; everyone agrees on that," Sims replied emphatically.

---

[346] In some ways this prophecy of August Sims is exactly the way things played out and are still doing so.

"And did they really achieve no results?"

"No results?" repeated Sims. "They had phenomenal success: In every way they had the confidence of the Indians. We government people do not have that. They had schools. Their enrollment was small, but all the children had been enrolled at the expressed wish of the parents. When we spoke of this last evening, you held that to be the ideal practice. Instead of using the police to bring in pupils, as we do, the missionaries even had Indians attending church on Sundays."[347]

And so the narrative of Harders' story goes. There are things that were prophetic in Pastor Harders' story. It did not happen within the time frame that Harders spoke of in his story. It would also not be fair to say that it happened with the result being the end of the work, but it does seem today that the work is in decline. At least it has happened that *Inashood* today does not have the presence on either the San Carlos Reservation or the Fort Apache Reservation that he once had. Times do change. In Christianity a certain ebb and flow has always been observable.

The threat of the mission closing because of lack of funds cast its scary shadow over those who worked. The minutes of a June 1909 conference in Fort Apache read: "There is presently a rumor circulating that funding for the work here is going to be cut off. Should this be a fact, the conference puts the following resolve before the commission in charge of our work: Should it be a fact that the Synod is considering stopping funding for the work here in Apacheland, we would ourselves take steps in our circles here to establish mission societies through which the work among the Apache by God's help could be carried on."[348]

This reading of Harders reflects the ongoing confrontations of the mission board in Wisconsin and the field. Paul Behn has his humorous chicken story (referred to already as the "Rooster Roster"), and the saga of the pipeline from Bylas to Peridot is remembered too. In that case the mission board suggested that the problem of water at Bylas could be solved by laying a pipe from Peridot where they had water! It is twenty-five miles across the desert! H. C. Nitz speaks of one of the mission board visits in 1924, "The last week in April, East Fork was visited by Pastor P. T. Brockmann of Waukesha, Wisconsin, Pastor F. E. Stern of Watertown, Wisconsin, and Mr.

---

[347] *The Apache Lutheran*, January 1993.

[348] From the translated minutes of the early pastors' meeting under Pastor Harders' leadership.

Fred F. C. Schroeder of Milwaukee. These men belong to the Mission Board under which our mission work among the Apaches is carried on. They visited all the mission stations. Then they returned to East Fork, where they met all the Indian missionaries in a conference." [349] Nitz also reported, "The Committee again discussed plans of a new Boarding School. More definite steps are to be taken at the next meeting. Relative to the Boarding School the Committee expressed its surprise about Nitz's silence as to where his thirty-six Boarding School pupils came from and where and how they are housed."[350] He also mentioned that he was reprimanded for making a trip to St. Louis and not first asking permission from the Committee.

Dual control was what the military called the situation. Pastor Edgar Guenther called the situation experienced by *Inashood* "The encumbrance of remote control." It was because of this "encumbrance of remote control" that Guenther resigned as superintendent of the field. During the 1930s, with the Depression running rampant, the mission board testily wrote in one of its letters back to the field, "Are these the same two tires and tubes now appearing on February 1 statement? If not, it appears to us that these two items need some thorough checking and explaining. To buy two tires and tubes for $25.00 per September 1 statement and then only a few months later present another bill for two more tires and tubes for the same truck is clearly a case of overestimating our ability to squeeze dollars out of the synodical treasury, which we are not entitled to under our budget for physical plant." To this Pastor Paul Behn replied (maybe also testily), "You did not pay for the tires and tubes of September - $25.00. What should we do, run on the rims? I wish you were here sometimes to help crack our problems. It is easy enough to say that we have to get along with this or that, but in this case the practical end does not work out."[351]

Paul Albrecht was assigned by the mission board to be pastor in Cibecue. He got into trouble because of the difficulty of travel into remote Cibecue and the expectations placed on him by the leadership. He also tangled with the superintendent's wife over the implementation of some building plans. The superintendent resigned as a result of the hard feelings the flap generated, and the board refused to accept his resignation so he continued. Alrecht ended up almost defecting; in fact, at one point he did desert and ended up in Lakeside, Arizona, where he found accommodation in the Arizona State Game

349 *The Apache Scout*, June 1925.

350 Committee minutes, Milwaukee, Thursday, October 1, 1925, at 2:00 p.m.

351 *Apache Lutheran*, March 1992, reminiscences of Paul Behn.

and Fish office. A person feels sorry for him having trouble coexisting with fellow workers and even existing as a missionary in this strange and foreign place. From their safe distance, the committee made their demands on Paul Albrecht. Pastor Henry Rosin in Peridot rose to Albrecht's defense. He spoke his mind about the heavy-handed treatment on the part of the mission board, "Since Paul Albrecht cannot satisfy the dictates of his conscience by returning to Whiteriver, your requesting him to do so would simply force him out of the service. This cannot be your aim. To be justified in forcing him out you must necessarily be absolutely certain that Albrecht is in the wrong. I believe you have not this certainty. In the interest of the mission do I write this and I beg you not to take any other action than such as will do justice to Albrecht and be for the good of the mission."[352] That would be the very sentiment of many missionaries. It was often spoken with a sigh. Sometimes it was spoken with eyes that sparkled angrily: "Do justice to the individual missionary, act in a way that is good for the mission, and please—please!—listen to us when we talk to you!"

Consider the following correspondence from Pastor Paul Behn. It is an example of some of the back and forth that happened—and some of the frustration expressed by those on the field trying to make things happen:

East Fork Mission, Whiteriver Arizona
March 9, 1939
Executive for Indian Mission
1608 So. 84th St.
West Allis, Wisconsin

Dear Brother R.:

As of yet I am unable to give a comprehensive report on the gasoline consumption, since with the statement of remittance, other things entered in that I am unable to answer at this time. That will follow as soon as I receive data necessary.

Perhaps the enormous gasoline purchases of October-November 1938 are partially answered by this time, after you have received the statements for the following months. May I call your attention to this fact once more that we cannot always obtain gasoline just when we want it. So it happens that the deliveries pile up during one period, while at another it strings along "catch as catch can." It has happened that the truck was expected on a day because they telephoned from Holbrook that

---

352 "Henry Rosin" (file) in the Synod Archives.

they were coming, but when he came he had made deliveries along the way and did not have enough left for us. To tide us over we have purchased in smaller quantities. Weather has been a factor in deliveries also, since the truck cannot possibly get to our supply tank when it is muddy. We have had two deliveries in one day, one barrel hauled by ourselves in the morning, and in the afternoon the truck came. Because of such irregularities we try to order the next consignment of gasoline when we have about fifty gallons in the storage tank. Oddly enough, we have run out a number of times before the consignment reached us.

Did you actually believe that 438 gallons of gasoline were consumed in October when a delivery of 208 gallons was made on the 27th? Then what did we use up to the 11th of November? Did you also believe that we used 518 gallons in November when a delivery of 163 gallons was made on the 28th? Then what do you suppose we used for fuel up to the 22nd of December? And so, 266 gallons on the December bills was consumed up to Jan. 21st, and the Jan. 30th delivery was consumed in February. It is also a fact to which I have referred before, that the F-M (the light plant generator) is consuming more gas per hour this year than a year ago. The statements to the State Highway Department testify to this also. Your statement "We are convinced that the F-M did not require 406 gals. of gas during this period of 1938. Then what was it used for?" leads me to believe that you did not believe my markings on the bills which show it was used for power, and that the statements to the Highway Department were sworn to falsely. That the average for monthly gasoline consumption from June-November 1937 is 342 gallons per month, and that from June 1938 to January 1938 averages 360 gallons per month is by no means an outrage. In fact, we held down the time of running the F-M this year, starting it 20 to 30 minutes later in the evening than we should, and have used candles instead to get along.

Oil consumption—You know how much of this there has been used during the past months. Would you believe that it is possible for a motor to suddenly quit using oil and go on a strict economy basis of less than one fourth the former consumption? Believe it or not, the F-M did. Already last fall we used kerosene to flush the crankcase and loosen carbon in the motor, but it availed us nothing. Not so long ago, Mr. Klaus gave it an overdose in the crankcase, in the combustion chambers and valves. It was enough to get into every crevice of the rings and *cut the carbon that kept them from expanding properly. The rings functioning properly again, it cut down on the use of oil. We did not believe it possible without dissecting the motor and doing an overhaul job, but it did. It has, however, not cut down on the consumption of gasoline. On a test this morning, using only a one-quart measure of gasoline, that quart was burned up in thirteen minutes.*

The gasoline and oil report for February is enclosed. It is early, but I am enclosing it to use together with the above report.

Sincerely,

P. B. [353]

The mission board did hard work, no doubt about it. One budget meeting in 1927 lasted from 2:15-9:30 p.m. The board had to try and manage the funding when the money was very scarce. They got the requisitions—or didn't get them. The men on the field bought things and then asked permission—and repayment. It sometimes was much easier to ask for forgiveness for an action taken rather than try and ask permission to do it in the first place. On Easter Monday, 1926, the Committee reported "East Fork had some unpleasant matters to report." In that meeting the Committee also reported that there had been no required reports from San Carlos and Peridot submitted. Missing! The Board also allowed the good judgment of E. E. Guenther and H. C. Nitz to prevail in the matter of choosing goats over cows, provided no thoroughbreds were bought! In the August 30, 1926, meeting it was noted that a number of the missionaries (three miscreants were pegged by name) had not used the proper report form in filing their monthly reports. The superintendent of the field was to see to it that they complied—and soon! There were squabbles and fights on the mission, and the mission board had to referee. Missionaries couldn't get along with each other. They had to stew in their own juices, and the brew wasn't pleasant. The mission board had to say, "You just have to get along!" They said it "in no uncertain terms," whatever that all meant.

Consider the following from Pastor Stern of the mission board, "As to the windmill request, Rosin's letter isn't quite clear to me. In one sentence he asks for a windmill, because an engine pump requires too much attention, and in the next sentence he states that East Fork has an engine which was too large for their windmill, and he asks the Board permission to keep it for Peridot." Does he want an engine and a windmill? I am at sea. Furthermore, he writes that

---

[353] *Apache Lutheran*, March 1992, reminiscences of Paul Behn.

the garden proposition is a speculation, which I cannot believe, if they have irrigation and sunshine in Arizona. But why then does he want the Board to consent to an outlay for a windmill and a pump that will be sufficient to pay for vegetables for a couple of years? But then I am not acquainted with geographical and climatic conditions. If you think he ought to have it and the other missionaries have such an irrigation plant, I am fully satisfied with what you do."[354]

And there were salary discussions. Aren't there always salary discussions? Pastor Rosin: "No indeed! I am not alarmed nor hurt because of the reduction in salary, be assured. Mr. Uplegger mentioned to me that that had been done. Nor do I care what other missionaries are getting, so as they can get by on what they do get. To be exact though, my salary was never $121.66 (as had been maintained in an earlier letter from the mission board). It was $111.66. How the $1.66 got in, I do not know. The sum of $110.00 was the sum allowed married men. Those that had children were to receive five dollars more for each child under sixteen years of age. The Lord gave us a child but I never received the five dollars, which in seven years amounts to $420. The ten dollars added to my check was given for the labor and expense we had in preparing the school dinners. The ten dollars do not cover the hire of the woman who cooks, which is a dollar each school day or about 20 dollars each month. We get those ten dollars twelve months in the year, however, which amounts to $13.33 for each school month. This woman helps Mrs. Rosin with the washing and other duties, which help comes on one or two days of each week. Whatever she gets above $13.33 we count our own expense. My salary according to the stipulation of the Mission Board should have been $115.00; it was $111.66. I think it has been the same with Rev. A. Uplegger's[355] salary. How the Board overlooked the above, I do not know. I reluctantly write about my financial status, but I take this opportunity to say that the above omission is perhaps the cause of my running short at the rate of about $75.00 every year. If Synod's financial account stood any better than mine I would ask for $25.00 more a month, but as it now is I do not ask for any. For my part I wish to bear my part of the burden and suffer with the rest. One of our great sins in the Wisconsin Synod is, I believe, a great lack of charity."[356]

You read above the missionaries' query, "What happens if you won't support our work?" And you heard their answer

354 Letter from F. E. Stern to P. T. Brockmann, dated February 6, 1925, Watertown, Wisconsin. Synod archives.

355 Henry Rosin was close to Alfred Uplegger. Alfred was the brother to Henry's wife, Johanna, and lived down the road in San Carlos.

356 Rosin letter to Executive Board, Rice, Arizona, August 15, 1929. Synod Archives.

to the authorities, "Then we will do it ourselves." It didn't happen often, but it did happen that individual pastors did work on their own bill. Listen to the history of Immanuel Lutheran Church in Springerville and you will hear it:

By the 1950s and early '60s Pastor Paul Schliesser was serving a small group of Apaches in Eager. They met at the home of Fannie John and her husband. Fannie was from Cibecue, but her husband worked at the sawmill. Their home was not far from the mill. Most of those who attended also lived in the same area. There were families that came from Bylas, Whiteriver, and Cedar Creek—Lester and Libby Casoose, Eugene and Angelina Nozie, Wayne and Neva Armstrong, Nelson and Gretchen Ethelbah, and a few others as well. In the early '60s Pastor Schliesser, who lived at the East Fork Mission and served Canyon Day and Cedar Creek, accepted a call to Henry, South Dakota.

The Apache Mission Board had Alfred Burdette, an Apache interpreter who lived at East Fork Mission and served various congregations and areas under the direction of Pastor H. E. Hartzell, to hold services and visitations at Eager for those who were working there—all of whom had previous contact with our Apache missions. Alfred served also Canyon Day and Cedar Creek as Pastor Schliesser had. By the late '60s, however, Alfred moved back to his home between Peridot and San Carlos after having served the Apache missions on both the San Carlos and Fort Apache reservations as teacher, interpreter, and pastor (although he was never formally ordained).

For a short time after Alfred left, Orville Sprengeler, the son of the late pastor at East Fork Mission who passed away in September of 1957,[357] was asked to continue contact with the members of our churches who were living in Eager. Orville had grown up at Bylas and East Fork and spoke fluent Apache. He served in many capacities as an interpreter and is still active in our church at Canyon Day.[358] However, in 1969, the Mission Board decided to terminate the work in Eager and so informed Pastor Hartzell, who was serving

---

[357] Pastor Sprengeler died in the end bedroom of that parsonage home across from the church at East Fork. The yellow Ford stopped outside that parsonage in April of 1958.

[358] Orville has also since died (2012) and is buried with his wife Inez not far from Pastor Ernie Sprengeler in the haphazard little cemetery behind the mission compound at East Fork Mission.

McNary and Holbrook as well as East Fork, and who supervised the interpreters that had been going to Eager a couple of times a month.

After the Synod ceased to support the work, Pastor Eugene Hartzell asked if he might continue it on his own twice a month with the permission of the McNary congregation. At that time, Pastor Hartzell worked at McNary each Tuesday having Sunday School, instruction classes, and Bible Study (during Lent and Advent there were worship services). The Board did not object but warned that no financial support was to be expected or asked. When the congregation at McNary was asked if they would permit their pastor to have services in Eager every other Tuesday in the evening, they immediately consented. Thus, in a sense, was born Immanuel of Springerville. This congregation, which from that moment has been self-supporting, began to worship in the home of Libby and Lester Casoose. This was in 1969, or thereabouts.

In 1958 Pastor Edgar Hoenecke, whose name became synonymous with mission work in the Wisconsin Synod, wrote the following in a report to the church at large: "Your chairman considers this matter of first importance and, therefore, the discussion of the book *Missions at the Crossroads*, by T. Stanley Soltau, D.D., presenting 'The Indigenous Church – A Solution for the Unfinished Task,' has been placed upon the agenda as the first matter to be considered. Several suggestions have been received for expediting the realization of indigenous churches in our foreign fields. One suggests the calling of a pastor by the various executive committees to stay in the foreign fields for any length of time necessary to deliberate with the men in the fields and to help to inaugurate the policy of the indigenous church. He would work in one field after another, after which the board would be free to terminate his call. Other suggestions have been made verbally. At this session the Foreign Board ought to make some practical provision to take care of this matter. A summary of the 'Soltau Plan' is attached." And Edgar Hoenecke ended his correspondence and affixed his name and title: Chairman.[359]

There has been reference to the Indigenous Church of Stanley Soltau before in this book. The word "indigenous" is still bandied about in the Apache Mission today. It probably is still what the authorities who are responsible for running the work today are thinking, as they philosophize about the nature and emphases of the

---

[359] This was in line with the Soltau Plan mentioned here.

work. When Stanley Soltau spoke in a lecture he gave in 1956 he said about the aim of Missions, "It is the proclamation of the Gospel to the unconverted everywhere, according to the command of Christ, with the view to the establishing of an indigenous church."[360] It was he who said about *Inashood* (the foreign missionary) that he is "an expensive and inefficient stop-gap." He also said, "It is completely out of harmony with the program of an indigenous church that any foreign missionary becomes a pastor of a congregation. He has been sent out to evangelize and to train others to carry on the work." It was he also who defined the indigenous church as **1)** self-governing, **2)** self-supporting, and **3)** self-propagating. The missionary was to show up and immediately strive toward establishing a church that was self-supporting. "The mission dare not give any money for salaries to nationals nor any money towards the erection of buildings." So those who had the power of remote control operated from distant sidelines to make the work go the way they thought it should and the Soltau Plan suggested.

Edgar Guenther's description of the "encumbrance of remote control" continues to the present day to be endemic to the work. It manifested itself in the 1980s, when the time came to choose the new principal of the grade school and high school at East Fork. The word was that this decision should come from the Apache people themselves. They should be the ones to choose who it would be. At the preliminary meetings, however, it was made very clear who the visiting authorities thought it should be and even insisted that it would be as the process went along. The committee wanted the people to come up with and choose the committee's own recommended candidate. When it didn't happen that way, and the people chose someone who was very likely, to be honest, a substandard teacher and leader, the committee came back again and essentially overturned the decision of the people on the field and the missionaries who had been "in charge" of the voting process. The whole lot—missionaries and people—were asked to sit and listen like truant school boys as they were told how it would be. One Apache man[361] in frustration said, "You white men come here and tie a rope on my hand like this (and he demonstrated it in the air) and when you want you pull the rope so that my hand goes up." So much for indigenous self- government and local leadership.

The dominant philosophy said, "If missionaries are willing to pay salaries and put up buildings the nationals will not object, but

---

[360] Stanley Soltau, "Lecture by Dr. T. Stanley Soltau, D.D.," May 24, 1956.

[361] This man was elected by the people for a stint as the vice chairman of the Fort Apache Reservation.

the missionaries are not succeeding in building up a strong church by so doing. Furthermore, the source of funds always determines the basis of authority. Mission funds prevent a group from assuming authority. Worst of all, mission funds are a barrier between the missionary and the nationals." And it was in black and white how the change over in thinking and policy should happen: "We must first sell the Mission Board. The Mission Board in turn must sell the missionaries and must insist on it that *every missionary is willing to abide by this new program.*[362] Thereafter the nationals must be sold, and they in turn must sell the national church."

So opportunities for other work off the reservation and in other places came, and missionaries rendered as "not team players" read the handwriting on the wall and left. Their leaving was a little like General George Crook at the end of his military tether respectfully asking that he be relieved of his duties. "Please fall on your own sword and do it quietly," was the message the leaving missionary heard.

Most of the *Inashood* thought of themselves as pastors to the individual people and congregations they had been called to serve. That's what their education at the seminary had taught them. That's what a pastor was supposed to be and do by the very definition of the word *pastor.* Many of the pastors didn't want to be perceived as property of the mission board to be moved around to other stations on the field as the remote mission board saw the need and saw fit. Probably from the beginning the philosophy considered the missionaries as initial proclaimers who would get things started and then move on. There was a kind of mantra that was pushed and published by mission boards, "Always be working yourself out of a job." Missionaries were to be essentially administrators who established an "indigenous" church that would then do the actual preaching and teaching, and they would move on to repeat the work somewhere else. This no doubt was the hope of the early mission boards—and the later. They didn't think the missionaries would become fixtures in the work and spend fifty and sixty years among the people. They didn't even want that to happen because it was at variance with Soltau's vision and their own philosophy of what was best for the field. The perseverance of many years in the work that seemed to some a wonderful blessing was not in line with the philosophy of others. Over the years of the Apache mission work there were so many humble pastors and teachers and lay workers who worked long and faithfully. (Just four of the missionaries of the first 100 years totaled among themselves

---

362 This was emphasized in the copy by those who presented this to the missionaries on the field.

over 200 years of service!). This general longevity of service is what happened, and it was what the Apache people then understood about *Inashood*. *Inashood* would be someone who would come and live with them and be with them and be their pastor into the indefinite future, if not even into the very distant future. Missionary as the mission board understood it and wanted it was different than that. This was a rub that would chafe throughout the work. It is especially so these days with the philosophy of the work being along the lines of the indigenous church. It is interesting to see that the very word chosen and championed by those who wanted to establish "indigeneity" in the Apache church was a word that English computer spell checkers didn't recognize and that even most English-speaking people didn't understand. Apaches thought they were saying, "Indianization," and perhaps they really were.

CHAPTER TWENTY

Three Stories

*My eyes have seen all this, my ears have heard and
understood it. What you know, I also know;
I am not inferior to you* (JOB 13:1,2).

This story of *Inashood* is not a story about theory or even of history. It is not the story of philosophy in the sky on how to do the work,
but it is the story of the pastoral practice on the ground and how
things actually happened. It is the story (and the ongoing story) of
relationships between *Inashood* and his people. The following three
stories come from the private writing of an *Inashood*. They are true
stories. The names have, of course, been changed.

The bizarre
Some people have bizarre things happen to them, even in
church—perhaps especially in church. So do I. Tuesday evening
was one.
We managed to get to Sunday School on time at Canyon Day. In
fact, the sun was still up when we started, a sure sign that spring
is coming. I have noticed it on the mountains where the sun slips
away in the evenings. The setting sun has passed to the north of Kelly's Butte. It is miles to the north now from the cliff off Seven Mile
Hill where it nestled in December. I called the children's attention to
the sunlight before we started our singing in Sunday school— which
was actually Tuesday school for us in Canyon Day. After the Bible
story and the consequential sprinting to the battered door of the little yellow school bus we used, we left to take everyone home. It was
dark by now, only a faint glow remained in the west. We stopped at
Seven Mile Store for treats. Because I had only the mission kids, and
these were the faithful ones who hadn't missed our Tuesday school
and because I had enough money for them all to have a can of pop, I
announced it. They all trooped in with me and picked out their drink.
But low and behold! Ryan and David wanted to have water. Imagine
it! Water instead of pop! To be sure, it must have been the fancy con-
tainer that held the water that they were really after, but still!

I swung on around in the mission and got Bibles to take to the counseling session I had scheduled for after class. A brother and a sister upriver wanted to have a double wedding. I had been there the weekend before and had talked to them. They had sat somber and quiet on the couch as I talked to them. I had never seen Robert before. He was Jeanine's mate. He had big eyes and a kind of surly way about him. He sat there with his foot up on the coffee table and then halfway through seemed to remember that maybe he wasn't making a good impression on anything but the coffee table and kind of snuck his foot away. I was treading gingerly because both couples were already living together. Two little boys were the product of the one union. Jeanine and Robert had nothing visible yet. I hoped there was nothing invisible. But they wanted to get married, all of them, and I was glad (mostly) to be able to at least get things on a legal footing. I explained that they were doing right in wanting to be married. In my talking with them I even used the term I had heard the past week, "Illicit cohabitation." The words even had an evil ring to me. That was how the state looked at what they were doing. But good, we were going to do something good about that. "I would like to be able to talk to all of you. Is that alright? Tuesday evening after Sunday school? Fine."

I pulled up to the house and parked off to the side in the large driveway. (It was for a two-car carport. The house itself had five bedrooms. It was huge, but all the rooms were filled with children illicitly cohabiting, and it was new. It looked nice, and Lorraine was doing a good job keeping things nice. I was happy for her that she finally had a place.) I wanted to leave room for the truck to get out because it seemed to me they might be wanting to leave. Jerome, the father, was walking around quickly when I got there. He had something on his mind, I thought. And there was something on his mind. Dennis and Charlene weren't there yet, but they had gone up the hill (as we say in Whiteriver for those going to Show Low) to get a new car. Dennis put down his income tax money so Lorraine could get it. "Fine," I thought, "but we did plan to have our counseling session tonight." "Go on into the house," I was told, and I did.

Jeanine wouldn't look at me. Robert was walking around in the house. I couldn't see his face well. Lorraine was busy getting room for me on the couch and getting the children to turn off the television. There were a bunch of them. Jeanine came walking in and then walked back out again. I sat down on the couch, and Jeanine and Robert came and sat down. "How are you, Robert?" I asked. "Not good," came the reply from his face staring down into his lap. Jeanine mouthed to me, "He's been drinking." My heart sank. Then there was an excited announcement behind me, "The new car is here!" Dennis and Charlene were back and everyone went outside. I asked Robert, who had indeed been drinking, if I could talk to him, and we stepped out onto the porch.

He started crying right away. It was his friends, he said. They told him, "Drink with us," and all the while he stupidly punctuated his speech with flailing arms. "Something made me do it," Robert said. "I have to find out why. Do you know about *chin*? (*Chin* is the Apache word for devil.) I think it is *chin*. The people at the sunrise dance always move back from me when I am singing and have to leave (to urinate). I was a Lutheran Pioneer for Guenther for eight years. (Pastor Arthur Guenther was in Whiteriver.) I think I should have a peyote dance. But I think it is *chin*." It was drunk talk but drunk talk is usually true talk (*in vino veritas*). At least it wasn't censored talk. "I have to make bathroom," Robert said and walked back into the house.

Dennis and Charlene had made it back in the new car. It was for Lorraine. They went quickly into the house and sat down on the couch where they had sat last Saturday when we had first talked. Jeanine was trying to get Robert to sit down, so we could begin our session of counseling. Then there was a general movement which suggested that Jerome Jr. and Delores were leaving to go back to McNary. Theirs was the pickup in the carport where I had parked off to the side. Robert came out from "making bathroom," and I went outside with him again. I just couldn't imagine having him in the counseling session, intoxicated as he was. It was making a mockery of the whole thing.

"Would you move the van, Pastor? Jerome Jr. and Delores are ready to leave." I pulled up farther into the left stall, watching carefully to my left that I didn't hit the eave coming down over the porch. But I forgot that my yellow van was a school bus van and very high in the front. Crash! I backed up again. No one seemed to notice, but I suspected they all noticed but weren't going to show it. There it was. The fascia board I had hit was all splintered. Jerome Jr. and Delores backed around and drove off. I couldn't help but wonder why they hadn't done that in the first place.

Back in the house drunken Robert was on the phone and talking loudly to one of his friends. Jeanine kept telling him to be quiet, but of course he wasn't and wouldn't. I started the session. Dennis and Charlene were ready. Maybe Jeanine would get something out of it I reasoned, but I knew that I wasn't going to be able to help Robert and I knew that he wasn't someone Jeanine should marry. Besides that, on my mind now was the mess I had of the broken fascia board outside. I told Jerome before I had come back into the house about what I had done to his new house. He said with a wry smile that it was okay. I also said to him, "Jerome, this marriage between Robert and Jeanine isn't going to work. He's drunk!" "I know that. Talk to my wife Lorraine about it," Jerome said. Jerome is a low-key dad for sure. He works hard and he comes to church with his wife, but as for direction and decision "talk to Lorraine" is about the way it is.

We started our premarital counseling by reading in Genesis 1 and 2. Marriage is there all right, and it is perfect. Marriage today is the original and only relic of the pre-sinful world. There was companionship, help, and children intended in that first marriage and in all subsequent marriages. These were the reasons God caused marriage to be. Then we went to the Old Testament book of Malachi to talk about divorce right away. We might as well face what will no doubt be at least a temptation. Do it right away so that when that argument or fight happens and the words are spoken, "I think I'll just get a divorce," that at least the folks have heard that the Lord hates divorce. Some place in our discussion, Robert came back into the house and flopped down next to Jeanine on the couch. That shoved Jeanine up against me on the couch, an unhappy sandwich to be sure. But Robert left again shortly and tried dialing someone else on the phone. To top it off, one of the contact lenses I was wearing had slid off my eye and I was having trouble reading in the dim light. It was not a pretty counseling session at all.

After herculean effort in the session I said, "Let's try again next Tuesday evening." It was okay with Dennis and Charlene. They went back out to the new car. Lorraine had returned with it and all the children who had mercifully left to go with her. I asked Lorraine if I could talk to her. I pointed to the broken fascia board first. She smiled in an embarrassed and shy way and said that the crew had just come that very day to check on repairs needing to be made on their new house, and that they could fix it. Then she took off on Robert. "Robert's no good. I told him not to come back here. I even got a restraining order on him, but the police never showed up. I didn't want him around, but Jeanine took him back. He talked good and said that he loved Jeanine. He said he was going to help with things here. He gave us a little money he had made fighting forest fires. We chased him away. Fred even threw him out of the house, but he always comes back to Jeanine's bedroom." "Lorraine," I said. "This just isn't going to work. I have asked Robert, and he said he will let me take him back to his mother's place in Whiteriver."

As we were driving along in the old school van on our way to Whiteriver, Robert talked on and on. "I think I'll just end it all," he said suddenly. "Lorraine said I should never come back again." Now, with Robert suicidal, I just couldn't dump him off some place and have him commit suicide at my expense. So I swung by Pastor Guenther's place. The light was on in the parsonage. I left Robert in the van and told him we were going to talk with Pastor Guenther. He had mentioned the Lutheran Pioneer stint before. Maybe Pastor Guenther could hold him until we could get the police so he wouldn't be free to "end it all." Pastor Guenther wasn't there, but his wife Gloria was. She came to the door and talked and in the middle of trying to figure out what to do, in walked Robert and started his drunken gesticulations, like a puppet on sticky strings. "Take me to my aunt's in Canyon Day," he said. That was the final opportunity, so we left in the van. I had to go to H Market first to get gas. I saw Timmy there while I gassed the van up. It was the first time I had seen him in two years. He wanted to talk about church and his confirmation. He dropped out of sight since the tribal election, which messed up his family. His mother was from the Lupe Family, his father was from the Johnson Family, and those two families had sparred in the last election. Robert was still in the van, so I left.

"Right there," Robert directed in the dark. "That is my aunt."

We were in Canyon Day, and I knocked at the door. A young teenage girl came and quickly eyed Robert, who had gotten out of the van and was standing behind me. "You can't stay here," she whispered hoarsely to Robert and then added to me, "The baby's inside the house." That didn't make any sense to me at all. Recita was inside the house in her wheelchair, and I went in. The young girl stayed outside with Robert. They were acquainted already, I could see. Recita had seen Robert when I knocked on the door. "He got my daughter pregnant," Recita said. "I don't want him to be here tonight. That is his baby there!" and she pointed to the little boy with big eyes looking back over his shoulder at me from his swing in front of the television. "That is Robert's baby all right," I thought. There was a marked resemblance.

I went back outside, but by this time it was as if I did not exist. This was the first time since the baby had been born that Robert had come back to talk. The girl was ecstatic! She came running back in and went up to her little boy in the swing with her face in his little wide-eyed face. "Your daddy has come back," she said in English. The baby didn't understand. Robert the drunken father didn't understand. I really didn't understand it all either. She went back outside. I asked Recita what we should do. She said she didn't want Robert around. I told her that he had threatened to kill himself. "That's the way he always does," she said.

So, I called the police. In the middle of the conversation, both Robert and the girl came back in. They heard the conversation. "Who did you call?" Robert demanded when I stopped. "I called the police, Robert. They are going to hold you until you get your mind back." Both Robert and the girl glared at me and then ran out into the dark again. Needless to say, when the police came, Robert was nowhere to be seen or found. The girl "didn't know" where he had gone. She started joking with Mark, the policeman in charge. "Two cars to get one person," she chided looking over the shoulders of the police at the cars with their lights flashing red and blue in our faces. "We have to use two cars these days because there are too many crazies around," Mark said. "I'm not crazy," she said, poking the arm of Mark affectionately.

I left shortly after that. It was late and I had had enough already three hours earlier.

Saturday night

Some people do exciting things on Saturday nights. They go to parties, they eat out with their wives and girlfriends, they anticipate sleeping in on Sundays. I do none of these things. In fact, Saturday nights usually end up being work for me. Not bad work, mind you, but work nonetheless: sermon work, study work, bulletin and readying work for the service the next day, filling Communion trays or posting hymns. Sometimes I even get to clean the church after several weeks of people forgetting, and when I go over to post the hymns I see everything is a mess.

The other Saturday night was work too, but it was pleasure as well. It was doing "my Father's business." I hope that was the case. I was almost done with the sermon. (I couldn't say it was coming along well.) It was already dark when the dog started barking. When the dog does that—bark, I mean—it irritates me. She barks at nothing for hours, and then when something worth barking at does come along—a pack of murderous dogs tearing through the wire and mangling all the rabbits in their cages, for instance—she does no barking at all. But tonight she was barking.

I looked out the window, and there was a gray pickup with its parking lights on. "What can they want on Saturday night?" I thought to myself unkindly. I felt unkind. When I got the dog quiet, Veronica came to the door. She walked slowly down the step by the stone planter and around to the side of the house. "Will you come and see Ed? His back is bad. He said he sprained it but I think it is his drinking. Will you come?"

"Yes, I will come in a little bit." The last paragraphs of the sermon continued to elude me, so I just changed my shirt, found my jacket and Bible, and left.

Ed was sitting on the edge of his bed, ramrod straight. He was hurting. He had no shirt on. His smooth brown skin really gave no hint of any muscles in his chest or stomach. He wasn't young anymore. Veronica had told me, "He's getting old," and it was true. He didn't look good. His nose had that rosy look from too much alcohol. His cheek twitched as he talked, and his neck muscles were pulling in shivers. It was the alcohol.

"It's bad. I'm never going to drink again. My back hurt when I stood up last evening. I was just sitting on the couch and stood up and it hurt. I can't even walk now. I can't even get into my truck," Ed said.

It could be kidneys, I thought. They have handled quarts and quarts of poison by now—and his liver! "Maybe you should have the doctors look at you," I suggested. The two women relatives who had been in the bed room started talking to each other and to Veronica in the next room. Ed and I could hear them. Veronica came back and said they were going to Seven Mile Store to phone for the ambulance. That was okay.

"Ed, you have to stop this drinking," I said. "Veronica loves you. She knows what you have done. How do you feel having gone with those girls and left her like you did?"

"It was bad. I am sorry I did that. I am not going to drink again," Ed promised.

Veronica came back into the bedroom. Ed was sitting there straight and miserable, the muscles in his face and neck pulling uncontrollably. She looked at him with pity in her eyes. On the dresser were some pictures. One was stuck in the corner of the dresser mirror. It was the picture of a little girl. The little grandson came in and peeked at me. He talked English and not Apache. His mother left him with Veronica. I had married the boy's parents, Erick and Vonda, half a dozen years before, and they had come to church for a while. Things had been good, but now both Erick and Vonda were living with others. The product of their lives together stood smiling happily before me.

"I'm very glad you came," Veronica said. She said it a number of times as Ed and I sat there in the bedroom talking about life—his life and Jesus' life.

The two relatives sat in their cars outside on the road. Their parking lights were on. I watched from the bedroom. Finally, I prayed with Ed and got up to leave. "Thank you for coming. I am very happy you came to see Ed," Veronica said. She said it again, and I was sure she meant it. I was happy I had been there. People were struggling with themselves and their lives and each other. Not many people besides myself had sat in Ed and Veronica's bedroom on the corner of their bed. Surely no other white man had sat there. But it was natural and right. I was their pastor. They felt alright having me there; in fact, they had invited me to be there.

The little boy followed me out onto the porch where the long-bodied hound dog sulked in the shadows. I had seen it on my way in. Often the dog would let you into the house and then bite you when you left. I had that happen several times. My little protector switched to Apache and made his best *"whishaant."* (The clumsy spelling is of the Apache word spoken to bad and mean dogs that says, "Get away" or "Get out of here!") The hound understood Apache. I was grateful, too, because of my little benefactor's care and contribution to my safety until I could get the truck door closed behind me and drive back to my waiting sermon.

The angel

It was night. I could see the car out by the gate and Jimmy at my door. "My mother would like to talk to you," Jimmy said. She got out of the car slowly and walked uncertainly to the back. It wasn't long ago that the meningitis had struck her. It was still taking its toll.

"Pastor, will you come and talk to us. It's Celeste. She just sits in the wheelchair. I offered to clean her room for her, but she doesn't say anything. We're down. Since those boys who were partying hit her with the car she just sits there. Will you come and talk to us? We're all down." The mother Katie asked this looking down. There was a catch in her voice, like she might cry.

I was thinking, "I just went to town to get wafers for the Lord's Supper tomorrow. It has been a week since the accident. You tell me of it now for the first time and it is Saturday evening. The accident happened almost a week ago. I need to be working on my sermon. I planned to be working on my sermon at this time."

"I'll come. Let me change my clothes and eat supper with my family. They are waiting for me." I tried to say it without letting my feelings show. "You don't have to change your clothes. Come just like that," Katie said as she turned slowly and started walking back to her car.

I went. Antone was at the house. So were Jimmy and his girlfriend. (I guess it was his girlfriend. He introduced me to her. He divorced his first wife against my wishes and my words.) Celeste was in the bedroom. "I'll bring her," said Katie.

The light flickered cold blue fluorescence on us all. In the corner, Shaquille O'Neal stood 7' 1" on a life-sized poster. Someone had given it to Sandy, the little boy in the house, for his birthday. Sandy showed me some pictures that he had drawn. They were good.

Both of Celeste's ankles were broken. The casts were tidy and clean, peeking out from under the blanket on her lap. The black thread was still in the sutures on her face. The drunks that had done this to her, smashing into her and her two friends and then running away, were still out running around someplace after they had insanely piled their stolen red truck into Celeste. "They haven't found them yet," she told me, looking at her hands on her lap. "Every time the police go there, they say they are not at home. We think the family is hiding them."

"Celeste, did they come here and say they are sorry for breaking your ankles?" I asked. "No," she said loudly. She had no anger apparent in her voice, just a "No" said loudly.

"Celeste, I would like to read you and your family the story of Stephen from the Bible," and I did. "Thank God you are alive. Jesus really did send his angels to keep you." (At this Celeste shook her head in a yes. Her mother Katie started noticeably.) "They killed Stephen. They did not kill you. Now, Celeste, the only way you can keep from becoming bitter, the only way you can now win in this bad thing that has happened, is to forgive those boys in the same way Stephen forgave those who hurt him. You say it in your mind and with your mouth, 'I am not going to hold this against them.' Ask Jesus to give you the strength to really do that."

We talked about this, and I prayed with them. The people were quiet and thoughtful. We talked about Sandy's pictures and drawings that they had shown me. The uncle came in with his wife. He had been sick. I had seen him at the post office, and he told me then that when he felt better he was going to come back to church. "No white blood cells are being produced in my bones," he said.

I rose to leave and shook the people's hands. They thanked me for coming. Katie followed me outside to the porch light and the cold night. "There is something I want to tell you that I have not told anyone but my husband," she said. "The night they operated on Celeste's feet, I left the room to get a drink of water. When I came back Celeste told me that someone had been there. She said it was a being. She could feel his presence, but she could not see him. He had come to the foot of her bed. Then he had moved to her side. He touched her arm and gently massaged her face and neck. Then she felt his hands going toward her broken legs. 'I'll scream if you touch my legs,' she told him. But when he touched her legs, it didn't hurt. He was gentle and soft. Then he came to her head again and wiped the tears from the corners of her eyes. Then he was gone."

"Celeste said to me, 'Mom, who was it?' I told her, 'It was an angel! God sent his angel to be with you!' Pastor, I think it was an angel. I haven't told anyone else about this, just my husband. But I wanted you to know," and her voice broke and caught again, just like it had done at the car earlier when she had said that they were all depressed.

"I think it was an angel too," I told her. "God says that he sends his angels to watch over us. That is what happened to Celeste. He protected her life from the red truck that blew up in flames when it hit her. Yes, I think it was an angel too."

When I said it I knew why Katie had jumped earlier when I had said that the angels came from God to protect Celeste.

CHAPTER TWENTY-ONE

Spencer

Be kinder than necessary, for everyone you meet
is fighting some kind of battle (UNKNOWN).

Spencer wasn't even four years old that day when our yellow Ford station wagon came across the cattle guard at East Fork Mission. He lived up the river, on the left side up against the red cliffs that came down toward the river. His mother always kept a tidy camp: she had a wickiup with its doorway facing up toward Rimrock, and there was a little frame house that later became Spencer's house. He came to

Spencer Forrest and donkey.
Hartzell photograph collection.

school with the rest of the upriver kids. There were years when the mission school bus went upriver to pick up the school children, and Spencer and the rest would get a ride. But there were also many years when they walked to school, some from four or so miles away. After school they all ran back up the river valley to go back home, the older children out in front and the rest of the group tailing along behind.

Spencer was in our sister's class in school, and she kept track of him over the years. He knew her by name later when we visited, and she attended his funeral when he died and was buried in Dove Street Cemetery. The cemetery was just downriver a little way from where Spencer grew up and lived. It used to be called *hawoo b'ishii'* (Dove Salt Flat). The donkeys grazed there sometimes, and there was an Anasazi ruin where remnants of pottery lay scattered on the ground. Pat Cruz was one of the pallbearers for Spencer's funeral, and one day many years before, when Spencer was a little boy and so were we, Pat's father Russell had ridden his white horse by that same place, when we were looking among the pottery pieces scattered there in the red dirt.

Spencer was a gentle soul. He didn't fight or threaten anyone. He wasn't devious, and he didn't dodge school like some of the upriver boys did. He had a shy smile and a kind way of nodding his head when he talked, and that mannerism stayed with him to the end of his life. He walked to church with his mother and then later caught rides in the back of someone's pickup.

The young man caught his kind ways from his mother, Edith. She was that way too, always with a bright and happy smile and an equally bright and colorful camp dress that dignified her approach. She kept her camp area spotless and tidy. Her woodpile was good too, thanks to Naado, the family donkey,[363] who carried the split cedar pieces down from the cliffs and slopes where she lived. She was one of the ladies who came regularly to the mission with Grace DeClay and Minnie Moody and Gussie Edwards and others and sewed buckskin booties for babies and put beadwork on the front. Each pair was decorated differently. The beadwork was bright and cheerful too, like Edith's camp dresses.

Spencer was there at Christmas time, as we all stood on the bleachers of the gymnasium at the mission school and recited our Christmas parts in the general Christmas program. In the gymnasium there were two big Christmas trees that Andrew Nash or some of the other men had dragged down with their horses from the high

---

[363] Spencer's father and the donkey shared the same name, and we all smiled when we thought about it.

359

hills around. The one tree on the south side of the gym had stacks of brown paper sacks of candy and nuts for every student. We filed by on our way out on those special evenings and got our sack. The tree on the other side of the gym was barricaded and buttressed by all sorts of brightly wrapped presents. The old-fashioned colored lights smiled benignly down on the treasures that lay beneath them. After our school Christmas service was over, men of the church and some of the teachers and the older high school boys went and got an armload of presents and started to distribute them, calling out the names. It was a happy bedlam. We sat on the bleachers until all the presents had been distributed. Once in a while we white kids would even get a present from someone. All the people up and down the river brought their gifts for their families and put them under the tree. No one had electricity at home to sport lights on a Christmas tree, so they brought their presents to the Christmas service, and that was their Christmas custom. In those days when you went up Seven Mile Hill in the night and looked down along the river valley in the dark, the only lights you saw were those at the mission and a few lights at the trading post. Those were the only lights in the whole valley.

Spencer stayed upriver after high school. He rode Naado down to the trading post to get things. The upper East Fork boys didn't have as big a group of donkey riders as the Seven Mile boys did, but they could occasionally be seen galloping by the mission on some errand of boyhood necessity. Spencer stayed in East Fork when I went on to school in Minnesota and Wisconsin. He stayed up East Fork while I went to school at the seminary and then spent six years in Zambia, Africa. Some people said that my life at East Fork had prepared me for my life and work in the bush of Africa at Mwembezhi. Maybe it did.

I came back to East Fork in 1982 to be the pastor on the reservation at the very church my father had served for twenty-five years. Spencer was not quite thirty years old when I got back. He was beginning to suffer from ailments and afflictions that would eventually get the best of him. He was my parishioner, and I was his *Inashood*. I visited him up East Fork at the same old place where he and his family had lived when he was a boy. He had gotten the little frame house at the family homestead there by the red cliffs.

One time in the fall when I visited Spencer, we talked in his little house. It was immaculate, and he took good care of it. His bed was carefully made. I asked him how he stayed warm when it got really cold, and he sheepishly pointed at his bed and said, "I have twelve blanket!" I remember that his wood stove had one of the legs missing, and it sat on that corner on a cement block. (I wondered at the time how it was possible to break the leg on a wood stove.) To my knowledge Spencer never married. I never saw him under the influence of alcohol, although there were few around him who could have had that said of them. Then in 1986 our school burned down, and the gym where we had stood together and recited our Christmas memory parts was forever gone. The explosion that caused the fire that burned it all down actually blew the 2 x 12 wooden bleachers away from the walls, the very bleachers that Spencer and I had stood on when we had recited the Christmas story all those years before.

Then for me came twenty years in Georgetown, Texas, not far from Austin. When I told the people at Canyon Day that I was going to be moving to Georgetown, Texas, they all started laughing because Georgetown was the nickname given to the favorite drinking place in Canyon Day down by the river.

I tried to visit Spencer when I came back to see family in the White Mountains of Arizona where we all had lived. His health was starting to fail him, and I found him at various care centers in either Globe or in the Show Low area. I was always glad to see him. It hurt my heart to see him lose his legs—both of them—to diabetes. He never complained about it or felt sorry for himself. He did tell me one time that someone in the care center had stolen one of his blankets. He didn't need twelve blankets on his bed anymore, but it was a loss to him that was hard to take—and for the first and last time I saw Spencer get angry. When I visited him I liked to leave a little cash, so he could buy himself some treats: diet coke and potato chips.

He started sending me *The Apache Scout*, the reservation political rag.[364] He was religious about sending me those *Scouts*, and I have to say that I enjoyed getting the scoop on goings-on in my old stomping grounds. He kept a calendar in his room, and he marked it when the next date the *Scout* would come out so that he could send it to me. With his meager funds he managed to get manila envelopes that would hold the issues and then used his stamps to send them to me. When I came to visit him he always got his calendar and showed me when I could expect the next issue. That was important to him, and it was important to me.

School had been challenging for Spencer. Classmates remembered him as always moving his legs because he had to fidget. In the care facilities he didn't move his legs anymore because they were no more. Diabetes is cruel. But he wrote me about going around the

[364] The reservation church's newspaper was at first entitled *The Apache Scout* by Edgar Guenther who wrote most of it. But that name gave way to *The Apache Lutheran*. The tribe then took the name *The Apache Scout* to be its political voice in the community. That's what Spencer sent to me.

facility in his "wheelie" chair. He told me when I could expect the next *Apache Scout*. He told me how the weather was: if it was raining or snowing or the sun was shining. If anyone who read the letter felt compelled to criticize any spelling or grammar discrepancies, just let that person remember that Spencer was bilingual and could make himself understood in two languages.

Living in Globe enabled me to see Spencer more often than before. At that time he was no longer in Globe but was in Lakeside at the facility there. When I was up that way seeing family, I tried to stop and see my friend Spencer. He still sent me *The Apache Scout*. On the envelopes I got from him in Globe, Devereaux St. got to be Deverzux St. The mailman never had any trouble with that, nor did I. Life got harder and harder for Spencer. Finally, he was not able to make the two van trips a week to Winslow to get on a dialysis machine. He told me, "It just makes me sick." So he stopped going, and the end was not long in coming.

Spencer Forrest, cowboy, funeral bulletin cover

Toward the end I came to see him later in the evenings, as I went back home to Globe after a day at East Fork or Lakeside. The nurses on duty came to recognize me in my work clothes and directed me down the proper wing to where Spencer was. He would be sleeping, looking very pale and quiet and small. He didn't care anymore if someone lifted one of his blankets. I touched his shoulder, and his eyes opened. For a moment they were blank and it didn't register, but then he smiled and knew me and talked with me. Actually, I shouted at him because he was almost deaf. With the same boyhood demeanor he shook his head in that same polite and gentle way as I talked. We talked about Naado and the other donkeys of our childhood. There was Boots from Seven Mile with her deformed back feet. Morris was the Moody donkey with one ear hanging at half mast because of an altercation with a logging truck. Adays had a gray donkey with a black stripe on the shoulder. Kino Edwards' donkey was white and he was mean. Simon Wycliffe's donkey was named after its brand.[365] And so we talked, and we also spoke of the little frame house with the bed decked out in twelve blankets. We spoke of the mission school and our telling the Christmas story while standing in rows on those 2 X 12 gymnasium bleachers. On the second-to-last evening that I was with him, he suddenly raised his head up from the pillow and pointed at the drawer by his bed. His calendar was there, and the date was Xed when the next *Apache Scout* would come, and he nodded when I saw it.

The last time I saw my friend Spencer was later in the evening. Everyone else in the home was quieted down for the night. A few were still watching television in the lobby down the hallway. I came alongside his bed. "Spencer," I whispered hoarsely as I touched his shoulder. His eyes came open, not because I had whispered but because I had touched his shoulder, and there was a moment of unrecognition before he said my name, "Eric!" My name rolled out into the room in a happy and familiar way. I will always remember how he said it. It was the way a friend who had not seen his friend for a long time might say his friend's name when he saw him unexpectedly again. However it was that Spencer said my name, he was my friend and my very good friend at that.

And I was *Inashood*. At the end of our "talk" that last evening I said to Spencer, "Spencer, just say the name: JESUS!" He heard me and in a sure and certain way looking me squarely in the face, he said it back to me: "JESUS!" Even then his face had that kind and happy look that carried the persona of my friend Spencer.

---

[365] It was Y something. I don't remember anymore.

That was all. I left him on that late evening and drove off in the dark toward Globe. I was in San Diego several days later for a pastors' conference when I heard that the angels had come into that very room and had taken my friend Spencer home. No more need for a "wheelie" chair. One more of God's saints home safely forever.

Goodbye, Spencer, my friend. I will see you again!

CHAPTER TWENTY-TWO

The End

No memory of having starred
Atones for later disregard
Or keeps the end from being hard
(ROBERT FROST, PROVIDE, PROVIDE).

In 1954, 50 years after Paul Mayerhoff left Apacheland, he wrote a letter to Pastor Edgar Guenther. "One thing is sure and clear in my mind, that I always feel homesick for my Apache friends and neighbors." He wanted to come back and see the place one more time. In fact, he gathered money to come and buy something important for the work at East Fork Mission, where he had spent those eight unforgettable years of his early ministry and life. (The money actually was spent to purchase a house trailer that was to be used to accomodate guests of the mission when they came to visit.)

The cedar tree where he had pitched his tent all those years before was still standing there. It was as if the old tree was waiting for him. Things had surely changed over all those years, but the cedar tree hadn't changed much. As the slowest aging thing around, it took its part in nature, and as Isaiah the prophet said, *"All the trees of the field will clap their hands"* (55:12). The shaggy arms of our cedar tree had clapped and waved as the seasons and storms passed and as the *Inashood* came and went. Alchesay was gone, and Pastor Guenther himself had gotten weathered and old. The mission compound had waxed and waned like the moon that came up over Rimrock. Rimrock's ancient cliff face hadn't changed at all to those who cared to look up that way. Paul Mayerhoff had looked up at that ancient face from his tent door under the cedar tree over fifty years earlier. Few wickiups glanced that way anymore toward the rising sun as they stood resolutely and waited for dawn to come. Modest wooden houses and shacks had replaced the wickiups. And then came the government housing areas nicknamed for their appearances and causing people to smile and nod: "Ben Gaye City" for the elderly; "Ready-to-Go" on this side of the cemetery and "One Step Beyond" on that side; "Rainbow City" and "Lifesavers," with their repeating multicolored arrangements; "A Six Pack and Two Quarts" with its clump of six smaller houses and two bigger ones; "Graceland" where Elvis lived (not Elvis Presley), and "Corn on the Cob" where Flora Cobb and her family lived along the road with many other houses on each side. In fact, someone had made a display wickiup for tourists at Fort Apache, but they had its entrance facing the west instead of the east. Mores had moved on, but Mayerhoff's Cedar had stayed.

Paul Mayerhoff didn't make it back to this place that remained in his head and his heart. The death of his wife, old age, and ill health prevented him from ever making the trip. Instead, he gave talks and raised money for the Apache missions, and in October of 1957 he wrote his friend Pastor Guenther a final letter.

> "Well, I am 87 and 8 months along. I hope to live to my next birthday, February 20, 1958. My best wishes to you and mother (Mrs. Minnie Guenther) and all other missionaries. God bless and keep you all in health and successful labor for the Lord and the Apaches. God be with you all, body and soul, disposition and reason since through God alone you can be shielded and protected!
>
> Inashood Hastin *(elderly missionary)*
>
> Paul S. Mayerhoff"

He did not make it to his birthday. Two days before Thanksgiving in 1957 he died. His niece wrote to tell Pastor Guenther the news. She noted that Mayerhoff's eyesight and hearing failed, but his mind had stayed sharp. She regretted that he was unable to see the reservation one last time and then concluded, "But all his love was for the Apache mission."

It was one year later in 1958 that the big cedar witnessed the yellow Ford station wagon cautiously come across the iron cattle guard and the family get out there by the church and go to their new home, where they would be for the next half century. Today it is almost sixty years since then, and the cedar is still there. The other day I was up there to work on a wall by the old church that still stands to serve ongoing Apache generations. The old church has been renovated and looks better than ever. On Friday mornings it is full of school children and their parents and teachers, as they sing and listen to the Word that does not change. Groups of children ran under the old cedar tree at their recess time. They shouted and screamed and scampered about like only school children can do at their recess times. Their happy voices were music to our ears. Probably even the old tree could hear them and rejoice.

And in a personal way something else wonderful happened, as another bending line came full circle. Pastor Eric Hartzell got to move back to Globe and to St. Peter's Lutheran Church on Devereaux Street, with its faithful membership of mostly Apache believers. Classmates from East Fork were some of those who came. After twenty years in Texas he was called back to serve this congregation, where everything had started for him and his family in the 1950s, when Pastor Mayerhoff went to heaven and the Ford station wagon had departed with the family bound for East Fork Mission. God is good! *Inashood* Hartzell gets to live in the very parsonage his father designed and built next to the church in Globe, the very building he grew up in. Noftsger Hill School building still stands across the canyons. One ancient picture of Alfred Uplegger showed its outline on the hill behind him. The date over the front door of the old school, which is now a bed and breakfast place, still says, "1917." That's the date that Alfred Uplegger and Henry Rosin had come to the work. And there on the study door of St. Peter's Lutheran Church today are the marks still of target arrows, shot sixty years before from a little boy who would learn that Apache warriors could shoot seven arrows into the air before the first one came to ground.

Appendices

Appendix 1

The following is a letter written to the writer while he was still in Texas. Delores Cassadore was sharing her recollections of the mission work primarily at Cibecue. Delores taught at Cibecue, so the recollections were firsthand.

To Eric Hartzell
January 21, 2015

Early Missionaries

The Uplegger Family: Dr. Francis Uplegger circa 1902-1963(?) He arrived, they say, from the East and started the church at Old San Carlos (now Coolidge Dam) with his sisters Johanna and Dorothy, his son Alfred Uplegger. The once-a-Lutheran church just has piles of stones and cement at Old San Carlos. They say his wife died. Later Henry Rosin came to assist him and he married Johanna. Later at Peridot Rupert Rosin was born went to College (*sic*) and become principal at Cibecue somewhere 1953-1957? They had three girls; Beth the oldest.

At Peridot they said Rev. Rosin had an interpreter name Clarence Bullis, a graduate from an Boarding Institute Carlisle Indian School at Pennsylvania. Later Clarence's son took over the late Reese Bullis. Before Clarence Bullis there was an artist Rankin Rogers who painted all the pictures of Jesus. Rev. Alfred Uplegger spoke Apache so he did not need any native speaking person, but they help keep the yards clean for him. Pastor Ernie Sprengeler one of the first Sem-graduate 1931 had an interpreter, his name was Alfred Burdette. This way the people heard two language and maintained their language. Rev. Schliesser had someone in Canyon Day. The preachers at Whiteriver and East Fork held church services for the unchurch on Sunday evenings and Thursday evenings at McNary, Maverick, and Cedar Creek.

At Cibecue Pastor William Bein had the late Norman Janeway. They drove to Show Low and at the Carrizo Junction toward Cedar Creek. They all had their Missions. Rev. Hartzell only had Daniel Victor as a guide and helped him with names. Also Homer Aday was his maintenance man and a man named Cooper fixed things for him, a car transmission. These folks all have passed on.

There was much prejudice among women missionaries, but not your mother. Probably it was more of a misunderstanding like why do missionaries pay more attention to people? Just like Doctors having to leave home a lot.

They put all their love and effort in this work to spread the Word of God that Jesus died for us on the Cross.

I wish I had more sense to say thank you to them for all the love they showed us and tried to comfort us in our sorrows and happiness. Now all we have is the memory of them. Their wives cooked from scratch and made hearty meals like tamale pie, chicken dumplings, cabbage and bell pepper rolled in hamburger and seasonings also home baked bread, rolls, cookies made simple and tasty.

(Pastor E. E. Guenther said to *The Apache Scout* in 1939, "Missionary Krueger was a faithful teacher and conscientious camp worker. One therefore wonders all the more where he found the time and energy to apply his mechanical skill in making Lower Cibecue station the attractive place that it is now. It would be hard to estimate the amounts his skillful hands saved the budgets of yesterday. Ruskin says that full many a flower is doomed to blush and bloom unseen, or words to that effect. I feel these can be applied to Mrs. Krueger. Very few are privileged to know the hardships she endured as a missionary's wife at this frontier post, and fewer still know of the work she did: cooking a daily meal for years for a famished group of thirty to forty school children—and she has three children of her own; sewing and cooking classes for the school girls; a class for mothers in homemaking and the care of children; and as a registered nurse ministering to the needs of the sick in camp near and far, etc." That was the way Pastor Guenther knew the work at Cibecue and also knew the Kruegers. It was also to this Mrs. Krueger that Delores Cassadore made her reference of "tamale pie, chicken dumplings, cabbage and bell pepper rolled in hamburger and seasonings also home baked bread, rolls, cookies made simple and tasty." And Delores in her letter finished her recounting of the history she had experienced.)

Jesus loves us and sent these folks to us to keep up reading our Bibles. They said Mr. Arthur Krueger, a pastor at Lower Cibecue 1954 (?) lost one son skating on broken ice. His children lived in Albuquerque, Caroline (?) Charles and Bobby.

"There is a book called *Yalaan* Harder (sic) one among the first missionaries at Old San Carlos. He must have spoken Apache because some books were written in Apache at the University library at Phoenix and at Tucson. Also Francis was fluent in Apache language. They said he spoke German, Norway, Polish, English, Latin and Apache. Francis was made an honorary Native Apache with rights, arrangement was made by tribal government that government cooks served him and his family meals 3 times a day until he died at the boarding house.

Delores Cassadore

Appendix 2

And another historical note from Delores Cassadore:

January 22, 2015

Dear Pastor Hartzel,

I know that your book will be very useful, especially for those who will be interested about how the Lutheran Missions came about in the wilderness and among unchurched people. Rev. Uplegger said in his time, that the only road to Whiteriver was the rough shortcut dirt road which took him all day morning to evening in his jalopy which was cranked in the front, and if he had a flat, he would take everything apart to glue the tube with a sticky tape.

Whiteriver in those days had Apache chairmen who helped the missionaries, later Catholic came to chairmanship, and they no longer continue what was started by Chief Alchesay. Chief Alchesay has a granddaughter; Lydia Baha Alchesay. Lydia is at the rest home in Globe. She was taken in, as they say, by the Guenthers when all relatives were dying of an epidemic.

They say our pastor is young. I thought I knew all things when I was sixteen. He keeps home, his wife continues to work. She's due they say in February.

Millie (Mrs. Hartzell) loved everybody at E.F.

God bless you and your family.

Delores Cassadore

Appendix 3

(The following is a love letter written by Bonnie Lewis, who taught pre-school at East Fork Lutheran Nursery for four years, and has since taught at East Fork Lutheran Grade School. It is included here by her permission.)

Dear Pastor Hartzell,

One of the greatest jobs that I've had here on earth is the one I am holding now, which will end on May 24, 1993.

What is so great about it is I was able to teach my favorite, the love of Christ.

I remember the day you came over to my house. It was at the end of July, a sunny afternoon. My boys and I were crushing cans outside my house. I knew your truck, and when it drove into my driveway, I only thought it was a wrong turn and that you might ask me where somebody lived. But I was wrong, for you came up to me and asked if I could work for the nursery as a preschool teacher. I don't know if you knew, but I was really happy to get that call! So happy that when you left, I went into my room and said a prayer: "Thank you, God, for the job I just received, I am greatly overjoyed and honored to accept. In Jesus' name I give thanks. Amen."

So on August 19, 1989, I started working at the nursery. First, getting things ready. Looking through all sorts of materials, and getting my room ready.

Then came the teaching. The children were so young, at first I didn't know if what I had planned would work, but of course, I should have. Because before I left for work that August, I prayed that this teaching would work for me. That I will be careful on handling the children, and even with the Bible stories that I would be able to let the little ones understand me. Please, Holy Spirit, may I say the right things. Help me. And should I do good, that I know I didn't do it on my own, but that it was the Holy Spirit within me.

Today I am happy after four years of teaching that God has used me to do his work, to follow his commandment of loving, caring, and letting others know of his Son Jesus Christ, of passing on his word. And in my case, what a better way it was, to work with whom I know how to work with, the children. Especially at a young age of 4 or 5, when they are so ambitious, when they are still at the point of gathering knowledge in their minds, at that prime age. Then getting them to know and love Christ at the best time of their life. These children are so trusting, so believing, and so obeying God's Word. It is such a blessing to me!

Through thick and thin, I have loved the job I had and will on to the end. I would like to say it was the best job I ever had.

Pastor, I thank you for that wonderful 4 years I had working for the East Fork pre-kindergarten. As I go on my way I will keep asking the Holy Spirit to be with me each day, as I have my own children to teach besides relatives and friends. And that the teaching of the love of God will not end for me.

East Fork, pre-k, with what I taught there is one thing that really made me strong in my belief. That is what it did for me. That I am thankful for also.

May there be many more blessings for our Apache children besides what wonderful things the nursery has done and to all our pastors.

With my thanks.
Boni Lewis.

Appendix 4

The Centennial

There was that very first Saturday that missionaries Plocher and Adascheck spent among the Apaches. We can imagine how it was. Apprehensive. Wondering. Tomorrow is Sunday. We have no congregation, but we are pastors and we have come here to make congregations. How will it ever be in this strange place that we will have a congregation where we can preach God's Word?

Tomorrow is Sunday! They must have thought it, those first two.

One hundred years of Saturdays later, on October 2, 1993, the spiritual descendants of the first pastors and their first people gathered at the same place. The same white dust clung to the shoes of the people who climbed the hill to the church. The same Triplet Mountains looked down from the distance. The same kind of people were there, Apache people and white people, who both called themselves brothers and sisters in the faith. They were all there to remember and to celebrate.

Pastor William Meier preached the sermon to a full church. Some stood outside and at the entrance. Some prepared the meal. The estimate was that there were about 600 people altogether.

120 miles away (as the car flies!) the beef was going into the barbecue pit. The oak wood was being prepared for the fires to cook the bread. It was Saturday evening. Tomorrow would be Sunday, October 3, 1993. It was going to be one hundred years of Sundays, on toward 6,000 Sundays since the first two missionaries had their brave first Sunday. Like the East Fork stream flowing nearby, the River of Life had not gone dry in the hundred years.

The people came for church in the morning. The members of the Board for World Missions attended church at Whiteriver. Their fall meeting was scheduled in Phoenix, so they could attend the festivities at both celebrations. And they were treated to the sight of between 800 and 900 people packed into the gymnasium at East Fork to hear President Karl Gurgel speak. "Teach them!" he encouraged. "Into the next one hundred years, teach them!"

At this high time of our lives, there were highlights. The children sang. The Apaches themselves sang "Jesus Loves Me" in Apache. Apache men from the congregations braved the fear of a podium staring at hundreds of faces and spoke of their faith and their joy. We were touched by what they said. There were so many people to encourage us all that this work is near and dear to the hearts of many. And friends were there, old friends and new friends. Former workers and teachers were there and talked of old days.

One common expression was heard: "The place has changed so much!" The first missionaries in their wildest dreams could not have imagined such a plant of buildings and lawns. God has been good to us! The people of the Wisconsin Synod who have given their gifts to support this work have been good to us through their offerings of love.

The Word hasn't changed, though. It still has the same street down the middle of the city, the same river running down the middle of that great street from the throne, the same tree of life on each side of the river bearing its twelve crops of fruit. The Word and the Promise haven't changed one bit. After 100 years of change, we celebrate that the really important things haven't changed.

(E. Hartzell, *The Apache Lutheran*, October 1993)

Appendix 5

At the 125th anniversary celebration in Peridot, October 27, 2018.
And because I love you.

125 years ago God said something to the people of the San Carlos and Fort Apache Reservations in eastern Arizona. He said to them what it was that caused him to do for them what he did for these past 125 years, *"Since you are precious and honored in my sight, and because I love you..."* (Isaiah 43:4). He said those words first to his people Israel, who were facing deep water crossings and hot blazing fire. But he also said those words most certainly to the people of the San Carlos and Fort Apache Reservations in eastern Arizona, who faced floods of regret and hopelessness and fear, and who faced fires of bitterness and anger and hate. Because these people were precious and honored in the Father's sight, he sent them his Son Jesus. And it all came to be for that one reason: because he loved them.

It was just like our God was saying the very words, "And because I love you, I am sending spokesmen to you from me who will tell you about my Son Jesus." It was so, and the first missionaries came in 1893 to the mountain shadows of the Triplets there by the Gila River. The people living there had been banished to live in that place that one of the officials of General George Crook called "stinking malarial flats." A most remarkable and miraculous thing happened too because God loved these people: he caused them not only to be loved by those who spoke of Jesus to them but to love those people back. It was love that saw past skin color. Right from the beginning it was so. Pastor Harders in Globe described the feeling he had for his people on these reservations as greater and stronger than the love a man has for a brother.

And the people realized it was true. There were not many of the dominant culture in 1893 who loved those who lived on the Gila River flats, but Apache people quickly came to know that they were loved. They were loved first of all by the One who made the sun go by the Triplet mountains every day, and by this same One who sent his Son to be with them there. They were also loved by those who came to serve them and live with them and in many cases, be buried with them. The list that started with John Plocher and George Adascheck is long. Over 125 years literally hundreds of men and women worked and lived there on the reservations of eastern Arizona.

So the day of celebration came after the clock had ticked for 125 years. It was Saturday, October 27, 2018. Busloads of connected and interested people came. There were presentations of historical interest and pictures and displays looking to the future. Under some friendly mesquite trees ladies were making fry bread in the way that only they can make it. Local artisans and workers displayed their talents and their wares. Choirs came. Cars drove cautiously into the parking lot in front of the church (the same place where the foundation blocks of the first school are still visible), and then the cars were directed up the hill to the baseball field to park. That parking field was the same field where Pastor Henry Rosin and other missionaries played baseball on Sunday afternoons with worthy opponents on the baseball field.

And so many times during the day someone might hesitantly say to someone else, "Do you remember me? I used to teach school here at Peridot." And probably as many times someone would say, "Do you remember me? I was your student in second grade when you taught school here." Those who had given of their time and talent to upgrade buildings and church and had done so elsewhere on the mission stations came to see those who had helped them and benefited from their work.

There were back-to-back historical presentations. There were attempts made to encapsulate and explain what had happened and was still happening during the 125 years. Dr. William Kessel presented Apache Christian voices from the past. He did so from his grandfather Edgar Guenther's missionary diary and recollections—and from his own. The presentations were made in the Peridot church, and it was full for nearly five hours of back-to-back presenting.

The crowning joy of the day came at 4:30 p.m. to see everyone packed into the big high school gymnasium that had been rented for the occasion. The choirs came to sing for the service, stationed at strategic positions in the bleachers. There were more Apache believers than white believers, and that was as it should have been. Pastor Gary Lupe spoke carefully and well to everyone about Jesus being his Savior, that he was proud and happy to say that he was a Christian, and that he believed in Jesus and followed Jesus and stood with Jesus. It was wonderful to hear it! WELS President Mark Schroeder was last to speak after two hours of service and many speakers! How is it possible for speakers to limit themselves to their recommended five minutes? (It wasn't possible!)

And when it all came to an end in the early evening, there was one thing that stood as the reason why there were 125 years to celebrate and be thankful for. This one thing that occasioned and caused it all was what had happened 125 years earlier when God himself had spoken to his people on the San Carlos and Fort Apache Reservations and said, "*Since you are precious and honored in my sight, and because I love you...*" (Isaiah 43:4).

Should this world continue on for another 125 years this Lord of ours will be true and faithful. It is our prayer and it is our hope that he will—because he loves us!

(Pastor Eric Hartzell, Globe, Arizona)

Appendix 6

Mr. Norbert Manthey wrote the following note regarding the history of his home congregation in Columbus, Wisconsin:

> I am not sure whether or not I sent this piece of history regarding mission work in Apacheland. The excerpt is from the history of Zion Lutheran Church of Columbus, Wisconsin.

> Pastor Otto H. Koch[366] was a son of my home congregation, Zion Lutheran Church of rural Arlington, Wisconsin. He was born in Barnimslow, Pomerania, on September 21, 1854, and came to America when he was one year old. He graduated from Northwestern College and then Concordia Seminary in Springfield, Illinois. He served first (1878) in Lewiston, Minnesota, and then in Columbus from 1884 until 1920. Pastor Koch died on March 26, 1933, in Columbus.

> The reason for the mention of this note is that it connects to the Apache mission work. In the historical record of Zion Lutheran Congregation of Columbus, Wisconsin, we read the following:

> "In 1892 Pastor Koch, together with Pastor Theodore Hartwig, was appointed by the Wisconsin Synod to explore mission possibilities among the Indians of New Mexico and Arizona, with special instructions to locate a tribe which had not yet been reached by any Christian missionary. The congregation granted Pastor Koch another leave of absence for this purpose and thus played its part in the establishment of the Wisconsin Synod's first foreign mission field which since 1893 it has maintained among the Apache Indians of Arizona."

---

366 Norbert Manthe wrote this biographical sketch.

Appendix 7

The Players

In an attempt to list the different pastors who carried the name *Inashood* in roughly the first century of the work, the following names are given. Norb Manthey is to be thanked here for his extensive historical work to identify the pastors and their time served as *Inashood*. This is not a complete listing up to the present date but stops toward the close of the millennium.

John Plocher, 1893-1899
George Adascheck 1893-1894
Paul Mayerhoff, 1895-1904
R. Kurtz, 1903-1904
Henry Haase, 1904-1906
Otto Schoenberg, 1904-1912
Gustav Harders, 1906-1917
Emil Recknagel, 1907-1910
Carl Guenther, 1900-1912
Carl Toepel, 1912-1916
Edgar Guenther, 1911-1961
A. Zuberbier, 1913-1919
Alexander Hilmer, 1913-1916
Gustav Fischer, 1916-1918
Alfred Uplegger, 1917-1984
Henry Rosin, 1917-1967
Martin Wehausen, 1918-1923; 1956-1976
Henry C. Nitz, 1919 to 1929
A. Albrecht, 1919-1920
Francis Uplegger, 1919-1964
Roy Gose, 1920-1921
Martin Zimmermann, 1921-1923
E. Arnold Sitz, 1921-1923
F. Weindorf, 1920-1923
Melvin Croll, 1923 to 1926
Arthur C. Krueger, 1923-1939 and 1959-1970
Albert Meier, 1926-1929
Paul Albrecht, 1919-1923
Eric LaHaine, 1923-1925
Gustav Schlegel 1920–1926
Arthur Arndt, 1925-1928
Alex C. Hillmer, 1926-1929
Paul A. Behn, 1926-1940
Christian Albrecht, 1929-1934
Rudolph Otto, 1934-1941

Raymond Riess, 1939-1946
Arthur P. Kell, 1941-1946
Waldemar Zarling, 1941-1943
Arnold Niemann 1928-1941
Waldomar Zarling 1941-1948
Adalbert Schultz 1943-1946
E. Adelbert Binger 1946-1947
Allyn Schuppenhauer, 1947-1951
Ernst Sprengeler 1930-1957
Paul Schliesser, 1941-1959
Frederic H Nitz, 1946 and 1948-1952
Edward Rasmussen, 1951-1952
Joel Sauer, 1952-1956
David Worgull, 1952-1955
William Bein, 1955-1959
Carlton Palenski, 1956-1961
Arthur Guenther, 1950-1997
Howard Eugene Hartzell 1958-1983
Paul Pankow, 1958-1962
Richard Paustian, 1962-1965
Alfred Burdette, 1959-1963
Johannes Hering, 1961-1968
Myron Schwanke, 1968-1971
Lyle Sonntag, 1968-1982
Mark Hallemeyer, 1969-1972
Richard Pagels, 1970-1976
Quincy Wiley, 1973-1982
Orlin Wraalstad, 1973-1985
Reuben Stock, 1976-1982
David Miller, 1982-1985
Dennis Meier, 1972-1983
Burgess Huehn, 1977-1979
George Pavia, 1981-1983
Larry Pontel, 1983-2000
Eric Hartzell, 1982-1996
Leonard Bernthal, 1983-1986
Kirby Spevacek, 1986-1991 and 1997-2007
Glenn Seefeldt, 1984-1998
Paul Schulz, 1985-1997

(1967 marked the beginning of vicars serving at Canyon Day under the supervision of Pastor Eugene Hartzell at East Fork. The following were the vicars: Thomas Schmidt, 1967-68; Richard Pagels, 1968-69; Kurt Mahnke, 1969-70; Dennis Meier, 1970-71; David Haeuser, 1971-72; Karl Kuenzel, 1972-73.)

Appendix 8

Pastor Eugene Hartzell writes of Alice Taipa, then the oldest known living Apache:

> Alice Taipa, widow of A-100, well known Apache of years ago, was baptized on 22 June 1958. It is one of the few dates that are known in her life. No one knows when she was born, but a good estimate is 1870. She does not know when she moved from the Gila River to Seven Mile in the East Fork area, but she was a young girl holding a cradleboard on her horse, and in that cradleboard was her baby brother who many years later would be the interpreter for Missionary E. E. Guenther in his early years at East Fork. She does

Alice Taipa, widow of A-100
(Picture taken in 1964 by Eugene Hartzell, Hartzell Family collection.)

not know when it was that her future husband would bring three horses to her father's camp in the hope he could win this young girl for his wife. She does not know the years when her children were born, nor does she know when she first heard about Jesus, but when she was asked before her baptism, "When you hear the name of Jesus what do you think?" she answered, "I think—He is the true one" (and she used a word which could be translated "The Amen One").

Alice is too feeble to get to church, but the missionary still visits her. Years ago she told him, "Other missionaries come to my house. I cannot see good so I can not tell who they are. When you come call me "Shi Cho" (my grandmother) and I will know it is you—the real missionary.

Appendix 9

I am a parent of two girls who attend East Fork Mission. I am very thankful that they can go to a school where the foundation is based on religion, the true teachings of the Bible and how they can be saved through Jesus Christ.

I went to school at East Fork Mission since kindergarten. There are things I have learned from the Bible that have stayed with me throughout my life.

Like, for instance, it surprises me that I can still remember Bible verses and hymns after all these years. My two daughters may be sitting around the house and memorizing songs or verses from the Bible, and if they come across something they need help with, I automatically jump in with the words or phrases needed. It amazes them and they ask, "Mom, how did you know it?"

For that I'm very thankful that I went to school at East Fork Mission.

The Apache word for "believe" is the same as the English word for "drink." I "drank" in the teachings of the Bible and now it lives inside of me.

Proverbs 22:6 says, "Train up a child in the way he should go and when he is old he will not depart from it."

I know this is very true because I have experienced it.

Once that child has grown up with the proper teachings, he will realize how true Psalm 19:7-10 is.

- The law of the Lord is perfect, reviving the soul;
- The testimony of the Lord is sure, making wise the simple;
- The precepts of the Lord are right, rejoicing the heart;
- The commandment of the Lord is pure, enlightening the eyes;
- The fear of the Lord is clean, enduring forever;
- The ordinances of the Lord are true, and righteous altogether.
- More to be desired are they than gold, even much fine gold;
- Sweeter also than honey and drippings of the honeycomb.

L. C.

(The writer wrote this wonderful letter after the school burned. She is keeping the faith! For sure!)

Bibliography

Betzinez, Jason (with Wilbur Sturtevant Nye). *I Fought with Geronimo.* Lincoln and London: University of Nebraska Press. 1959.

Bourke, John Gregory. *On the Border with Crook.* Lincoln and London: University of Nebraska Press. September, 1971. (The preface and text of the Bison Book edition are reproduced from the 1891 edition, published by Charles Scribner's Sons.)

Bourke, John Gregory. *The Medicine Men of the Apaches.* Glorieta, New Mexico: Rio Grande Press. Inc. 1983

Ball, Eve. *An Apache Odyssey, Indeh.* Provo, Utah: Brigham Young University Press. 1980.

Basso, Kieth H. and Ned Anderson. *SCIENCE: A Western Apache Writing System: The Symbols of Silas John.* (Reprinted from 8 June 1973, Volume 180, pp. 1013-1022.)

Basso, Kieth H. *Western Apache Language and Culture.* Tucson: University of Arizona Press. 1990

Brown, Lenard E. *The Arizona Apaches and Christianization: A Study of Lutheran Mission Activity, 1893-1943.* (A thesis submitted to the Department of History at The University of Arizona, 1963)

Browne, J. Ross. *Adventures in the Apache Country, A Tour Through Arizona and Sonora, 1864.* Tucson, Arizona: The University of Arizona Press. 1974 (First printed by Harper Brothers in 1869.)

Browning, Sinclair. *ENJU.* Flagstaff, Arizona: Northland Press. 1982

Ceram, C. W. *The First American, A Story of North American Archaeology.* New York: Harcourt Brace Javanovich, Inc. 1971

Clum, Woodworth. *Apache Agent: The Story of John P. Clum.* Lincoln and London: University of Nebraska Press. 1938

Collins, Charles. *Apache Nightmare, The Battle at Cibecue Creek.* Norman, Oklahoma: University of Oklahoma Press. 1999.

Comfort, Will Levington. *Apache.* Lincoln and London: University of Nebraska Press. 1931

Continuing In His Word. (History of the Ev. Lutheran Joint Synod of Wisconsin and Other States.) Milwaukee, Wisconsin: Northwestern Publishing House, 1951.

Cremony, John C. *Life among the Apaches.* Lincoln and London: University of Nebraska Press, 1983

Forrest, Earle R. *Arizona's Dark and Bloody Ground.* The Caldwell Printers LTD: Caldwell, Idaho. 1936

Found, Charles E. *The Cradle and the Crucible*. WELS. 2003

Gatewood, Charles B. (Edited and with additional text by Louis Kraft). *Lt. Charles Gatewood & His Apache Wars Memoir*. Lincoln, Nebraska: University of Nebraska Press, 2005.

Goodwin, Grenville and Neil Goodwin. *THE APACHE DIARIES: A Father-Son Journey*. Lincoln and London: University of Nebraska Press. 1931

Griffith, A. Kinney. *MICKEY FREE Manhunter*. Caldwell, Idaho: The Caxton Printers, Ltd. 1969

Guenther, Alchesay Arthur. *The Ministry among the Apaches after 100 Years* [Arizona Pastors' Conference at Grace Evangelical Lutheran Church, San Carlos, Arizona, May 4-5, 1993]

Harders, Gustav. *Dohashtida* (Translated by Alma Pingel Nitz). Milwaukee, Wisconsin: Northwestern Publishing House. 1958.

Harders, Gustav. *La Paloma*. Hamburg: Agentur des Rauhen Houses (Allein-Auslieferung fuer Nord-Amerika Northwestern Publishing House, Milwaukee). 1913.

Harders, J. F. G. *The Apaches Today*. Milwaukee, Wisconsin: Northwestern Publishing House. 1912. (Translated by John M. Drickamer, Lakeview, Oregon.)

Hinman, George W. *The American Indian and Christian Missions*. New York: Fleming H. Revell Company. 1933.

Hoenecke, Edgar H. *The End of an Epoch in the Apache Indian Mission*, (Alfred M. Uplegger 1892-1984 and Henry E. Rosin 1892-1982)

Hutton, Paul Andrew. *The Apache Wars*. New York: Broadway Books. 2016.

Ingstad, Helge. *The Land of Feast and Famine*. Alfred Knopf, New York, 1933.

Keiser, Albert. *Lutheran Mission Work Among the American Indians*. Minneapolis, Minnesota: Augsburg Publishing House. 1922.

Kessel, William B. *Apache Indians and Anglo Missionaries: A Study in Cross-Cultural Interaction*. (Presented at Native American Symposium; May 5-6, 1992; Tucson, Arizona.)

Kiessling, Elmer Carl. *Centennial Memoir*. Milwaukee, Wisconsin: Northwestern Publishing House. 1979.

Klaszus, Barbara Laila (Nee Peters). *East Fork, Arizona, 1948-1949*.

Koehler, John Philipp. *The History of the Wisconsin Synod*. St. Cloud, Minnesota: Sentinel Publishing Company (Printed for the Protestant Conference). 1970

Lane, Jack C. (editor). Chasing Geronimo - *The Journal of Leonard Wood, May – September 1886*. Lincoln and London: University of Nebraska Press. 1970.

Lockwood, Frank C. (Foreword by Dan L. Thrapp). *The Apache Indians.* Lincoln and London: University of Nebraska Press. 1938.

Machula, Paul R. *Tale of the Apache Kid. Globe,* Arizona. 2006 (For copies contact: zybt@yahoo.com.)

Machula, Paul R. *Pinal Mountain Legacies.* Globe, Arizona. 2007 (For copies contact: zybt@yahoo.com.).

Mails, Thomas E. *The People Called Apache.* Englewood Cliffs, N.J.: Prentice Hall, Inc. 1974.

Minutes of Meetings, Executive Committee for Indian Missions, September 29, 1924 to July 1, 1927, Synod Archives, Mequon, Wisconsin.

Nickens, Paul and Kathleen. *Images of America: Old San Carlos.* Arcadia Printing. 2008.

Nickens, Paul and Kathleen. *Terrell Victor, Sr. Apache Cattleman, Soldier, Councilman, and Tribal Elder with An Early History of the Victor Family of San Carlos, Arizona.* Prepared by Paul and Kathy Nickens with the assistance of Armstrong Victor. October 21, 2010.

Oswalt, Wendell H. *This Land Was Theirs.* John Wiley and Sons, Inc. New York, London, Sydney. 1966.

Ogle, Ralph H. *Federal Control of the Western Apaches, 1848-1886.* The University of New Mexico Press, 1970.

Samuels, David W. University of Massachusetts, 215 Machmer Hall, Amherst, MA 01003 (Samuels@anthro.umass.edu) He wrote "Bible Translation and Medicine Man Talk," an article about language and the translation work of men like our missionaries on the San Carlos reservation. His comments compare with what Alfred Uplegger said about *Nayenesgani* (Monster-Killer) and Somigo. See pages 191 and 192.

Sauer, Theodore A., project director. Editors: Harold R. Johne and Ernst H. Wendland. *To Every Nation, Tribe, Language and People.* Milwaukee, Wisconsin: Northwestern Publishing House. 1992.

Schroeder, Morton. *"Edwin Edgar Guenther: Missionary to the Apaches."* Northwestern Lutheran, October 1995, pages 12, 13.

Stockel, H. Henrietta. *On the Bloody Road to Jesus: Christianity and the Chiricahua Apaches.* Albuquerque: Univ. of New Mexico Press, 2004. Pp. viii, 314. (This book is the old line that Christianity was just about getting the Apaches away from their wonderful culture and that they never really bought in but did what they did because they had to. Geronimo's conversion was listed as a case in point.)

Sweeney, Edwin R. *From Cochise to Geronimo.* Norman, Oklahoma: University of Oklahoma Press. 2010.

The Apache Scout, Vol. 1-8. Milwaukee, Wisconsin: Northwestern Publishing House. (1923-1931)

The Apache Scout, Vol. 9-16. Milwaukee, Wisconsin: Northwestern Publishing House. (1931-1938)

The Apache Scout, Vol. 17-24. Milwaukee, Wisconsin: Northwestern Publishing House. (1939-1946)

The Philosophy for Cross-Cultural Ministry. Prepared and Adopted by The Multicultural Mission Committee of The Wisconsin Evangelical Lutheran Synod, 2929 North Mayfair Road, Milwaukee, WI 53222.

The Smoke Signal. *History of the Apache Indian Agency and Army Camp at Old San Carlos, 1873-1929*, December 2009, No. 87.

The Western Apache. Wikipedia

Thrapp, *Encyclopedia of Frontier Biography.* (Check this for Alchesay's biography.)

Thrapp, Dan L. *The Conquest of Apacheria.* Norman: University of Oklahoma Press. 1967

Tough Times in Rough Places. (Edited by Neil B. Carmony and David E. Brown.) Silver City, New Mexico: High-Lonesome Books. 1992

Trimble, Marshall. *Arizona, A Cavalcade of History.* Tucson, Arizona: Treasure Chest Publications. 1989.

Uplegger, Alfred M. On *"The Elevation of An Indian Native Worker to The Ministry."* (Prepared upon request for the Missionaries Meeting, July 10, 1959.)

Watson, Don. *INDIANS OF THE MESA VERDE.* Lithoprinted in the United States of America by Cushing – Malloy, Inc. Ann Arbor, Michigan, 1961

Wendland, Ernst H. *Reaching Out–100 Years Ago.* The Northwestern Lutheran, pp. 168, 169. June 1, 1983.

Wharfield, Col. H. B. Edited by John Alexander Carroll, Professor of History. The University of Arizona. Arizona Pioneers' Historical Society: Tucson, Arizona. 1965.

Worcester, Donald E. *The Apaches, Eagles of The Southwest.* Norman: University of Oklahoma Press. 1979